Property Assessment Valuation

Property Assessment Valuation

International Association of Assessing Officers

Library of Congress Cataloging in Publication Data

International Association of Assessing Officers.
  Property assessment valuation.

  Includes index.
  1. Real property tax. I. Title.
HJ4151.I57   1977   333.3'32   77-8155
ISBN 0-88329-009-X

Printed in the United States of America

Contents

The Assessment Function

Introduction

The assessor is the government official responsible for establishing the value of property for ad valorem tax purposes. He is known by many different names in the United States and Canada—evaluator, assessment commissioner, appraiser, and tax assessor (this text will use the term assessor). He may be elected, appointed, or under civil service.

The assessment function may be carried out at the state or provincial government level and/or at lower levels. At the state level, the function is carried out by individual administrators, members of a board, or commissioners. At the local level, the assessment jurisdiction may be the same as a county, city, township, or school district, or it may cross political boundaries under a consolidated government, such as a city-county or regional area. Both the governmental structure and the scope of the assessor's authority are delineated by the statutes of the individual states and provinces. Most assessors, however, have the same general responsibilities and duties.

The assessor is responsible for discovering, listing, and valuing all taxable property. This may include both real and personal property. (Real property may be loosely defined as land and all things attached to the land, and personal property as all other property.) In accomplishing this, the assessor is responsible to the individual property owner to ensure that the value is proper so that the owner pays no more than his fair share of the property tax. The assessor is further responsible to all the people in ensuring that no property escapes the assessment process or is underassessed and that no property owner receives unauthorized preferential treatment.

A summary of the duties of the assessor common among most jurisdictions is contained in the following list.

1. Location and identification of all taxable property in the jurisdiction.
2. Inventory of all taxable property, including quantity, quality, and important characteristics.
3. Determination of the extent of taxability of each property.
4. Estimation of the market value of each taxable property.
5. Calculation of the assessed value (sometimes a fraction of market value) of each property.
6. Preparation and certification of the assessment roll of the entire jurisdiction.
7. Notification to the owners of the assessed value of their property.
8. Upon appeal by the property owner, appearance and defense not only of the value of the property, but also of the methods used to establish value.
9. Repetition of all these steps periodically, usually annually.

In accomplishing the initial task of discovering property, the assessor will need a mapping system that shows each and every parcel of land. Without an adequate mapping system, it will be quite difficult to verify that all land has been discovered and that all measurements resulting in square-footage and acreage calculations are accurate. The discovery of buildings and other improvements attached to the land requires on-site inspection of each parcel in the jurisdiction. At the time of this inspection, the assessor records pertinent data regarding the buildings and other improvements and regarding the land as well.

The discovery of personal property normally requires two steps. First the property owner files a return with the assessor detailing any personal property that may be taxable. Then the assessor audits the property owner's records and makes a physical inspection and an appraisal of the property.

After property has been discovered, the assessor must be able to describe it in order to make an assessment. This is normally achieved through the development of a parcel-numbering system in which each property is assigned its own unique identifier.

The next step is to classify property according to its proper category. In most jurisdictions these classifications are real property, personal property, exempt property, and, in some cases, property owned or operated by a public utility. The classification may have bearing upon the manner in which the property is assessed. Sometimes real property is assessed on one portion of the assessment roll, personal property on another, and public utility property on another. Exempt property may or may not be assessed, depending on local regulations.

Property must also be identified as to situs. *Situs* has a dual meaning. In the case of real property, it refers to the physical location of the property. In the case of personal property, it refers to taxable location, since personal property often may be moved from place to place. An assessor mandated to value personal property such as boats, aircraft, and cattle must make a determination not only as to whether the property may be taxed within the jurisdiction but also in some cases as to the portion of the year for which it may be taxed. Such decisions often require reference to laws and court decisions.

Having discovered, identified, and classified all the property in the jurisdiction, the assessor must value each property. He collects general, specific, and comparative data on all types of property, analyzes the data, and processes them into indications of value for each individual property. The property is then assessed at its market value or at some legally authorized fraction thereof, known as the *assessed value.*

After making the assessment, the assessor normally notifies the property owner of the value. In addition, he may be required to notify various government agencies of the total value of different types of property. The assessment roll is then certified and surrendered to the appropriate agency so that the roll may be reviewed, taxes computed, bills sent, and moneys collected.

The assessment function is not yet complete. In most jurisdictions the assessor's value is subject to review. Property owners may request informal review by the assessor while he still has control of the roll, and the values may be reviewed and changes made. In some jurisdictions property owners may request formal review before a quasi-judicial appeals board, and in all jurisdictions formal review by the appropriate trial court may be requested. In a formal review the assessor may be called upon to give evidence to support the value and to support the methods used to arrive at the value.

The end product of the assessment process is the generation of tax bills to collect and pay for local government services. Tax bills generally are not the responsibility of the assessor and will not be discussed in this text.

The Property Tax

Since the assessment function is performed for the purpose of generating revenue through the property tax, some discussion should be devoted to this tax. Basically there are three kinds of tax—income, sales or excise, and property tax. The income tax is based on the income an individual or a corporation earns and may be imposed at any level of government. The sales tax is based on the price paid for a particular item. It is generally enacted at the state or provincial level, with local options added. The property tax is based upon the market value of property. Generally, the individual state or provincial statutes provide for the levying and collecting of property tax; however, the levying and collecting are usually accomplished at the local level.

The property tax is ad valorem—that is, it is based solely upon value. It is based neither upon the ability of the owner to pay nor upon the amount for which the property last sold. It is the primary means by which local government pays for the services it provides, such as police and fire protection, schools, roads, parks, libraries, and the court system. More than half the local government revenue generated in the United States is accounted for by the property tax.

Before the amount of property tax for each individual property can be determined, it is necessary to know the amount of money to be spent by local government for one year (the budget) and the total assessed value of the assessment roll. The budget is obtained by totaling the tax moneys to be spent in three ways—bonded indebtedness, schools, and all other services. The total assessed value is provided by the assessor. The budget, less anticipated revenues from non–property tax sources, is divided by the assessed value to obtain the tax rate. An individual value is multiplied by the rate to obtain an individual tax bill. This may be illustrated as follows:

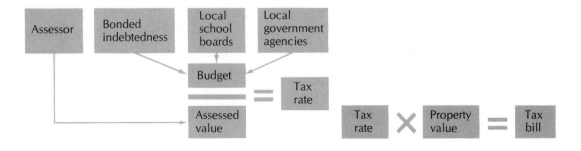

For example, suppose that the total assessed value is $2 billion, and the taxes to be collected amount to $250 million:

$$\text{Tax rate} = \frac{\$250,000,000}{\$2,000,000,000} = 0.125 \ .$$

This may be expressed as a 12.5 percent tax rate applied to assessed value. The tax rate is always a function of the budget and the total assessed value. If, for example, the budget goes up and the total assessed value remains constant, the tax rate will go up:

$$\text{Tax rate} = \frac{\$300,000,000}{\$2,000,000,000} = 0.150 \ .$$

If the assessed value goes up and the budget remains constant, the tax rate will go down:

$$\text{Tax rate} = \frac{\$250,000,000}{\$2,500,000,000} = 0.100 \ .$$

If the assessed value goes up and the tax rate remains constant, the amount of revenue has been increased:

$$0.125 = \frac{?}{\$2,500,000,000} \ ;$$

$$? = \text{Budget} = \$312,500,000 \ ;$$

$$\text{Budget increase} = \$312,500,000 - \$250,000,000$$
$$= \$62,500,000.$$

Tax rates are generally expressed in one of three ways: as millage, in dollars per $100 of assessed value, or in dollars per $1,000 of assessed value. Millage is a simple concept when properly explained. It is simply the tax rate expressed in mills (thousandths of a dollar) per dollar.

$$1 \text{ dime} = \$0.10, \text{ or } \tfrac{1}{10} \text{ of } \$1 \ .$$

$$1 \text{ cent} = \$0.01, \text{ or } \tfrac{1}{100} \text{ of } \$1 \ .$$

$$1 \text{ mill} = \$0.001, \text{ or } \tfrac{1}{1,000} \text{ of } \$1 \ .$$

In the first example shown above, the result $0.125 per dollar is equal to 125 mills per dollar. To convert dollars to mills, simply move the decimal point three places to the right:

$$\$0.125 = 125. \text{ mills} .$$

To convert the result in the example above to dollars per $100 of assessed value, simply move the decimal point two places to the right:

$$\$0.125 \text{ per } \$1 = \$12.50 \text{ per } \$100 .$$

This is the same as multiplying $0.125 by 100. The tax per $1,000 of assessed value is obtained by multiplying $0.125 by 1,000, that is, $125.

Once the tax rate has been determined, it is a simple matter to calculate the individual tax bills. The calculation involves multiplying the individual property's assessed value by the tax rate.

Examples:

A. Assume an assessed value of $10,000 and a tax rate of 125 mills per dollar.

    1. Convert mills to dollars by moving the decimal point three places to the left (or divide by 1,000):

$$125. \text{ mills} = \$0.125 .$$

    2. Multiply the assessed value by the dollar amount, 0.125:

$$\$10,000 \times 0.125 = \$1,250.00 .$$

B. Assume an assessed value of $10,000 and a tax rate of $12.50 per $100 of valuation:

    1. Divide the assessed value by $100:

$$\frac{\$10,000}{\$100} = 100 .$$

    2. Multiply the result by the tax per $100:

$$100 \times \$12.50 = \$1,250.00 .$$

Chart 1.1
The Assessment Process

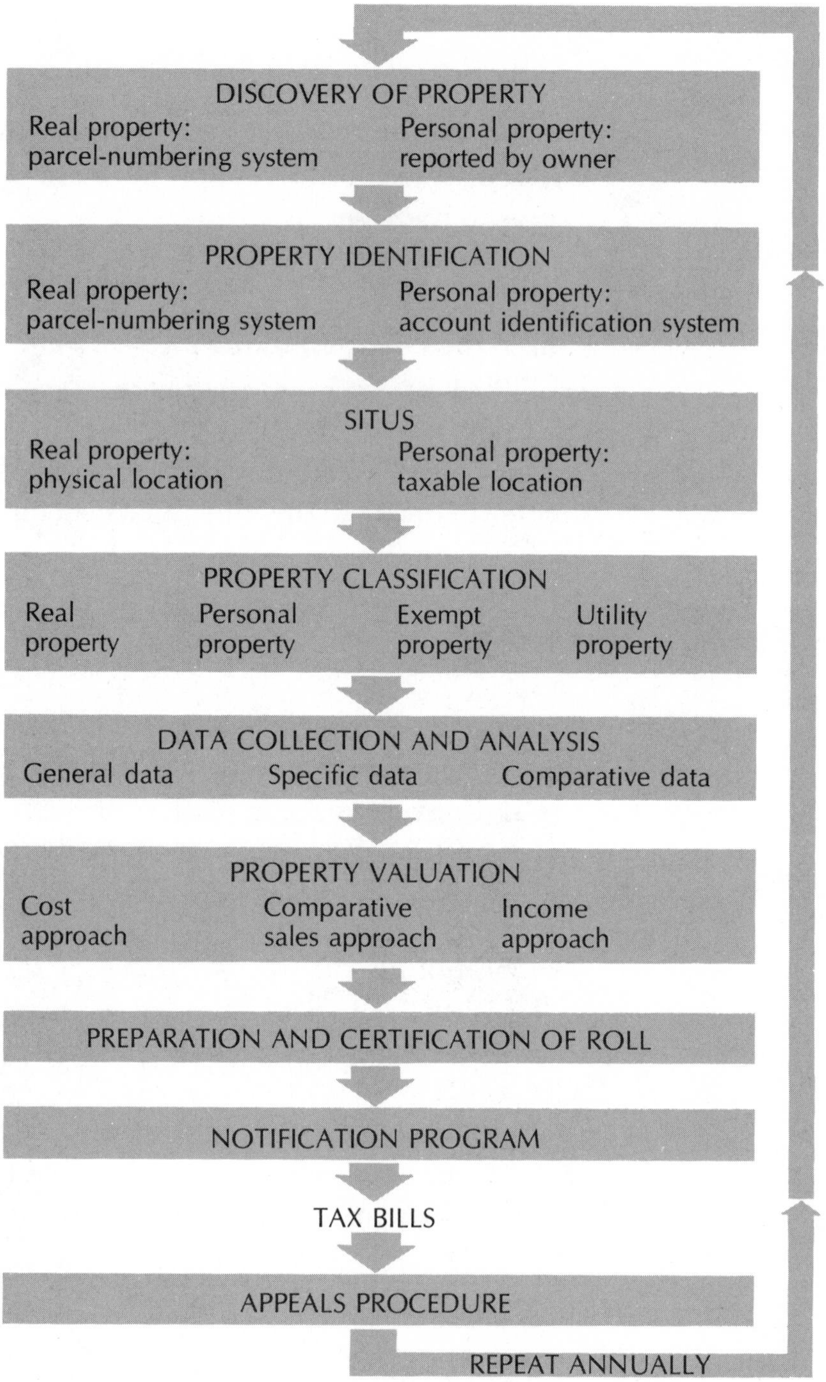

DISCOVERY OF PROPERTY

Real property: Personal property:
parcel-numbering system   reported by owner

PROPERTY IDENTIFICATION

Real property: Personal property:
parcel-numbering system   account identification system

SITUS

Real property: Personal property:
physical location   taxable location

PROPERTY CLASSIFICATION

Real   Personal   Exempt   Utility
property   property   property   property

DATA COLLECTION AND ANALYSIS

General data   Specific data   Comparative data

PROPERTY VALUATION

Cost   Comparative   Income
approach   sales approach   approach

PREPARATION AND CERTIFICATION OF ROLL

NOTIFICATION PROGRAM

TAX BILLS

APPEALS PROCEDURE

REPEAT ANNUALLY

Summary

The assessor is the government official charged with discovering, listing, and valuing all taxable property in the jurisdiction. The assessor's authority is derived from the constitution and statutes of the state or province in which the jurisdiction is located. The assessor is usually a local government official.

The assessment process is summarized in chart 1.1.

2 Property and Value

Before the assessor can undertake his responsibilities and duties properly, he must be familiar with the legal framework in which his function is performed. It is necessary to be acquainted with the nature of value and property and with the basic economic principles that serve as the foundation of the valuation process.

Concepts of Property and Property Rights

A discussion of property and property rights should begin with a definition of property. When the layman thinks of property, he tends to think of a thing. Legally, however, property is the *right* of any person to possess, use, enjoy, and dispose of a thing. *Property*, then, is a broad term expressing the relationship between persons and their rights in and to possessions. "A property," on the other hand, refers to the unit to be valued by the assessor.

All property may be divided into two major categories—real property and personal property. *Real property* is defined as the sum of the tangible and intangible rights in land and improvements. It refers to the interest, benefits, and rights inherent in the ownership of physical real estate. A synonym for real property is realty. *Real estate*, on the other hand, is the physical land and everything permanently attached to it. *Personal property* consists of movable items not permanently affixed to, or part of, the real estate and is commonly known as "personalty" or "chattels."

Real estate may be divided into two categories: land and improvements. *Land* may be defined as the surface of the earth together with everything under its boundary and everything over it, extending indefinitely into the heavens. The shape of a parcel of land can be described as an inverted pyramid with its apex at the center of the earth and extending upward through the surface into space. Certain legal limitations have been imposed throughout the years by the courts, such as the right of aircraft to fly over the land. *Improvements* (land improvements, such as paving, fencing, structures, and landscaping) consist of immovable items affixed to and becoming part of the real estate. "Permanently affixed" refers to the economic life of the improvements rather than "forever."

In discussing the distinction between real estate and personal property, the term *affixed* was used. Defining *fixture* has been the subject of much litigation, and the courts do not always agree. Generally speaking, personal property annexed to land is called a fixture. Chattels that have been annexed to the land so as to lose their character as chattels become real estate for ad valorem taxation purposes. In determining the nature of the annexation of personal property, there are two basic considerations: first, the adaptability of the personal property to the use of that part of the realty and, second, the person by whom the annexation is made and his interest in the land and the personal property.

Courts tend to agree that, if the chattel is affixed to the land so that it loses its original physical character and cannot be restored to its original condition as a practical matter, it loses its nature as personal property and becomes real property. In some cases there are two basic tests to determine whether personal property becomes real property: (1) the intention of the person who put the item in its place and (2) whether the item may be removed from the real estate without damaging either the item or the real estate. For example, if a tenant places a screen in front of a fireplace, there is no intent of permanent installation, and the screen can be easily removed when the tenant leaves. The screen is therefore personal property. However, if a property owner installs a light switch in the wall, the wall would be damaged by its removal. The light switch is considered part of the real estate. In more difficult cases involving this question, state statutes and court decisions should be the reference sources.

Another important distinction in property is that of tangible and intangible property. *Tangible property* consists of actual physical property. *Intangible property* is evidence of ownership of property rights. Examples of intangible property are patent rights, copyrights, notes, mortgages, deeds of trust, and stock certificates.

Ownership of Property

There are six basic rights associated with the ownership of property:

1. The right to use.
2. The right to sell.
3. The right to lease or rent.
4. The right to enter or leave (real property).
5. The right to give away.
6. The right to refuse to do any of these.

These are rights included in what is known as the *bundle of rights,* which is the ownership of all the legal rights obtained with fee-simple title. The bundle of rights may be compared to a bundle of sticks, each representing ownership of one property right. Basically property rights are divisible. Property ownership is transferred in many circumstances without the exchange of the full bundle of rights.

Unless property is owned by the government, it is subject to certain public and possibly private restrictions. The United States and other nations impose certain limitations for the common good. These public, or legal, restrictions thrust limitations on the full bundle of rights. Four rights, or "sticks," have been removed from the full bundle in favor of governmental control.

- *Taxation*—the right to tax the property for support of the government.
- *Eminent domain*—the right to take the property for public use provided that just compensation is paid.
- *Police power*—the right to regulate the use of property for the public welfare in the areas of safety, health, morals, zoning, building codes, and traffic and sanitary regulations.
- *Escheat*—the right to have property revert to the state for nonpayment of taxes or where there are no legal heirs of a decedent who dies intestate.

Some of the private limitations which affect fee-simple ownership of property are (1) the rights of other co-owners of the property; (2) covenants, conditions, and restrictions that are found in the chain of title to the property; (3) mortgages (a mortgage is a written instrument pledging specified real estate as a guarantee for the repayment of a loan used to purchase property); (4) easements and rights of way (an easement is a right held by one person to use the land of another); (5) liens and judgments (a lien is a legal right to hold property or to have it sold or applied for a payment of a claim); and (6) leases.

Estates in Property

Estate may be defined as the legal position or status of an owner with respect to the property and the degree or quantity of interest owned with respect to the nature of the right, its duration, or its relation to the rights of others. Estates in real property may be categorized according to the quality and duration of the property rights. The two main divisions in estates are freehold and nonfreehold. A *freehold estate* is one which is to endure for an uncertain period of time but which usually lasts during the life of some person. *Nonfreehold estates* endure for a specified period of time and may be subject to immediate termination. There are three basic types of freehold estates: fee simple absolute, fee tail, and life estates.

An estate in fee simple is one which has been given to an individual and his heirs without any end or limit put to his estate. *Fee-simple title* is the greatest possible degree of ownership. It is title free and clear of all encumbrances, including easements, rights of way, liens, and so forth. In other words, it is the ownership of all legal rights. With certain statutory exceptions, fee-simple title is the only estate which the assessor values. Personal property is always valued by the assessor as free and clear of all encumbrances.

A *fee tail* is an estate which descends to a person and his heirs, or some particular class of such heirs, until the extinction of the last heir. This estate violates the rule against perpetuities (control of property after death) and, as a result, has been abolished by most states or curtailed by the conversion to fee-simple estate.

A *life estate* is granted with ownership limited to the life of the owner or that of another party. An assessor may be called upon to value a life estate if required by law or if the remaining interest is owned by an exempt government agency.

Examples of nonfreehold estates are various types of tenancy, such as tenancy at will that can be canceled by either landlord or tenant and has no definite term. A special type of interest in land that may fall within categories of nonfreehold estates is possessory interest. *Possessory interest* may be defined for assessment purposes as the possession of, claim to, or right to the possession of taxable land or improvements when uncoupled with the ownership of tax-exempt land or improvements by the same person. Possessory interests present special valuation problems to the assessor.

Estates in real property may also be categorized according to the way in which title is held: tenancy in severalty indicates ownership interest by one owner; tenancy in common indicates ownership by more than one person where the interest is not divided and descends individually to each owner's heirs; tenancy by the entirety indicates joint ownership by husband and wife where ownership reverts to the survivor and cannot be disposed of individually during the lifetime of either. There are many different types of tenancy in which the assessor is interested primarily for the purpose of keeping ownership records up to date.

Nature of Property Value

The word "value" is an abstract word, generic in nature, with many acceptable definitions and meanings. The term defies exact definition to suit all circumstances. In a broad sense, value is defined as the relationship between an object desired and a potential purchaser. It is the ability of a commodity to command another commodity (money) in exchange. For purposes of real estate appraisal, *value* may be described as the present worth of future benefits arising from the ownership of real property.

A major distinction must be made between value in use and value in exchange. A property may have one value in use and a significantly different value in exchange. *Value in use* embodies the objective premise which maintains that value is within the object itself. A hose rack built into a fire station is a useful and valuable item as long as the building is used as a fire station. If use as a fire station is abandoned, however, the hose rack probably will not add value to the property unless it can be used for an almost identical purpose. Under the concept of *value in exchange,* the subjective element is accentuated. It is a subjective concept which holds that value is within the mind of man. For example, meat is valuable only if hunger exists; stated differently, meat is desirable and therefore valuable because it satisfies hunger when and if hunger exists. The value-in-use concept easily accommodates cost. In an economic sense, value in exchange is the primary concern for the assessor because this value—market value—indicates the actions and reactions of buyers, sellers, and investors.

In order for property to have value, it must have utility, scarcity, and desirability. *Utility* is the capacity of goods to excite desire for possession and should not be confused with usefulness. Diamonds possess utility in that they excite a desire for possession in the minds of most people and usefulness in that they are the hardest substance known and have many industrial uses. Utility is a subjective concept, in the mind of man; usefulness is an objective concept, inherent in the property.

Scarcity is the second requirement for value. The air we breathe has utility, but it is not valuable, primarily because it is not scarce. There are two economic forces that determine scarcity: supply and demand. As demand increases or supply decreases, the value of the goods will increase. Conversely, if the supply increases or the demand decreases, the value of the goods will decrease.

Utility and scarcity by themselves do not confer value on an object, unless the desire by the purchaser is present, a desire backed by purchasing power.

A comparison of the terms "cost" and "price" is useful in a discussion of value. *Cost* may be defined as the sacrifice made in the acquisition of property. It may be incurred in either the purchase of an existing property or the construction of a new property. *Price* may be defined as the amount of money given or expected in the exchange for property. Cost and price may be the same. If a purchaser pays $10,000 to buy a property, it may be stated that the property costs the purchaser $10,000. However, while price is defined in terms of money, cost is expressed as a sacrifice. A sacrifice may be in terms of money, labor, or time. Also, when a property is sold, the price may be either above or below the owner's cost.

Market Value

While the term "value" remains quite difficult to define, the term "market value" does not suffer from the same limitation. The constitutions and statutes of the states and provinces have many different definitions of market value. They also have different definitions of value for property taxation, eminent domain, corporate reorganization, and public utility rate regulation.

Neither the United States Supreme Court nor the United States Circuit Court of Appeals has defined market value of real property in an ad valorem tax case. The Supreme Court, however, provided a definition of market value for personal property in an 1865 case involving ad valorem duties upon imports. In this case the Supreme Court approved the trial judge's instructions to the jury, as follows:

The market value of goods is the price at which the owner of the goods, or the producer, holds them for sale; the price at which they are freely offered in the market to all the world; such prices as dealers in the goods are willing to receive, and purchasers are made to pay, when the goods are bought and sold in the ordinary course of trade. You will perceive, therefore, that the actual cost of the goods is not the standard.[1]

1. *Cliquot's Champagne,* 70 U.S. 125 (1865).

For a definition of market value as it relates to real property we must borrow from the field of eminent domain cases. In a 1934 case the United States Supreme Court had the following to say:

In respect of each item of property that value may be deemed to be the sum which, considering all the circumstances, could have been obtained for it; that is, the amount that in all probability would have been arrived at by fair negotiations between an owner willing to sell and a purchaser desiring to buy. In making that estimate there should be taken into account all considerations that fairly might be brought forward and reasonably be given substantial weight in such bargaining. The determination is to be made in the light of all facts affecting the market value that are shown by the evidence taken in connection with those of such general notoriety as not to require proof. Elements affecting value that depend upon events or combinations of occurrences which, while within the realm of possibility, are not fairly shown to be reasonably probable, should be excluded from consideration, for that would be to allow mere speculation and conjecture to become a guide for the ascertainment of value.[2]

In an eminent domain case decided in 1878, the United States Supreme Court had the following to say regarding the use of the property as it affects market value:

In determining the value of land appropriated for public purposes, the same considerations are to be regarded as in a sale of property between private parties. The inquiry in such cases must be what is the property worth in the market, viewed not merely with reference to the uses to which it is at the time applied, but with reference to the uses to which it is plainly adapted; that is to say, what it is worth from its availability for valuable uses. Property is not to be deemed worthless because the owner allows it to go to waste, or to be regarded as valueless because he is unable to put it to any use. Others may be able to use it.[3]

2. *Olson* v. *United States*, 292 U.S. 257 (1934).
3. *Boom Co.* v. *Patterson*, 98 U.S. 407 (1878).

A definition of the value of public utility property may be borrowed from a rate regulation case, since the rate a public utility is permitted to charge is based upon the value of its property. In a 1926 case the United States Supreme Court stated:

But in determining present value, consideration must be given to prices and wages prevailing at the time of the investigation; and, in the light of all the circumstances, there must be an honest and intelligent forecast as to probable price and wage levels during a reasonable period in the immediate future.

If the tendency or trend of prices is not definitely upward or downward and it does not appear probable that there will be a substantial change of prices, then the present value of lands plus the present cost of constructing the plant, less depreciation if any, is a fair measure of the value of the physical elements of the property.[4]

Three definitions of market value may be restated as follows:

• *Personal property*—Market value is the price that dealers in the goods are willing to receive and purchasers are willing to pay when goods are bought and sold in the ordinary course of trade.

• *Real property*—Market value is the amount of money that probably would be arrived at through fair negotiations between a willing seller and a willing buyer, taking into consideration the uses to which the property may be put.

• *Public utility property*—The market value of the physical property (excluding value of franchises) is the present value of lands plus the present cost of improvements less depreciation taking into consideration the probable income and expenses for the immediate future.

In reviewing the two remaining definitions, the following important points regarding market value should be noted:

4. *McCardle et al.* v. *Indianapolis Water Co.,* 272 U.S. 408, 411 (1926).

- It is the most probable price. It is not the highest, lowest, or average price.
- It is expressed in terms of money.
- It implies a reasonable time for exposure to the market.
- It implies that both buyer and seller are informed of the uses to which the property may be put.
- It requires an arm's-length transaction in the open market.
- It requires a willing buyer and willing seller, with no advantage being taken by either buyer or seller.
- It recognizes the present use as well as the potential use of the property.

These points may be combined into the following definition of market value:

Market value is the most probable price expressed in terms of money that a property would bring if exposed for sale in the open market in an arm's-length transaction between a willing seller and a willing buyer, both of whom are knowledgeable concerning all the uses to which it is adapted and for which it is capable of being used.

Compare this definition with the one handed down in 1892 by the Supreme Court of Kansas:

The market value means the fair value of the property as between one who wants to purchase and one who wants to sell, not what could be obtained under peculiar circumstances when a greater than its fair price could be obtained, nor its speculative value; not a value obtained from the necessities of another; nor, on the other hand, is it to be limited to that price which the property would bring when forced off at auction under the hammer. It is what it would bring at a fair public sale, when one party wanted to sell and the other to buy.[5]

It is important to keep in mind that the assessor should refer to the definition of market value found in the stat-

5. *Kansas City, W & NWR Co.* v. *Fisher*, 49 Kans. 18 (1892).

utes and court decisions of the state or province in which his jurisdiction is located.

Highest and Best Use

The way in which property is used plays an essential role in its value. In 1894 the United States Supreme Court stated: "The value of property results from the use to which it is put and varies with the profitableness of that use, present and prospective, actual and anticipated. There is no pecuniary value outside of that which results from such use."[6]

Almost all property is subject to competing uses. Rural land is subject to the competition of farming and grazing. Urban land is subject to many competing uses: a single parcel of land may be sought after as the site for a store, gas station, apartment building, or office building. When one is estimating market value, it is necessary to determine which of the competing uses is the highest and best use.

Highest and best use may be defined as that use which will generate the highest net return to the property over a period of time. Further amplification of this definition is necessary for a clear understanding of the term.

The highest and best use must be a legal use. This means not only that the use cannot be criminal but also that it must be permitted under local administrative regulations, such as zoning. Assuming that zoning regulations are strictly enforced, the highest and best use may be limited. If it is easy to obtain a change or variance in zoning, uses not permitted by current regulations must be considered along with the probability that zoning will be changed. The use also must not be prohibited by enforce-

6. *Cleveland, C.C. and St. L. Ry. Co.* v. *Backus,* 154 U.S. 445 (1894).

able restrictions contained in the chain of title to the property.

The use must be a probable use and not a highly unlikely or speculative one. There must be a demand for the use either in the present or in the near future. This, of course, is determined by persons in the market and not by a bias on the part of the assessor. It is important to consider as well that the highest and best use may be the present use or an entirely different one. It may even be a combination of uses over a period of time. Imagine, for example, a site in a good downtown location on which stands a three-story store with a 75 percent vacancy factor. Assume that the site could be developed with a modern fifteen-story office building. However, since there is currently too much unrented office space on the market, the highest and best use of the property might be as a parking lot for the next five years. Once the excess office space is absorbed, its highest and best use could be as an office building.

The highest and best use will be a complementary rather than a competitive use. For example, if there are gas stations on three of four corners, a fourth gas station will reduce the customers that are available to all four stations. However, suppose that on the fourth corner a fast-food restaurant were established. The restaurant would draw business from the gas station customers. Conversely, the gas stations would draw business from the restaurant's customers.

The highest and best use must be the most profitable for the entire property—land, buildings, and other improvements—since the market deals with the total property unit and land and buildings usually are not sold separately. Also, when estimating highest and best use, the assessor should not combine parcels of common ownership that are used independently for different purposes.

The highest and best use generates the highest net return over a reasonable period of time. A use that yields a very high immediate income but one of short duration may not be as valuable as a use that results in a lower but more prolonged income stream. Just as everything changes with time, the highest and best use of property will change. The character of a neighborhood may be altered, thereby creating demands for different uses. The assessor periodically reviews conclusions as to highest and best use and revises them according to the data that are collected.

Properties in transition present a difficult appraisal problem. Not only must a new highest and best use be found for the property, but an estimate must be made as to when the property will begin the new use. Occasionally, there will be an interim use prior to the future highest and best use. In order to estimate the value of these consecutive uses, the benefits must be identified, valued, and summed. The total value is the sum of

1. The present worth of the income stream from the interim use for the period of that use less the cost of erecting interim improvements.
2. The present worth of the salvage value of the interim improvements less the present worth of removing them.
3. The present worth of the income stream from the future use less the present worth of erecting the future improvements.

For example, assume that a vacant parcel of land downtown has a highest and best use as a parking lot for five years and as a twenty-five-story office building thereafter. The sum of the future benefits is shown as pluses and minuses in the following example:

Plus	*Minus*
1. Present worth of parking-lot income for five years	1. Cost of erecting parking-lot improvements: paving, fencing, and small office

2. Present worth of salvage value of parking-lot improvements deferred five years

3. Present worth of sixty-year income stream from twenty-five-story office building deferred six years (one year for construction)

2. Present worth of demolition cost of parking-lot improvements deferred five years

3. Present worth of cost of erecting twenty-five-story office building deferred six years.

Basic Principles of Value

These principles, which have evolved from economic doctrine, are generally—although not universally—accepted as having a direct effect on the modern concept of value. It should be emphasized that these principles rarely if ever can be considered in isolation; it is typical to conceive of them in an interrelated setting, for they tend to complement and accompany one another (see fig. 2.1). It should also be pointed out that highest and best use is neither an economic principle nor an isolated concept but rather the interrelationship among the basic appraisal principles.

Principle of Anticipation

Market value is the present worth of all the anticipated future benefits to be derived from the property. The benefits may be in the form of an income stream or amenities. Anticipated future benefits are those benefits anticipated by the market. The assessor should not allow personal opinion to influence the determination of anticipated future benefits. Past sales of the property and past income are of importance only when they are an indication of what may be expected in the future. The principle of anticipation works in conjunction with the principle of change.

Principle of Balance

The principle of balance has dual significance. When applied to an individual property, the principle states that maximum market value is reached when the four agents of production—labor, coordination or management, capital, and land—attain a state of equilibrium. In the case of individual properties, the principle works in conjunction with the principles of contribution, increasing and de-

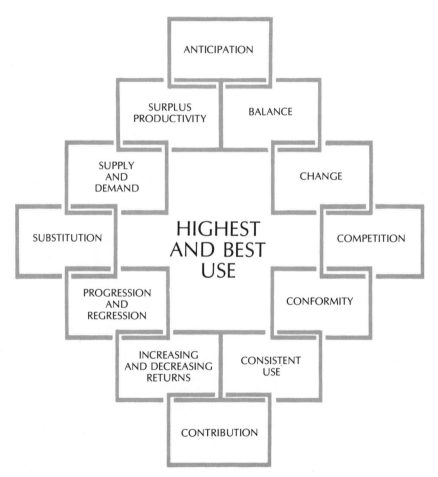

Fig. 2.1.—Interrelation of basic principles of value

creasing returns, and surplus productivity. When applied to a neighborhood, the principle of balance indicates that maximum market value is reached when the complementary uses of land attain an equilibrium. For example, a single-family residential neighborhood requires commercial facilities such as grocery stores, gasoline stations, drugstores, and so forth. It also needs residential support facilities such as churches, schools, recreational facilities, and the like. When these complementary uses are in balance, the individual properties (and the neighborhood) achieve maximum market value. When the principle of balance is applied to a neighborhood, it works in conjunction with the principle of competition.

Principle of Change

This principle states that market value is never constant, because economic, social, and government forces are at work to change the property and its environment. In addition, property itself is constantly changing. For example, the quality of the soil can be changed by the forces of nature, and improvements change by aging. Because change is continuous, the estimate of market value is valid only on the day it is made. The principle of change works in conjunction with the principle of anticipation.

Principle of Competition

The principle states that when substantial profits are being made, competition is created. This leads to the aphorism that profit tends to breed competition and that excess profit breeds ruinous competition. A neighborhood can support only a certain number of bowling lanes, department stores, gasoline service stations, and shopping centers. An excess of any one type of facility will tend to decrease the value of most, if not all, other such facilities.

Principle of Conformity

This principle states that maximum market value is reached when a reasonable degree of economic and social homogeneity is expected in the foreseeable future. When the principle is applied to improvements, reasonable homogeneity implies reasonable similarity, not monotonous uniformity. When it is applied to the residents, it means similarity in age, income, background, education, attitudes, and so on. Conformity works in conjunction with the principles of progression and regression.

Principle of Consistent Use

This principle states that the property must be valued with a single use for the entire property. It is improper to value a property on the basis of one use for the land and another use for the improvements. This is not to say that consecutive uses for the entire property would violate the principle of consistent use. The principle of consistent use is especially applicable to a property in transition from one use to another.

While the improvements on a parcel ready for a higher use may theoretically have a long physical life, their economic life may have already terminated. In this case the improvements may have a negative value, namely, the cost of demolition.

Principle of Contribution

This principle states that the value of an agent of production (or a property component) depends upon its contribution to the whole. This is another way of saying that cost does not necessarily equal value.

Examples:

1. Ten thousand dollars is spent on labor, which is a cost.

What has the $10,000 worth of labor contributed to the value of the property—less than $10,000, $10,000, or more than $10,000?

2. An owner spends $2,500 to erect a garage for use with the home. The market value is thereby increased by $1,500. In this case $1,500 is the value contribution of the garage. In the case of income-producing properties, the value of an agent in production (or property component) can be measured by the amount it contributes to net income, since net income can be capitalized into value. For example, assume that the owner of a small retail store finds that, by spending $2,000 for an air-conditioning unit, annual gross income from rents can be increased by $650. Additional operating expense due to the air-conditioning unit will be only $400, including amortization of the investment. Consequently, installation of this unit will add value to this property in excess of its cost. If the additional annual income were less than $400, the expense would not be practical.

This principle is the basis for the adjustment process of the comparative sales approach to value and the direct sales comparison method of land valuation, for determining whether physical deterioration and functional obsolescence are curable or incurable, and for justifying remodeling and modernization.

The principle of contribution works in conjunction with the principles of balance, increasing and decreasing returns, and surplus productivity.

Principle of Increasing and Decreasing Returns

This principle states that when successive increments of one agent of production are added to fixed amounts of the other agents, future net benefits (income or amenities) will increase up to a certain point (point of decreasing returns), after which successive increments will decrease future net benefits. For example, assume a number of hypothetical buildings, each constructed on the same site.

A $10,000 building that can earn 1.4 percent on its cost;

A $20,000 building that can earn 5.5 percent on its cost;

A $30,000 building that can earn 8.0 percent on its cost;

A $40,000 building that can earn 5.8 percent on its cost;

A $50,000 building that can earn 1.2 percent on its cost.

Larger inputs of capital produce increasing returns up to the point of $30,000 in this illustration. Beyond this point, additional investment contributes diminishing returns. The principle of increasing and decreasing returns works in conjunction with the principles of balance, contribution, and surplus productivity.

Principles of Progression and Regression

Progression indicates that the value of a lesser object is enhanced by association with better objects of the same type. For example, a $12,000 house among $25,000 homes could probably bring a higher price in the market. The principle of regression states that when there are dissimilar properties within the same general classification and in the same area, the better property will be adversely affected. Thus, when a $50,000 house is located in an area where the typical home is in the $25,000 category, the market value of the former will tend to fall. The $50,000 house, in this example, is an overimprovement for the neighborhood. The principles of progression and regression work in conjunction with the principle of conformity.

Principle of Substitution

A property's market value tends to be set by the cost of acquiring an equally desirable and valuable substitute property, assuming that no costly delay is encountered in making the substitution. This principle serves as the basis of the three approaches to value—cost, comparative sales, and income.

Principle of Supply and Demand

This principle states that market value is determined by the interaction of the forces of supply and demand. A sudden increase in the population of an area would increase demand. If, at the same time, mortgage interest rates rose sharply, demand might lessen.

Principle of Surplus Productivity

This principle states that the net income remaining after the cost of the agents of production—labor, coordination, and capital—has been paid is considered surplus productivity. The surplus productivity is the income earned by the land. The agents in production must be satisfied in the following order: labor (wages), coordination (management), capital (improvements), and land. As a result, land value tends to be set by the cost of labor, coordination, and capital. The principle of surplus productivity works in conjunction with the principles of balance, contribution, and increasing and decreasing returns.

Summary

This chapter has dealt with basic concepts of property and value and has discussed the ingredients of market value. Highest and best use and the basic economic principles of value have been shown, with particular emphasis on their interrelationship.

Concepts of Property

1. Real property is the sum of tangible and intangible rights in land and improvements. Real estate is the physi-

cal land and everything permanently attached to it. Personal property consists of movable items not permanently affixed to, or part of, the real estate.

2. Land is the surface of the earth together with everything under its boundary and everything over it. Improvements are movable items affixed to and becoming part of the real estate.

3. The six basic rights associated with the ownership of property are the rights to use, sell, lease or rent, enter or leave, give away, and refuse to do any of these.

4. The four limitations imposed by governments on the private ownership of property are taxation, eminent domain, police power, and escheat.

5. Fee-simple title is the greatest possible degree of ownership and is title free and clear of all encumbrances.

Concepts of Value

1. Value in use embodies the objective premise which maintains that value is within the object itself. Value in exchange holds that value is within the mind of man. Value in exchange—market value—is the primary concern for the assessor.

2. For property to have value, it must have utility, scarcity, and desirability.

3. Market value is the most probable price, expressed in terms of money, that a property would bring if exposed for sale in the open market in an arm's-length transaction between a willing seller and a willing buyer, both of whom are knowledgeable concerning all the uses to which it is adapted and for which it is capable of being used.

4. Estimating market value is dependent upon determining the highest and best use of the property. Highest and best use is defined as that use which will generate the highest net return to the property over a period of time.

5. The determination of highest and best use requires the proper application of the twelve interrelated appraisal principles.

3 Assessment and the Appraisal Process

Although the responsibilities of the assessor include more than the appraisal of an individual property or properties, the basic theories and principles, as well as the elements of the appraisal process, are equally pertinent to the assessor and to the fee appraiser. This chapter will review the appraisal process and at the same time will expand upon portions of it in order to show how the assessor deals with the different steps. By necessity, the assessment process and the appraisal process are integrated throughout the chapter, with expansion on both the appraisal process chart in this chapter (chart 3.1) and the assessment process chart at the conclusion of chapter 1 (chart 1.1).

An appraisal is an opinion; it is an estimate of value. A convincing appraisal is based on the integrity and competence of the assessor and the soundness and skill with which the available pertinent data are processed.

The appraisal process is a systematic, logical method of collecting, analyzing, and processing data into intelligent, well-reasoned value estimates. It is used by both the assessor and the appraiser in estimating the value of property. Even though the assessor must appraise a large number of properties in a short period of time, no steps in the appraisal process may be omitted. The appraisal process chart (chart 3.1) outlines these steps, an explanation of which follows.

Chart 3.1
The Appraisal Process

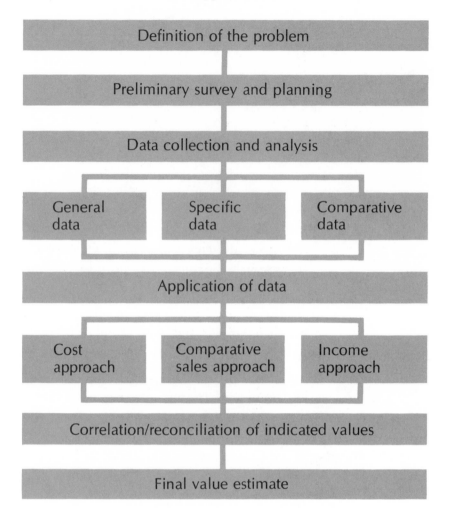

Definition of the Problem

Five individual steps are useful in the definition of the problem, which is the start of the appraisal process.

1. Identification of the property.
2. Property rights involved.
3. Purpose and function of the appraisal.
4. Date of appraisal.
5. Definition of value.

Identification of the Property. There are several ways to identify a property: street address, legal description, and assessor's parcel identifier. Legal descriptions appear in several forms—the rectangular survey system, the lot and block system, the metes and bounds system, and the geodetic survey system (see chap. 5).

A good mapping system is the foundation upon which a property identification system is laid. The mapping system may take the form of a simple drafting system or a sophisticated, computerized one. While it is feasible to rely on ground surveys for a simple drafting system, more accuracy may be obtained through the use of aerial photography. The drafting system will produce reasonably accurate blue-line and black-line maps, which must be kept up to date by adding all the new parcels created by subdividing or by splitting and combining of parcels.

The product of an assessor's mapping system is the identification of both individual parcels and neighborhoods. The normal procedure is to assign a unique identifier (usually a number) to each parcel and neighborhood. To facilitate the location of the number on the map, it is common practice to use most of the number to identify the individual map and indicate where the map may be found.

The assessor will also use the street address of the property and its legal description, which facilitate its location for on-site inspection. The legal description will be used as a secondary identifier, in abbreviated form, to keep the assessor's ownership records up to date.

Property Rights Involved. Normally the assessor will be concerned with appraising all the rights that may legally be owned—that is, fee-simple title. Most state and provincial statutes require the assessor to assign all value-contributing rights to the title owner of the land. Where valuation of fractional interests is permitted, the assessor must identify such interests.

Purpose and Function of the Appraisal. The purpose of all appraisals is to estimate value. Although the assessor must determine the type of value sought, normally it will be market value. Other appraisal specialists may be involved with other types, such as insurance value, mortgage value, and condemnation value. The function of the appraisal refers to the use to which it is put, such as obtaining a mortgage loan or obtaining insurance. The assessor normally uses the appraisal as a basis for property taxation.

Date of Appraisal. The opinion of value, strictly construed, is effective only on the date of appraisal. As indicated by the principle of change, conditions, trends, and factors may be altered in a short period of time, sometimes drastically, thus affecting value.

Definition of Value. The assessor must isolate the exact value that is sought—whether market value, insurance value, or some other kind. A precise definition of the value sought is necessary as well.

Preliminary Survey and Planning

This portion of the appraisal process should include at least the following considerations: a tentative or final estimate of highest and best use, an inventory of required data to be collected, selection of the dominant approach to value, and allocation of time and resources to accomplish the assignment.

The estimate of the highest and best use is of great importance. At this stage in the appraisal process the assessor may not always have enough information for a well-defined estimate of highest and best use, but he probably can make a tentative judgment. A final decision on highest and best use will be made after full consideration of the items cited thus far, as well as of physical, economic, governmental, and social forces and the site and improvement descriptions of the subject property.

Each appraisal problem will require that a certain amount of information be gathered. The type of property will determine the extent and areas of data collection. At the same time, the probable dominant approach to value will present itself. Not all approaches will necessarily be pertinent in every appraisal. Again, the nature of the property usually will dictate the most relevant approach. Another significant factor is the amount of information available to process each approach. Since the assessor must, by the nature of his position, handle many properties, he must prudently budget his own time and resources as well as those of his staff. More time and effort, obviously, must be dedicated to the more complicated properties. Although the assessor is involved primarily with mass appraisal, there is no excuse for neglecting the important elements of the appraisal process.

Data Collection and Analysis

Data to be collected, analyzed, and processed can be divided into three categories: general, specific, and comparative. General data include trends that work to affect value and may occur on the national, regional, and neighborhood levels. They also include physical, economic, governmental, and social factors that affect value; these are discussed in chapter 4. Comparative data consist of recent sales, cost, and income information. Specific data consist principally of site and improvement data and are discussed in detail in chapters 5 and 7, respectively.

Data are collected in a variety of ways by the assessor. Cost, comparative sales, and income and expense data are gathered either through interviews or via questionnaires. A field visit with thorough inspection of the property is required to capture the neighborhood characteristics and site and improvement data. These data are usually recorded on a property record card. When improvement data are collected, special attention is given to condition and functional utility.

Using cost data, the assessor must develop cost manuals and depreciation schedules. The cost data may also be used as historical cost for individual properties and as a basis for developing up-to-date factor tables to make historical costs current. From sales data, basic adjustments are developed, such as time and location and gross rent multipliers. As a result, benchmark properties for comparison purposes are established. From income and expense statements, the assessor may develop economic rents, vacancy and collection loss allowances, and discount, tax, and recapture rates. Chapters on each of the three valuation approaches expand on comparative data.

Data collection and analysis are illustrated in chart 3.2.

Application of the Approaches to Value

As indicated in chart 3.1, the three approaches to value are the cost approach, the comparative sales approach, and the income approach. Chart 3.3 shows the valuation step as it relates to the assessment process.

Not all three approaches to value are pertinent and useful in the valuation of all properties. For instance, the income approach does not lend itself to the valuation of single-family residences, which are not typically purchased for their income-producing abilities. The cost approach is not applicable to the valuation of vacant land. The comparative sales approach can usually be eliminated in the valuation of a public library or zoo where no useful sales information is available. Following is a brief description of the important steps in each approach and how the assessor uses them in the assessment process. These steps are expanded upon in the chapters devoted to each approach as well as in chapter 13, "The Mass Appraisal Process."

Cost Approach. To the estimated value of the land, preferably derived from sales data, is added the current depreciated reproduction or replacement cost of the improvements. The value estimate is the sum of the depreciated improvement cost and the site value. The principle

Chart 3.2
Data Collection and Analysis

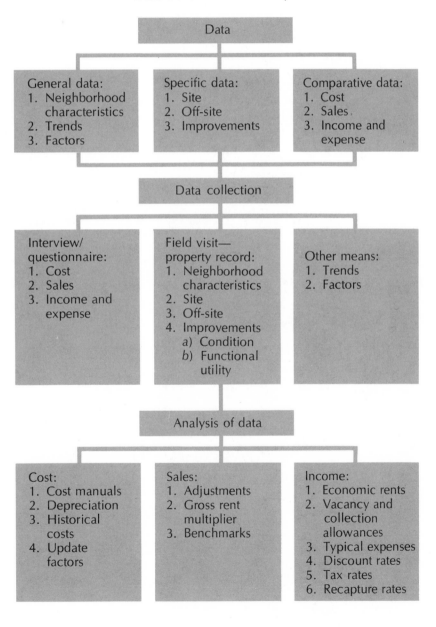

of substitution is pertinent in this approach. The steps in the cost approach include the following:

- Value estimate of the land as if vacant and marketable.
- Estimate of the reproduction or replacement cost of all improvements to land as of the date of appraisal.
- Deduction of the estimate of accrued depreciation from all causes.
- Addition of the current depreciated reproduction or replacement cost of all improvements to the estimated land value.

Comparative Sales Approach. Based on the subjective concept of value in exchange, the comparative sales approach to value provides for the comparing of similar

Chart 3.3
Valuation in the Assessment Process

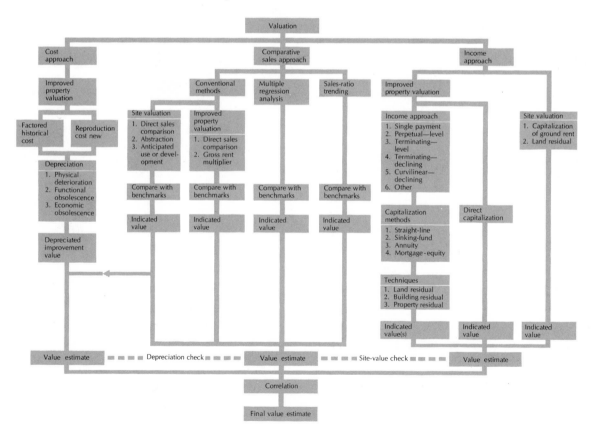

properties sold in the recent past with the property under appraisal. The market evidence gained from the sales is analyzed as to similarity applied to the subject of appraisal. Value indications derived from this approach are usually considered particularly significant because the reactions of buyers and sellers in the real estate market are expressed. The comparative sales approach is used to value any property, whether improved or vacant, as long as that type of property is being exchanged periodically in the market. There are four basic steps in the approach:

- Discovering and analyzing the data.
- Selecting appropriate units of comparison.
- Making reasonable adjustments based on the market.
- Applying the data to the subject of appraisal.

The assessor uses conventional appraisal methods to value vacant and improved properties. The assessor may also use two sophisticated methods to value these properties—multiple regression analysis and sales-ratio trending. These methods are discussed in chapter 13.

The five conventional methods employed to value a site are direct sales comparison, abstraction, anticipated use or development, capitalization of ground rent, and land residual capitalization. Improved property is valued by using the adjustment method and the gross rent multiplier method. Whichever of the latter methods is used, the assessor should compare the results with established benchmark properties. The values indicated by the use of multiple methods are correlated into a single estimate for the comparative sales approach.

Income Approach. A restatement of the definition of market value in terms of the income approach provides that value is the present worth of future benefits arising from the ownership of a property. This is an exemplification of the principle of anticipation. Income-producing real property typically is purchased for the right to receive the future income stream of the property. The assessor seeks to evaluate this income stream in terms of quantity, quality, and duration and then to convert it by means of appropriate capitalization rates into an expression of present worth of market value. There are five major steps in this approach:

- Estimate of gross income from market data.
- Analysis and estimate of operating expense.
- Estimate of net income.
- Selection of appropriate capitalization method, technique, and rate structure.
- Computation of value by capitalization.

The income approach may be used also to value both vacant and improved properties, provided that the properties are leased or rented in the market or are capable of being leased or rented. The assessor may use conventional analytical methods in this approach, or he may enlist the computer.

Correlation and Final Value Estimate

When the value indications from the three approaches have been reached, the final step in the appraisal process is taken. It would be unusual, in actual practice, for the value indications resulting from the three approaches to be exactly the same. These value indications must be judged in three categories: (1) the amount and reliability of the data collected in each approach, (2) the inherent strengths and weaknesses of each approach, and (3) the relevancy of each approach to the subject of the appraisal.

In weighing the evidence, the assessor takes into consideration the purpose of the appraisal and the kind of value sought. It is indefensible merely to average the three value indications. The degree of reliance on one or two approaches should lead the appraiser to a logical and supportable value conclusion. The correlation may tell the assessor that he must go back into his appraisal process and make modifications before the final conclusion of value can be reached.

The Appraisal Report

The tangible evidence of the appraiser's work is the appraisal report. This report should lead its reader through the appraisal process to a convincing estimate of value.

There are usually two types of appraisals—the form appraisal and the narrative appraisal. The form appraisal is made upon a special form designed to record pertinent data and value conclusions. Such forms may vary from checklists to special building and property records. Many government agencies, such as assessors' offices, the Veterans Administration, and the Federal Housing Administration, employ the form appraisal, as well as many nongovernmental organizations, such as banks and savings and loan associations. The narrative appraisal leads the reader through the appraisal process to a convincing estimate of value. It is a summary of the techniques used to process data to arrive at the value estimate, within the framework of the appraisal process. The letter-type appraisal is an abbreviated form of the narrative appraisal.

In view of the assessor's multiplicity of responsibilities, it is recognized that not every appraisal can be reported in the detail required of the narrative appraisal. For many appraisals the assessor uses the same regional and city data, the same cost schedules, and the same comparable sales and rentals. Even though the assessor may present his appraisal on a one- or two-page form, the analysis behind each appraisal should include the facts considered in the formal narrative appraisal.

Summary

This chapter provides an overview of the appraisal process and shows how the assessor integrates the steps in his work with the assessment process. The assessment process is different from the appraisal process in that the former encompasses the latter and includes duties and responsibilities in addition to the appraisal process. At the same time, the assessor must deal with the *total* number of properties in his jurisdiction and perforce applies the appraisal process to his duties in a practical manner.

The essential points in this chapter may be summarized in the following list of six steps in the appraisal process.

1. Definition of the problem.
2. Preliminary survey and planning.
3. Data collection and analysis.
4. Application of the approaches to value.
5. Correlation or reconciliation of value estimates.
6. Final value estimate.

The assessor must concern himself with the varieties of methods and techniques employed in carrying out these steps within the assessment process.

4 General Data

There are three categories of data that are essential to the appraisal process: general, specific, and comparative. This chapter will deal with the trends and factors that work to affect real property value and are included in the overall category of general data. It is the responsibility of the assessor to recognize those forces occurring on the national, regional, or neighborhood level that influence the value of property and, in addition, to understand the four great forces—physical, economic, governmental, and social—by which value is created, maintained, modified, or destroyed.

Trends Affecting Property Value

A trend is a series of changes brought about by a chain of causes and effects. Since values represent anticipated benefits to be received from property ownership, these trends, typically economic in nature, play an important role in the future of the property. The direction of a trend, its limit, and its future value impact must be taken into account. Trends affecting a neighborhood can produce an immediate effect on the value of a property. Some of the major trends are discussed below.

The Economy

The status of industrial, commercial, and agricultural activity establishes the general pattern of the nation's economic health. The total economy consists of the sum of the various regional economies. Trends in the economic pattern are most obvious on the local or neighborhood level. The assessor should be attuned to the trends of the general economy so that he may be aware of their result on the local level.

Price Levels and Building Costs

The trends in general price levels, costs of construction, and current and projected costs of commodities can be analyzed through such statistical presentations as the cost-of-living index and the wholesale price index. The trend in building costs will influence the value of improved real estate.

Business Cycles

The economic history of the United States and other countries demonstrates that there are periods of underproduction and overproduction in industry and agriculture that result in inflationary cycles and recessions. Industrial overexpansion, inventory surplus, and governmental controls are examples of trends to be observed in this category.

Population

The principle of supply and demand serves as the basis for the importance of population trends. Normally, greater population will create more demand. Projections of birth rates and death rates and of shifts in population are significant.

Purchasing Power

The amount of money in circulation is a force affecting purchasing power, which is the economic ability of a population to satisfy desires and needs. Disposable income is a useful criterion to develop levels of purchasing power. The trends in wage levels and employment levels are important, as is the number of real estate transactions.

Financing

A projection of the availability of mortgage funds and the rates required for borrowing has a pronounced effect on decisions to buy real estate. Monetary policies and regulations of government agencies are trends to be watched.

Taxes

Emphasis on the property tax is becoming increasingly prominent in real estate valuation. Value levels of real property vary from community to community, depending to some extent on the property tax burden. Industry includes real estate taxes and their probable trends among items to be considered in a decision to relocate or expand.

International, National, and Regional Data

The value of property is affected indirectly by many forces external to the property. At the international level, some of these forces are balance of payments, war, the price of gold, foreign tariffs, and the stability of foreign currency. On the national level, forces include Federal Reserve policies, Treasury policies, interest rates, competition for financing, the Federal Housing Administration and Veterans Administration policies, income taxes, and national tariffs.

At the regional level, the forces begin to have a more direct effect on property values. Some of these forces include the unemployment rate; income levels; population increases, decreases, and shifts; availability of financing; and local imports and exports.

The collection and analysis of the foregoing data have been termed *economic base analysis,* which also consists of determining the impact of the forces upon a local area. While many appraisal texts cite the need for the collection and analysis of international, national, and regional data and usually identify some of the forces, they fail to explain the methods used in analyzing the data. Perhaps this is due to the fact that, with a few exceptions, such data are not only difficult to identify but almost impossible to analyze with any degree of reliability.

The analysis of economic base data is important in the prediction of the future income stream of a property. It is also important in predicting changes in property values, since it is expected that people dealing in the market have considered economic base data in establishing list prices, offers, and sales prices. However, if the market does not appear to recognize the trends found in analyzing data, the assessor must rely upon the market as the best evidence of market value.

Neighborhood Data

A *neighborhood* may be defined as the environment of a subject property that has a direct and immediate impact on its value. The term is primarily an urban and suburban concept; however, it may be extended for appraisal purposes to rural areas covering many counties. Residential neighborhoods are characterized by the activities or operations that are carried on in the neighborhood.

The boundaries of a neighborhood must be delineated for the purpose of analysis. The three types of boundaries are natural, man-made, and political. Natural boundaries include rivers, lakes, hills, ravines, and undeveloped land areas. Political boundaries are usually those established for governmental purposes, such as city limits, school districts, zoning districts, and assessment districts. In the man-made category are streets, highways, freeways, railroad tracks, and major utility rights of way.

There are four forces, or sets of factors, to be dealt with in neighborhood analysis: physical, economic, governmental, and social. They must be analyzed in reference to the neighborhood and the property under appraisal. The factors are probably indeterminate in number and frequently are in some process of change. The assessor, operating within a limited geographic or governmental jurisdiction, has a distinct advantage over fee appraisers, who must expend extensive time and effort identifying and evaluating the factors in many localities. Familiarization with these factors assists the assessor in establishing benchmarks for value decisions.

The four forces affecting value will be discussed within the framework of four property classifications: residential, commercial, industrial, and rural. Before extensive analysis can be accomplished, the assessor usually classifies the property that is the subject of appraisal. The principle of highest and best use is important in this step, because reference to it will be necessary for a correct determination of the class of property that is being appraised.

Residential

Physical Factors. In general, the most important physical factor affecting value is location. All other factors are subordinated to, or considered in relation to, location. If location is not attractive and all other factors are positive, the property will probably have a negative value basis. Other physical factors include those discussed briefly below.

Size of Neighborhood. The physical size of the neighborhood involves the homogeneity theory: the larger the area, the less homogeneous in nature.

Topography. Generally, low- and middle-income housing is located on flat or gently rolling land. Property of higher value may be located in hilly areas or in wooded, isolated locations.

Appearance. The attractiveness of the neighborhood has a definite influence on the value of the individual properties.

Size, Shape, and Lot Area. Older neighborhoods in urban locations tend to have small, narrow lots, while newer neighborhoods will tend to vary in the size and shape of lots. The more expensive neighborhoods will naturally tend to have larger lot areas.

Street Pattern. Older neighborhoods tend to have grid patterns, while modern ones exhibit more planning: curved streets, dead ends, and culs-de-sac. Heavy traffic flow is routed away from residential areas into main arteries.

Soil and Subsoil Conditions. The condition of the soil and subsoil will determine the type of building foundations within a neighborhood.

Drainage. Drainage refers to the capability of the neighborhood as a whole to handle heavy rainfall, which is contingent primarily upon the adequacy of the storm-sewer systems.

Hazards. Hazards take many forms: flooding, forest fires, industrial explosions, and airplane crashes. As the possibility of hazards increases, property value decreases.

Climate. The climate of an area can vary considerably over a distance of a few miles. Variation in climate will indicate what types of heating or air conditioning will be required for homes.

Utilities. Better neighborhoods not only have all utilities but normally have the electric and telephone lines located underground.

Conformity of Houses. The conformity of the houses will have a direct bearing on the appearance of the neighborhood.

Proximity to Supporting Facilities. Residential neighborhoods require proximity to schools, churches, and shopping and recreational facilities. The quality and location of these facilities have a direct bearing on the value of the properties.

Nuisances. Any noise or odors from commercial or industrial activities will have an adverse effect upon the values in the neighborhood.

Economic Factors. Some of the more important economic factors affecting residential properties are noted below.

Population Growths, Shifts, and Declines. The number of residents in a neighborhood and the family size set the character. The ages of the family members and the number of families with children normally determine the market for new purchasers.

Patterns of Use. Individual property values are increased

when there is balanced land use in the neighborhood. In addition to normal residential support facilities, such as churches and schools, there should be sufficient commercial facilities, such as grocery stores and gas stations.

Amount of Vacant Land. The amount of vacant land will normally determine the amount of room available for growth in a neighborhood.

New Construction. New construction in a neighborhood is a mixed blessing. It indicates that the area is growing economically; however, when there is new construction, there is need for more support facilities. It also places a strain on local government to provide the necessary services in the way of fire and police protection, sewers, and garbage collection.

Employment of Residents. The type of employment, its stability, and the location of jobs will have a strong impact upon the property values in the neighborhood.

Family Income. The level and stability of family income will affect the property values in the neighborhood. In this respect, it will also determine the level of income of the purchaser likely to be interested in the property in that neighborhood.

Ownership-Tenancy Ratio. The ratio of ownership to rental properties will often determine the character of the neighborhood. The owners of a property are likely to take pride in its care and maintenance. Tenants do not have any permanent investment and therefore may not exercise the same degree of maintenance as owners.

Turnover and Vacancy. A good neighborhood will show low turnover and vacancy rates. There should be some turnover, however, since it indicates that the neighborhood is attractive to prospective purchasers and tenants.

Price Levels. The overall price levels of a neighborhood will affect the individual property levels within the neighborhood and will also limit the market of prospective purchasers.

Rent Levels. Like overall price levels, overall rent levels will tend to set the maximum and minimum rental value of any one particular property in the neighborhood. As such, they will also tend to determine the type of tenant who will be interested in the property.

Lender Attitudes and Policies. The quality of a neighborhood is often determined by the availability of financing. If conventional lenders, such as savings and loan associations and banks, readily advance the financing required, it is an indication of a desirable neighborhood.

Foreclosure Rate. This is a guide to how well the lenders have done in making loans in the area. A high foreclosure rate will make lenders review and perhaps curtail their loan activities in a neighborhood.

Assessments. It is of primary importance that assessments be fair and uniform. If the overall assessment pattern within a neighborhood is not uniform, individual properties will be penalized. If a neighborhood is underassessed in comparison with other neighborhoods, it will have a competitive advantage in reference to the sale of individual properties.

Real Estate Taxes. The level of real estate taxes will be determined primarily by the tax rate established by local government.

Special Assessments. The existence of special assessments indicates that the local government has not provided the necessary off-site improvements required by the neighborhood. Such off-site improvements may consist of streets, street lighting, sanitary sewers, and storm sewers.

Utility Costs. This is not as important with residential properties as it is with other types of property. Generally, the modern trend is to have utilities provided across geographical and political boundaries. This will usually result in standardized cost over wide areas. However, if utilities cost less in one neighborhood than in another, this fact will have a bearing upon property values within both neighborhoods.

Fire Insurance Rates. Fire insurance companies normally set their rates on the basis of the location of fire hydrants and the quality of service provided by the local fire department. There are many different levels of fire protection, from sophisticated systems in larger cities to volunteer fire departments in local areas. The fire insurance rates may effect property values in a given neighborhood.

Governmental Factors. The third category of factors that affect the neighborhood consists of governmental, or legal, factors. Some of the governmental factors affecting residential properties are listed below.

Municipal Services. The availability and adequacy of municipal services have an important effect upon the desirability of a neighborhood. These municipal services include fire protection, police protection, schools, refuse collection, and recreation.

Planning. Good planning should provide for the integrity of the neighborhood and for growth that may be expected within it.

Zoning. One of the results of good planning is adequate zoning regulations. An adequate zoning plan will encourage the harmonious use of properties within the neighborhood. Good zoning enforcement will allow for minor variances but at the same time will make obtaining a different use difficult.

Building Codes. Building codes will have a direct effect upon the cost of new construction, remodeling, and modernization. Some localities have modern building codes that permit the best features of construction at the lowest possible cost. Other localities have antiquated building codes that increase cost. Like zoning regulations, building codes must be enforced to be of value.

Development Regulations. Development regulations can take many different forms. Some concern the development of new subdivisions and require that the developer install all streets, utilities, sewers, and other services. Some require that recreational land be set aside. Others may impose a moratorium on new construction.

Assessments. The policy of state government toward the valuation of property for ad valorem tax purposes will often dictate how well local assessors do their jobs.

Taxes. The policy of state government toward the taxation of real estate has an important bearing upon establishing the tax base. It is often to the advantage of the people to exempt certain properties from taxation when those properties are used for religious, charitable, or philanthropic purposes. However, when some properties are exempted from taxation, the taxes must be increased upon the remaining properties to make up the loss in revenue.

Special Assessments. The policy of local government will determine whether or not developers are required to provide necessary support services and whether property owners must replace existing services when they wear out.

Social Factors. The fourth category of factors that affect the value of property is social. Some of the social factors affecting residential property are the following.

Characteristics of Residents. The age of the residents, size of families, and educational and cultural background will have a direct bearing on the character of the neighborhood.

Population Densities. Usually the greater the population density, the greater the land value. This is not, however, always true of property values.

Crime. The crime rate in a neighborhood is one of the prime concerns of a purchaser of residential property. Both physical security and the attitude of residents toward the protection of their neighbor's property will have a bearing on the purchaser's decision.

Commercial

The element of income becomes pronounced when commercial properties are appraised. Many of the factors influencing residential properties also affect commercial real estate.

Physical Factors. Again, location is the predominant physical factor for commercial property. The size of the neighborhood, topography, the size, shape, and area of lots, and hazards all affect value in commercial neighborhoods. Some physical factors of particular note are listed below.

Street Patterns. Strip-type commercial properties tend to be located upon straight streets. This has an advantage in that shoppers passing by in automobiles can view merchandise in the windows.

Soil and Subsoil Conditions. Soil conditions will have an effect upon the site's ability to accommodate the style, story height, and kind of foundation of proposed buildings.

Drainage. It is important that parking areas for customers have adequate drainage.

Parking. Parking has a great effect upon shopping centers, since it may limit the amount of business a shopping center can do. Downtown shopping areas generally get by with fewer parking facilities because of public transportation. Outlying strip-type area developments require some parking in addition to on-street parking.

Traffic Patterns. Location plays a part in the effect of traffic patterns because the better strip-type commercial developments allow for both pedestrian and auto traffic to observe the display windows of the stores. In this respect it is desirable to keep the automobile traffic moving at slower speeds.

Nuisances. Nuisances are not as detrimental to commercial neighborhoods as to residential ones, since a moderate amount of noise is to be expected. Shoppers tend to avoid areas with obnoxious odors, however.

Economic Factors. As in the case of residential neighborhoods, assessments, taxes, and special assessments affect value. In addition, the following are some important economic factors affecting commercial property.

Population Changes. Growth, decline, or shifts in population will determine the number of customers available to shop in a commercial area.

Direction of Growth. Almost invariably the direction of growth of any city is outward; this has an adverse effect upon the downtown shopping areas. Outlying shopping areas will be directly affected by the direction of growth. Those in the line of growth will naturally show an increase in business.

Compatibility of Development. Just as a residential neighborhood needs some commercial property, a commercial neighborhood needs residential neighborhoods nearby.

Rents. The level of rents within a commercial area tends to determine the type of business that will be located in that area. Conversely, the type of tenants and the business generated in that commercial neighborhood will tend to set the levels of rent.

Vacancy Factor. The level of vacancy is an indication of the strength of a commercial neighborhood. Good commercial neighborhoods tend to have very low vacancy rates.

Property Expenses. The expense level of doing business within a neighborhood will tend to set its character. All other factors being equal, businessmen tend to locate in areas where there are low fixed expenses.

Competing Commercial Neighborhoods. When two commercial neighborhoods are located close to each other, both may suffer high vacancy rates: there are simply not enough customers to go around. There is also competition between downtown shopping areas and outlying shopping centers. Since the development of modern shopping centers, downtown areas have tended to lose business. This is due partly to the availability of free parking in shopping centers.

Business Failure and Turnover Rate. While the failure rate for new businesses in the United States is quite high, location in a good commercial area will provide a better chance for success. A low failure and turnover rate indicates a better commercial neighborhood.

Lender Attitudes and Policies. In addition to real estate financing, there must be a sufficient supply of commercial money for business purposes.

Governmental Factors. Governmental factors affecting commercial property are essentially those that affect residential neighborhoods: municipal services, planning, zoning, building codes, development regulations, assessments, taxes, and special assessments.

Social Factors. Several social factors in addition to crime and population affect commercial neighborhoods.

Shopping Attitudes. For food and small items, shoppers tend to go to neighborhood commercial establishments. For other purchases, the shopper has the choice of neighborhood commercial areas, downtown shopping areas, and shopping centers. In making their decision, shoppers will consider transportation, parking, and price.

Characteristics of Shoppers. The shopper's standard of living, level of income, and attitude toward spendable income will have a direct bearing upon the business conducted in a commercial neighborhood.

Industrial

Industrial concerns tend to have considerable mobility on a local, regional, national, and even international scale. The nature of industry presents, on a periodic basis, the necessity of deciding whether to move its location completely or to expand in its existing circumstances. The principle of change as it relates to technology reminds the assessor that factors affecting the decisions of industry must be identified.

Physical Factors. Location becomes the focal point of all factors—physical, economic, governmental, and social —when applied to industrial property. It is the paramount factor, which contains within itself most of the other factors. Some industries must be located on a river, in a port city, on a major railroad line, near air transportation, or in restricted climates. Other physical factors include size of area and topography. Of particular note are the following.

Size and Shape of Sites. The size of a site depends upon the activity that takes place there. Modern industrial park properties tend to be regular in shape, whereas older neighborhoods tend to fit the improvements to the available land whatever its shape.

Street Pattern. It is important that streets be fairly straight and wide, so that trucks taking freight in or out of the property are able to do so with ease.

Hazards. The primary hazard in industrial neighborhoods is the handling or manufacture of dangerous materials, such as explosives and flammable or corrosive substances.

Climate. The climate has a direct bearing on the expenses involved in the industrial process. In extreme climates, owners will have to spend more on heating or air conditioning.

Utilities. Manufacturing properties typically require an ample supply of gas and electricity.

Waste Disposal. Disposal of waste, which may take the form of liquid waste in sewage systems or solid waste to be trucked out, is important in the manufacturing process. Environmental considerations are of increasing concern as well.

Transportation Facilities. Of prime importance to an industrial neighborhood are transportation facilities: wide streets, railroad spur lines, airport location, and waterways. Raw materials must be brought in and finished products taken back out, both with relative ease.

Location of Labor. Since any industrial use requires the employment of labor, an adequate labor supply nearby is essential.

Economic Factors. Among the economic factors to be considered in industrial neighborhoods are rents, property expenses, lender attitudes and policies, assessments, and special assessments. Of particular interest as they pertain to industrial property are the following factors.

Wage Rates. Since wages are one of the major items in the cost of production, favorable wage rates will cause industry to locate in the area. Higher wages may cause relocation.

Union Attitudes. The attitudes of unions and union members will be a strong factor in the decision of an industry to locate or remain in a particular industrial neighborhood.

Cost of Utilities. In some localities utility rates are reduced for large consumers. This naturally has a beneficial effect upon the cost of doing business.

Transportation Costs. Any industry involved in the manufacturing process will have heavy transportation costs. Although it is ideal to locate plants close to both the source of supply and the customer, in reality this is seldom done. Plants usually are located close to one or the other.

Taxes. Many jurisdictions that wish to attract industry either totally or partially exempt new businesses from paying real estate taxes for a period of time.

Governmental Factors. The governmental factors are essentially the same as those affecting residential and commercial property: municipal services, planning, zoning, building codes, development regulations, assessments, taxes, and special assessments.

Social Factors. In addition to crime, the major social factors affecting industrial property are population growth, shifts, and density and the labor force. The level of the population will determine whether or not the necessary labor force can be provided to support an industrial neighborhood. The educational level, attitudes toward training, and membership in unions will have a direct bearing upon the cost of doing business.

Rural

Many of the factors affecting urban properties are also substantial in rural properties. Factors that are particularly prominent in the case of rural property include the following.

Physical Factors. The following physical characteristics have special relevance for rural property.

Topography. The use to which rural property may be put is often determined by topography. Flat and gently rolling land may be used for farmland, whereas steeper land might have to be used for grazing of livestock.

Climate and Weather. The climatic conditions of an area will often determine which crops are to be planted. Different crops require different growing periods and levels of rainfall.

Soil Condition. The condition of the soil will also be a deciding factor as to which crops may be planted.

Irrigation. Irrigation may affect rural property in the sense that, if water is available in ample supply at a low cost, the owner is in a competitive position with other properties not requiring irrigation. The type of crops raised may also be limited by expensive irrigation.

Proximity to Market. The proximity to the market will determine transportation cost to the property owner.

Availability of Residential Support Facilities. Like residential properties, rural areas need schools, churches, and recreation facilities.

Economic Factors. Some important economic factors that affect rural properties are listed below.

Family Income. When family income falls to an unreasonable level, the owners are more willing to sell out to large farming corporations or real estate developers.

Ownership-Tenancy Ratio. As with residential property, a high level of ownership will indicate stability in the neighborhood. A great deal of tenant farming will suggest a low economic level for the area.

Rent Levels. Rentals on rural property generally are limited to the use of the property for agricultural purposes. Rental income may not be a good indicator of the market value of the property.

Lender Attitudes and Policies. In addition to real estate financing, a sufficient quantity of money must be available for agricultural purposes.

Taxes. In rural property, real estate taxes play a major part in promoting the property to more intensive use. Jurisdictions may provide for assessments of the value-in-use type to prevent the fall of rural land to suburban development.

Land Capabilities. The land capability of a rural neighborhood has a direct bearing upon its economy. Some of the factors that will be determined are the type and value of crops to be raised and other uses to be made of the land.

Operating Costs. Some of the special operating costs for rural property are fertilization, irrigation, and farm machinery and equipment.

Governmental Factors. Governmental factors affecting other types of property also affect rural property. Two factors of particular note are taxes, particularly governmental policies dealing with in-lieu taxes or value-in-use assessments, and federal farm policies. The multitude of federal policies and programs, such as price supports, soil-bank programs, crop diversions, and the land-bank system, have a direct bearing on the well-being of rural economies.

Collection and Analysis of General Data

Most physical factors affecting a neighborhood may be determined through an inspection of the neighborhood. Information on some factors may also be obtained from such sources as local chambers of commerce. Some sources for economic, governmental, and social factors include the United States Bureau of the Census, public records, private surveys, utility companies, colleges and universities, banks and other lending institutions, and real estate brokers.

Summary

This chapter has covered trends and factors that influence value. Particular emphasis has been given to the effect that these trends have on neighborhood analysis and to the four great forces to be dealt with by the assessor.

1. The major trends are in the economy, price levels and building costs, business cycles, population, purchasing power, financing, and taxes.
2. A neighborhood is the environment of a subject property that has a direct or immediate impact on its value.
3. In the analysis of a neighborhood there are four forces, or sets of factors, to be analyzed: physical, economic, governmental, and social.

Later chapters will discuss comparative data in conjunction with the three approaches to value.

5 Land Valuation

When appraising real estate, the assessor must deal with two separate entities: land, which is the nonwasting portion; and improvements, which are the wasting form of the asset subject to various forms of depreciation. Land and improvements are frequently valued separately so that the trends and factors affecting each can be studied. In fact, many statutes require separate valuation of land and buildings. If the land is a site with improvements, the total property must, in the final analysis, be considered as an integral unit.

This chapter is devoted to the methods of land identification, analysis, and valuation. The first step in land valuation is identification of the property, since it is essential that the assessor know how much land he is dealing with and where it is located. Once the land has been properly identified and described, analysis of the subject is undertaken. This should include the study of trends and factors influencing value, the data collection program, and the physical measurement of the site. (The term *site* differs from *land,* in that a site is a parcel of land that has been made ready to use for the purpose for which it was intended.) Once the subject is analyzed, the assessor must value the land after determining highest and best use, utilizing one of the five generally accepted methods of land valuation.

Land Identification and Assessment Mapping

The assessor must deal with a wide variety of appraisal-related data. It is therefore advantageous to utilize tools that provide methods for modern and efficient presentation of these data. An assessment map is such a tool. It can be used to give tangible meaning in visual form to land-related data such as the location and limits of each individual appraisal unit. It may also be used to depict land use, socioeconomic patterns, sales data, school districts, legal ownership, or any other desired data conglomerations. These data are of primary importance to assessors, for they have been given the responsibility of making equitable appraisals on all property within their jurisdiction; however, without maps, they cannot be sure all property has been discovered and appraised. It is therefore necessary for the assessor to foster the development of assessment mapping in order to fulfill this responsibility.

Legal Descriptions

Assessment maps provide the assessor the location and delineation of legal land descriptions for the purpose of appraisal. All legal descriptions of land are based on surveys, which may be purely visual or highly mathematical recitations of the limits of the land. Assessment maps are therefore the net result of delineating the variety of methods used to describe the land. The following are land identification systems commonly in use.

Metes and Bounds. The earliest form of land description was the "bounded" description. This type of description totally disregarded the regularity or permanence of the land unit. It was often thought sufficient if land was described by naming adjacent property owners and/or features of the terrain—for example, "bounded on the north by French Creek, bounded on the east by the land of Ezra Jones, bounded on the south by a wooden fence, and bounded on the west by a line of trees." Little thought was given to the fact that a wooden fence or a line of trees would someday cease to exist.

As the land became more valuable and disputes over unclear "bounds" became more numerous, it was apparent that better methods were needed to describe the land. A general surveying practice began to evolve, which took into consideration the compass direction and distances along and between these bounds. Boundaries of property being described in this manner were said to be described by "metes and bounds"—*metes* meaning measurements and *bounds* meaning boundaries that included features of the terrain in conjunction with compass bearings and distances. A survey made today in the foregoing manner, but utilizing more modern equipment, might read as follows:

Beginning at a point on the center line of Palomares Canyon Road, formerly Stony Brook Road or County Road No. 7784, 50 feet wide, distance thereon, northerly 427.10 feet from the southern line of Section 35, Township 2 south, Range 1 east, monumented base and meridian, and running thence along said center line of Palomares Road, north 0°53′45″ east 199.88 feet; thence south 81°26′ west 266.64 feet; thence south 5°03′15″ east 162.22 feet to a line drawn south 89°39′45″ west from the point of beginning; and thence north 89°39′45″ east 246.26 feet to the point of beginning.

In assessment mapping, the foregoing description would be interpreted as shown in figure 5.1.

Rectangular Survey (Section, Township, and Range). The rectangular survey system is based upon existing law and was devised with the object of marking upon the ground and fixing for all time legal subdivisions for purposes of description and disposal of the public domain under the general land laws of the United States.

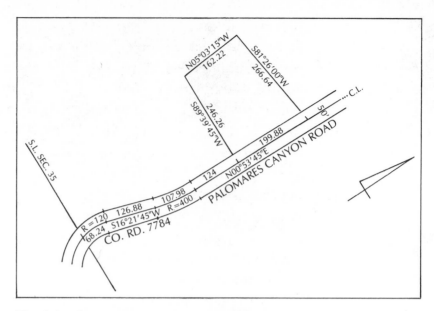

Fig. 5.1.—Interpretation of metes-and-bounds description

An ordinance passed in May 1785 was the first of many to be passed by Congress that would regulate the surveying, marking, and disposing of public lands in the United States in accordance with the rectangular survey system. The original ordinance called for the establishment of townships 6 miles square, each containing 36 sections, and each section being 1 mile square. The first divisions of land in accordance with the foregoing ordinance were those north of the Ohio River.

As shown in figure 5.2, surveys of the rectangular system are located with respect to an initial point or origin (usually a prominent geographic feature) through which pass true meridians and parallels of latitude respectively called principal meridians and baselines. The principal meridian is a true north-south line that passes through the geographic poles of the earth, while the baseline is a line that runs east and west parallel to the equator.

Once a principal meridian and baseline have been established, additional divisions are created. This is accomplished by establishing townships that are approximately 6 miles square, as shown in figure 5.3. Each 6-mile division

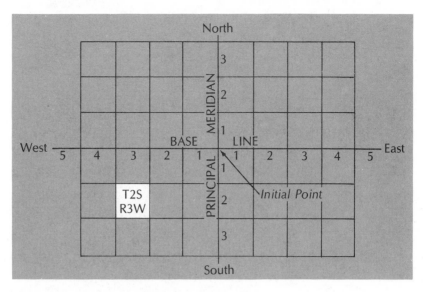

Fig. 5.2.—Township grid (rectangular survey system)

Township 2 South, Range 3 West   Section 14

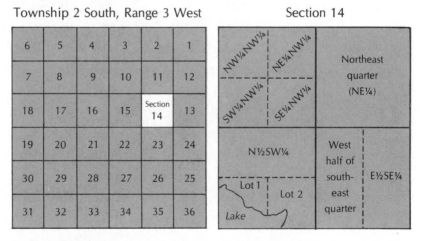

Fig. 5.3.—Subdivision of a township (rectangular survey system)

either north or south of the baseline is called a township north or a township south. Each 6-mile division either east or west of the principal meridian is called a range east or a range west. Each township and range is further divided into 36 sections each approximately 1 mile square. In the United States the sections are numbered consecutively, beginning with the section at the northeast corner of each township and continuing west to the northwest corner.

Then the sequence of numbers drops down one row and runs back east, and so on until the entire township is numbered, with Section 36 in the southeast corner. (In Canada the numbering system begins at the southeast corner of the township and ends at the northeast corner.) The divisions of areas of the rectangular survey system are approximate because of the convergence of meridians toward the poles. This often results in irregular-sized townships and sections. This discrepancy, as well as others due to errors in measurement or alignment, is thrown into the most westerly half of the township. Shortages in acreage are thus found on the west and north sides of townships. They become evident in fractional sections and in subdivisions of fractional sections. (A full explanation of this matter may be found in the *Manual of Instructions for the Survey of the Public Lands of the United States,* issued by the Superintendent of Documents, Washington, D.C.)

As can be seen in the following description, further divisions can be made by reference to the halves and quarters of a section: "The NE¼ of the NW¼ of Section 14, Township 2 south, Range 3 west, monumented base and meridian." An assessor's initial contact with this type of description can be traumatic. Take for example this description: "The NE¼ of the NE¼ of the NW¼ of the NW¼ of Section 14, Township 2 south, Range 3 west. . . ." In analyzing this description, it is necessary to note that the first ¼ section (the NE¼) mentioned is the property of primary interest, and all subsequent mention of ¼ sections relates only to the divisions necessary to locate the property. The key to the foregoing description is found in reading it backwards (see fig. 5.4). By progressively delineating it in this manner, we have now solved the location of the descriptions within the given section.

Lot and Block. During the late 1800s, land was being developed at a rapid rate. Cities and towns were being established, and large landholders within these areas were

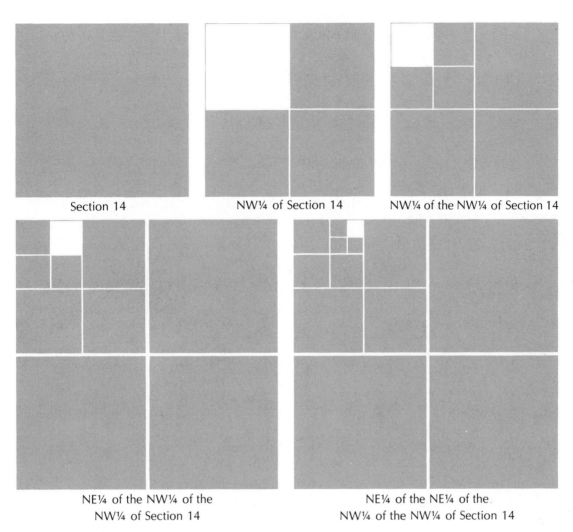

Section 14

NW¼ of Section 14

NW¼ of the NW¼ of Section 14

NE¼ of the NW¼ of the
NW¼ of Section 14

NE¼ of the NE¼ of the
NW¼ of the NW¼ of Section 14

Fig. 5.4.—Analysis of description of property location (rectangular survey system).

subdividing their land for purposes of sale. In most cases, this included making a survey of the property and its various sales divisions (lot and/or block), preparing a map of the property, and recording the map in the office of the local recorder. Although the map actually contained a metes-and-bounds survey of the property to be sold, it was possible, by adding numbers to each sale unit, to describe the property legally by simple reference to the units and their numbers as shown on the map. The following is an example of this type of description in verbal form: "Lot 7,

Block 2, Tract 1523, filed February 24, 1955, in map book 35, at page 52 Office of the Recorder." Figure 5.5 provides a graphic example.

Other Methods of Description

The enumerated methods of describing the land are used primarily to describe the location and extent of the land legally for the purpose of public record. The public record is created by the recording of land descriptions and provides the assessor with a current and historical reference to the ownership transfers and encumbrances of real property. In surveying and mapping there are additional methods of describing the land. These methods, however,

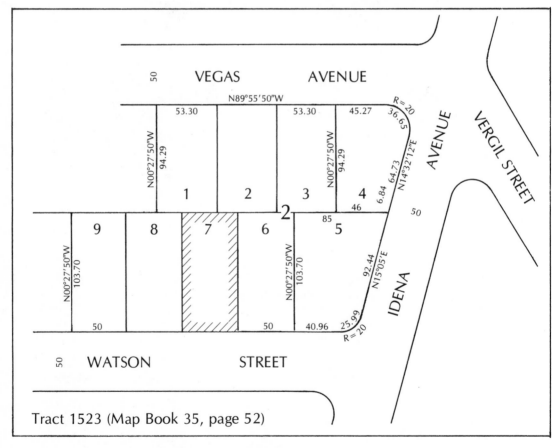

Fig. 5.5.—Example of lot-and-block description

are not extensively used for the purpose of legal description. A discussion of each of these methods and the reasons for their development follows.

Longitude and Latitude. Scientifically, militarily, and commercially there will always be a need to know the relative position of one continent in relation to other continents of the world. Geodetic surveying takes into account the shape of the earth and is used primarily to survey extremely large areas. The national network of horizontal geodetic control is composed of monument points from the accumulated geodetic surveys made by various federal, state, and local agencies since 1916. In the United States these surveys are conducted primarily by the United States Coast and Geodetic Survey and provide measurements of the interrelation of distances, direction, and location of monumented points. The geographic location of these points is expressed in terms of longitude and latitude.

The national system of interrelated points is called a horizontal control network because the correlation of other surveys is derived from and controlled by the network. All geodetic control surveys of the United States, Canada, and Mexico are referenced to this network, which is commonly known as the North American Datum of 1927.

X, Y Coordinates. In the surveying of smaller areas, the assumption is made that the earth's surface is a plane. It therefore is necessary to use a more local system of listing geodetic stations using plane rectangular coordinates expressed in feet and decimal fractions of a foot. In 1933 the United States Coast and Geodetic Survey worked out a grid system to fit the size and shape of each of the states. This system has become known as the state plane coordinate system. Just as geodetic points are referenced to a horizontal control network by longitude and latitude, points on the state plane coordinate system are referenced to a local network or grid by *X* and *Y*.

As shown in figure 5.6, the *Y*-axis of the grid is a true north-south reference line that passes through a point of origin. The *X*-axis of the grid is an east-west line perpendicular to the *Y*-axis and passing through the same point of origin. A point is located on this grid by reference to its distance north or south along the *Y*-axis and east or west along the *X*-axis as measured from the point of origin. The actual location of this point then becomes the intersection of lines drawn perpendicular to the *X*- and *Y*-axis lines. The additional application of geometric principles allows the calculation of the angle and distance between any two points that are referenced to the state plane coor-

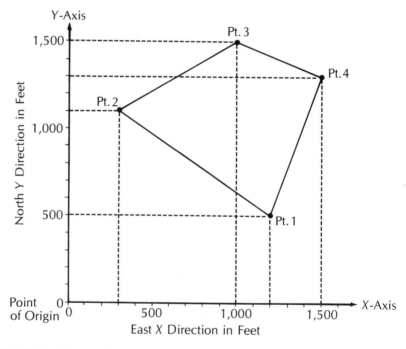

Fig. 5.6.—Description of land using state plane coordinate system.

Description by Coordinates

Pt. 1: $X=1,200$, $Y=500$
Pt. 2: $X=300$, $Y=1,100$
Pt. 3: $X=1,000$, $Y=1,500$
Pt. 4: $X=1,500$, $Y=1,300$
Pt. 1: $X=1,200$, $Y=500$

Coordinates Converted to Bearings and Distances

Pt. 1 to Pt. 2: bearing N56°18′36″W, distance 1,081.66 feet
Pt. 2 to Pt. 3: bearing N60°15′18″E, distance 806.22 feet
Pt. 3 to Pt. 4: bearing S68°11′55″E, distance 538.52 feet
Pt. 4 to Pt. 1: bearing S20°33′22″W, distance 854.40 feet

dinate system. This means that theoretically one could describe a piece of land using the X, Y values of the angle points within its boundaries.

Parcel Identification Systems. The parcel identification system is the tie between ownership, tax maps, and tax-roll entry. It is in essence the taxpayer's account number and, as such, requires uniqueness. Identification systems are basically unique numbering schemes allowing for positive identification of all properties in the taxing jurisdiction. They reduce lengthy legal descriptions to numerical expressions.

Like tax mapping, identification systems vary significantly in level of quality. The more elementary schemes use a sequential numbering technique employing the use of hyphen-suffix identifiers to identify property changes, such as segregations or subdivisions of acreage. The main disadvantage of this system can be traced to inherent maintenance problems and confusion resulting from the use of hyphenated numbers as properties are segregated.

Various sequential numbering system "takeoffs" are presently being used, the most noteworthy being the map-page system. This system basically entails the incorporation of the assessment map itself into the numbering system. A typical identifier resulting from such a system might appear as 1-22-15, where the first number indicates that the parcel is located in the book of tax maps labeled 1, the second number indicates the page of the property, and the third number specifically identifies the property on the page. The map-page system is subject to the same criticism leveled at the sequential system in respect to maintenance problems. In addition, if the system is not developed with foresight, chaos may result when urbanization takes place, necessitating extensive remapping.

Geocode parcel identifiers, although not presently in wide application in the United States, demonstrate real

promise in solving assessment needs. Geocodes are referenced to one of three alternative grid systems: (1) longitude and latitude, (2) state plane coordinates, and (3)
universal transverse Mercator coordinates. Complexities,
however, limit practical application of longitude and
latitude in the development of tax parcel identification
systems.

Coordinate parcel identification systems are characterized by: (1) an x, or east-west, coordinate and (2) a y, or
north-south, coordinate. Both are referenced to a known
point. Figure 5.7 illustrates the geocoding principle. This
simple illustration of a coordinate system clearly demonstrates the theory behind geocoding. Parcel identification
is based upon the distance the indicated dot lies to the
right of the origin, the x coordinate, and the distance it lies
above the origin, the y coordinate. The coordinates of the
property illustrated are therefore (4, 5). In this example,
the reference point is the center of the street frontage of
the parcel, but alternatives exist. For example, it is possible to establish the identifier as the centroid of the parcel

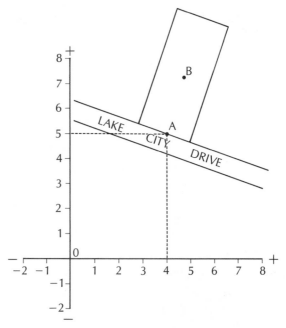

Fig. 5.7.—Example of geocoding principle

or even to identify two or more points. Through the identification of two points, more information (e.g., frontage) can be captured by the system.

Coordinate numbering systems have the following advantages over the others discussed: (1) in addition to providing a one-to-one relationship, they are easily maintained; (2) property identifiers resulting from systems directly relate properties to one another geographically; and (3) geocodes lend themselves to multiagency use.

Methods of Surveying

Two basic surveying methods are used in mathematically and legally determining the extent of landownership. The most common method is the field survey, where crews of trained personnel physically traverse the land using modern survey equipment to lay out angles and distances that will be used to describe a given ownership. The other method is a combination of limited field surveying and photogrammetrically adjusted photography. A brief description of photogrammetry is given here for the purpose of familiarizing the assessor with this survey method and the way in which photography can be used advantageously in the appraisal of land.

Photogrammetry. Photogrammetry is the science, art, and technology of obtaining reliable measurements and quantitative information from photographs. Photogrammetry dates back to the 1800s and the first attempts to use land-based (terrestrial) photographs to fashion topographic maps. The United States Geological Survey, an agency responsible for the majority of maps prepared in the United States, uses photogrammetry as the primary method of topographic compilation and mapping. Advantages of photogrammetric mapping include speed of coverage of an area, ease of obtaining topographic detail, and reduced likelihood of data omission because of photographic detail. As previously mentioned, the principles of photogrammetry combine limited field surveying and adjusted photography. Photography may be terrestrial or aerial. In photogrammetry, the field survey work is normally limited to establishing a minimum number of lines of known angles and distances within the area to be surveyed. Once these lines have been established, the endpoints are marked in such a manner (usually with large white crosses) that their position can readily be determined in a photograph. After the photographs have been taken, the known angles and distances between the white crosses are used as a mathematical basis for adjusting and removing error or distortion factors attributed to aircraft movement and camera irregularities. The final result is a photograph or group of photographs from which reliable measurements may be taken. Aerial photography, whether adjusted or unadjusted, can be a powerful research tool to the assessor. Photography can be used to give validity to the location of structures, fences, orchards, and so forth, and, if accurately prepared, photographs may be used for obtaining land measurements and the subsequent preparation of assessment maps. Appraisal data, such as square footage or acreage, use type, sales data, and income and expense data, are often delineated upon overlays. These data often make a useful, graphic appraisal tool when so displayed.

Versatility through Assessment Mapping

Earlier the visual presentation of data through the use of mapping and the assessment map's role as a vehicle for this presentation were discussed. Because of the versatility of the assessment map, its importance in the appraisal process cannot be overstressed. It must be remembered, however, that the assessment map is not a cure-all for the problems of land appraisal. Eventually, the increasing demand for the delineation of appraisal data will begin to place a burden on existing maps. New or better methods must therefore be utilized to prolong a map's useful life while facilitating the unrestricted delineation of land-related data.

One of these methods is the use of overlays. By overlaying an assessment map with a transparent sheet, appraisal data may be added without altering the configuration of the underlying map. A group of overlays may be used for each map, and yet the map may be removed at any time to be updated. Colors may be used on an overlay to represent a specific type or group of appraisal data. The overlay, combined with the assessment map, provides the assessor with a method for the delineation of land-related appraisal data without compromising the integrity of the underlying assessment map.

The preparation of maps is a very time-consuming job. Size, scale, and area coverage must be considered prior to preparation. Unfortunately, at some point the original criteria used in the development of a map will no longer meet the needs of its users. The map must therefore be redrawn. This will occur again and again or as often as the users' requirements change. It can therefore be said that inflexibility is the direct result of the current manual methods used in the preparation of maps. In assessment mapping this is especially true, for, as assessors apply new and more scientific methods to the appraisal process, they will find that the inflexible structure of current mapping is no longer applicable to their problem. Fortunately, map-makers have become increasingly aware of this problem. There has been a slow but steady increase in the replacement of manual drafting skills through the application of a new and more advanced technology. This technology employs the use of the computer in conjunction with recently developed specialized peripheral equipment for the automated preparation of maps. This process, known as *computer graphics,* should once and for all destroy the last serious limitation of mapping and provide an unstructured and totally flexible format for the dissemination of land-related data.

Site Analysis

Trends and Factors

The classification of land is basic to the study and analysis of trends and factors. At least a tentative decision on classification and highest and best use should be made at this point. The land may be classified as residential, commercial, industrial, land in transition, undeveloped, farm or ranch, or special-purpose. The nature of the physical, economic, governmental, and social factors will assist in developing regional, city, neighborhood, and site data and in selecting the appropriate valuation method.

One of the more important factors to be considered in appraising land, particularly urban land, is zoning data. Zoning ordinances often describe in detail exactly what uses are permitted for the property. Highest and best use may be predetermined with the assistance of zoning ordinances. Zoning ordinances may also specify how many units may be built upon a site, or they may limit the height of a building.

Site Data

In addition to title data, specific site data to be collected include frontage, width, depth, shape, area, topography, slope, drainage and soil condition, and off-site improvement.

Frontage. Frontage is the distance which a property abuts a street or other public way. It is normally expressed in front feet.

Width. Width is normally measured along the front of a parcel. With regular-shaped lots, the width and frontage are almost the same; with irregular-shaped lots, width will be an average measurement either larger or smaller than the frontage. When the parcel is irregular, the standard method is to add together the front and rear measurements and divide by 2 to determine the average width.

Depth. Depth is the distance from the front to the rear line of a parcel.

Shape. The shape of a site may be categorized as regular, slightly irregular, or very irregular. The shape of a lot may have a direct bearing on its value.

Area. The area of a parcel is one of the most important characteristics affecting value. It is important to consider the effective area—that is, the area within which a building may be built. Zoning and deed restrictions often require that buildings be set back from the front, rear, and side property lines. This may have a major effect upon a site because of the reduction of usable land for improvements.

Topography. Topography will often dictate the use to which a site may be put. It may also determine the size of the foundation, the type of construction, and the location of the building on the site.

Slope. It is necessary to determine whether the slope of the property is uphill, downhill, or side-to-side. The slope will determine what site improvements may be needed in the way of retaining walls and fill.

Drainage and Soil Condition. The condition of the soil and subsoil will determine the feasibility of construction. In order to build on sites with fluid subsoil, it may be necessary to have special footings. *Percolation* refers to the ability of the soil to accept moisture. Poor percolation may require special drainage features. The soil condition may also determine whether ordinary landscaping may be used or whether additional cost will be required to improve the condition.

Off-Site Improvements. The value of a site is strongly influenced by the value of the off-site improvements, such as streets, sidewalks, street lighting, and traffic patterns. Street width is of special importance to commercial and industrial property for transportation needs; traffic flow may affect residential property due to the effect of noise and traffic hazards. The utilities available to the property, including water, gas, electricity, telephone, and sewers, will also have an effect upon the value of the site.

Units of Comparison

It is often necessary to analyze differences in size and shape of comparable sale properties in order to apply uniform methods of valuation and to compare directly sites of varying size and shape. Five basic units of comparison are used to value sites: (1) front foot, (2) square foot, (3) acre and section, (4) site (lot), and (5) units buildable. Care must be exercised in selecting the unit of comparison. The assessor must ascertain from the market the appropriate unit or units in terms of which sites are bought and sold.

Front Foot. Use of the front foot as a unit of comparison is based upon the premise that frontage significantly contributes to value. A *front foot* is a strip of land 1 foot wide, fronting on a street, railroad siding, or body of water, and continuing to the rear of the parcel. This distance is frequently measured in terms of a standard depth.

The front-foot method is useful in the valuation of downtown commercial property, where the amount of frontage a property enjoys is important because of the exposure it gives for display area. It may also prove useful in the valuation of industrial property that fronts on a railroad siding in light of the requirements of the industrial firm. Likewise, the amount of frontage on a body of water may contribute to the value of a residential lot for swimming, boating, or the view. The "effective" frontage of irregularly shaped lots is calculated according to formula and will be discussed later. An example of the front-foot method is as follows: A downtown commercial lot has 60-foot frontage on Main Street and a depth of 100 feet. By analyzing comparable sales, it has been determined that similar lots with 100-foot depth are selling for $1,000 per front foot. Therefore, the lot would have a value of $60,000 (60 front feet × $1,000 per front foot).

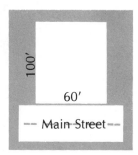

Square Foot. This unit of comparison is used for irregularly shaped parcels and where frontage is not a dominant factor in the valuation process. It is used for sites that sell for an average price per square foot of land area. This method can be used to value residential, commercial, and small industrial sites. For example, a subject property consists of 20,000 square feet. Comparable properties of similar size are selling for 50 cents per square foot. The indicated value of the subject site is therefore $10,000 (20,000 square feet × $0.50 per square foot = $10,000).

In this example 50 cents is the average selling price per square foot; however, in many cases the assessor may not be able to find comparable sales of similar size. In the adjustment process, consideration should be given to the minimum site necessary for the improvement (dwelling, retail store, etc.) and the amount of excess land, if any. Through the analysis of sales, the square-foot values should be developed for the minimum site as well as for any excess land. As an illustration, suppose that the minimum lot size required by zoning in the previous example is 15,000 square feet. After an analysis of various-sized properties with similar characteristics, an estimate of the minimum-lot value is 60 cents per square foot, and the excess-land value is 20 cents per square foot. The indicated value of the minimum site is $9,000 and that of the excess land $1,000.

Minimum site (15,000 square feet × $0.60)	$ 9,000
Excess land (5,000 square feet × $0.20)	1,000
Total site (20,000 square feet × $0.50)	$10,000

Acre and Section. Acres may be calculated by dividing square footage by 43,560 and are used in the valuation of large industrial sites, shopping centers, and rural and farm properties. There may be a breakdown between acres that front on a public thoroughfare and rear acres: in many circumstances front acres are more valuable.

A section consists of 640 acres and is a unit of comparison used to value ranch and farm properties, primarily in the western part of the United States and Canada.

Site. The site, or lot, unit of comparison is used when the market does not indicate a significant difference in lot value even when there is a difference in lot size. This method is becoming more prevalent and is found in residential subdivisions such as cluster developments and planned unit developments. It may also be used in valuing industrial sites located in industrial parks.

Units Buildable. This unit of comparison is used when the market indicates that a site is sold on a unit basis, such as an apartment property where the unit of comparison is selling price/buildable apartment or a parking-garage site where the unit of comparison is selling price/car. The units buildable may be either a theoretical or an actual number of units. The probable number of units to be built may be different from the theoretical number permitted by zoning ordinances. Consideration should be given to market demand, setback limitations, topography, height limitations, and other limiting factors.

As illustration, a subject site consists of 25 acres, and zoning ordinances permit 10 units per acre. The site has no limitations. There is one comparable sale of a property consisting of 30 acres with an allowable density of 10 units per acre. The property was purchased for $560,000 with the knowledge that because of a topographical problem only 280 units would be built. On the basis of this information, the subject site value can be estimated at $500,000.

Subject ...... Units buildable: 25 acres × 10 units/acre = 250 units
Comparable .. Units buildable: 280 units (actually built)
Value/unit ... Comparable: $560,000/280 = $2,000/unit
Subject ...... 250 units × $2,000/unit = $500,000

The unit price of $2,000/unit should be used because the developer purchased the property with the knowledge that only 280 units could be built.

Formulas, Tables, and Rules

Through the analysis of market data, formulas, tables, and rules have been designed to assist in dealing with changes in parcel size, shape, and location. They include depth tables, irregular-lot valuation tables, and corner-influence tables. It is important to bear in mind that these formulas, tables, and rules are only guides and must be supported by evidence from the local market.

Depth Tables. Depth tables assist in the measurement of changes in value caused by variation in lot depths where land is typically purchased on a front-foot basis. They are based on the observation that the front section of a lot is more valuable on a unit basis than the rear portion. As depth increases, the value unit decreases.

The least complex basis for computing depth tables is the "4-3-2-1 rule." This rule states that the first 25 percent of depth of a lot represents 40 percent of the total lot value, the second 25 percent of depth represents 30 percent of the value, the third 25 percent of depth represents 20

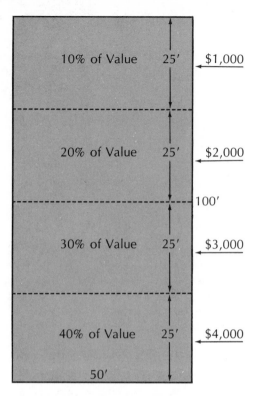

Front-Foot Price = $200

Fig. 5.8.—4-3-2-1 rule. The estimated lot value is $10,000. The 4-3-2-1 rule assumes that the first 25 feet of depth is worth 40 percent, or $4,000; the second 25 feet is worth 30 percent, or $3,000; the third 25 feet is worth 20 percent, or $2,000; and fourth 25 feet is worth 10 percent, or $1,000.

percent of the value, and the fourth 25 percent of depth represents 10 percent of the value. Figure 5.8 illustrates the value of a 50-foot × 100-foot-deep lot having a front-foot value of $200.

Some depth tables may show small variations from this standard. Table 5.1 is a sample depth table, based on a standard depth of 100 feet. Using this same depth table, the value of a lot 65 × 125 feet can be computed. Assume that the unit foot value for lots with standard depth of 100 feet is $50. According to the table, the depth factor for a lot 125 feet deep is 108 percent, or 1.08. Therefore, the lot value is $3,510.

Table 5.1

Sample Lot Depth Table (100 Feet Standard Depth)

(Percentages of Front-Foot Value for Lots 1–400 Feet Deep)

1–40		41–80		81–120		121–160		161–400	
Depth	Per-cent	Depth	Per-cent	Depth	Per-cent	Depth	Per-cent	Depth	Per-cent
1	7	41	66	81	92	121	106	161	116
2	9	42	67	82	92	122	107	162	117
3	11	43	67	83	93	123	107	163	117
4	13	44	68	84	93	124	107	164	117
5	15	45	69	85	94	125	108	165	117
6	17	46	70	86	94	126	108	166	117
7	19	47	71	87	95	127	108	167	117
8	21	48	71	88	95	128	108	168	118
9	23	49	72	89	96	129	109	169	118
10	25	50	73	90	96	130	109	170	118
11	27	51	74	91	96	131	109	175	118
12	29	52	75	92	97	132	110	180	119
13	31	53	75	93	97	133	110	185	120
14	33	54	76	94	98	134	110	190	120
15	35	55	77	95	98	135	110	195	121
16	37	56	78	96	98	136	111	200	121
17	38	57	78	97	99	137	111	205	121
18	40	58	79	98	99	138	111	210	121
19	41	59	79	99	100	139	112	215	121
20	43	60	80	100	100	140	112	220	122
21	44	61	81	101	100	141	112	225	122
22	46	62	81	102	101	142	112	230	122
23	47	63	82	103	101	143	113	235	122
24	49	64	82	104	101	144	113	240	123
25	50	65	83	105	101	145	113	250	123
26	51	66	84	106	102	146	113	260	124
27	52	67	84	107	102	147	114	270	124
28	53	68	85	108	102	148	114	280	125
29	54	69	85	109	103	149	114	290	125
30	55	70	86	110	103	150	114	300	126
31	56	71	87	111	103	151	114	310	126
32	57	72	87	112	103	152	115	320	127
33	58	73	88	113	104	153	115	330	127
34	59	74	88	114	104	154	115	340	128
35	60	75	89	115	104	155	115	350	128
36	61	76	89	116	105	156	115	360	129
37	62	77	90	117	105	157	116	370	129
38	63	78	90	118	105	158	116	380	130
39	64	79	91	119	106	159	116	390	130
40	65	80	91	120	106	160	116	400	131

65×125-foot lot size;

1.08 depth factor × $50 unit foot value = $54 per unit foot;

65 front feet × $54 unit foot value = $3,510 lot value.

Irregular-Lot Valuation Tables. The utility of a lot may be seriously affected by its shape. The size or shape of a proposed building can be affected by setback requirements, as previously discussed. The purpose of irregular-lot valuation tables is to convert the actual frontage of irregular-shaped parcels to effective front footage. The 65/35 rule is based on the premise that a right-angle triangular-shaped lot with its base on a street has 65 percent of the value of a rectangular lot and that a right-angle triangular-shaped lot with its apex on a street contains 35 percent of the value of a rectangular lot. Figure 5.9 is an illustration of the 65/35 rule. In this figure, the effective front footage of Lot A is 65 feet (100 feet actual frontage × 65 percent) and that of Lot B is 35 feet (100 feet actual frontage × 35 percent).

Corner-Influence Tables. Corner-influence tables are constructed on the premise that the greatest extent of value is at the corner of two streets and that value decreases with

---

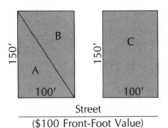

($100 Front-Foot Value)

Fig. 5.9.—65/35 rule.

Lot A: Right triangle with base on street; use 65 percent factor.
100 feet × $100 (front-foot value)
    = $10,000 × 100% (depth factor) = $10,000;
$10,000 × 65% (triangle factor) = $6,500 lot value.

Lot B: Right triangle with apex on street; use 35 percent factor.
100 feet × $100 (front-foot value)
    = $10,000 × 100% depth factor = $10,000;
$10,000 × 35% (triangle factor) = $3,500 lot value.

Lot C: Rectangular lot.
100 feet × $100 (front-foot value)
    = $10,000 × 100% depth factor = $10,000 lot value.

---

the distance from the corner. These tables consist of percentages that show an increase in value due to the assumption that a corner location affords more prominence, light, and air and makes the site more accessible to pedestrian traffic. Corner-influence tables do not necessarily apply to residential lots, but an analysis of sales may indicate that, in some communities, buyers pay a premium for corner residential sites. As is the case with all formulas, tables, and rules, they must be localized or extracted from the local market to be of benefit.

Assemblage and Plottage

Two terms commonly confused in appraisal terminology are assemblage and plottage. *Plottage* is the process of combining two or more sites under a single ownership in order to develop one site having greater utility and unit value than the aggregate when each is separately considered. *Assemblage,* on the other hand, is simply the merging of adjacent properties into one of common ownership or use. Generally, when the new site has a greater utility than the sum of the old sites, the new site will have increased value. This value increment is known as *plottage value.* Occasionally the assemblage of land will result in the creation of a new site with lesser utility, normally resulting in lesser value. This value decrease is known as *negative plottage.*

Land Valuation

The comparative sales approach is the most reliable method of land valuation. It involves comparisons and assumes that market evidence is available. Unfortunately, good, reliable sales data are not always available for use. For this reason, the assessor must resort to other methods of valuation. The five generally accepted methods discussed in this chapter are (1) direct sales comparison, (2) abstraction (allocation or distribution), (3) anticipated use or development, (4) capitalization of ground rent, and (5) land residual capitalization.

Direct Sales Comparison Method

This method compares the subject property with comparable vacant parcels that have sold recently and processes the sales prices into indicators of value for the subject property by adjusting the sales prices for differences between the properties. The process involves four major steps: discovery and verification, selection of appropriate units of comparison, adjustments to sales data, and application of adjustment techniques.

Discovery and Verification. A listing of all pertinent information connected with the sale to be used for comparison is necessary. Among the data to be recorded are name of grantor and grantee, date of sale, description and location, price verification and recorder fee, and mortgage terms. It is useful to build and maintain an up-to-date file system of land sales. Sources of information include recorded deeds; newspaper reports; published sales listings, such as multiple listing services; and interviews with brokers, attorneys, and bankers. It is preferred practice to verify every sale with either buyer, seller, broker, or attorney involved. Knowledge of the motives of buyers and sellers is mandatory.

Units of Comparison. Once comparable sales have been analyzed and listed, the process of comparison with subject site requires units of comparison, as discussed in the previous section. It should be noted that, in addition to physical units of comparison, there are economic units used by buyers and sellers in the real estate market, such as units buildable, discussed earlier. Ranchers are primarily interested in how many animal units can be developed on the land. If the quality of the land is such that 5 acres are required per animal unit, this will probably serve as the basis for the price. Farmers growing corn are highly motivated by the productivity of the soil. The price will probably be contingent on the number of bushels per acre realized. These economic units of comparison are tied directly to the concept of highest and best use.

Adjustments. Since no two parcels of land are exactly alike, at least as to location, there will be differences to compensate for when the sale property is compared with the subject property. Typical differences are in time of sale, location, and physical characteristics. Other differences become apparent with the study of the physical, economic, governmental, and social factors affecting the sale property and the subject property.

The adjustment process is an analysis designed to eliminate these differences. The sale property is likened as much as possible to the subject property. In adjusting the sale property, lump-sum dollar amounts or percentages are customarily employed. Adjustments are always applied to the sale property, not to the subject property. If the sale price is inferior in some respect to the subject property, it is increased by a dollar amount or a percentage. If the sale property is superior in some category, it is decreased. The adjustment process, then, uses the sale price of the comparable property as modified by the application of adjustments to render a value indication for the subject property.

Adjustment Techniques. Adjustments may be made to sales prices in one of three ways: (1) adding and subtracting dollars, (2) adding and subtracting percentages, and (3) multiplying percentages. For the following examples, assume a residential lot, 100 × 125 feet in size, that sold five years ago for $5,000. There is no alley, and the street has concrete pavement with curb, gutter, and sidewalk. The market for this type of land has increased 10 percent during the past five years. If a lot on the next street is to be valued, this sale may be considered a comparable sale. The subject lot is the same size, but there are an alley and a gravel street with no curb, gutter, or sidewalk. Adjustment of this comparable sale might be made as follows:

Adding and Subtracting Dollar Amounts

Selling Price	Time	Street Improvements	Alley	Indicated Value of Subject
$5,000	+$500	−$325	+$250	$5,425

In this example, sales data analysis indicates that the pavement is worth $325; the alley influence, $250; and the time of sale, $500. The value influence of these factors should be measured by checking various sales with and without cited conditions. The total of the plus factors is $750; the minus factors totaling $325 are subtracted, for a net plus of $425. This total, added to the selling price of the comparable lot, results in an indicated value for the subject lot of $5,425. After selecting several sales and making appropriate adjustments for differences, several value indications for the subject lot will result. The greatest weight is normally given to the sale which requires the least adjustment.

When percentages are used, it is possible to add and subtract or to multiply. A slightly different value indication will result when percentages are multiplied, but the difference is not sufficient to affect the value indication substantially. For example, using the same values as in the previous illustration but reducing them to percentages, the results would be as shown in the accompanying tabulation.

Selling Price	Time	Street Improvements	Alley	Composite Factor	Indicated Value of Subject
$5,000	+10%	−6½%	+5%	+8½%	$5,425

Selling price $5,000× 8½% composite factor = $425
$5,000 + $425 = $5,425

Multiplying Percentages

Selling Price	Time	Street Improvements	Alley	Composite Factor	Indicated Value of Subject
$5,000	1.10	×0.9350	×1.05	1.08	$5,400

Selling price $5,000 × 1.08 composite factor = $5,400

An expanded discussion of adjustment techniques can be found in chapter 6, "The Comparative Sales Approach."

Abstraction Method

The abstraction, or allocation, method of site valuation may be helpful when no vacant sales are available for comparison. It is based on the principle of balance, which states that there is a sense of proportion in the four agents of production (see chap. 2). Land, as one of the agents of production, should have a logical value relationship to total property value.

Under the concept of allocation, a portion of total property value may be assigned to the site. A fair allowance is estimated, based on knowledge of the market for properties of the class under appraisal. Typical relationships are established from sales of improved properties. To establish proper ratios, the following are usually considered: (1) site values in previous years, (2) land-building ratios in similar neighborhoods, and (3) analysis of new construction on similarly classified sites.

Estimate, for example, that site should represent about

20 percent of the total property value in a given area, classified as single-family residential. The allocation is 4:1; there are four parts building to one part land. In a $40,000 property, land typically represents one-fifth, or 20 percent, of the total. The site in this example would be valued as follows: $40,000 × 20% = $8,000.

Abstraction, as opposed to allocation, employs elements of the cost approach in the analysis of an improved property sale. The method involves subtracting the depreciated replacement cost of improvements from the sale price of an improved property. The remainder is an indication of land value for that property. The following example clarifies this method.

Value of property as indicated by sale		$40,000
Estimated replacement cost new of building ...	$50,000	
Accrued depreciation of all types	18,000	
Estimated value of improvements		$32,000
Indicated site value		$ 8,000

Similar analysis with several sales of improved properties in a neighborhood may yield a pattern of site values as follows:

Sale Number	Sale Price	Replacement Cost New	Accrued Depreciation	Improvement Value	Indicated Site Value
1	$35,000	$28,000	$ 8,000	$20,000	$15,000
2	31,000	27,000	10,000	17,000	14,000
3	40,000	29,000	3,000	26,000	14,000

It may be estimated from this analysis that typical sites in this neighborhood have a value in the $14,000–$15,000 range.

This method should be employed with caution; it is a poor substitute for the direct sales comparison method and is useful only in certain restricted circumstances.

Anticipated Use or Development Method

The anticipated use, or development, method may be considered in cases where there are limited useful sales data. It is used primarily to value land in transition from agricultural use to residential or commercial use. For example, with the highest and best use of a tract established as residential, the assessor hypothetically develops the site. The total development costs are subtracted from the projected sales prices of the developed lots to indicate value for the raw land. The result is the price a prudent developer is willing to pay for the land in its present undeveloped condition.

As an illustration, a 20-acre tract is zoned for single-family residence, which is its highest and best use. The tract may be developed four lots to the acre, including streets. An analysis of the supply and demand as well as the purchasing power of typical homesite buyers indicates a selling price of $3,000 per lot, or a total sale price of $240,000 for the sites when completely developed. Technical assistance may be required to calculate all development costs. A study might demonstrate the following: (1) 25 percent for site development, including streets, sewers, water service, site preparation, and planning; (2) 25 percent for overhead and sales expense, such as commissions, title work, advertising, general office expense, accounting, and legal expense; and (3) 25 percent for profit and interest costs during development and a consideration for a time lag, since all 80 lots will be sold over a period of time, not simultaneously. If this is the breakdown demonstrated by the study, the remaining 25 percent of lot sales can be attributed to the contributory value of the raw land:

$$\$240,000 \times 0.25 = \$60,000 \; ;$$

$$\$60,000 \div 20 \text{ acres} = \$3,000 \text{ per acre.}$$

It must be emphasized that, while this method may serve as a secondary, backup method to assist in the substantiation of a value estimate gained by the direct sales comparison method, it is a substitute only when useful sales data are not available. The method is frequently criticized because of its hypothetical nature. Practitioners may fall into the indefensible habit of simply selecting an arbitrary percentage of projected sale price as the indicated value of the raw land. Many of the development costs are relatively constant regardless of the value of the land. In the foregoing illustration, the following is projected.

Projected sale price of lots ($3,000 × 80 lots)		$240,000
1. Site development: streets, sewers, water service, site preparation, planning	$60,000	
2. Overhead and sales expense	60,000	
3. Profit, interest, and time lag	60,000	
		$180,000
Indicated value of undeveloped land		$ 60,000

In this example, the indicated value of the undeveloped land is 25 percent ($60,000 ÷ $240,000) of the projected sale price of lots. If there is another 20-acre parcel of higher-quality, better-located land available for development, many development costs would remain the same, while others would be directly related to the projected sale price of developed lots. For example:

Projected sale price of lots ($6,000 × 80 lots)		$480,000
1. Site development	$ 60,000	
2. Overhead and sales expense	120,000	
3. Profit, interest, and time lag	120,000	
		$300,000
Indicated value of undeveloped land		$180,000

Here the indicated value of the undeveloped land is 38 percent ($180,000 ÷ $480,000) of the projected sale price of the lots. In other words, the developer's investment requirements can be satisfied even if he pays $180,000 for the raw land. If this parcel can be acquired at a lesser price, the developer's potential profit will be increased. Any arbitrary "thumb rules" used in this method destroy its credibility.

Capitalization of Ground Rent

This method employs the income approach to value, which is based on the premise that value is the present worth of future benefits of property ownership (see chaps. 9–12). The method may be desirable in central business districts where no vacant land sales can be found. If there are market data available to estimate the income potential of area parking lots, for example, this income can be converted, or capitalized, into an expression of value. Assume that comparable rental data indicate that the subject site would rent or lease for a net income of $800 per year to the owner. (Net income is the result of the deduction of all operating expenses from gross income.)

There are many instances where land, particularly commercial land, is leased on a net basis. Rental data comparisons may be made on a per square foot or per front foot basis. Farmland may be leased on a per acre basis. Once the market rent of the subject site is established, a net income is calculated and a capitalization rate selected. For purposes of demonstration, assume that a market study indicates that the proper land capitalization rate is 8 percent. The net income is capitalized into a value as follows.

$$\$800 \div 0.08 = \$10,000 \text{ value} .$$

This method is only as reliable as the estimate of highest and best use, market rent, and correct capitalization rate for the subject property.

Land Residual Capitalization

Another use of the income approach to value to estimate site value is land residual capitalization. This method somewhat parallels the anticipated use or development method of land valuation, in that the highest and best use of the land is projected. It may be an office building, apartment house, or shopping center, and it may or may not be the existing type of use. A new building, hypothetical or actual, representing the most profitable use, is projected.

The net income earned by the total property (land and building as a unit) is estimated from market data. The cost, or contributory value, of the building and other improvements is established. The income attributable to the building and other improvements is calculated and deducted from the total net income. The remaining net income is attributable to land and is capitalized at the appropriate rate for a value indication.

Net income generated by the total property	$10,000
Building cost or value ($50,000) × 12% rate	6,000
Income attributable to the land	$ 4,000
Value indication for land ($4,000 ÷ 0.10)	$40,000

With the exception of forecasting a hypothetical building, the method is the same as the land residual capitalization technique used for improved properties and discussed in chapter 12.

Summary

Land valuation is basic to real estate appraisal. It encompasses three separate functions: identification, analysis, and valuation. Within the identification function, the assessment map is of paramount importance to the assessor. Both site analysis and valuation encompass principles and techniques pertinent to the three approaches to value, as illustrated in future chapters.

Land Identification

1. Legal descriptions—based on surveys or on visual or mathematical recitations of the limits of the land.

   a) Metes and bounds—earliest form of land description; describes land using adjacent property owners and/or features of the terrain.

   b) Rectangular survey (section, township, and range)—based upon law and devised to mark and fix legal subdivisions for purposes of description; originally established township 6 miles square.

c) Lot and block—originated as communities grew; derived from surveys of property and various divisions (lot and/or block) for sale; numbers added to each sale unit and recorded.

2. Other methods of description—additional methods in surveying and mapping, rarely used for legal description.

a) Longitude and latitude—result of geodetic surveying; geographic points expressed in terms of latitude and longitude; national system of interrelated points known as horizontal control network.

b) *X, Y* coordinates—local system of listing geodetic stations using plane rectangular coordinates expressed in feet and decimal fractions of a foot.

c) Parcel identification systems—the tie between ownership, tax maps, and tax-roll entry.

3. Methods of Surveying.

a) Field survey—physical traversing of the land to lay out angles and distances to describe ownership.

b) Photogrammetry—the science, art, and technology of obtaining reliable measurements and quantitative information from photographs.

Site Analysis

1. Data—include trends, factors, and specific site data.

a) Trends and factors—land classification; highest and best use; physical, economic, governmental, and social factors; development of regional, city, and neighborhood data.

b) Site data—frontage, width, depth, shape, area, topography, slope, drainage and soil condition, off-site improvements.

2. Units of comparison—analysis of differences of size

and shape in order to apply uniform benchmarks for valuation.

a) Front foot—use based on the premise that frontage contributes to value.

b) Square foot—used for irregularly shaped parcels where frontage is not a dominant factor.

c) Acre and section—acre equal to 43,560 square feet; section equal to 640 acres.

d) Site—used when the market does not indicate a difference in lot value even when there is a difference in lot size.

e) Units buildable—used where the market indicates that a site is sold on a unit basis.

3. Formulas, tables, and rules—designed through the analysis of market data to assist in dealing with changes in parcel size, shape, and location.

a) Depth tables—used to assist in measurement of changes in value due to variation in lot depths where land is purchased on a front-foot basis.

b) Irregular-lot valuation tables—used to convert actual frontage of irregular-shaped parcels to effective front footage.

c) Corner-influence tables—constructed on the premise that the greatest value is at the corner of two streets.

Land Valuation

There are five generally accepted methods of land valuation.

1. Direct sales comparison—compares the subject property with comparable vacant parcels that have recently sold and processes the sales prices into indicators of value by adjusting them for differences among the properties.

2. Abstraction (allocation)—based on the principle that land has a logical relationship to total property value; a

proportion of the total property value is allocated to the land.

3. Anticipated use or development—used primarily to value land in transition from agricultural use to residential or commercial use; total development costs are subtracted from the projected sales prices of developed lots to indicate value for land.

4. Capitalization of ground rent—employs the income approach; income is converted, or capitalized, into an expression of value.

5. Land residual capitalization—involves estimating net income earned by a total property, establishing the cost of the building, and calculating and deducting from total net income the income attributable to the building; the remaining income attributable to the land is capitalized to a value indication.

6 The Comparative Sales Approach to Value

An understanding of the comparative sales approach to value involves the realization that the indication of sales—namely, prices—must be critically analyzed to indicate properly the value of property under appraisal and that all the conditions of the term *market value* must be satisfied. This approach to value utilizes application of data from the market and is frequently called the market data or sales approach.

The comparative sales approach rests on the principle of substitution, which states that no commodity has a value greater than that for which a similar commodity —offering similar uses, similar utility, and similar function—can be purchased within the reasonable time limits that the buyers' market demands. Properties subjected to the comparison process, both subject and comparables, must have at least the potential of a similar, if not identical, highest and best use if a valid value estimate is to result. In other words, all the properties compared must possess the capacity of satisfying the needs and desires of the same buyer.

The basic steps in the comparative sales approach are (1) collecting and analyzing the data, (2) selecting appropriate units of comparison, (3) making reasonable adjustments based on the market, and (4) applying the data to the subject of appraisal.

Analysis of Subject Property

A thorough familiarity with the property under appraisal is essential. The description and classification of the subject property, knowledge of its highest and best use, and awareness of the purpose and function of the appraisal help establish the framework within which the assessor enters the real estate market to procure comparative sales data.

Description and Classification

The inspection of the subject property is usually recorded on the property record card or the assessor's worksheet. A complete physical description of the site and improvements is taken into consideration, along with the nature of the neighborhood, in order to classify the property. The classifications discussed in this chapter include residential, commercial, industrial, and farmland.

Site may be valued separately in the comparative sales approach in order that the site value obtained may be utilized in the cost and income approaches. The elements of comparison for improvements include the following:

- Overall quality
- Architectural attractiveness
- Age
- Size (square footage, stories, number of units, number of bedrooms, and baths)
- Amenities (special-purpose rooms, garage, swimming pool, parking)
- Functional utility (architecture and appearance, layout, equipment)
- Accrued depreciation (physical deterioration, maintenance, modernization, including remodeling and additions)

Highest and Best Use

Frequently the present use of an improved property is its highest and best use. A search for the type of typical buyer will lead the assessor, in most cases, to the highest and best use for the subject property. It is almost impossible to project a highest and best use for a property if there are no potential buyers to base purchase decisions on such use. The projection of highest and best use, therefore, is market-oriented. An error in the selection of highest and best use for the subject property will eventually lead the assessor to comparable data that will be misleading.

If a vacant, old, and obsolete multistory industrial property is the subject of appraisal, the estimation of highest and best use is extremely critical. Who are the typical buyers of such properties? To what uses are such properties put? Does the building contribute any value to the site? Does the building detract from the value of the site? A miscalculation here on highest and best use certainly will lead to an erroneous value conclusion.

In the comparison of single-family residences, the estimate of highest and best use of the subject property may be, for example, as the family home of a young couple having children in the two-to-ten age bracket. This residence must be compared with the sales of residences having similar appeal to the same type of family grouping. It should not be compared with residences that would be in demand by buyers wanting a home for retirement, or by buyers wanting a status neighborhood, or by buyers with a full-grown family. Typical buyers and their motives lead the assessor to the highest and best use.

Purpose and Function of the Appraisal

Almost exclusively, the purpose of the appraisal for the assessor is market value. Does the property under appraisal lend itself to value measurement using the comparative sales approach to value? What do the statutes have to say about using market data to serve as indications of value? If the subject property is classified as one that is normally traded in the real estate market, it probably is desirable and mandatory to employ the comparative sales approach to value. For the assessor the function of the appraisal is to establish a basis for assessment and, ultimately, for the property tax burden. Market data are essential if uniformity and equality in assessments are to be realized. What better evidence of market value can be provided than actions of buyers and sellers in the market?

Collection and Analysis of Comparative Sales Data

Comparative data consist of recent sales, cost, and income information on individual properties. The assessor collects sales and income data for use in the comparative sales and income approaches to value. Cost data are collected for the purposes of determining whether the costs obtained from outside sources are accurate and for the preparation of cost manuals. Cost data collection will be discussed in detail in chapter 7.

The discovery of such comparative data as sales, options, asking prices, offering prices, leases, and rentals constitutes the essence of the first step in the comparative sales approach.

Sales are of all types and reflect all attitudes of people, all ideas, and all possible conditions under which sales are consummated. Thus they need to be examined closely. The imperfect nature of the real estate market makes each sale property subject to scrutiny to learn how closely it conforms to the definition of market value. Before a sale may be used as an indicator of market value, it must meet the following criteria: (1) it must be a sale on the open market, (2) neither party may enter into the sale under undue stimulus, (3) a reasonable time must be allowed for selling, (4) both buyer and seller must be reasonably knowledgeable of the property's use, (5) consideration should be in cash or its equivalent, and (6) there must be no "love and affection" consideration (as in a sale to a relative).

Other types of data that must be collected on individual sales include the following:

- *Actual sale price*—the price for which a property sells without any adjustments.
- *Date of sale*—the date the deed is recorded.
- *Date of agreement to sell*—the date on which the buyer and seller enter into a contract.
- *Cash down payment*—the amount of money that the buyer pays for the property from equity funds.
- *Financing*—the amount of money borrowed from a lender to complete the purchase price. The effect of financing is discussed in chapter 9.

In terms of bracketing the market, or developing a range of value, such data as options, asking prices, and offering prices have limited application. An *option* is an agreement which permits one to buy, sell, or lease a property within a stipulated period of time in accordance with terms that frequently call for a payment for such privilege. The option need not be exercised, but this typically results in the forfeiture of any payment. It is some evidence of value but not as indicative as an actual sale. In the absence of sales data, the option can be helpful for a general value indication.

Asking prices of property owners generally establish the upper limit of value, since it would be unusual to have a property sell for more than its asking price. Conversely, *offering prices* by buyers normally establish the lower limit of value. Asking and offering prices, then, tend to establish the range of value for a property. Market information on *leases and rentals* is essential in the income approach to value as well as in the comparative sales approach when gross rent multipliers are used (to be discussed later in this chapter).

Sources of Data

A working familiarity with the sources of sales data is essential for the proper application of the comparative sales approach. Most commonly used are office files. A proficient assessor will have in his office a historical record of the marketplace indexed and cross-indexed so that relevant facts can be rapidly discovered. Another source is the public record of deeds and contracts, which can be examined directly or sometimes may be more rapidly analyzed by the use of title companies. Atlases, survey maps, and lease records are important sources of market data.

A source often overlooked is *published news.* The assessor should read newspapers, magazines, professional journals, and multiple listing service reports. He may index and correlate published real estate news. *Classified ads* and *listings* should not be overlooked. *Real estate brokers* and *appraisers* are excellent sources of sales data, as are *attorneys* and *bankers* and other lenders.

A direct interview of the *buyer* or *seller,* preferably both, is the best source of documentation of sales data. In such an interview, one can ascertain how long the buyer looked for the property, what he located that was comparable, what made him decide on the particular property, how he arrived at his price level, what his demands were, how close he came to fulfilling his demands, how important financing was, and the extent of compulsion on him to buy the property. In confronting the seller (usually a better target for an assessor), the assessor may discover why he wanted to sell, the importance of any pressure to sell, how long the property was exposed to the market, how the price was established, and how important sale terms were to him.

One method that works well for the assessor is the questionnaire. While questionnaires are inflexible in that questions are standardized, a well-planned and tested questionnaire will generally provide the assessor with a great deal of required information.

Verification of Data

Verification of comparative data is often a problem for the assessor concerned with a large quantity of sales and rental information, as it is often not possible to verify every data item. However, it is fundamental that the verified sale is more reliable than the unverified sale. It is important that *key* data be verified. Ideally, transactions should be verified with both buyer and seller, as time may obscure the recollection of the details of the transaction. Sometimes the individual participants are the only ones who know the true motivating factors in a transaction.

Elements of Comparison

Comparison Process

The assessor's objective in the comparative sales approach is to estimate by interpreting data on comparable sales the price that the property being appraised would probably bring in the market. The number of sales selected should be sufficient to set a pattern and will be dependent upon the appraisal problem itself and the degree of comparability of sales. Similarities and dissimilarities between subject and comparable properties must be recognized. Utility in function, the ability to excite desire backed by purchasing power, and the extent of supply and demand form the starting point for the comparison process.

This process is essentially a bracketing of the market —that is, the setting up of a series of value levels and a gradual narrowing of these value levels into one value area in which the value of the subject property is found. Comparable sales must be visually inspected. With an actual physical examination of the comparables, the assessor will develop knowledge that will enable him to make an accurate analysis of the sales that have been selected.

Factors and Trends

The subject property and comparable sales are subject to analysis for comparability with one another. Attention should be directed to the factors and trends that influence value. Reference to the law of supply and demand is beneficial. The greatest degree of comparability is achieved when the properties involved in the comparison process are influenced to a similar extent by economic trends and physical, economic, governmental, and social factors. When one property is heavily influenced by one set of factors while a second property is significantly affected by dissimilar factors, there probably is no comparability. The assessor does not attempt to compare apples with oranges. A review of the various factors and trends is necessary at this stage of the comparative sales approach. The question of whether the comparable sales are really comparable must be answered. It is not acceptable procedure, for instance, to compare a sale of 5 acres of woodland with that of a property containing 250 acres. Nor is it useful to compare buildings constructed in 1976 with one built in 1925. The greater the areas of similarity, the better the comparable sale.

Units of Comparison

Reference to chapter 5 will indicate that appropriate units of comparison for the valuation of vacant land include the section, the acre, the square foot, and the front foot. With improved property, sales are broken down into useful units so that reasonable and logical comparisons can be made. For residential properties, typical units of comparison are per dwelling unit, per square foot of building, per room, and per bedroom. For apartment houses, the unit, room, or square foot of building including land are appropriate units of comparison. For industrial properties, the square foot and cubic foot of building are used.

One economic unit of comparison in general use with commercial and apartment properties is the *gross rent multiplier*. A gross rent multiplier expresses a relationship between gross rent and the value of a property. It is calculated by dividing the property value or selling price by the property's gross income at the time of sale. A typical application of the technique entails the gross rent potential without vacancy at the time of sale. As is the case with all units of comparison, the quantity and quality of the available comparative data to develop the unit establish its reliability. The use of the gross rent multiplier in the valuation process, discussed later in this chapter, can be a valuable technique if adequately supported with data.

Examples of units of comparison are demonstrated by the following example. A 40-unit apartment building recently sold for $350,000. It contains 34,000 square feet of living area, there are 160 rooms, and the gross annual rental is $60,000.

Sale price per square foot: $\dfrac{\$350,000}{34,000} = \$10.29$;

Sale price per unit: $\dfrac{\$350,000}{40} = \$8,750$;

Sale price per room: $\dfrac{\$350,000}{160} = \$2,188$;

Gross rent multiplier: $\dfrac{\$350,000}{\$60,000} = 5.83$.

Methods and Techniques

There are two generally accepted methods of valuation of improved properties in the comparative sales approach —the direct sales comparison method (also called the adjustment method) and the gross rent multiplier method.

Direct Sales Comparison Method

The direct sales comparison method compares the improved property with improved comparable properties that have sold recently. This approach processes sales prices into indicators of value for the subject property by making adjustments. Most of the adjustments, in typical appraisal practice, involve physical factors. Adjustments are usually made for physical characteristics, location, and time of sale. Other typical adjustments are made for terms of sale, financing, vacancy rates, and rent levels.

One important thing to bear in mind is that the total adjustment is made by a series of individual adjustments for each item in the sale. A single adjustment from sale to subject property cannot be made in one mental leap. The adjustment process that produces a final value decision consists of a series of smaller decisions.

The adjustments, whether expressed on a lump-sum or on a percentage basis, are always applied to the sale property; adjustments are never made to the subject property in the comparison process. This technique, in effect, amends the price of the sale property so that it becomes a better indication of value for the subject property. If the comparable sale is inferior in some category, it is adjusted upward. If the comparable sale is superior in some respect to the subject property, the comparable is adjusted downward.

In recognition of the principle of contribution, the preferred practice is to allocate the amount of the adjustment by its contributory value to the total property rather than by its individual cost. Sales data should be employed to discern the contributory value of individual items. For example, assume that one house has a fireplace and a second house does not; also assume that it is possible to install a fireplace in the second house. The amount of the adjustment is the dollar difference that the presence or absence of a fireplace makes in the selling price or value of a house, not the cost of installing a fireplace. Although installation cost may not contribute anything to property value, the absence of the fireplace might reduce the sale price or value by twice the cost of installation.

Adjustment Methods. Following is a discussion of the various mechanical methods that may be employed to determine the amount of adjustments in several frequently encountered categories. The foundation of adjustments in the real estate market cannot be overemphasized. Where comparative data are not available for analysis, the assessor must draw upon his experience and upon other experts to estimate the amount of adjustments.

Time Adjustment. The principle of change states that change is continually affecting the real estate market. During an inflationary period, the value level tends to rise; during deflationary times, value levels tend to fall. Perhaps the best evidence of the required adjustment for time is the resale of the same property. Assume that a downtown retail property sold as follows:

Original sale (two years ago)	$40,000
Sale of sale property (present time)	$44,000
Increase in value over two-year period	$ 4,000
$44,000 ÷ $40,000 = 110\%; increase = 10\%	

The indicated time adjustment is +5 percent per year. This exercise is valid if the assessor assures himself that no other changes, physical or otherwise, have occurred to modify property value. This time adjustment may be applied to other comparable sales data.

Location Adjustment. The objective here is to find two similar properties—apartments, for example. The only significant difference is location. Both properties sold about the same time.

Apartment 1 (better location): sale price per unit $20,000	
Apartment 2 (poorer location): sale price per unit $16,000	
$20,000 ÷ $16,000 = 125\%$; difference = 25\%	

If the subject property has a location similar to that of apartment 1, then a +25 percent adjustment to apartment 2 is required if it is to be used as evidence of value for the subject property.

Physical Condition Adjustment. Two similar light industrial buildings sold at the same time. They are quite similar in size. One has considerable deferred maintenance (curable physical deterioration). Functional utility and location are comparable.

Property 1 (good physical condition): sale price $30,000	
Property 2 (poor physical condition): sale price $27,000	
$30,000 ÷ $27,000 = 111\%$; difference = 11\%	

This example demonstrates, in addition to the amount of the adjustment, that the comparative sales approach measures and compensates for accrued depreciation.

Contributory Value of Component. Assume two similar single-family residences recently sold. Amenities are about the same, except that residence 1 has a detached one-car garage.

Residence 1 (with garage): sale price $24,500	
Residence 2 (without garage): sale price 23,000	
Indicated contributory value of garage .... $ 1,500	

Farmland. Two nearby farms sell in the open market at about the same time. The soil productivity of farm 1 is better than that of farm 2. How much better?

Farm 1: sale price per acre $300	
Farm 2: sale price per acre $270	
$300 ÷ $270 = 111\%$; difference = 11\%	

The market, according to this analysis, will pay 11 percent more for the better land.

Adjustment for Time and Location. Five comparable warehouse sites are being analyzed in order to make adjustments for time and location when comparison is made with the subject property. This example assumes that time and location are the only two adjustments required.

Sale	Price	Area (Sq. Ft.)	Unit	Time	Location*
1	$15,400	26,500	$0.58	Current	Same
2	11,300	18,200	0.62	Current	Same
3	18,000	27,700	0.65	One year	Better
4	9,000	11,765	0.765	Current	Better
5	9,900	18,330	0.54	Two years	Same

* When compared to subject property.

The following comparisons among sets of sales are used to provide an indication of the necessary adjustments for passage of time. These sales are judged to have the same location attributes as each other and the subject.

Sales 1 and 5, $0.58 ÷ $0.54: +7.5% for 2 years, or 3.75% per year;

Sales 2 and 5, $0.62 ÷ $0.54: +14.8% for 2 years, or 7.4% per year.

Sales 3 and 4 have better locations than the subject property and sales 1, 2, and 5. Using the approximate range of 4–7 percent, it is reasonable to conclude that there is an indicated upward adjustment of 5 percent per year for the passage of time in this rising real estate market. Adjusting for location, sales 3 and 4 are judged to be better located than the subject site. Since sales 1, 2, and 4 are current, there are no time differences, and the location differences can be isolated:

Sales 1 and 4, $0.58 ÷ $0.765: −24% adjusted for sale 4;

Sales 2 and 4, $0.62 ÷ $0.765: −19% adjusted for sale 4.

Sale 4 is decreased by approximately 20 percent to account for locational differences when compared to subject site. On a prorated basis, an approximate 8 percent adjustment is indicated for sale 3. Adjustments are summarized as follows:

Sale	Unit	Time Adjustment	Location Adjustment	Total Adjustment	Adjustment Unit
1	$0.58	0%	0%	0%	$0.58
2	0.62	0	0	0	0.62
3	0.65	+ 5	− 8	− 3	0.63
4	0.765	0	−20	−20	0.61
5	0.54	+10	0	+10	0.59

Application of Adjustment Methods. The final major step in the comparative sales approach to value is application of the data to the property being appraised. The data frequently may be presented in grid analysis form, thus providing a clear and logical display of the information. Adjustments may be treated on a lump-sum or on a percentage basis. The percentage adjustments in each category may be added and subtracted or multiplied to arrive at a total or composite adjustment. The assessor always works from the sale property toward the subject property. For instance, if the subject property is 10 percent better on location, the factor of 110 percent for location would be applied to the sale property price.

Residential Properties. The following example demonstrates the lump-sum adjustment method and the percentage adjustment method. The subject property is a single-family residence on a 50 × 127-foot site in a good neighborhood. The building is a one-story frame dwelling built ten years ago, containing 923 gross square feet on the main floor and a partial basement and one-car garage. Four comparable sales are used. A grid presentation of the pertinent information is displayed in table 6.1.

Table 6.1
Grid Display of Comparative Sales Data

	Subject	Sale 1	Sale 2	Sale 3	Sale 4
Sale price	...	$26,200	$26,200	$26,800	$27,100
Date of sale	...	3 years	2 years	1 year	Current
Age of improvements ..	10 years	9 years	11 years	9 years	10 years
Condition of improvements	Good	Good	Good	Good	Good
Lot size (ft.)	50 × 127	50 × 117	50 × 100	50 × 156	50 × 115
Floor area (sq. ft.)	923	962	977	1,008	936
Full basement*	No	Yes	Yes	Yes	Yes
Garage	Yes	None	None	None	None
Quality	Good	Good	Good	Good	Good
Utilities	Average	Average	Average	Average	Average
Site improvements	Average	Average	Average	Average	Average
Location	Good	Good	Good	Good	Good

*Subject dwelling has only partial basement because of outcropping of ledge.

Table 6.1 demonstrates that adjustment is necessary in several areas. The unit of comparison is the dwelling itself. Adjustments will be required for time, floor area, basement, garage, and lot size. The lump-sum adjustments given in table 6.2 are abstracted from available market data, heeding the principle of contribution as shown.

Table 6.2
Lump-Sum Adjustments and Adjusted Prices for Comparable Sales

Adjustment	Sale 1	Sale 2	Sale 3	Sale 4
Time	+$ 1,575	+$ 1,050	+$ 535	...
Lot size	...	+ 100	− 100	...
Floor area	− 250	− 300	− 400	...
Basement	− 625	− 625	− 625	−$ 625
Garage	+ 500	+ 500	+ 500	+ 500
Total adjustment	+$ 1,200	+$ 725	−$ 90	−$ 125
Sale price	26,200	26,200	26,800	27,100
Adjusted price .	$27,400	$26,925	$26,710	$26,975

The adjustments are based on the following observations:

1. Time—advance in the market of 2 percent per year.
2. Lot size—depths of 115 to 130 feet are typical ($100 less

for 100 feet of depth and $100 more for 156 feet of depth); all frontages are 50 feet.

3. Floor area—for a significant number of square feet, $4.50 to $6.50 per square foot is the contributory value.

4. Basement—sales reveal penalty of $625 for ledge in basement.

5. Garage—$500 contributory value from market data.

All dwellings have two bedrooms.

The value indicators for the subject property provide a range from $26,710 to $27,400. Since sale 4 required the fewest adjustments, it should be considered the strongest value indicator. The other adjusted sales bracket this value indicator of $26,975. The range of adjusted sales is narrow. All adjusted sales are generally good value indicators for the subject property. They tend to substantiate a $26,975 value, rounded to $27,000. The lump-sum adjustments could have been shown in percentages (table 6.3).

Table 6.3
Percentage Adjustments and Adjusted Prices for
Comparable Sales

Adjustment	Sale 1	Sale 2	Sale 3	Sale 4
Time	+6 %	+4 %	+2 %	...
Lot size	...	+0.5	−0.5	...
Floor area	−1	−1	−1.5	...
Basement	−2.5	−2.5	−2.5	−2.5%
Garage	+2	+2	+2	+2
Total % adjustment	+4.5%	+3 %	−0.5%	−0.5%
Sale price	$26,200	$26,200	$26,800	$27,100
Adjusted price .	$27,380	$26,985	$26,665	$26,965

Industrial Properties. Improved industrial properties are valued by using a two-step procedure for the processing of sales data. Independent site value is estimated, and the contributory value of the improvements is calculated. In this example, a small light industrial property is the subject. It is twenty years old and contains 22,000 gross square feet on 1 acre of land. Office space is 1,100 square feet. Typical units of comparison are square feet of building and the gross rent multiplier. The square-foot comparison method is demonstrated here. Some of the most important physical factors to compare are column spacing, door openings, ceiling clearances, percent of office space, loading and unloading facilities, and, of course, location. Subject site value, by comparison, is estimated at $10,000. Three comparable sales are studied.

Sale	Price	Land Value	Building Value	Building Square Feet	Office Square Feet	Price per Square Foot of Building	Date
1	$70,000	$10,000	$60,000	20,000	1,000	$3.00	2 years
2	95,000	15,000	80,000	25,000	1,225	3.20	1 year
3	75,000	15,000	60,000	18,000	875	3.33	Current

Adjustments are required for time, location, and building quality. Others features are similar. Office space is about 5 percent of total space in all sales and subject property.

Sale	Time	Location	Building Condition- Utility	Net Adjustment	Adjusted Price of Building per Square Foot
1	106%	98%	101%	105%	$3.15
2	103	. . .	98	101	3.23
3	. . .	. . .	97	97	3.23

Further analysis leads to the conclusion of $3.20 per square foot for the subject property; 22,000 square feet × $3.20 per square foot = $70,400; addition of site value of $10,000 gives an indicated property value of $80,400.

Farm and Ranch Properties. Agricultural and grazing lands usually are compared on a per acre basis. Economic units of comparison relate to the production of crops or the ability of ranchlands to sustain animal units. Buildings and other land improvements, such as farm service buildings, wells, and fences, normally comprise a small percentage of total property value. In some cases, old and obsolete buildings make no contribution at all to the property value. In many areas, small farms and ranches sell on a higher unit basis than large farms and ranches. With rapid advances in technology and fewer individual farms, buyers have been eager to add smaller tracts to their existing properties. If supportable values can be assigned to the farmhouse or ranch house and other service buildings, the comparison process can be used with land alone. In some real estate markets, buildings and land are considered together on a unit basis. The following is an example of the comparative sales approach on an improved property. The subject property contains 150 acres with farmhouse and service buildings valued at $10,000. A grid presentation of available sales data includes units of comparison.

Sale	Price	Date	Acres	Building Value	Land Value	Price per Acre Overall	Price per Acre Land Only
1	$69,600	3 years	160.05	$ 3,800	$65,800	$435	$411
2	75,000	4 years	145.40	25,000	60,000	516	413
3	44,100	3 years	115.85	12,000	32,100	381	277
4	75,000	1 year	163.75	10,000	65,000	458	397

Each of the farms is about a quarter-section in size, except for sale 3. Buildings are in the same general value category, except for sale 1. Indicated adjustments are made as follows.

Sale	Time	Productivity	Sales Condition	Location	Net Adjustment
1	109%	105%	. . .	. . .	114%
2	112	105	. . .	95%	112
3	109	. . .	110%	. . .	119
4	103	105	. . .	. . .	108

The adjustment process reveals that, on a unit basis, all sales are considered inferior to the subject property, which explains the upward net adjustments. Further investigation of sale 3 indicates that there was considerable pressure on the seller, who needed to liquidate assets. It is the judgment of the assessor that sale 3 is not an acceptable value indicator, and it is eliminated here from further consideration. Comparing first on an overall price per acre including buildings, we have the following.

Sale	Price per Acre	Net Adjustment	Adjustment per Acre
1	$435	114%	$496
2	516	112	578
4	458	108	495

Since no consideration was given to the contributory value of the buildings in the adjustment process, some weight must be given to this factor here. The subject property has buildings valued at $10,000, the same as for sale 4. Sale 4 is also the most recent sale and has the smallest adjustment. It probably should be selected as the best value indicator—that is, for the subject property, 150 acres × $495 = $74,250. On a land-only basis, observe the following.

Sale	Price per Acre	Net Adjustment	Adjustment per Acre
1	$411	114%	$469
2	413	112	463
4	397	108	429

Again, sale 4 is the best value indicator—for the subject property, 150 acres × $429 = $64,350; adding $10,000 building value gives a total property value of $74,350.

Special-Purpose Properties. The use of the comparative sales approach for special-purpose properties has application when suitable comparable sales are available and worthwhile units of comparison can be developed. Golf courses may be sold at so much per hole. Other units of comparison include, for theaters, per seat; for bowling alleys, per lane; for garages, per vehicle; for grain elevators, per bushel; for storage tanks, per gallon. There are at least some occasional sales in these categories. Some specialized properties almost never sell and therefore do not lend themselves to valuation by the comparative sales approach.

Gross Rent Multiplier

The use of the gross rent multiplier (GRM) requires certain assumptions. The first is that the highest and best use of the property will not change over the remaining economic life of the property. It is also assumed that the property will remain rented at a constant rate with no unusual vacancy factor. A further assumption is that the subject property and the comparables are truly comparable in that they are subject to the same market influences, are competitive with one another, have similar operating expenses, and have similar utility and amenities. It is finally taken for granted that any differences in the subject and comparables are reflected in the rents of each property.

The GRM gives a simple, direct estimate of value and eliminates the complex adjustments of the direct sales comparison method. However, there are limitations in the use of GRMs. Before they can be derived, a volume of sales and rental data is needed on the same properties. The GRM does not allow for abnormal physical deterioration, unusual operating expenses, or differences in zoning. The GRM's application to single-family residential properties has doubtful validity because amenities of owner occupancy may not be reflected in the rentals as they would be in sales.

The mechanics of the GRM method are simple. GRMs are derived by dividing the sale price by gross annual income. To estimate the value of the subject property, the annual economic rental of the subject property is multiplied by the GRM. For instance, if a property has an annual income of $30,000 and sold for $210,000, the gross rent multiplier is derived as follows:

$$\frac{\text{Sale price}}{\text{Annual income}} = \frac{\$210,000}{\$30,000} = 7 \text{ (GRM)}.$$

If the subject property has an annual income of $25,000

and the GRM is 7, then

Annual income:	$25,000;
GRM:	7;
Value ($25,000 × 7):	$175,000.

The GRM can also be developed for use with monthly rentals. Since single-family residential properties normally are not purchased for income purposes, there is no authentic income approach to value for this class of property. However, the assessor uses the monthly GRM to assist in the formation of an opinion of value. For example:

Sale	Sale Price	Monthly Income	Monthly GRM
1	$24,000	$200	120
2	22,000	190	115.8
3	27,000	215	125.6

The multipliers range from 115.8 to 125.6. It is judged that the subject property is better than sale 2 and almost as good as sale 1. If the economic rent of the subject property is $195 per month and the monthly multiplier selected is 120, the value indication is $23,400 ($195 × 120). The use of this multiplier can serve as a check on the comparative sales and cost approaches in valuing single-family residential properties. It is important to be consistent and use gross rents for unfurnished residences when the objective is to value the real property.

Purchases of apartment properties must be studied in direct relation to the income they are capable of producing, since these purchases are based on the proposition that value is the present worth of the right to receive the future income that the property will generate. An example of the GRM used in conjunction with other units of comparison is as follows: The subject property is a middle-aged, 45-unit apartment building with 202 rooms. There are 28,000 square feet of building. The gross annual rent is $50,000. The land area is 90,000 square feet. The building does not have all the contemporary features but competes well with other similar properties. A detailed analysis will include examination of four current comparable sales.

Sale	Building Square Feet	Apartments	Rooms	Gross Income	Sale Price
1	30,000	50	175	$63,000	$425,000
2	26,250	44	172	48,000	340,000
3	21,000	32	120	41,000	300,000
4	17,500	27	128	35,000	242,000

In apartment property appraisal, several units of comparison can be developed: per square foot of building including land, per apartment unit, per room, or GRM.

Sale	Per Square Foot of Building	Per Unit	Per Room	GRM
1	$14.17	$8,500	$2,429	6.75
2	12.95	7,727	1,977	7.08
3	14.29	9,375	2,500	7.32
4	13.83	8,963	1,890	6.91

In this example the assessor has difficulty developing adjustment factors from market data. However, he can make some reasonable estimates. Examination reveals that no adjustments are required for land area and time. Adjustments should be made in the following areas:

Sale	Location	Utility	Physical Features	Net Adjustment
1	95%	. . .	95%	90%
2	95	105%	95	95
3	95	95	. . .	90
4	95	. . .	95	90

The net adjustment will be applied to each unit of comparison to arrive at a value indicator.

Sale	Per Square Foot of Building	Net Adjustment	Adjusted per Square Foot of Building
1	$14.17	0.90	$12.75
2	12.95	0.95	12.30
3	14.29	0.90	12.86
4	13.83	0.90	12.45

The need for further analysis of the sales and subject property presents itself. The relative sizes of the apartments and the number of rooms per apartment should have some bearing. The relative average size of rooms is pertinent.

Sale	Apartments	Rooms	Rooms per Apartment	Building Square Feet	Square Feet per Apartment	Square Feet per Room
1	50	175	3.5	30,000	600	171
2	44	172	3.9	26,250	597	153
3	32	120	3.8	21,000	656	173
4	27	128	4.7	17,500	648	137
Subject	45	202	4.5	28,000	622	139

On a square foot per apartment basis, sales 1 and 4 are the most comparable to the subject property. These two sales indicate a range of $12.45–$12.75 per adjusted square foot of building for the subject property. If $12.45 were adopted as a reasonable estimate, the value indicator for the subject property would be 28,000 square feet × $12.45 per square foot = $348,600. On a per apartment basis:

Sale	Per Apartment	Net Adjustment	Adjusted per Unit
1	$8,500	0.90	$7,650
2	7,727	0.95	7,341
3	9,375	0.90	8,438
4	8,963	0.90	8,067

The subject property has 4.5 rooms per unit. Sale 4 has 4.7. Again, it appears to be most comparable. Taking the price for sale 4 as an estimate, we have 45 apartments × $8,067 per apartment = $363,015. On a per room basis, the adjustments are processed as follows:

Sale	Per Room	Net Adjustment	Adjusted per Room
1	$2,429	0.90	$2,186
2	1,977	0.95	1,878
3	2,500	0.90	2,250
4	1,890	0.90	1,701

Sale 4 seems most comparable, with 137 square feet per room as compared with 139 square feet per room for the subject property. The adjusted value is given by 202 rooms × $1,701 = $343,602.

No adjustments are applied to the GRM because it is a factor that expresses a relationship between income and value. Actually, all factors that affect the property in an adverse or a beneficial way should be summed up in the gross rents. All proper adjustments are contained in the property's ability to produce rent. In this example, all sales are current. If the GRMs were developed over a period of a few years, older indicators would not be as useful as current ones, since many conditions affecting the properties would have changed, particularly the finance-mortgage market. In this example, consistency dictates that the GRM developed from sale 4 is most useful. Therefore, we have $50,000 (gross rent of subject property) × 6.91 = $345,500.

Reconciliation of Values Indicated by Comparative Sales Approach

In both site valuation and improved property valuation the methods will have indicated value estimates for the subject property. These value indications must be reconciled into a single indicator of value for the comparative sales approach. Hopefully the value indications will be within a narrow range. In selecting the single value estimate, it is not proper to average the results. Rather, the process is one of reviewing the adjustments made and placing the greatest reliance on that value indicated by the most comparable property with the least adjustments.

Correlating the information found in the last series of examples, we see the following.

	Value
Square-foot-of-building comparison	$348,600
Apartment-unit comparison	363,000
Room comparison	343,600
GRM	345,500

The four GRMs (6.75, 7.08, 7.32, 6.91) fall within a narrow range around 7. The adjustments applied to the other units of comparison are not of the best quality, suggesting less reliance on these units. A supportable value indication is $345,500.

Benchmarks

Benchmarks are normally established for typical properties of each use type that have sold. For example, benchmarks may be established for various residential properties within a neighborhood, based upon the main variables in an appraisal, that is, quality of construction, size of improvements, size of the site, age of the improvements, and other factors. All other properties being appraised will require adjustments from the benchmark properties.

Summary

The fundamental strength of the comparative sales approach to value is that it reflects the actions of the marketplace and what buyers and sellers are actually doing and paying. This approach places less reliance on subjective judgments and the opinion of the appraiser because the data are taken directly from the market and related directly to the subject. The comparison of actual sales is generally recognized as good appraisal practice by courts and other review authorities.

It is important to note that the comparative sales approach is not unique in its attempts to deal with the facts of the market. In future chapters it will be seen that in the cost approach to value considerable market data can and should be used. Market information, particularly concerning rents and lease levels and capitalization rates, is an essential element in the income approach to value.

A review of the comparative sales approach reveals a number of important steps as detailed in this chapter.

Analysis of Subject Property

1. Description and classification—inspection and a complete description of the site and improvements.
2. Highest and best use—a projection of highest and best use based on the market.
3. Purpose and function of the appraisal—market value.

Collection and Analysis of Comparative Sales Data

Data such as sales, options, asking prices, offering prices, leases, and rentals must be collected. The sales must be analyzed to determine whether market-value criteria are met.

1. Sources of data—assessors' files, published news, ads, listings, attorneys, brokers, buyer and seller via interviews and questionnaires.
2. Verification of data—key data verified, ideally with both parties to transaction.

Elements of Comparison

1. Comparison process—the setting up of a series of value levels and a gradual narrowing of value levels into one value.
2. Factors and trends—properties influenced to a similar extent by factors and trends have the greatest degree of comparability.
3. Units of comparison—useful units into which sales are broken down so that reasonable comparisons can be made.

Methods and Techniques

1. Direct sales comparison—processes sales prices into indicators of value for the subject property by making adjustments.
2. Gross rent multiplier—gives a simple, direct estimate of value and eliminates complex adjustments.

7 The Cost Approach to Value: Cost Estimation

The cost approach to value, also known as the summation approach, provides a value indication that is the summation of the estimated land value and the depreciated cost of the building and other improvements. The cost approach to value is based upon the principle of substitution—that a rational, informed purchaser will pay no more for a property than the cost of acquiring an acceptable substitute with like utility, assuming that no costly delay will be encountered in making the substitution.

The primary use of the cost approach is to obtain a value estimate that can be compared with value estimates from the other two approaches. However, this is an ideal situation, for at times there are no sales data available. This is especially true for special-purpose properties, such as schools, hospitals, and churches. Assessors are particularly interested in the cost approach because, properly used, it is applicable to most classes of property and serves as a good foundation for uniformity and equality in assessments. The cost approach can be readily adapted to mass appraisal projects if current cost and depreciation schedules are market-oriented (see chap. 13).

The steps in the cost approach to value are as follows: (1) estimate site value, as if vacant; (2) estimate replacement cost new or reproduction cost new of the improvements; (3) estimate the amount of accrued depreciation; (4) subtract estimate of accrued depreciation from estimated cost new; and (5) add estimated site value to estimate of depreciated replacement or reproduction cost. This chapter will concentrate on the estimation of replacement or reproduction cost new; chapter 8 will expand upon the estimation of accrued depreciation. In the treatment of cost estimation, consideration will be given to improvement analysis and methods of cost estimation.

Improvement Data

An inspection and a suitable description of the site improvements, including the building, should be the first step in the cost approach. The assessor, armed with a description and a value estimate of the site, usually has property record cards that assist in making a thorough inspection of the building. It is necessary to observe the quality, condition, and adequacy of each component and of the whole. Generally, the following elements should be rated as to quality, workmanship, and special physical characteristics.

- Overall quality
- Use type (residential, commercial, etc.)
- Construction (light, standard, better)
- Structure (foundation and framing)
- Exterior
- Roof (type, pitch, cover, gutters, and eaves)
- Wiring and fixtures (type and grade)
- Windows (type, screens, storm windows)
- Plumbing (type and grade)
- Heating and air conditioning (type and capacity)
- Special features
- Equipment
- Room and finish detail (floors, walks, and trim)
- Bath details (number, type, and grade)

- Construction record (year built, effective age, remaining economic life)
- Miscellaneous improvements

In addition to recording and rating the above features, the assessor should make a sketch of the building dimensions and square-foot and/or cubic-foot areas.

After rating and recording the quality of the individual components, the assessor must be concerned with functional utility. Functional utility is the overall usefulness and desirability of a property; the ultimate criterion is whether the improvement efficiently satisfies the wants and needs of the market. Elements to be considered in determining functional utility are architecture and appearance, layout, systems, and equipment. Poor or inappropriate architecture, wasteful floor plans, bad natural lighting, inappropriate room sizes, and inadequate heating or cooling capacity should be judged by the assessor as to deficiency in functional utility.

Cost Estimation

Cost estimation is the process by which the replacement cost or reproduction cost of improvements is obtained. The process begins after all the pertinent physical data regarding the improvements have been collected.

Elements of Cost

Cost consists of all the direct labor and materials and indirect expenditures required to complete the construction of a structure. From the viewpoint of the builder or developer, cost includes all the components of expense incurred in the manufacture of the building. The builder or developer intends to recapture all these costs, including overhead and profit, if he places the property for sale. Likewise, a builder constructing a building for the owner of a site will charge a price that allows him to recoup his expenditures, including a reasonable sum for such items as overhead and profit. If cost is to represent value, it is necessary that all appropriate costs be included in the estimate. The goal of the assessor is not cost; it is value. Cost is merely the avenue to value in this approach.

Cost may be divided into two categories—direct and indirect. Examples of direct costs include labor, materials, supervision, electrical and water service, equipment rental, installation of components, and utilities. Indirect costs include (but are not limited to) architecture and engineering, building permits, title and legal expenses, insurance, real estate and other taxes during construction, construction loan fees and interest payments during construction, overhead, profit, advertising, and sales expense. When using manuals or actual cost submissions, the assessor must learn to what extent all direct and indirect costs are reported.

Concepts of Cost

There are two concepts of cost: reproduction cost and replacement cost. *Reproduction cost* is the cost of producing an exact replica of a building or improvement using the same or very similar materials, design, and workmanship. *Replacement cost* is the cost of producing a building or improvement having the same utility, but using modern materials, design, and workmanship.

The primary difference between replacement cost and reproduction cost is that reproduction cost includes the cost of reproducing such obsolete features as high ceilings, excessive foundations, out-of-date features, and poor, inefficient design, while replacement cost new excludes the cost of such items.

There is a difference of opinion among appraisal practitioners as to which concept of cost is preferable to use. Those who hold that reproduction cost is preferable argue that physical deterioration must be charged against the subject improvement rather than against a hypothetical improvement. Those who favor replacement cost respond that an informed purchaser would not pay more for the subject property than an acceptable substitute of like utility lacking the built-in obsolescence. It is argued that the cost of reproducing obsolete features should not be included when it must be subtracted later as part of the accrued depreciation.

An argument for the use of replacement cost is that an item which is classified as functionally obsolescent should not be charged partly to physical deterioration and partly to incurable functional obsolescence. For example, a subject property has a 12-foot ceiling in a market that pays only for an 8-foot ceiling. If reproduction cost is used, the cost factor is for the full 12 feet; deduction is then made for physical deterioration for 12 feet and a second charge for 4 feet of functional obsolescence less the charge for 4 feet of physical deterioration. If replacement cost is used, the cost factor is based upon an 8-foot ceiling. On the other hand, it might be argued that the replacement cost factor does not account for the functional obsolescence deduction (which cannot be subtracted from the replacement factor) and is therefore a short-cut method of measuring functional obsolescence.

Replacement cost should be used for structures of considerable age, which cannot be physically or economically reproduced today. In some cases, materials are no longer available to reproduce an existing building, and new construction techniques and materials may make it possible to build a structure of equal utility at less than reproduction cost. In such cases the assessor can use replacement cost, recognizing that he may be excluding some or all of the functional obsolescence in the actual structure under appraisal.

Reproduction cost can be used for most buildings. Most published cost manuals (discussed later in this chapter) are based upon reproduction cost.

The usefulness of cost as a representation of value must be kept in its proper context. The assessor should remind himself that the objective is value, not cost. Cost estimating is not appraising; it is only one step in the appraisal process. Appraising is an orderly and disciplined method of estimating the most probable selling price of a property. Cost estimation, while stating the development cost of a new property, does not indicate the ultimate value of the property. As has been discussed previously, other factors (the general economy, the market, supply and demand, and location) influence value and must be accounted for.

Methods of Estimating Cost

The methods of estimating current cost may be placed in four categories: the quantity survey method, the unit-in-place method, the square-foot or cubic-foot method, and the factored historical cost method.

Quantity Survey Method. This is a complete cost itemization of all the direct and indirect costs incurred in the construction of a building. It is the method generally used by contractors, cost estimators, and builders; it is accurate and reliable. Because it requires a great amount of detailed work and is consequently time-consuming, the method is seldom used by the assessor in normal practice. However, he should be familiar with the method because he probably will be presented with schedules of quantity survey costs by contractors or builders for study and analysis. Table 7.1 illustrates a construction cost estimate for a single-family dwelling using the quantity survey method.

The general building description is as follows: The dwelling is a five-room one-story ranch-style house with two bedrooms, living room, kitchen, and bath. The exterior walls are concrete block, painted, and the interior walls are frame and plaster. The roof has asphalt shingle cover, with two-inch rock-wool insulation. The subflooring is concrete slab. The house has steel casement windows. Heat is electric, and there is a 40-gallon automatic electric water heater. Floors are carpeted, except for the kitchen and bathroom, which are tiled.

Table 7.1
Construction Cost Estimate for a Single-Family Dwelling Using
the Quantity Survey Method

Item No.	Type of Construction	Material	Labor	Total
1	*Excavation*			
	Layout and forms	$ 45.00	$ 50.00	$ 95.00
	Excavation 6.41 cu. yd.: labor 6.41 cu. yd. × $7.00	. . .	44.87	44.87
	Gravel fill 24.7 cu. yd.: 24.7 cu. yd. × $3.00	74.10	. . .	74.10
	Gravel fill labor	. . .	120.00	120.00
2	*Foundation*			
	⅝-inch rods 364 lin. ft. × $0.20	72.80	. . .	72.80
	Labor 364 lin. ft. × $0.05	. . .	18.20	18.20
	Footings 4.3 cu. yd. × $40.00	172.00	. . .	172.00
	Labor 4.3 cu. yd. × $4.00	. . .	17.20	17.20
	One course dapped out block	75.00	. . .	75.00
	Labor 98 × $0.39	. . .	38.22	38.22
3	*Chimney—masonry*			
	Brick	100.00	70.00	170.00
	Flashing	15.00	22.00	37.00
4	*Exterior walls*			
	Concrete blocks 98 per tier × 12 tiers = 1,176 × $0.45	529.20	. . .	529.20
	Labor 1,176 × $0.39	. . .	458.64	458.64
	Gable ends 400 blocks × $0.45	180.00	. . .	180.00
	Labor 400 blocks × $0.39	. . .	156.00	156.00
	Steel rods 364 lin. ft × $0.20	72.80	. . .	72.80
	Labor 364 lin ft. × $0.05	. . .	18.20	18.20
	Concrete lintel 2.13 cu. yd. × $40.00	85.20	. . .	85.20
	Labor	. . .	10.00	10.00
	Mortar 1,576 blocks × $0.10	157.60	. . .	157.60
	Labor—forms, removal	. . .	50.00	50.00
5	*Floor construction*			
	Membrane (felt, hot mopped) 1,000 sq. ft. × $0.10	100.00	. . .	100.00
	Labor 1,000 sq. ft. × $0.05	. . .	50.00	50.00
	Wire mesh 1,100 sq. ft. × $0.07	77.00	. . .	77.00

Table 7.1—*Continued*

Item No.	Type of Construction	Material	Labor	Total
	Labor 1,100 sq. ft. × $0.01	...	$ 11.00	$ 11.00
	Exposed joint 156 lin. ft. × $0.20	$ 31.20	...	31.20
	Labor 156 lin. ft. × $0.025	...	3.90	3.90
	Concrete slab 12.4 cu. yd. × $40.00	496.00	...	496.00
	Labor 12.4 cu yd. × $3.50	...	43.40	43.40
	Bolts 31 × $0.30	9.30	...	9.30
	Labor 31 × $0.11	...	3.41	3.41
	Finishing	6.00	100.00	106.00
6	*Partitions*			
	Sole plate (2 × 4) 126 lin. ft. × $0.38	47.88	...	47.88
	Labor 126 lin. ft. × $0.20	...	25.20	25.20
	Studs (2 × 4) 423 bd. ft. × $0.25	105.75	...	105.75
	Labor 423 bd. ft. × $0.18	...	76.14	76.14
7	*Ceiling framing*			
	Top plate (2 × 6) 130 lin. ft. × $0.40	52.00	...	52.00
	Labor	...	22.00	22.00
	Joists 870 sq. ft. × $0.28	243.60	...	243.60
	Labor 870 sq. ft. × $0.20	...	174.00	174.00
	Bridging (1 × 3) 177 lin. ft. × $0.08)	14.16	...	14.16
	Labor 177 lin. ft. × $0.12)	...	21.24	21.24
	Rough and finish not included	224.00	...	224.00
8	*Roof framing*			
	Bolts 32 × $0.29	9.28	...	9.28
	Labor 32 × $0.14	...	4.48	4.48
	Top plate (2 × 4) 126 bd ft × $0.25	31.50	...	31.50
	Labor 126 bd. ft. × $0.19	...	23.94	23.94
	Fascia (1 × 6) 80 lin. ft. × $0.39	31.20	...	31.20
	Labor 80 lin. ft × $0.29	...	23.20	23.20
	Boxed cornice 126 bd. ft × $0.30	37.80	...	37.80
	Labor 126 bd. ft. × $0.21	...	26.46	26.46
9	*Roofing*			
	Rafter (2 × 6) 1,040 bd. ft. × $0.25	260.00	...	260.00
	Labor 1,040 bd. ft. × $0.19	...	197.60	197.60
	Purlins (2 × 4) 47 bd. ft. × $0.28	13.16	...	13.16
	Labor 47 bd. ft. × $0.24	...	11.28	11.28
	Bracing (2 × 4) 103 bd. ft. × $0.28	28.84	...	28.84
	Labor 103 bd. ft. × $0.24	...	24.72	24.72
	Roof decking 1,628 bd. ft. × $0.24	390.72	...	390.72
	Labor 1,628 bd. ft. × $0.18	...	293.04	293.04
	Roofing (felt 2 layers) 1,628 bd. ft. × $0.04	65.12	...	65.12
	Labor 1,628 bd. ft. × $0.03	...	48.84	48.84
	Roofing 13.33 sq. ft. × $19.00	253.27	...	253.27
	Labor 13.33 sq. ft. × $10.00	...	133.30	133.30
	Eave drip 80 lin. ft. × $0.14	11.20	...	11.20
	Labor 80 lin. ft. × $0.07	...	5.60	5.60
10	*Gutters and downspouts*			
	Material	85.00	...	85.00
	Labor	...	85.00	85.00

Table 7.1—*Continued*

Item No.	Type of Construction	Material	Labor	Total
11	*Windows*			
	Windows 11 × $63.00	$693.00	. . .	$ 693.00
	Labor 11 × $13.00	. . .	$ 143.00	143.00
12	*Entrance and exterior detail*			
	Outside doors 2 × $90.00	180.00	. . .	180.00
	Labor 2 × $25.00	. . .	50.00	50.00
	Screen doors 2 × $26.00	52.00	. . .	52.00
	Labor 2 × $12.00	. . .	24.00	24.00
	Louvers 2 × $20.00	40.00	. . .	40.00
	Labor 2 × $6.00	. . .	12.00	12.00
13	*Insulation rock wool*	115.00	80.00	195.00
14	*Interior wallboard*			
	Gypsum board 386 sq. yd. × $2.10	810.60	. . .	810.60
	Labor 386 sq. yd. × $1.90	. . .	733.40	733.40
15	*Carpeting*			
	Material 97 sq. yd. × $7.00	679.00	. . .	679.00
	Labor 97 sq. yd. × $2.00	. . .	194.00	194.00
16	*Tile flooring*			
	Kitchen—vinyl-asbestos: material 11 sq. yd. × $10.00	110.00	. . .	110.00
	Labor 11 sq. yd. × $6.00	. . .	66.00	66.00
	Bathroom—ceramic: material 4.5 sq. yd. × $20.00	90.00	. . .	90.00
	Labor 4.5 sq. yd. × $10.00	. . .	45.00	45.00
17	*Interior door and trim*			
	Exterior walls baseboard 130 lin. ft. × $0.24	31.20	. . .	31.20
	Labor 130 lin. ft. × $0.15	. . .	19.50	19.50
	Exterior walls molding 130 lin. ft. × $0.10	13.00	. . .	13.00
	Labor 130 lin. ft. × $0.06	. . .	7.80	7.80
	Interior partitions baseboard 202 lin. ft. × $0.24	48.48	. . .	48.48
	Labor 202 lin. ft. × $0.10	. . .	20.20	20.20
	Shoe mold 202 lin. ft. × $0.10	20.20	. . .	20.20
	Labor 202 lin. ft. × $0.05	. . .	10.10	10.10
	Interior doors 10 × $47.00	470.00	. . .	470.00
	Labor 10 × $25.00	. . .	250.00	250.00
18	*Cabinet work*			
	Base 8 ft. and Formica top and splash 8 lin. ft. × $34.00	272.00	. . .	272.00
	Labor 8 lin. ft. × $11.00	. . .	88.00	88.00
	Wall cabinets 12 lin. ft., labor and materials @ $20.00	. . .	. . .	240.00
	Medicine cabinet	40.00	10.00	50.00
	Shelves and rods	30.00	20.00	50.00
19	*Painting and decorating*			
	Undercoat and finish material 3,556 sq. ft. × $0.09	320.04	. . .	320.04

Table 7.1—*Continued*

Item No.	Type of Construction	Material	Labor	Total
	Labor 3,556 sq. ft. × $0.12	. . .	$ 426.72	$ 426.72
	11 windows @ $18.00	. . .	198.00	198.00
	Exterior walls and gable	. . .	220.00	220.00
20	*Plumbing*			
	Plumbing (total contract with guarantee)	$900.00	. . .	900.00
	Labor	. . .	1,050.00	1,050.00
21	*Heating*			
	Electric heat 45 lin. ft. × $7.20	324.00	. . .	324.00
	Labor 45 lin. ft. × $4.80	. . .	216.00	216.00
22	*Electric*			
	37 outlets (materials and labor)	150.00	220.00	370.00
	Service	105.00	. . .	105.00
	Labor	. . .	125.00	125.00
	Range and heater wiring	45.00	80.00	125.00
	Fixtures	. . .	. . .	140.00
23	*Miscellaneous*			
	Water supply—under construction	. . .	. . .	75.00
	Building permit	. . .	. . .	60.00
	Electrical service—under construction	. . .	. . .	50.00
	Site clearance	. . .	. . .	70.00
	Architect's fee	. . .	. . .	125.00
Total material and labor cost		. . .	. . .	$17,291.00
Add: field overhead @ 4%		. . .	. . .	691.64
				$17,982.64
Contractor's profit and overhead @ 22%		. . .	. . .	3,956.18
Total construction cost		. . .	. . .	$21,938.82

The primary problem for the assessor is to establish the gross floor area of the building and to calculate each of the costs on a unit basis, comparing them with others on file in order to establish that these costs are reasonably correct.

In order to analyze these costs, the assessor should break the building down into its component parts, such as foundations, column footings, floor area, exterior walls, interior partitioning, roof, roof framing, roofing, interior finishes, and so on. The assessor must then list their appropriate areas, building materials, and labor, adding all indirect costs.

This analysis leads the assessor into the next step, the unit-in-place method, with which records of normal building costs for all of the many components of building construction can be established.

Unit-in-Place Method. This method is a modification of the quantity survey method that is frequently used by architects, appraisers, and assessors who require a considerable degree of accuracy. This method combines direct and indirect costs (labor, materials, and overhead) into a single *unit in place*, which, when multiplied by the area of the portion of the building being priced, results in a total cost estimate for that portion. Every building component is similarly calculated and added together for a cost of the total structure. Table 7.2 shows an example of the construction cost of an industrial building by the unit-in-place method.

Table 7.2
Illustration of the Unit-in-Place Method
(Construction Cost Estimate of an Industrial Building)

Building dimensions: 282 ft. × 401 ft. 8 in. × 27 ft. 3 in.
Floor area: 113,270 sq. ft.
Description: one story, no basement, full steel frame

Component	Quantity	Unit Cost	Total Cost
Excavation, for foundation walls and column footings, yards of material	933 yd.	$ 1.75	$ 1,633
Column footings, concrete, including reinforcing and form work	86 yd.	42.50	3,655
Wall footings, 20 × 8 inches including light reinforcing	1,367 lin. ft.	0.93	1,271
Foundation walls, 12-inch reinforced concrete; includes form work, concrete, and reinforcing	5,468 sq. ft.	2.40	13,123
Column piers, reinforced concrete	22 yd.	113.00	2,486
Structural steel, 88 columns, plus girders	4,191 cwt.	22.00	92,202
Cost of steel, erected in place; 280 long-span steel joists regulated at 40 feet ..	280 ft.	200.00	56,000
Flooring, 6-inch concrete on sand fill, wire-mesh reinforcing, cured finish ...	113,270 sq. ft.	0.95	107,607

NOTE.—Total cost figures are rounded.

Table 7.2—*Continued*

Component	Quantity	Unit Cost	Total Cost
Roof, 1¾-inch metal deck, 2-inch rigid insulation ...	113,270 sq. ft.	$ 0.75	$ 84,953
Roofing, tar and gravel plus flashing	113,270 sq. ft.	0.70	79,289
Exterior walls:			
4-inch brick face, 8-inch concrete	8,490 sq. ft.	3.00	25,470
Block backing, 12-inch concrete block	20,606 sq. ft.	1.40	28,848
Continuous factory steel sash	3,820 sq. ft.	3.50	13,370
Fascia: ¼-inch asbestos board, 1-inch insulation, on wood frame	1,790 sq. ft.	1.10	1,969
Doors: wood slab (3 × 7)..	13	65.00	845
Overhead doors, wood, sectional 8 × 10 feet ...	6	160.00	960
Electrical operation	6	500.00	3,000
Overhead steel shutter door	352 sq. ft.	10.00	3,520
Electrical operation	1	1,000.00	1,000
Entrance, plate glass in aluminum frames; includes 2 doors 3 × 7 feet	80 sq. ft.	20.00	1,600
Partition walls:			
10-inch concrete block .	8,900 sq. ft.	1.20	10,680
8-inch concrete block ..	2,100 sq. ft.	1.00	2,100
2 × 4 wood stud, framing plywood, 2 sides ...	5,300 sq. ft.	2.00	10,600
4-inch concrete block	300 sq. ft.	0.80	240
Doors, plywood slab (3 × 7 feet)	20	50.00	1,000
Wall finishes:			
Gypsum lath and plaster	1,200 sq. ft.	0.65	780
Glazed tile	640 sq. ft.	1.50	960
Office ceiling, suspended T-bar, acoustic lay-in panels	3,900 sq. ft.	0.50	1,950
Flooring, vinyl-asbestos tile	7,100 sq. ft.	0.35	2,485
Terrazzo	1,560 sq. ft.	1.50	2,340
Heating plant, gas-fired forced air, unit blowers suspended from roof, no ductwork	104,611 sq. ft.	0.80	83,689
Offices, heating, hot water, radiation	8,660 sq. ft.	1.50	12,990

NOTE.—Total cost figures are rounded.

Table 7.2—*Continued*

Component	Quantity	Unit Cost	Total Cost
Package air conditioner, ductwork, 10-ton capacity .	8,660 sq. ft.	$ 1.50	$ 12,990
Sprinkler system, open . . .	113,270 sq. ft.	0.30	33,981
Plumbing and drains; fixtures include roughing in, drains, and installation . . .	45 fixtures	600.00	27,000
Electrical wiring and lighting, office area, 4 walls . . .	8,660 sq. ft.	2.00	17,320
Plant area 2 walls	104,611 sq. ft.	1.00	104,611
Dock levelers, hinged, spring 6 × 7 feet	8	750.00	6,000
			854,517
Contractor's overhead and profit	15%	. . .	128,178
			982,695
Architectural and engineering fees	5%	. . .	49,135
Total construction cost	. . .	. . .	$1,031,830

The assessor can take this type of survey one step further by combining several items of each portion into one element—for example, totaling the several items included in structural cost into an elemental cost that can be related to gross floor area.

Square-Foot or Cubic-Foot Method. Many cost manuals are composed of tables in which all construction costs are combined into a single unit, either the square foot or the cubic foot, according to the quality and types of construction and on the basis of comparison with known costs. These methods are essentially the same, except that the square-foot method is based upon floor area, while the cubic-foot method is based upon volume. These methods are not considered as accurate as the quantity survey and unit-in-place methods, but they are easily understood and quickly computed. Consequently they are widely used. The cubic-foot method is used primarily when the ceiling height varies within a class of building, such as a warehouse or industrial structure. The square-foot method generally is used for residential buildings and other structures which typically have uniform story heights.

Factored Historical Cost Method. This method of cost estimating is especially useful for unusual or special-purpose structures. It requires the date and cost of the original structure. Care must be taken to verify that the original cost was typical at the time and representative of existing construction rates. Using cost schedules for former years from recognized building pricing manuals, trending factors can be developed to bring the original cost to current cost.

Example:

Subject property: 200-bed general hospital.
Original cost, 9 years ago: $3,995,000.
Nonresidential building cost index using fourteen years ago as the base year:

Construction Year	Factor
14 years ago	1.000
9 years ago	1.211
Today	2.525

Conversion factor to today: 2.525 ÷ 1.211 = 2.085.
Current indicated reproduction cost: $3,995,000 × 2.085 = $8,329,575 (rounded to $8,330,000).

The factored historical method is a substitute method to be used only when other, more accurate methods are not available. It may be used, however, as a valuable check against other methods.

The Classification System

As will be seen in chapter 13, mass appraisal requires a fast, reasonably simple and accurate method of cost estimating. The key to cost estimating in a mass appraisal system is the building classification system. It recognizes that buildings of similar design and construction quality have similar costs per construction unit.

The use of a classification system is particularly advantageous in that the basis of the cost determination—the quality class of the building—remains constant through all changes and variables of cost due to fluctuations of material and labor prices and through locational differences. The classification system overcomes difficulties due to such changes and differences. The use of the classification system has many advantages. It is fast, simple, and, more important, it promotes uniformity. It also facilitates bringing cost manuals up to date.

There are several varieties of classification systems. A system may recognize five principal characteristics that influence costs: design type, construction type, quality class, floor area, and building shape. Basic building costs are estimated by classifying buildings according to each of these characteristics and using these classifications as a reference to a table of square-foot costs to be applied to the building area.

Design Types. Buildings are first classified on the basis of the use for which they are designed. The four basic design types are residential, commercial, industrial, and rural. Square-foot cost of buildings varies considerably depending on the type. Two buildings may be alike in area, shape, quality, and type of construction but have different square-foot costs because of differences in structural components or quality of finish detail. Each basic design type may have several subtypes, as follows.

1. Residential
    a) Single-family
    b) Apartments
    c) Condominiums
    d) Hotels, motels[1]
    e) Churches[1]
    f) Funeral homes[1]

1. Sometimes classified as commercial construction.

2. Commercial
    a) Stores
    b) Supermarkets, discount houses
    c) Department stores
    d) Financial institutions
    e) Office buildings
    f) Medical and dental buildings
    g) Hospitals
    h) Restaurants
    i) Theaters
    j) Service stations, garages
3. Industrial
    a) Warehouses
    b) Light industrial buildings
    c) Heavy industrial buildings

Construction Types. Construction type refers to the structural characteristics of a building. The letters A, B, C, D, and S are frequently used to designate five recognized structural types. These types may be identified by the following descriptions.

• *Class A structures*—Buildings have fireproofed structural steel frames carrying all wall, floor, and roof loads. Wall, floor, and roof structures are built of noncombustible materials.

• *Class B structures*—Buildings have fireproofed reinforced concrete frames carrying all wall, floor, and roof loads. Wall, floor, and roof structures are built of noncombustible materials.

• *Class C structures*—Buildings have exterior walls built of a noncombustible material. Interior partitions and roof structures are built of combustible materials. Floor may be of concrete or wood frame.

• *Class D structures*—Buildings have wood or wood and steel frames.

• *Class S structures*—Specialized buildings that do not fit in any of the above categories.

Quality Classes. Quality classes rank buildings according to the types of materials used and the quality of workmanship. If two buildings are of the same design, construction type, size, and shape, and one has better materials and workmanship, it will have a higher square-foot cost. Each class remains constant throughout the life of a building, provided that no major remodeling is done or additions made. Changes in costs are provided by updating cost factor tables. In this way the accuracy and equality of the cost estimation remain constant through varying conditions in varying locations.

Of the five characteristics according to which a building may be classified, that of quality class is the most difficult. The relative quality of a building is not as obvious as its design type, construction type, shape, or size. The assessor must study the specifications of each quality qualification very thoroughly, relating them to examples of actual buildings. Table 7.3 is a sample set of specifications for an average-quality single-family residence.

Table 7.3
Building Specifications for Average-Quality Single-Family
Residence ("D" Construction)

Components	D6 Quality
Foundation	Concrete perimeter foundation with continuous foundation under interior bearing walls or interior piers
Floors	Concrete slab or 2 × 8 wood joists, 16-inch on center with ⅝-inch ply subfloor; medium-quality asphalt tile or carpeting
Walls and exterior	2 × 4 studs, 16-inch on center, wire and paper; average-quality stucco or medium quality ½-inch plywood siding over 2 × 4; 24-inch on-center studs
Windows	Medium-quality aluminum sliding
Front doors	1¾-inch hardwood veneer slab door
Roof	2 × 4 frame, 24-inch on center; wood shingle, light shake, or medium-quality composition shingle or built-up tar and rock
Overhang	16-inch unsealed
Gutters	Painted galvanized iron over entrances
Interior walls	Sheetrock textured and painted; some inexpensive wallpaper

Table 7.3—*Continued*

Components	D6 Quality
Doors and trim ...	Average hollow-core slab or flat-panel doors; average base and casing
Electrical	Romex wiring; average quality fixtures
Plumbing	Average amount of medium-quality fixtures
Bathroom:	
Walls	Sheetrock and enamel
Floors	Sheet vinyl covered
Shower	Over tub with tile wainscot and glass door
Vanity	Small with average-quality tile or Formica top and splash
Kitchen:	
Walls	Well-applied Sheetrock and enamel
Floors	Coved average-quality sheet vinyl
Cabinets	Ample amount; average quality
Counters	Tile or rounded and coved Formica with 6-inch splash
Closets	Wardrobe bedroom type with average-size linen closet

Floor Area. The fourth classification is floor area. Considering size only, on a square-foot basis the smaller building in a class is more expensive than the larger. The reason for this is the amount of outside wall area required to enclose a building, which is usually expressed as a ratio of 1 lineal foot of enclosing wall to 10, 15, 20, or 30 feet of floor area enclosed. To illustrate:

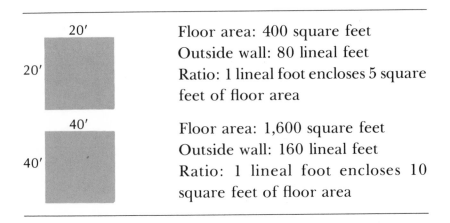

Floor area: 400 square feet
Outside wall: 80 lineal feet
Ratio: 1 lineal foot encloses 5 square feet of floor area

Floor area: 1,600 square feet
Outside wall: 160 lineal feet
Ratio: 1 lineal foot encloses 10 square feet of floor area

The variation in floor area may be treated in two ways. Cost tables may be developed to provide individual square-foot costs for various increments of area, as shown in table 7.4.

Table 7.4
Cost Tables for Increments of Floor Area

Class	Square-Foot Area										
	500	600	700	800	900	1,000	1,100	1,200	1,300	1,400	1,500
6.5 ..	25.30	24.05	22.80	21.65	20.55	19.60	18.85	18.25	17.75	17.30	16.85
6.0 ..	23.05	21.90	20.80	19.70	18.70	17.85	17.25	16.65	16.15	15.70	15.35
5.5 ..	20.95	19.90	18.85	17.85	16.95	16.20	15.55	15.00	14.55	14.20	13.85
5.0 ..	19.40	18.35	17.35	16.35	15.50	14.80	14.25	13.75	13.25	12.90	12.60
4.5 ..	17.45	16.45	15.55	14.80	14.15	13.55	13.00	12.50	12.05	11.70	11.40
4.0 ..	15.90	14.95	14.20	13.45	12.80	12.20	11.75	11.30	10.95	10.60	10.40
3.5 ..	14.40	13.65	12.95	12.25	11.65	11.15	10.65	10.30	9.95	9.60	9.45
3.0 ..	12.90	12.25	11.60	10.95	10.40	9.95	9.50	9.10	8.90	8.60	8.40
2.0 ..	11.70	11.10	10.50	9.90	9.30	8.80	8.45	8.15	7.90	7.70	7.45
1.5 ..	10.65	10.00	9.35	8.85	8.35	7.95	7.55	7.35	7.10	6.90	6.70
1.0 ..	9.90	9.25	8.60	8.10	7.70	7.30	6.95	6.70	6.45	6.25	6.20

Area Modification Table

Area	Factor
500	1.29
600	1.23
700	1.17
800	1.10
900	1.05
1,000	1.00
1,100	0.97
1,200	0.93
1,300	0.90
1,400	0.88
1,500	0.86

Alternatively, a single cost factor may be developed for each quality class with an area modification table, so that the cost factor can be easily calculated as follows:

Use type .... Single residential
Construction class .... D
Shape .... A
Base area .... 1,000 square feet

Class	Base Cost	Class	Base Cost
6.5	19.60	3.5	11.15
6.0	17.85	3.0	9.95
5.5	16.20	2.0	8.80
5.0	14.80	1.5	7.95
4.5	13.55	1.0	7.30
4.0	12.20		

To find the square-foot cost of a single-family residence of D6 (average) quality having 1,450 square feet of floor area, the following calculation is made.

D6 base cost factor	$17.85
Area modifier	× 0.87
	$15.53
Rounded to	$15.50

Building Shape. The shape classification considers any cost difference as caused by variations in building outlines. The most economical building to construct is a square building. The greater the deviation from the square shape, the higher the square-foot unit cost of construction. This is an extension of the effect on cost per square foot of the ratio of lineal feet of wall to enclosed floor area. It also reflects the higher cost of constructing building corners. In addition, shape classification considers differences in cost of various types of roofs. The least costly is the flat roof; the most expensive is the steep-pitched, cut-up roof with many ridges, valleys, and dormers.

Cost Manuals

Several good cost services and manuals are available, with costs produced through an analysis of the construction market of many large metropolitan areas. These usually come with a list of indexes or factors to localize these costs to other metropolitan areas throughout the United States and Canada. While these services provide a great quantity of technical assistance, the assessor will gain a more thorough knowledge of the complexities of costing and of the construction market in general by participating in the development and maintenance of a cost manual.

Cost Data. The first step in the preparation of a cost manual is gathering cost data, which will consist principally of construction contract costs showing a breakdown of all costs by trade for as many types of buildings as possible. When construction cost is analyzed, it should be kept in mind how the construction market acts. When work is plentiful and contractors are busy, costs tend to rise; conversely, when there is little work, contractors' prices tend to fall.

The assessor's office should maintain complete files of construction costs by year and have these related to gross floor area of each building. All data should be recorded as complete specifications. These data form the basis of valuable backup and the beginning of a manual of square-foot cost. In order to make it possible to extend these costs to other similar buildings, more analysis must be carried out.

Data Analysis. Analyzing all construction costs by means of developed unit-in-place costs is a first step in the analysis of construction costs received from building owners, developers, and others. The cost used is made up of labor, materials, and productivity. Productivity refers, for example, to the amount of material that a bricklayer and a helper can place in a working day. Thus the cost of labor and materials and the amount of material, when totaled and divided by the total units of materials in place, determine the cost per unit. Other costs, such as contractor's on-site expenses, overhead, and profit may be included in this cost or may be added in at the end of the cost calculation. The next step is to bring some of these individual costs into a loose, flexible series of elemental costs with detailed sets of specifications for each element.

Building Components. A Class A or Class B multistory building may be separated into the following components: substructure, superstructure, exterior walls, partitions, interior finishes, mechanical components, electrical components, vertical access, conveying systems, special equipment, and building extras.

Substructure. Included in the substructure are the following: excavation, foundations, columns and beams, bottom floor, suspended floors, and exterior walls. The costs corresponding to these are affected by area, shape (ratio of lineal feet of enclosing wall to enclosed floor area), floor height, and the number of stories of superstructure supported by the substructure.

Superstructure. Included in the superstructure are the following: foundations, columns and beams, bottom floor (assuming no basement), suspended floors, roof and roofing, and staircases. The costs are affected by the floor area, the number of column bays and aisles (as the number increases, costs per square foot diminish slightly), the average height per floor, and the number of stories comprising the structure.

Exterior Walls. When the structural frame is treated separately from the exterior walls, the adjustments to cost per square foot caused by the variable relationship of enclosing walls to enclosed floor space are largely eliminated. However, there is a smaller effect on the cost of structural frames: the effect of the number of column lines required. Commencing at the smallest number of column lines required by a structure, each additional bay decreases the overall cost per square foot until a structure size is reached such that the difference in cost for each additional bay becomes too small to have an effect.

The base number of stories is significant, since the optimum saving in construction cost occurs in buildings of ten to twelve stories. Below this level, the effect of the cost of the roof and the bottom floor on the overall cost per square foot causes an increase; above this level, the structural strength and bracing required to support more stories cause the structural cost to increase greatly.

Costs for many exterior wall types used by industrial plants, apartment buildings, commercial office buildings, hotels, and institutional properties may be calculated on the basis of cost per square foot wall area, including normal amounts of windows, entrances, insulation, and so on. These wall types are compiled, and listed, to be added separately to the costing project when and where required.

Partitions. The costs of various types of partitioning can be calculated and recorded. These costs should include the walling, doors, windows, and hardware costs. Partitioning is classified as to materials and cost and can be applied on a use basis. For example, normal office buildings require 1 lineal foot of partitioning to every 15, 20, or 30 square feet of floor space; hospitals require about 1 lineal foot of partitioning for every 8 feet of floor space. In use types requiring little partitioning, the partitioning can be accounted for on an individual basis.

Interior Finishes. Interior finishes include ceilings, flooring, and wall and column facings.

Mechanical Components. Mechanical costs may include plumbing fixtures, piping, drains, sprinkler systems, heating and air conditioning, and ventilation. These costs vary greatly from one building type to another. Ordinary warehouses usually require minimal heating and plumbing fixtures, while industrial plants require plumbing fixtures for many employees. Offices, stores, and institutional buildings have higher heating requirements, usually with ventilating and air-conditioning systems. The highest mechanical costs are usually found in research laboratories and some types of hospitals.

Electrical Components. The frequency and intensity of lighting varies with building use and can be calculated and costed on that basis.

Vertical Access. Vertical access includes elevators, escalators, and dumbwaiters.

Conveying Systems. Conveying systems include conveyors, pneumatic tubes, and chutes.

Special Equipment. Special equipment includes hospital paging systems, public address systems, refrigerators (walk-in type), bank vaults, security doors, and dock levelers.

Building Extras. Building extras include entrance porches, truck doors, ramps, tunnels, overhead bridges, and incinerators.

A compilation of the foregoing costs on the basis of square-foot floor area or on a per unit basis, in separate sections and by use type, is what is termed an elemental cost manual. It is one of the simplest manuals to understand and apply and can be expanded to almost any use type. By compiling an elemental cost manual, one can gain a greater understanding of the role of cost.

Summary

When the cost approach to value is used, a few basic points must be considered. First, cost is not necessarily value, nor does it create value. As has been discussed previously, many other factors enter into the estimation of value. On the other hand, the cost approach is a comparative approach. Not only are cost data derived from newly constructed comparable properties, but, as will be seen in the following chapter, market reaction to comparable properties is used as a standard from which to estimate accrued depreciation.

A review of the cost approach reveals a number of important facets as detailed in this chapter.

Improvement Data

1. Inspection and description—observing the quality, condition, and adequacy of each improvement component and recording data.

2. Rating characteristics—as to overall quality, use type, construction, structure, exterior, roof, wiring and fixtures, windows, and plumbing.

3. Functional utility—considering overall usefulness and desirability of a property and of the various components.

Elements of Cost

1. Cost—consists of all direct labor and materials and indirect expenditures required to complete construction.

2. Direct costs—labor, materials, supervision, equipment rental, components, and utilities.

3. Indirect costs—architecture and engineering, building permits, title and legal expenses, insurance, real estate and other taxes, loan fees, overhead, profit, advertising, and sales expense.

Concepts of Cost

There are two concepts: reproduction cost and replacement cost.

1. Reproduction cost—the cost of producing an exact replica of a building or improvement using the same or very similar materials, design, and workmanship.

2. Replacement cost—the cost of producing a building or improvement having the same utility as the original but using modern materials, design, and workmanship.

Methods of Estimating Cost

1. Quantity survey method—consists of a complete cost itemization of all direct and indirect costs incurred in the construction of a building.

2. Unit-in-place method—combines direct and indirect costs into a single unit in place, which, multiplied by the area of the portion of the building being priced, results in a total cost estimate for that portion.

3. Square-foot or cubic-foot method—combines construction costs into a single unit, either square foot or cubic foot, according to the quality and types of construction and on the basis of comparison with known costs.

4. Factored historical cost method—develops trending factors to bring original cost to current cost by using cost schedules for former years from recognized building pricing manuals.

Classification System

The key to cost estimating in a mass appraisal system is the building classification system, which may recognize five principal characteristics influencing costs.
1. Design types—basic types include residential, commercial, industrial, and rural.
2. Construction types—refer to the structural characteristics of a building, sometimes designated by letters A, B, C, D, and S.
3. Quality classes—rank buildings according to the types of materials used and the quality of workmanship.
4. Floor area—provides individual square-foot costs for various increments of area or single cost factors for each quality class with an area modification table.
5. Building shape—considers cost differences as caused by variations in building shapes.

Cost Manuals

Development and maintenance of a cost manual include the following.
1. Cost data—gathering and analyzing construction contract costs, having a breakdown of all costs by trade for as many buildings as possible.
2. Data analysis—analyzing all construction costs by means of developed unit-in-place costs and bringing them into a flexible series of elemental costs with detailed specifications.
3. Building components—include substructure, superstructure, exterior walls, partitions, interior finishes, mechanical and electrical components, vertical access, conveying systems, special equipment, and building extras.

8

The Cost Approach to Value: Depreciation

Depreciation is the loss from the upper limit of value, from all causes, of property having a limited economic life. It does not apply to land, since land continues into perpetuity. *Accrued depreciation,* which is used only in the cost approach, is the difference between reproduction or replacement cost new of a property and its market value as of the date of appraisal. It is a deduction from the cost new as of the date of appraisal. It may also be described as a loss in value from any cause except *depletion,* which is the loss of value of property due to consumption and is properly applied to oil, gas, precious metals, and timber. Distinction should be made between accrued depreciation and recapture, which is the recovery of a capital investment from a property (discussed in chap. 10).

Accrued depreciation is applied to the wasting asset in real estate—the building and other site improvements. Any structure that is not new suffers from at least one of the several types of accrued depreciation. The task of the assessor is to identify, classify, and measure these influences on value. The true test of the extent of accrued depreciation is the effect on marketability of the property. The assessor must determine how buyers and sellers in the market react to conditions of decreased desirability and how decreased desirability affects market prices.

Causes of Depreciation

The causes of accrued depreciation fall into three general categories: physical deterioration, functional obsolescence, and economic obsolescence. Physical deterioration and functional obsolescence are inherent in the property itself, while economic obsolescence is extrinsic to the property, that is, from without the property.

Physical Deterioration

Physical deterioration is the loss in value due to wear and tear in service and the disintegration of a reproducible property from the forces of nature. All man-made objects begin a slow process of deterioration as soon as they are created. Decay may be due to normal chemical changes in the material's composition or may result from mechanical causes. Among the most common causes of physical deterioration are wear and tear through use, breakage, negligent care, infestation of termites, dry rot, moisture, and the elements.

Physical deterioration may be subdivided into the classifications of curable and incurable. *Curable physical deterioration* can be called deferred maintenance. An item may be considered curable when the cost of repair or replacement is at least offset by the value added to the property—in other words, the cure is economically justified. Examples of curable physical deterioration are broken windowpanes, cracks in plaster, leaky plumbing, worn-out floor covering, and flaky and faded exterior and interior paint work.

Incurable physical deterioration is deterioration that is not generally economical to repair or replace. It affects those physical components of a structure which are not easily discernible by normal inspection, such as structural framework, foundation, and subflooring. Other examples include ceiling structures and heat transmission systems.

Functional Obsolescence

Obsolescence is the loss of value in a property improvement due to changes in style, taste, technology, needs, and demands. *Functional obsolescence* is the impairment of functional capacity or efficiency and is a loss in value brought about by such factors as overcapacity, inadequacy, and changes in the art that affect the property item itself or its relation with other items composing a larger property. It is the inability of a structure to perform adequately the function for which it is currently employed.

Functional obsolescence may also be categorized as either curable or incurable. *Curable functional obsolescence* is obsolescence that is economically prudent to correct. The curing cost must be justified in increased value, at least equal to cost (which is a demonstration of the principle of contribution). Examples of curable functional obsolescence include old-fashioned bathroom and kitchen fixtures, inadequate hot-water or heating systems, inadequate placement of electrical outlets, low-hanging pipes in commercial or industrial buildings, and absence of ventilating facilities.

Incurable functional obsolescence includes conditions that are physically or economically impractical to correct. Theoretically, any functional deficiency can be corrected by the expenditure of money. The assessor must examine the real estate market and judge whether potential buyers would base their pricing decisions on correcting the inadequacy or would make a lower offer and accept the inutility as a permanent condition. Some examples of incurable functional obsolescence are poor room arrangements, superadequacies such as extra high ceilings, inadequate column spacing in a warehouse, multistory construction in an old industrial building, and undesirable shape or location on a site of a commercial structure.

Economic Obsolescence

Economic obsolescence is the impairment of desirability or useful life arising from economic forces, such as changes in highest and best use and legislative enactments that restrict or impair property rights and changes in supply-demand relationships. It is sometimes referred to as *locational obsolescence*. Since this type of accrued depreciation is seldom if ever curable, it is generally classified as incurable. Some examples of economic obsolescence are encroachment of inharmonious land uses, location of obnoxious commercial or industrial businesses in a residential neighborhood, narrow streets with poor traffic access, and lack of adequate parking in a retail business district.

After the assessor, through a physical inspection of the subject neighborhood and property, discovers and identifies the various types of accrued depreciation, the next step is selection of a method to measure this loss in value.

Methods of Measuring Depreciation

The translation of the value loss from accrued depreciation is one of the most questionable aspects of the appraisal process. There are six methods used to measure accrued depreciation; each has advantages and disadvantages and varies in reliability. They are categorized as follows.

Indirect Methods
1. Comparative sales data method
2. Capitalization of income method

Direct Methods
3. Overall (age-life) method
4. Engineering breakdown method

5. Observed condition (breakdown) method
6. Depreciation tables

Comparative Sales Data Method

This method of estimating accrued depreciation borrows from the comparative sales approach to value and is particularly useful in mass appraisal work. In this method the replacement cost new of subject building is estimated. Buildings of similar age, condition, and desirability that have been sold recently are found, and the site values are deducted. Contributory building values are deducted from reproduction cost or replacement cost new of each sale property. The amount remaining is the measure of accrued depreciation. For example, a comparable sale is analyzed as follows:

Estimated replacement cost new		$27,500
Value of property by comparison	$25,000	
Less estimated land value	10,000	$15,000
Accrued depreciation		$12,500

Not all properties have the same replacement cost new even when they are closely comparable. For this reason the accrued depreciation of the sale property should be converted to a percentage figure before an attempt is made to apply it to the subject property. The accrued depreciation percentage is obtained by dividing the lump-sum accrued depreciation by the replacement cost new. Continuing with the last example:

$$\frac{\text{Accrued depreciation}}{\text{Replacement cost new}} = \frac{\$12,500}{\$27,500} = \text{Approximately } 45\%.$$

This accrued depreciation percentage may then be used to calculate the accrued depreciation for the subject property. Assuming that the subject property has a replacement cost new of $26,000, then, replacement cost new times accrued depreciation percentage equals lump-sum accrued depreciation:

$$\$26{,}000 \times 45\% = \$11{,}700 \ .$$

In valuing the property, the assessor is usually more interested in determining the replacement cost new less depreciation (RCNLD) than in determining the lump-sum depreciation. This may be accomplished in two different ways. The first method estimates accrued depreciation before finding RCNLD. The second method finds RCNLD without estimating accrued depreciation. Table 8.1 compares the two methods:

Table 8.1
Two Methods of Finding RCNLD

Sold Property:
Replacement cost new (RCN) $27,500
Value of property by comparison . . . 25,000
Land value 10,000
Subject Property:
RCN $26,000

Method No. 1	Method No. 2
RCN $27,500	Value $25,000
Value $25,000	Land value $10,000
Land value . $10,000	Value remaining $15,000
Value remaining $15,000	
Accrued depreciation . $12,500	
Accrued depreciation ÷ sold property RCN = $12,500 ÷ $27,500 = approx. 45%	Value remaining ÷ sold property RCN = $15,000 ÷ $27,500 = approx. 55%
Subject RCN × accrued depreciation percent = subject accrued depreciation: $26,000 × 45% = $11,700	Subject RCN × percent value remaining (percent good) (RCNLD) = $26,000 × 55% = $14,300
Subject RCN less accrued depreciation (RCNLD) = $26,000 − $11,700 = $14,300	

The comparative sales data method has a number of disadvantages. It does not produce a breakdown or allocation of physical deterioration, functional obsolescence, and economic obsolescence. It requires ample sales data of truly comparable properties. If the assessor has to make many adjustments to the sales prices of the comparables, the reliability of the method is adversely affected. In addition, it requires accurate estimates of replacement cost new and site values for each comparable. It has two primary advantages. First, it is probably the most reliable method because it has market justification. Second, it is a relatively fast method. Since the assessor must value the comparable properties as well as the subject property, the determination of replacement cost new and site values for each comparable property is usually accomplished without additional burden.

Capitalization of Income Method

Since capitalized income is actually a direct method of estimating value, the accrued depreciation estimate is a by-product. In the income approach, accrued depreciation is provided for in the process of estimating the quantity, quality, and duration of the income and, ultimately, the property value (see chap. 10). By this method, an estimate of depreciation may be calculated by capitalizing the net income of the subject property into an estimate of value, deducting the site value, and providing the indicated building value, which is then compared with the estimated replacement cost new to provide an indication of the percentage of building value remaining. Table 8.2 on page 164 gives an example.

The capitalization of income method should provide an estimate of accrued depreciation that is almost as accurate as that obtained by the comparative sales data method. The capitalization of income method also has market justification when income and expense information is derived from the market. This method has the disadvantage of being part of the income approach. For this reason, it plays no part in the independent development of accrued depreciation via the cost approach. It can, however, be used as a check against the results of the cost approach.

Table 8.2

Estimate of Depreciation by Capitalization of Income Method

Replacement cost new		$500,000
Gross annual income	$96,000	
Less operating expenses	20,000	
Net income	$76,000	
Capitalization rate:		
Discount 8.00%		
Taxes 3.00		
Building recapture 1.34		
12.34%		
Indication of property value: $76,000 ÷ 0.1234	$615,883	
Rounded value	615,000	
Site value (deducted)	250,000	
Value remaining to building........................		$365,000
Indicated amount of depreciation		$135,000
Depreciation expressed as a percentage		27%
Value remaining to building..........................		73%

Overall (Age-Life) Method

This is the so-called straight-line depreciation method. This method allocates a uniform percentage of value loss each year over the useful life of the building. It is a mechanical method of handling depreciation borrowed from the accountant. However, whereas the accountant is interested primarily in book depreciation or in allocating a penalty against original cost over a number of time periods, the appraiser is concerned with the actual loss in value as of the date of the appraisal.

In dealing with the overall (age-life) method, the following terms are important.

• *Effective age*—Effective age is the number of years indicated by the condition of the building. If a building has had better-than-average maintenance, its effective age may be less than the actual age; if there has been inadequate maintenance, it may be greater. A fifty-year-old building may have an effective age of twenty-five years due to rehabilitation or modernization.

• *Remaining economic life*—Remaining economic life is the

number of years from the date of appraisal to the date when the building becomes economically valueless.

- *Total economic life*—The total economic life is the estimated period over which it is anticipated that a property may be profitably used. This may be described as the sum of effective age and remaining economic life. Total economic life can never exceed, and is generally shorter than, the physical life of the property.

In this method, an estimate is made both of the effective age of the building and of its remaining economic life. The effective age and remaining economic life together comprise the life span of the building. The ratio of the effective age to the life span, times the replacement or reproduction cost new of the structure, is a measure of the depreciation. Example:

Actual age	15 years
Effective age	10 years
Estimated remaining economic life	40 years
Reproduction or replacement cost new	$200,000
Depreciation: $10 \div 50 = 20\%$; $0.20 \times \$200,000 = \$40,000$	

Effective age may or may not represent actual or chronological age, since maintenance, design, and location are factors that may increase or decrease the aging process. The remaining economic life of the building will in most cases represent something less than the remaining physical life. Within the same building-use type, location will be an important consideration in the determination of economic life. For many uses, economic life in a large, fast-growing, and relatively new city will be much shorter than economic life expectancy for the same property use in an older, smaller city.

Tables have been evolved through statistical processes in an attempt to determine the average life spans of various types of improvements. There is danger in the application of such tables, because individual situations are not reflected in an arithmetical average. These tables are discussed later in this chapter.

The overall (age-life) method has the advantage of being very simple. But it is deceptively so. This is because too many elements have been lumped together without being given individual attention. An error in estimating effective age is critical. This method ignores all curable deficiencies and short-lived components, and it assumes straight-line depreciation. It does not make any allowances for unusual functional or economic obsolescence. For these reasons, the assessor must exercise discretion in its use.

Engineering Breakdown Method

The engineering breakdown method is actually a detailed age-life method. It is based on the physical life expectancy of the components of the structure, and it uses a combination of observed condition and chronological age to estimate the loss in value of each of the components. An example of the engineering breakdown method, involving the replacement cost new of a ten-year-old industrial plant, is given in table 8.3.

As can be seen from the table, the engineering breakdown method eliminates one of the disadvantages of the overall (age-life) method—namely, the lack of attention to the individual components. It still suffers from all the other disadvantages of the overall (age-life) method. In addition, the engineering breakdown method is very time-consuming and is not readily adaptable to the mass appraisal process. It normally does not render a measurement of obsolescence, since it concentrates on physical deterioration.

Observed Condition (Breakdown) Method

The observed condition method requires a separation of elements of accrued depreciation into various categories. During the physical inspection of the neighborhood and

Table 8.3

Engineering Breakdown Method: Ten-Year-Old Industrial Plant

	Current Replacement Cost	Life Expectancy (Years)	Percent Remaining	Depreciated Cost
Column and wall footings	$ 4,926	200	95	$ 4,680
Foundation walls ...	13,123	200	95	12,467
Column piers	2,486	200	95	2,362
Structural steel	148,202	200	95	140,792
Floor—concrete	107,607	100	90	96,846
Roof	84,953	100	90	76,458
Roofing	79,289	20	50	39,645
Exterior walls— brick and block	54,318	100	90	48,886
Windows and doors	26,264	50	80	21,011
Partitions:				
Concrete block ...	13,020	100	90	11,718
Wood stud	10,600	50	80	8,480
Doors	1,000	40	75	750
Ceilings, wall, and floor finishes	8,515	50	80	6,812
Heating—suspended units	83,688	30	67	56,071
Heating—radiation .	12,990	40	80	10,392
Air conditioning	12,990	20	50	6,495
Sprinklers, plumbing, and drains	60,981	75	87	53,053
Electrical wiring and lighting	121,931	50	80	97,545
Dock levelers	6,000	20	50	3,000
Subtotals	$ 852,883	...	...	$697,463
Weighted average: 697,463 ÷ 852,883 .	...	...	81.8	
Excavation	$ 1,632	...	81.8	$ 1,335
Contractor's overhead and profit	128,177	...	81.8	104,849
Architect's fees	49,134	...	81.8	40,192
Totals	$1,031,826	...	...	$843,839
Rounded to	$1,032,000	...	...	$844,000

subject property, the causes of accrued depreciation are segregated into classes and types described in chapter 7. This method can be the most complete and accurate way of handling the problem of depreciation, and a thorough understanding of this method is an excellent way of acquiring an understanding of the problems posed by the calculation of depreciation and its relationship to market value. Although it is not particularly adaptable to the mass appraisal process, its value to the assessor is its deep penetration into the specific causes and individual measurement of accrued depreciation. A working knowledge of the breakdown, or observed condition, method permits the assessor a better understanding of both the causes of accrued depreciation and the methods of measuring depreciation. The principal techniques that may be used to measure physical deterioration, functional obsolescence, and economic obsolescence are as follows.

Curable Physical Deterioration. This type of depreciation is measured by the cost to cure the defect. The amount to deduct from reproduction or replacement cost new is the cost to correct or repair the defect. If, for instance, the curable physical deterioration is due to a damaged linoleum floor, and it will cost $250 to replace or repair the linoleum, then $250 is the amount of curable physical deterioration. In order to fall into this classification, the defect must be in such condition that it should be cured as of the date of appraisal. A roof that is 50 percent deteriorated would not be cured as of the date of appraisal, nor would an exterior paint job that will last for two more years; they are not curable items.

Incurable Physical Deterioration. This refers to the normal wear and tear on the principal structural elements of the building. Much of this deterioration is not visible. The assessor must be careful to keep the categories of curable and incurable distinct. Those items that are curable are those that are exposed and easily accessible for repairing or replacement. Those items of a building that come under the category of incurable are typically not easily accessible and are not easily replaced. When repairs and/or alterations are being considered for the basic structural framework of a commercial, institutional, or industrial building, it is always a major job involving considerable cost. Therefore, feasibility studies are usually carried out first to determine whether the capital cost involved can be recovered in a reasonable period of time in order to justify incurring the cost. With commercial buildings and income-producing industrial buildings, this means that, upon completion of the work, the cost incurred will be covered by the increase in rental income. With institutional buildings and owner-occupied industrial buildings, however, the project is for the purpose of increasing the efficiency of the building's service, without thought to the financial return from the buildings.

To calculate incurable physical deterioration, the first step is to separate the components of the building into basic structure and short-lived items. For example, the classification of the components of a small office building might be as follows:

Basic Structures	Short-lived Items
Excavation	Floor covering
Foundation	Ceiling
Frame	Interior walls, doors, trim
Floor structure	Plumbing fixtures
Interior partitions	Heating unit and controls
Piping	Electrical fixtures
Heat ducts	Roof cover
Electrical wiring	Exterior walls, doors, and
Exterior wall structure	windows
Insulation	
Roof structure	

The next step is to calculate the replacement or reproduction cost new of both the basic structure and the short-lived items. Finally, the incurable physical deterioration of the basic structure is calculated, as well as the short-lived items, and the resulting figures are summed to obtain a single lump-sum total. This calculation may be made by applying either the overall (age-life) method or the engineering breakdown method.

Curable Functional Obsolescence. This form of deficiency can be measured by the cost to cure. The technique is similar to the handling of curable physical deterioration. Assume, for example, that old-fashioned bathroom fixtures adversely affect the marketability of a residential building. The cost of replacing these fixtures with similar, contemporary-style conveniences is $550. This is the measure of this type of curable functional obsolescence.

Incurable Functional Obsolescence. This form of obsolescence adversely affects the value of the buildings but is considered too costly in the market for the cure to be justified. Buyers who can live with the deficiency will accept the condition when they are compensated in the form of a lower purchase price. When the assessor concludes that it is not economically prudent to cure a functional deficiency, the condition may be categorized as incurable functional obsolescence. One method of measurement is accomplished by direct market comparisons. For example, consider a residence with a poor room arrangement classified as incurable. This condition adversely affects the marketability of the property. A study of comparative sales data may indicate to the assessor that, through prices paid for similarly affected properties, typical buyers have demonstrated that $1,000 is the measure of this type of depreciation.

Similarly, market data could reveal the following: a 1,000-square-foot ranch-style single-family residence on a 75 × 100-foot lot has no apparent functional deficiencies. It recently sold for $28,500. A similar residential property having all comparable conditions and features except for poor room arrangement also sold recently for $27,500. The marketability of the second property is decreased by $1,000 and is charged to poor room arrangement. This is an example of measuring incurable functional obsolescence.

Frequently, reliable sales data are not available to estimate this form of depreciation by comparison. The capitalization of a rent loss can be useful in many circumstances. Consider an aging retail-store building that has high ceilings, poor placement of electrical fixtures, and inadequate doorway widths. Investigation reveals that these conditions cannot be economically cured at the time of the appraisal. A prudent buyer would realize that the rent capability is affected by this condition. A prospective tenant would pay less rent for this space than for comparable space without these deficiencies. By a market rental study, it can be determined that the functional deficiencies will cause a monthly rental loss of $50. This rent loss can be converted into an estimate of capital value loss with the use of a gross rent multiplier.

Example:

Monthly rent loss: $50 per month × 12 months ..	$600 per year
Annual GRM developed by comparative sales data	7
Capitalized value loss (7 × $600 per year)	$4,200

Economic Obsolescence. This type of accrued depreciation usually is classified as incurable, since it is caused by factors external to the property. Market comparisons similar to those used to estimate incurable functional obsolescence can likewise be used to measure economic obsolescence. The capitalization of a rent loss is handled in a fashion similar to that used for incurable functional obsolescence, with one significant alteration. Since economic obsolescence affects the total property—building and land—the obsolescence attributable to the building must be isolated. The site value, if correctly estimated, would have taken into consideration the economic obsolescence factors affecting it. However, caution must be exercised not to penalize land twice (see application of land-building ratio below).

Assume that an appraisal is being made of a single-family residence in an area zoned for residential use. A special permit has been issued, and a gasoline service station is constructed on the adjoining property. The marketability of the residence is adversely affected. An analysis of similar residences reveals that $220 per month is typical rent. This adverse condition limits rent of the subject property to $190 per month. Market analysis further reveals that residences of this nature in this area typically sell for 120 times the monthly rent. The monthly gross rent multiplier is 120.

Estimated monthly rent of subject property if unaffected ... $220
Less estimated monthly rent of subject affected property ... 190
Estimated monthly rent loss .... $ 30

$30 × 120 (GRM) = $3,600
Ratio of land to building: 1:4
Land = 20%; building = 80%; 80% of $3,600 = $2,880

Therefore, the amount of economic obsolescence is $2,880.

When using this breakdown, or observed condition, method of calculating depreciation, the assessor will realize that there is sometimes a thin line between curable physical deterioration and curable functional obsolescence. Also, the identification of a deficiency as incurable functional obsolescence or economic obsolescence can sometimes be difficult. The identification of the cause of depreciation obviously determines the method of measurement. Significant errors can result from incorrect identification.

The observed condition method requires considerable skill to use, especially as the improvements get older. Care must be exercised to avoid depreciating building components twice. Given below is an example of estimating accrued depreciation by the observed condition method.

ILLUSTRATION OF THE OBSERVED CONDITION (BREAKDOWN) METHOD

Description and Condition of Property. The subject property consists of two three-story apartment buildings constructed thirty-four years ago. Each building contains 40 apartment units with a gross floor area of 17,124 square feet (34,248 square feet total). The property is located in the peripheral older residential-commercial area surrounding the core of a larger city. The exterior walls are 10-inch brick-faced masonry with concrete block backing. Casement-style wood-sash windows account for approximately 16 percent of the wall area. The brick is of good quality but needs considerable pointing. The window sash has deteriorated. The ground floor, two upper floors, and the roof are all composed of wood joist and deck construction. The roofing is built-up tar, felt, and gravel on 1-inch rigid insulation. There are no basements, but located in each building is a furnace room having a floor level 5 feet below that of the ground-floor level and about 3 feet below grade level. There is a crawl space below the ground floor for piping. The interior dividing walls are of concrete block, and the apartment partitioning is of wood studs and gypsum board, plastered. The flooring is ⅜-inch strip hardwood, the ceilings are lathed and plastered and attached to the wood joists above, and the wall finishing is plaster. The doors and frames are of good-quality wood paneling, with good-quality hardware, and the baseboard and trim are of hardwood. The buildings are heated with hot-water furnaces using cast-iron radiators. Each apartment is furnished with electric stoves and refrigerators, with the exception of one building, in which the tenants are still using the old-fashioned wooden built-in refrigerators connected to one central compressor. Apartment finishing also includes ceramic tiling in the bathrooms and built-in kitchen cupboards and counters.

Although the improvements are thirty-four years old, they are in fairly good physical condition, the maintenance is good, and the interiors are in fair condition. The effective age is thirty years. The remaining economic life is estimated to be thirty years. The roofing is ten years old; the furnaces were each replaced ten years ago, but the radiators and piping are original, as are the plumbing fixtures and drains. The domestic hot-water system was replaced ten years ago in both buildings. The stoves are ten years old, while the newer refrigerators are five years old.

Cost Approach to Value: Depreciation   173

Estimate of Reproduction Cost New

Summary of Building Costs

Grading and excavation	$ 1,883
Structural costs—foundation and foundation walls, interior masonry, bearing walls, floors, and staircases ...	131,854
Roofing	5,308
Exterior walls:	
Masonry	61,650
Pointing	6,850
Wood-sash windows	16,428
Entrances	2,383
Chimneys, brick with tile flues	9,619
Partition walls	61,911
Interior finishing ceilings, walls, and flooring	78,733
Electrical wiring and fixtures	27,013
Heating:	
Furnaces	10,000
Hot-water radiation	25,283
Drains	9,132
Plumbing fixtures, plus roughing in	93,139
Domestic hot water	7,448
Built-in cupboards and counter	19,200
Stoves	14,896
Refrigerators:	
Modern (personal property)	0
Built-in	5,320
Bathroom tiling	13,193
Fire escapes	1,170
	$602,413

NOTE.—Contractor's overhead and profit and architectural fees are included in costs.

Depreciation

Summary of Cost and Physical Deterioration

Item	Cost	Class*	Effective Age	Remaining Economic Life	Total Economic Life	Percent Depreciated
Grading and excavation ...	$ 1,883	B.S.	30	30	60	50
Structural costs	131,854	B.S.	30	30	60	50
Roofing	5,308	S.L.	10	10	20	50
Exterior walls—masonry ..	61,650	B.S.	30	30	60	50
Exterior walls—pointing ..	6,850	S.L.	5	0	5	100
Wood-sash windows	16,428	S.L.	30	0	30	100
Entrances	2,383	S.L.	30	10	40	75
Chimneys	9,619	B.S.	30	30	60	50

* B.S. = basic structure; S.L. = short-lived.

174

Item	Cost	Class*	Effective Age	Remaining Economic Life	Total Economic Life	Percent Depreciated
Partition walls	61,911	B.S.	30	30	60	50
Interior finish	78,733	S.L.	20	10	30	67
Electrical wiring and fixtures	27,013	S.L.	20	10	30	67
Furnaces	10,000	S.L.	20	10	30	67
Hot-water radiation	25,283	S.L.	10	20	30	33
Drains	9,132	S.L.	10	10	20	50
Plumbing	93,139	S.L.	20	20	40	50
Domestic hot water	7,448	S.L.	10	10	20	50
Cupboards and counters ..	19,200	B.S.	30	30	60	50
Stoves	14,896	S.L.	10	10	20	50
Refrigerators—built in	5,320	S.L.	30	0	30	100
Bathroom tiling	13,193	B.S.	30	30	60	50
Fire escapes	1,170	B.S.	30	30	60	50
Total	$602,413					

* B.S. = basic structure; S.L. = short-lived.

Physical Deterioration—Curable
(Items That Are 100 Percent Depreciated)

Item	Amount of Depreciation
Pointing—exterior walls	$ 6,850
Wood-sash windows	16,428
Built-in refrigerators	5,320
Total	$28,598

Physical Deterioration—Incurable: Short-lived Items

Item	Cost	Percent Depreciated	Amount of Depreciation
Roofing	$ 5,308	50	$ 2,654
Entrances	2,383	75	1,787
Interior finish	78,733	67	52,751
Electric wiring and fixtures .	27,013	67	18,099
Furnaces	10,000	67	6,700
Hot-water radiation	25,283	33	8,343
Drains	9,132	50	4,566
Plumbing	93,139	50	46,569
Domestic hot water	7,448	50	3,724
Stoves	14,896	50	7,448
Total	$273,335	...	$152,641

Physical Deterioration—Incurable: Basic Structure

Item	Cost	Percent Depreciated	Amount of Depreciation
Grading and excavation	$ 1,883	50	$ 942
Structural costs	131,854	50	65,927
Exterior walls—masonry	61,650	50	30,825
Chimneys	9,619	50	4,810
Partition/walls	61,911	50	30,956
Cupboards and counters ...	19,200	50	9,600
Bathroom tiling	13,193	50	6,597
Fire escapes	1,170	50	585
Total	$300,480	...	$150,242

Physical deterioration—incurable: short-lived items	$152,641
Physical deterioration—incurable: basic structure	150,242
Physical deterioration—incurable	$302,883

Functional Obsolescence—Curable

Removal of old refrigerators and compressors	$800
Salvage value	0
Installation of new electric refrigerators (personal property)	0
Total cost—functional obsolescence curable	$800

Functional Obsolescence—Incurable. As is typical in older apartment houses of this age group, there is a lack of adequate closet space as measured by contemporary standards. Physically and economically, more closet space cannot be added to the apartments. It is a condition classified as incurable. After surveying other rental apartment houses in the area, it is estimated there is a $7 per month per apartment rent loss attributable to this lack of adequate closet space. A market analysis indicates that the local gross rent multiplier for this class of property is 6. Therefore:

Rent loss ($7 per apartment × 80 apartments × 12 months)	$ 6,720
Value loss (annual rent loss of $6,720 × 6 [GRM])	40,320

Economic Obsolescence. The subject property is an older type of apartment building, located in what was formerly a very harmonious neighborhood. Since then, a modern indoor arena has been erected on a nearby block, in which professional hockey, basketball, and traveling shows perform. This arena seats approximately 18,000 persons and is operated on a year-round basis. It has caused many old residences in the neighborhood surrounding the subject property to be demolished and replaced by vast stretches of parking lots. These are floodlighted at night, but, despite this, the intrusion of the crowds, the gas fumes, the noise, the loiterers, and the inevitable vandalism are causes of concern to the tenants. As a result, a rental loss of $10 per unit is attributed to the property. This is in addition to the $7 rent loss attributed to the closet space. Because of this low rental, vacancies have not as yet become a big factor. The subject building is situated on high-priced land, and the valuation split between land and building is approximately equal. Therefore:

Rent loss (80 apartments × $10 per month per apartment × 12 months)	$ 9,600
Indicated loss of value ($9,600 × 6)	57,600
Loss attributable to the building ($57,600 × 0.50) = total economic obsolescence	$28,800

Summary. The following tabulation summarizes the foregoing example.

Current cost of reproduction		$602,413
Less:		
Physical deterioration—curable	$ 28,598	
Physical deterioration—incurable	302,883	
Functional obsolescence—curable	800	
Functional obsolescence—incurable	40,320	
Economic obsolescence	28,800	
Total accrued depreciation		$401,401
Value of improvements indicated by the cost approach		$201,012
Rounded to		$201,000

Note that all modern refrigerators were treated as personal property in this illustration. As such, they had no bearing on the calculation of accrued depreciation of the building.

The observed condition method, when performed by a skilled cost estimator, is a reliable method of estimating accrued depreciation. Its primary disadvantage is that it is not adaptable to mass appraisal because of the time required. Still, it is a tool which the assessor should possess and use in those situations where other methods do not provide satisfactory results. The assessor will find this method most applicable to those larger, owner-occupied, special-use properties that rarely sell.

Developing Depreciation Tables

Since no two parcels of real estate are identical, it is logical that depreciation will vary from property to property. Depreciation will also vary with the type of property and from one locality to another. However, there are groups of properties which exhibit like value trends. These groups show similar physical deterioration and are similarly affected by typical functional and economic obsolescence.

Empirical tables, based on experience and available market data, may be established to provide a schedule of typical standards with which to measure or estimate depreciation. Straight-line depreciation allocates a uniform percentage of value loss each year over the useful life of the building. These tables are based simply on estimated economic life, which is based on type of construction, quality of construction, and use.

Market studies have established several things. First, actual depreciation in the market is not straight-line but follows a more irregular path. Upon completion of construction, depreciation commences quickly at first, and then reaches a plateau where, with normal maintenance, there is little change for many years. This period can be extended for very long periods of time with good maintenance. Second, depreciation changes pace with different occupancies. Some occupants show pride of ownership and maintain an older building well, while others take all the return out and put a bare minimum in. Third, with good maintenance, many buildings outlive the economic life normally expected.

The assessor may obtain depreciation tables from various sources. Before using any of these tables, he must test them to see that they reflect typical local market conditions.

Table 8.4
Depreciation Table for Small Stores of Average Quality

Sale	Effective Building Age (Years)	Sale Price	Site Area (Sq. Ft.)	Site Value	Residual to Building	Replacement Cost New	Depreciation	Depreciation (%)	Percent Good
1	5	$65,000	8,000	$15,000	$50,000	$55,000	$ 5,000	9.1	90.9
2	10	50,700	5,000	10,000	40,700	47,000	6,300	13.4	86.6
3	20	45,000	5,500	10,000	35,000	48,000	13,000	27.0	73.0
4	18	47,000	5,000	10,000	37,000	45,000	8,000	17.8	82.2
.	.	.	.	.	.	.	.	.	.
.	.	.	.	.	.	.	.	.	.
25	15	51,000	5,600	10,000	41,000	50,000	9,000	18.0	82.0
26	25	47,000	6,000	12,000	35,000	60,000	25,000	41.7	58.3
27	28	43,000	5,300	10,000	33,000	58,000	25,000	43.1	56.9
28	32	43,000	5,200	10,000	33,000	60,000	27,000	45.0	55.0

Table 8.5
Percent Good for an Average-Quality Store

Effective Age	Percent Good
0	100
1	98
2	96
3	95
4	93
.	.
.	.
.	.
20	71
21	70
22	68
.	.
.	.
.	.
50	26
52	22
56	20
60	10

The assessor may also prepare depreciation tables when sufficient sales data exist. For example, a depreciation table is being developed for small stores of average quality. The data shown in table 8.4 have been developed with the comparative sales data method (all sales are in the same year).

Next the data are plotted with effective age as one axis and percent good as the other. The sales would appear on the graph as demonstrated in figure 8.1. The next step is to draw a line through the plots to represent the mean (fig. 8.2). The final step is to complete a percent good table with effective age in one column and percent good in the other (table 8.5).

The percent good may now be used as a factor to calculate remaining building value (replacement cost new less normal depreciation) on any average-quality store that has no "unusual" physical deterioration or obsolescence.

A word of caution: as in the case of all tables and for-

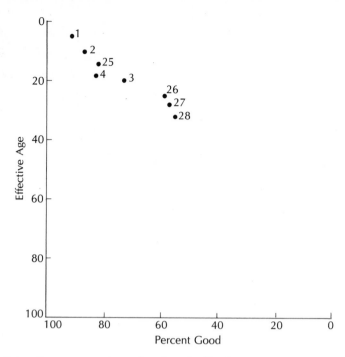

Fig. 8.1.—Representation of ratio of effective age to percent good of small stores.

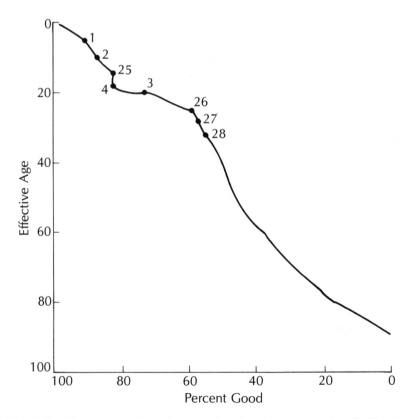

Fig. 8.2.—Representation of determination of mean ratio of effective age to percent good of small stores.

mulas, depreciation tables are not intended as a substitute for the need for a thorough examination of all the factors and forces that detrimentally affect the property, or for the exercise of judgment in evaluating the extent to which these factors and forces diminish the property's value.

Sometimes assessors will compensate for the the condition of the building by using a rule of thumb—for example, a scale such as poor, -10%; fair, -5%; average, 0; good, $+5\%$; and excellent, $+10\%$. While such adjustments aid in the use of depreciation tables based upon "typical" improvements, like the tables themselves, they must be used with discretion.

Summary

One of the limitations of the cost approach to value is in its applicability to old properties, because of the difficulty of estimating accrued depreciation. The methods thus far elucidated have demonstrated these difficulties. However, the assessor finds the cost approach particularly valuable when he is unable to procure reliable sales and income data. Since most statutes under which the assessor operates call for market value, it is necessary that the objective of the cost approach be value, not cost. As previously indicated, the test of accrued depreciation is the effect of this depreciation on the market and not simply the effect on cost.

A review of accrued depreciation reveals the following:

Causes of Depreciation

1. Physical deterioration—loss of value due to wear and tear in service and disintegration due to the forces of nature.

   a) Curable physical deterioration—deterioration affecting an item for which the cost to repair or replace is economically justified.

b) Incurable physical deterioration—deterioration that is not generally economical to repair or replace at the time of appraisal.

2. Functional obsolescence—the impairment of functional capacity or efficiency with a loss in value brought about by overcapacity, inadequacy, changes in the art, and other similar factors.

a) Curable functional obsolescence—obsolescence that is economically prudent to correct, that is, is justified in increased value at least equal to cost.

b) Incurable functional obsolescence—impairment of desirability or useful life arising from inutility; generally classified as incurable.

3. Economic obsolescence—the impairment of desirability due to factors external to the property, such as economic forces or environmental changes which affect supply and demand relationships; generally considered incurable. The obsolescence attributable to the building must be isolated from the total obsolescence of the property.

Methods of Measuring Depreciation

1. Comparative sales data method—reproduction or replacement cost new of subject property is estimated; comparable properties are found and site values deducted; contributory building values remain; contributory building values are deducted from reproduction or replacement cost for each sale property, yielding measure of accrued depreciation; accrued depreciation figure is converted to percentage and applied to subject property.
2. Capitalization of income method—income of subject property is capitalized into estimate of value, with site value deducted; indicated building value is compared with estimated reproduction or replacement cost new to provide indication of building value remaining.
3. Overall (age-life) method—allocates a uniform percent-

age of value loss each year over the useful life of the building.

4. Engineering breakdown method—based on the physical life expectancy of the components of a structure; uses a combination of observed conditions and chronological age to estimate loss in value of each component.

5. Observed condition (breakdown) method—requires a separation of elements of accrued depreciation into categories.

6. Developing depreciation tables—establishing empirical tables based on experience and market data to provide a schedule of typical standards with which to measure depreciation.

9 Real Estate Investments and Finance

Investments are considered in terms of risk and return. They are generally divided into two categories: fixed-dollar investments and growth investments. *Fixed-dollar investments* are exemplified by the savings account, where the investment is sound and the possibility of loss slight. The savings account earns interest on the amount deposited, while the deposit remains as a fixed amount. *Growth investments* are exemplified by the real estate purchase, where the possibility of loss is present as well as the opportunity for growth. Competition for investment dollars is ever present, and fixed-dollar investments are in competition with growth investments. It is reasonable to conclude that, if the risk of an investment is high, the return should also be high.

Real estate investments account for many billions of dollars of wealth. These investments result from business transactions between buyers and sellers of real estate, who comprise the market upon which real estate value is based. Real estate investors are motivated to buy real estate by the expectation of receiving a profit from ownership. Since large sums of money are involved in this ownership, methods of real estate financing have arisen out of the necessity to substitute for cash. Financing has also been used effectively by investors as a profit-making device known as *leverage,* which is the use of borrowed money to acquire property in expectation of a rate of return on the property higher than the rate on the borrowed capital. It is the advantage gained by using the money of others.

Real Estate Investments

Real Estate as a Competitive Investment

There are several types of investments that attract capital from investors. Included in a list would be the following:

- Bonds—certificates of ownership of specified portions of a debt due to be paid by a government or corporation to the holder(s), usually with a fixed rate of interest.
- Stocks—shares of a company.
- Life insurance.
- Loan company deposits.
- Mortgages and trust deeds (discussed in this chapter).
- Savings accounts.
- Real estate.

Just as single-family residential property is purchased for the amenities provided to the owner and is appraised on the basis of the relative amenities provided, an investment property competes with other classes of investments on the basis of the return anticipated by the owner and the risk involved in such ownership. In determining where capital should be invested, the investor must consider many factors. Following is an enumeration of these factors, showing the relative position of real estate to other possible investments, particularly the savings account.

Safety. An insured savings account is safe as regards the money invested and the rate of return. Neither is assured in real estate investment.

Liquidity. A liquid asset is one which is easily converted to cash. Since a demand savings account is already cash, conversion is no problem. Real estate, however, requires time to convert to cash.

Size of Investment. Real estate investment generally requires substantial sums of money. Savings accounts require only very small amounts.

Use as Collateral. Savings accounts ordinarily can be used as collateral in the full amount of the account. Although real estate may be used as collateral under certain circumstances, there are limitations.

Time. Some investors prefer long-term investments, whereas others prefer relatively short periods for investments. Real estate is usually a medium- to long-term investment.

Management. Real estate investment property requires management. This is an important factor, since management must be either accomplished by the investor himself or paid for by the investor. One consumes time, the other money. Investments requiring relatively little attention generally are preferred.

Appreciation. Real estate is likely to appreciate in value over the period of ownership; that is, its value will increase as a result of such factors as increased cost to replace, improved economic conditions, and increasing price levels. Money in a savings account is likely to lose purchasing power because of inflation. Real estate investments are considered a hedge against inflation.

Income Tax Advantages. Whereas return on a savings account is taxed directly, real estate provides a tax advantage to some owners through building depreciation, interest on mortgages, and other tax deductions, and by providing long-term capital gains.

When purchasing a $10,000 ten-year government bond that pays 7.5 percent interest annually, the investor anticipates receiving $750 per year interest for ten years and return of his $10,000 at the end of the ten years. In evaluating this risk, the investor realizes the high degree of safety and certainty of yield, reflecting the rate of return. The purchase of a common stock represents a situation where there is an investment objective of income and some growth, or capital gain. Suppose that 200 shares of a leading blue-chip utility stock are purchased at $50 a share, for a total investment of $10,000. A 7 percent dividend from the stock provides an annual income of $700. If the shares are sold ten years later for $11,000, there is a $1,000 capital gain in addition to the annual income, making an approximate annual yield of 8 percent on the investment. Since an investment of this nature involves more risk than an investment in a government bond as outlined above, the rewards are greater, for some of the safety of the investment is sacrificed in anticipation of greater appreciation from the investment.

Suppose that another $10,000 investment were made in real estate. The purchase price and income-producing ability of the property will largely determine the rate of return. Depending on the quality of the investment, a return of perhaps 8–10 percent may be realized. The investor also wants the return of his investment. Since real estate is composed of land (a nonwasting asset) and buildings or improvements (a wasting or depreciating asset), there are several methods whereby the investor receives the return of his investment.

If the property is sold at the end of a ten-year period, the rate of return can be calculated from the historical record. The rate could be 10 percent or higher, depending on resale value. Evaluating the risk in this investment at the time of purchase is of critical concern to the investor and, hence, to the assessor. Because of the degree of safety and lack of certainty of yield, estimates made about the rate at the time of the purchase are critical.

Factors Affecting Discount Requirements

Considerations of risk, return, management, liquidity, and other factors work together to affect the acceptable discount rate anticipated by the investor. (For the present, discount rate may be defined as the annual percentage rate reflecting the competitive rate of return on an investment. It is distinguished from interest rate, which is the rate of return on borrowed funds.) Recognition of these factors is found in the *summation concept* of analyzing the discount requirements for real estate investments. The following factors are considered in this analysis.

- *Safe rate*—The safe rate is the rate obtainable with the most safety and the least risk; in the summation concept, it should be taken from investments having the least risk.
- *Risk rate*—The risk rate is the return commensurate with the risk assumed by the investor; it is a component because the return on real estate is a desired return and may or may not be realized by the investor. Also, the property may depreciate, resulting in a loss when the property is sold.
- *Rate for nonliquidity*—The rate for nonliquidity is necessary, since an investment in real estate ties up money which cannot be quickly reconverted to cash. Therefore, real estate is considered a nonliquid asset.
- *Rate for management*—The rate for management is a necessary component in order to compensate for the time and cost involved in managing the real estate investment.

The above factors are reflected in the discount rate, as in the following example:

Safe rate	6%
Risk rate	2
Rate for nonliquidity	1
Rate for management	1
Total discount rate	10%

The total rate of 10 percent for this theoretical application should reflect the discount requirement expected from investments in real estate in the local jurisdiction. This method is difficult to document in the real estate market, however. Interest, discount, and selection of rates will be discussed further in chapter 11.

Real Estate Finance

The word finance simply means money, capital, or resources that make possible business transactions. Real estate financing is, therefore, the process of making money or credit available for real estate transactions. The major methods of financing real estate are cash, mortgage, trust deed, and land contract.

Cash. In this method the buyer simply pays cash for the real estate. The exchange involves cash or check for a general *warranty deed* (a document from seller to buyer transferring title free and clear of all encumbrances except those specifically spelled out or of public record).

Mortgage. This is the most common method of real estate finance. Mortgages are two-party agreements between the borrower (mortgagor) and the lender (mortgagee). A *mortgage* is a written instrument that pledges specified real estate as a guarantee for the payment of a loan used to purchase a property. Using this method, the buyer borrows money from a third party to use in paying cash for the real estate. The buyer then pledges the real estate to the lender as security for the loan.

Trust Deed. A trust deed is a three-party agreement: the borrower gives title to a third party (trustee), who holds the title in trust for the benefit of the borrower (trustor) and the lender (beneficiary). The main advantage of the trust deed is that, in case of default by the borrower, the trustee has the power to foreclose and sell the property to satisfy the debt. The arrangement does not require court action for the foreclosure and generally provides a reinstatement period for the borrower.

Land Contract. This method involves the exchange of cash and agreement between buyer (vendee) and seller (vendor) in a contract stating how the balance will be paid and how and when the buyer is to receive a warranty deed to the property. The buyer ordinarily takes possession of the property upon making the down payment and signing the contract. The land contract is sometimes used as a method of intermediate financing: the title does not pass to the buyer until stated conditions are met. This method is sometimes called "contract for deed" or "contract for sale."

Mortgages

Types of Mortgages. Many types of mortgages have developed as a result of the great variety of circumstances relating to the sale and development of real estate (the term *mortgage* as used here includes trust deeds). The type of mortgage involved in financing usually depends on the following:

- Purpose of the loan.
- Reliability of the borrower.
- Restrictions imposed by the lender.
- Terms required (time, interest rate, and repayment schedule).
- Amount of the loan.
- Priority of mortgage if the property is already encumbered.

There are several types of mortgages as well as mortgage sources. The types of mortgages are classified as follows:

First Mortgage. The first mortgage has the first claim on real estate securing the loan and generally covers the major portion of the property value. A typical loan ratio covers 60–95 percent of the property value.

Junior Mortgage. This type is often called second mortgage, third mortgage, and so forth, and is frequently used when the borrower requires more financing than the amount provided by the first mortgage. Junior mortgages commonly cover from 5 to 50 percent of the property value, and the interest rate normally can be expected to be higher than the interest rate for the first mortgage.

Construction Loan Mortgage. This is a short-term loan made for the purpose of financing new construction. Usually the land is initial collateral for the loan, and provisions are specified in the mortgage for disbursing funds as the project develops. Improvements on land provide additional security for the lender as the loan amount increases.

Purchase-Money Mortgage. This type of mortgage is given by the buyer to the seller or other lender to secure the purchase price. A purchase-money mortgage may be a first mortgage or a junior mortgage. A third party may also be involved.

Open-End Mortgage. This type allows the borrower to obtain additional money under the terms of the original mortgage for the purpose of providing funds for property improvements or other uses.

Package Mortgage. This type of mortgage covers real estate as well as personal property included with the real estate. It may be found on apartments where the stoves, dishwashers, and refrigerators are covered by the mortgage.

Chattel Mortgage. Chattel mortgages cover *only* personal property, such as stoves, dishwashers, and refrigerators.

Mortgage Repayment Provisions. Mortgages may also be classified according to the provisions for repayment. The three types are straight mortgage, amortized mortgage, and partially amortized mortgage.

Straight Mortgage. The straight mortgage is of short term, usually about three years. It has no requirement for *amortization* (the process of extinguishing debt or recovering a capital investment through periodic repayments of principal); requires level interest payments, usually monthly or quarterly; and requires that all unpaid principal and interest balance be paid at maturity. This last requirement is known as a *balloon payment,* which is the balance due on a note at the end of the loan term in excess of the regular payment amounts.

Amortized Mortgage. The amortized mortgage is commonly used with residential and commercial properties and has two typical patterns. First, there is a reduction of principal by constant payments plus interest on the declining principal balance. Second, there are required level, constant payments including principal and interest, with each payment applying first to the accrued interest, the remainder reducing the principal.

Partially Amortized Mortgage. The partially amortized mortgage has monthly or quarterly payments of interest and partial amortization of the loan balance, with a large balloon payment at the end of the mortgage.

Minimum Mortgage Requirements. Given below is an enumeration of requirements that can serve as a checklist for the minimum requirements for any mortgage.

- All mortgages must be in written form.
- Parties involved in the mortgage must be legally competent and have the right to contract.
- A legal description of the property must be included.
- The property interest mortgaged must be specified (e.g., fee-simple interest, leasehold interest).
- The mortgage must be signed by the borrower.
- All covenants, contracts, and agreements must be included.
- The obligation secured should appear in the mortgage, including a reference to the note.
- A "granting clause" should be contained in the mortgage, such as "mortgagor hereby mortgages and warrants to mortgagee the following described real property."
- The mortgage must be acknowledged, delivered to the mortgagee, and recorded.

Sources of Financing

Most residential, commercial, and industrial property loans are made by financial institutions. Two types of loans are in common use at the present time: conventional loans and Federal Housing Authority–insured and Veterans Administration–guaranteed loans. Conventional loans are generally more conservative, or less favorable to the borrower, than government-insured loans. The ratio of loan to value is generally less, the rate of interest higher, and the length of the loan generally shorter.

Listed below are the institutions prevalent in financing real estate investments.

Commercial Banks. The long-term lending activities of commercial banks are concentrated in their mortgage departments. Commercial banks usually make short-term loans with low loan-to-value ratios, except where the loans are FHA-insured.

Mutual Savings Banks. Mutual savings banks are located primarily in the northeastern part of the United States. They are very similar to the savings departments of commercial banks, except that they are independent mutual associations. Mutual savings banks generally lend money on FHA-insured mortgages.

Savings and Loan Associations. The savings and loan associations have grown to be the largest single source of money for single-family and multifamily residential sale and development in the United States. They also are involved to a great extent in the commercial loan field and are usually more active in conventional lending rather than FHA-insured loans.

Life Insurance Companies. Because of their resources and nationwide operations, life insurance companies are especially attracted to large development loans. They are also reasonably active in junior mortgage loans. Life insurance companies are important sources of financing for multifamily and commercial properties, although the activity of life insurance companies in the area of real estate finance fluctuates.

Mortgage Companies. Mortgage companies are organizations generally formed for the specific purpose of placing mortgages in their own name, but with commitments from large institutional lenders to cover the loans at a later date. Sometimes mortgage bankers act as agents for large lenders. Mortgage companies are often associated with life insurance companies in commercial loans. Mortgage bankers are also active in the junior mortgage market.

Effect of Financing on Mortgage Payment and Equity Requirements.

The effect of financing on the monthly investment payment required for a $1,000,000 apartment building is shown in the following example.

	Conventional Loan	FHA Loan
Loan-to-value ratio	75%	90%
Term of loan	25 years	30 years
Interest rate	9.00%	8.50%
Mortgage amount	$750,000	$900,000
Partial payment rate	0.00839	0.00769
Mortgage payment	$6,292.50	$6,921.00
Equity dollars required	$250,000	$100,000
Equity return of 13%: dollars required	$2,708.33	$1,083.33
Total monthly requirement, mortgage and equity return	$9,000.83	$8,004.33
Total annual requirement	$108,009.96	$96,051.96

Clarification of the above example follows.

Loan-to-Value Ratio. This is the ratio, as a percentage, of loan to total property value that each mortgage covers. A $750,000 mortgage on a $1,000,000 property indicates a loan-to-value ratio of 75 percent.

Term of Loan. This is the number of years covered by the mortgage. A twenty-five-year mortgage or a thirty-year mortgage has a term of twenty-five or thirty years.

Interest Rate. The mortgage has a predetermined interest rate stated in the agreement. The interest rate and the mortgage balance will determine the interest in dollars.

Mortgage Amount. When the property is new and no payments have been made, the mortgage amount is the same as the full amount of the loan. As payments are made, the mortgage balance decreases.

Partial Payment Rate. This rate is the monthly amount required to pay the mortgage principal and interest on $1.

When this rate is multiplied by the mortgage balance, the monthly payment for any mortgage amount can be calculated (partial payment rate). The partial payment rate is discussed in chapter 12.

Mortgage Payment. The mortgage payment is calculated by multiplying the partial payment rate by the mortgage amount.

Equity Dollars Required. Equity is the owner's interest in a property beyond the mortgage or other claims. The amount of equity dollars required is the difference between the property value and the amount of the mortgage. When the property value is $1,000,000 and the mortgage is $750,000, the amount of equity dollars required is $250,000.

Equity Return of 13 Percent: Dollars Required. In this example, the equity return is assumed to be 13 percent, and the amount of dollars required for equity return is calculated by multiplying the equity dollars required by 13 percent on an annual basis and 1.083 percent on a monthly basis.

Total Monthly Requirement: Mortgage and Equity Return. This is the sum of the monthly payments required for the mortgage and for the equity. This includes both interest and principal on the mortgage and yield on the equity investment.

Total Annual Requirement. The total monthly requirement multiplied by 12 gives the total annual requirement.

Although many points in this discussion will be clarified in later chapters, the example demonstrates the effect of different terms of financing on the same property. In this case, the more favorable loan produces smaller monthly payments. Smaller monthly payments will cause the cash flow to increase without an increase in gross income. The following should be pointed out.

- As the loan ratio goes up, the mortgage payment increases.
- As the loan ratio goes up, the required equity goes down.
- As the interest rate goes up, the payment increases.
- As the loan term (years) goes up, the mortgage payment decreases.
- As the loan term increases, the total amount paid over the loan term increases.

The discussion of real estate financing is important mainly because the price that real estate will bring if offered for sale on the open market is affected by the type of financing available to the buyer. This will become more apparent in subsequent chapters on the income approach to value. However, financing also affects residential properties and, as was indicated in chapter 6 ("The Comparative Sales Approach to Value"), is important sales data to be collected.

Adjustments for Financing: Sales Data Analysis

In many states the assessor must adjust the actual sale price of a property to cash, making fair cash value the objective of the sales analysis (some states prohibit such adjustments). On the whole, considerations of down payment, junior mortgages, terms of the loan, and interest rate affect the sale price less when the seller and lender are different parties. When the seller and mortgagee are separate, the seller receives cash for the property sold and is not concerned with the terms of the mortgage and their relation to the selling price of the property. There are, however, three cases where these considerations do affect the sale price: (1) when the seller and lender are the same party, (2) when the buyer assumes an existing mortgage, and (3) when the seller pays points.

In the first case, the seller may adjust the sale price in

order to receive a high rate of interest on the mortgage. The sale price would therefore be lower. On the other hand, the seller might accept a low interest rate and sell the property at a higher price. To determine whether either of these circumstances has occurred, it may be necessary to analyze the terms of the loan, comparing them with the existing loan market.

An example of an analysis of sales data to discover such a situation might be as follows. Suppose that there are four identical properties located side by side. Property 1 sells for $45,000 with no down payment (seller and lender are the same party), the seller carrying back a note and mortgage for the full amount of the purchase price. Property 2 sells for $40,000, with $5,000 down payment and a $25,000 conventional first mortgage (from a third party), with the seller carrying back a second mortgage at a low rate of interest for the balance. The third property sells for $37,500 cash to the seller.

Sale No.	Sale Price	Down Payment	Mortgage
1	$45,000	$ 0	$45,000 (full)
2	40,000	5,000	25,000 (first)
			10,000 (second)
3	37,500	0	0

Can the market value of the subject property be determined? The highest price paid is $45,000. In selecting this price as the highest, we are assuming that a $45,000 mortgage is worth more than $37,500 cash. But could the seller (and lender) sell his mortgage to an investor for $45,000 cash? What were the terms of the mortgage, and how were they reflected in the selling price of the property? In the case of the $40,000 sale, the seller receives $30,000 cash (including loan proceeds of $25,000) and a $10,000 second mortgage. How much of the risk inherent in such a mortgage is reflected in the selling price? Sale 3 is a cash sale and therefore does not require adjustment. Have the purchasers of sales 1 and 2 been penalized for not having paid cash? These questions must be answered and further analysis made of the terms of the sales before the market value of a subject property can be determined.

In cases where a buyer takes over a seller's mortgage instead of arranging a new one, the sale price may be influenced by both the cash value of the property and whatever difference there may be between the interest rate of the assumed loan and the going rate. The effect is similar to the effect of a seller/lender situation as previously described.

If a loan is insured by the FHA or guaranteed by the VA, the seller usually must pay prepaid interest for the buyer to obtain the loan. Lenders call this prepaid interest *points*. A point equals a 1 percent reduction in the face amount of the loan (not to be confused with points charged to the borrower as a loan-processing fee). The reason for this is that FHA and VA establish a ceiling on the rate of interest which the lender may charge the buyer. This ceiling is almost always below the going market interest rate. In addition, FHA and VA regulations prohibit the buyer from paying the difference. To bring the fixed interest rate to the market level, the lender will reduce the loan proceeds by the amount of prepaid interest necessary. Following is an example of converting an FHA sale to its cash equivalent.

	Face Value	Cash Equivalent
Down payment	$ 5,000	$ 5,000
First loan	25,000	. . .
4 points computation: $25,000 × 0.96	. . .	24,000
	$30,000	$29,000

Summary

Real estate is an investment. As such, it competes with other kinds of investments, demonstrating a number of advantages and disadvantages. The investor must weigh the factors inherent in the ownership of real estate and their relation to the possible benefits of investing money elsewhere. Once the decision is made, the investor must be concerned with financing. The assessor must be aware of the decisions made by investors in the market and also of the effects that terms of financing may have on the value of property under appraisal.

A review of real estate investments and finance follows.

Real Estate Investments

1. Real estate as a competitive investment.

a) Types of investment—divided into fixed-dollar investments and growth investments; include bonds, stocks, life insurance, loan company deposits, mortgages and trust deeds, savings accounts, and real estate.

b) Factors to consider with real estate investments —safety, liquidity, size of investment, use as collateral, time, management, appreciation, and income tax advantages.

2. Factors affecting discount requirements. The summation concept of analyzing the discount requirement consists of four factors.

a) Safe rate—the rate obtainable with the most safety and the least risk.

b) Risk rate—the return commensurate with the risk assumed by the investor.

c) Rate for nonliquidity—necessary rate for the fact that real estate is a nonliquid asset.

d) Rate for management—factor compensating for the time and cost involved in managing the real estate investment.

Real Estate Finance

1. Methods of financing.

a) Cash—exchange of cash or check for a general warranty deed.

b) Mortgage—a written instrument pledging specified real estate as a guarantee for payment of a loan used to purchase a property.

c) Trust deed—a three-party agreement in which the borrower gives title to the trustee to hold for the trustor and the beneficiary.

d) Land contract—exchange of cash and agreement in a contract stating how the balance is to be paid.

2. Mortgages.

a) Types—first mortgage, junior mortgage, construction loan mortgage, purchase-money mortgage, open-end mortgage, package mortgage, chattel mortgage.

d) Classifications according to mortgage payment provisions—straight mortgage, amortized mortgage, partially amortized mortgage.

3. Sources of financing.

a) Commercial banks—usually make short-term loans with low loan-to-value ratios.

b) Mutual savings banks—independent mutual associations, generally making loans on FHA-insured mortgages.

c) Savings and loan associations—largest single money source for single- and multifamily residential sales.

d) Life insurance companies—attracted to large development loans; active in junior mortgage loans and commercial mortgages.

e) Mortgage companies—often formed to place mortgages in their own name with loan commitments from large lenders.

4. Adjustments for financing: sales data analysis. There are three cases in which financing affects sale price.

a) Seller and lender same party—necessity for analyzing loan terms and comparing with loan market.

b) Buyer assumes seller's mortgage—sale price influenced by cash value and difference between assumed rate and market rate.

c) FHA and VA loans—loan proceeds must be reduced by amount of points to bring to market level.

10 The Income Approach: Income and Expense Analysis

Introduction to the Income Approach

The third method of valuation is the income approach, frequently referred to as capitalization of net income. The capitalization process restates market value by converting the future benefits of property ownership into an expression of present worth. The buyer of a single-family home makes the purchase in order to enjoy the benefits the property will afford to him in the future. Likewise, the buyer of an investment property pays the price in order to receive future benefits—the annual stream generated by rents. As in the case of the cost and comparative sales approaches to value, the principle of substitution applies: a property does not have a market value in excess of the amount upon which it is capable of producing a return consistent with that anticipated from investments with similar risk.

The assessor must be familiar with this approach to value for the following reasons.

• When no reliable sales data are available for the appraisal of, for instance, a commercial property, and the building is so old that the cost approach is inconclusive or unconvincing, the income approach is the best value indicator.

• Investors, the typical owners of income-producing

properties, place chief emphasis on the income approach in making decisions to buy or sell.

● The income approach is a valid check on the value indications in the cost and comparative sales approaches to value.

● Most statutes require the assessor to consider all factors that affect market value.

The basic steps in the income approach are as follows: (1) estimate potential gross income; (2) deduct for vacancy and collection loss; (3) add miscellaneous income; (4) determine operating expenses; (5) deduct operating expenses to determine net income before discount, recapture, and taxes; (6) select the proper capitalization rate; (7) determine the appropriate capitalization procedure to be used; and (8) capitalize the net income into an estimated property value. The discussion presented in this chapter covers the first five steps in this process.

This chapter deals with income and expense analysis, which is necessary in order to arrive at a net income figure that the property is capable of producing. One point should be emphasized: the income and expenses that are proper and acceptable for income tax purposes are not the same as proper income and expenses used by the assessor. This is important, since the investor is interested in both short-term and long-term profits even though the taxable income for income tax purposes for any given period may or may not be related to the real estate value in question.

Gross Income Estimates

The first step in the income approach to value is to estimate the potential gross income for the property in question. *Potential gross income* is economic rent for the property at 100 percent occupancy. *Economic rent* is the rent that is justified for the property on the basis of a careful study of comparable properties in the area. In other words, economic rent is market rent.

The following example will clarify potential gross income. A retail store that has 2,500 square feet rents for $5 per square foot per year. Assuming that $5 per square foot per year is economic rent, the potential gross income can be computed as follows:

2,500 square feet × $5 per square foot
$$= \$12,500 \text{ potential gross income.}$$

The potential gross income for this property is the economic rent of $5 per square foot times the number of square feet (2,500), which equals $12,500, or the maximum possible rent the property could produce if rented at economic rent and if fully occupied.

The rent that a property will command in the market depends on many different factors. Just as the assessor must examine all the terms and conditions surrounding the sale of a property when the comparative sales approach to value is used, so all the circumstances surrounding the comparable rentals used as a basis for establishing economic rent for the subject property must be examined in the income approach to value.

Rental Information Sources

In the search for comparable rental properties, many of the same sources utilized in the comparative sales approach may be considered. Typical sources of rental information are buyers and sellers of commercial property, commercial property managers, realtors, tenants, and public records.

A professional rapport should be developed with these information sources. This rapport can be established by making requests for information in a reasonable manner, by explaining the need and purpose of the information, and by maintaining the confidentiality of all information received in confidence.

Rental Market Data

Leases. Rental information may be recorded on leases that are a matter of public record. Leases ordinarily detail the terms and other important considerations between the tenant and the property owner. Listed below are the various types of leases.

Month-to-Month Lease. Month-to-month leases are short-term leases that may or may not be in written form. This type of lease provides no security for the tenant or the landlord, since the landlord has no guarantee of future occupancy and rent payment, and the tenant has no guarantee of the right to continue to occupy the premises.

Short-Term Lease. Short-term leases are generally written with the terms and provisions of the lease detailed. This type of lease is generally considered to be for periods of less than ten years. Usually it is for a period under five years.

Long-Term Lease. The long-term lease provides for terms extending more than ten years.

Percentage Lease. Percentage leases typically provide for rent payments to be based on a percentage of income from the sale of merchandise or services. Percentage leases have a stated minimum rent and sometimes a maximum rent provision.

Graduated Lease. The graduated lease provides for a stated rent level for a given period, followed by a change (usually an increase) in the rent level during stated subsequent periods.

Renewal Lease. Renewal leases provide for one or more extensions of the lease term in the original lease document at the option of the tenant. The rent under such renewals may be predetermined or negotiated at the time of renewal.

In comparing one rental property with another, the following factors are considered: (1) date of lease, (2) location of property, (3) physical characteristics of property, and (4) terms of the lease. From a thorough study and comparison of rental properties based on these factors, an accurate judgment as to comparability can be made. Since the income approach depends upon an accurate estimate of economic rent, the leases covering the subject property as well as those covering comparables in the area must be carefully analyzed.

The following list of considerations will provide helpful guidelines for comparing leased properties.

Date of Lease. As with the date of the sale in the comparative sales approach, the date of the lease must be known in making comparisons in the income approach. Leases negotiated several years earlier may not accurately reflect present prevailing conditions, and the rents paid may not be indicative of current economic rent.

Name of the Owner (Landlord or Lessor). The owner is the party who receives the rent.

Name of the Tenant (Lessee). The tenant is the party who occupies the premises and pays the rent.

Reference. The reference indicates where the lease is recorded.

Legal Description. The legal description or other identification includes a map, group and parcel number, and property address.

Lease Term. The lease term should state the beginning and ending date for the tenant's occupancy. The number of months and years remaining and covered by the lease can thereby be calculated.

Amount of Rent. The lease should contain a clause stating the amount of rent, how and when the rent is to be paid, and whether or not any percentages, graduations, or overages are applicable.

Owner's Responsibilities. Statements are included in the lease about the responsibility for maintenance, insurance, taxes, and all other items for which the property owner is responsible during the terms of the lease.

Tenant's Responsibilities. Statements in the lease relate to the tenant's responsibilities for taxes, insurance, utilities, and maintenance; provisions may call for escalation of rent payments due to an increase in the cost of these items.

Right to Sublease. There should be a clause stating whether or not the tenant may assign and/or sublease the premises and under what conditions. This statement should also indicate whether or not an assignment or a sublease would relieve the initial tenant from future responsibility under the original lease.

Option to Renew. This clause should give dates, terms, rent payments, and other provisions specified as the tenant's option.

Tenant Improvements. This clause should state the conditions under which the tenant can make improvements to the property being leased and whether or not the improvements are to remain or may be removed by the tenant at the end of the lease. The responsibility of the tenant for taxes on improvements should also be stated.

Security. This provision should state the amount of any damage deposit required along with advance rent. This clause should also include a provision for damage claims that may result from tenant abuse to the property.

Termination. This clause should indicate under what conditions the owner and/or the tenant can terminate the lease.

Special Provisions. This clause should include other special conditions or considerations that would have an effect on the tenant and/or the owner of the property during the term of the lease.

When analyzing leases and interviewing owners and managers, the assessor may come across such terms as "gross lease"; "net lease"; "net, net lease"; and "net, net, net lease." Although these terms have somewhat different meanings to different individuals, the most common understanding is that a *gross lease* provides for the landlord to pay all maintenance, utilities, insurance, and taxes. The *net, net, net lease* provides for the tenant to pay all property expenses. Net leases and net, net leases are degrees of the gross lease and the net, net, net lease that may require specified expenses to be paid by either tenant or landlord.

Types of Rent. Given below is an explanation of the various types of rent.

Contract Rent. Contract rent is the actual rent specified in the lease and is the rent that is actually paid by the tenant.

In the case of leases by month, year, and other periods (other than long-term leases), the lease need not be in writing.

Excess Rent. Excess rent is the difference between contract rent and economic rent and implies that the tenant is paying too much rent on the basis of comparable rents.

Percentage Rent. Percentage rent is based on a fixed or graduated percentage of gross sales, normally with a guaranteed minimum rent.

Minimum Rent. Minimum rent is the base or fixed rent provided for in a percentage lease.

Overage Rent. This type is rent over and above a guaranteed minimum under the terms of a percentage lease (not to be confused with excess rent).

Economic Rent. As previously indicated, economic rent is the rent justified on the basis of an analysis of other comparable rental properties. It should be stressed that economic rent is sought in the income approach, since it is the rent justified for the property on the basis of comparable rental properties in the area and upon past, present, and projected future rent of the subject property.

Rental Units of Comparison. If the rent from a property is to be considered in relation to property value, the rent must be expressed in terms of some common denominator. A judgment regarding the appropriate unit of comparison for the subject property must be made. There are several common units of comparison that are used for the various types of income-producing properties. Typical units of comparison are square foot, room, apartment, space, and percentage of gross business income of the tenant.

Rental Unit of Comparison	Type of Income-producing Property
Square foot	Shopping centers, retail stores, office buildings, warehouses, apartments, and leased land
Room	Apartment buildings, motels, and hotels
Apartment...........	Apartment buildings
Space	Mobile home parks, travel trailer parks, and parking garages
Percentage of gross business income	Retail stores, shopping centers, restaurants, and gas stations

When the square-foot unit is used with an office building or a shopping center, care must be exercised in the comparison process, since some leases refer to gross leasable area and others are negotiated on the basis of net leasable area. The *gross leasable area* (GLA) includes common areas such as halls, restrooms, and vestibules. The *net leasable area* (NLA) includes only the floor area occupied by the tenant. An office building with 100,000 square foot of GLA might have an NLA of only 80,000 square feet, which is a difference between GLA and NLA of 20 percent. When leases are compared, it must be known whether rent is based on GLA or NLA.

Rental units of comparison may be expressed in terms of rent per month or rent per year. Local custom and the type of income property will determine whether typical rent is specified per month or per year. The important consideration is to avoid comparing rent per month with rent per year. In the capitalization process, income, as well as expenses, is expressed on an annual basis.

Effective Gross Income Estimates

After making the complete analysis for determining potential gross income for the subject property, the next step in the income approach is to determine effective gross income. *Effective gross income* is potential gross income less vacancy and collection loss, plus appropriate miscellaneous income. To arrive at effective gross income, each of these factors must be examined.

Vacancy

Since it is highly unlikely that a property will remain fully rented for the entire period of its life, a deduction from potential gross income should be made for the vacancy that is expected to occur. The vacancy factor for any particular property must be determined by a study of other comparable properties and an analysis of their rental histories, as well as the recent history of vacancies in the subject property. In arriving at the appropriate deduction for vacancy, consideration should be given to the probability of competitive construction in the near future as well as the present demand for the type of property being appraised. The following example demonstrates the development of a vacancy rate from three apartment buildings having comparable rental units.

Apartment Building	No. of Units	Occupied	Vacant	Vacancy Rate (%)
A	120	112	8	6.7
B	150	139	11	7.3
C	160	148	12	7.5
Subject	130	(?)	(?)	(?)

The vacancy percentage is found by dividing the total number of units vacant by the total number of units. The example shows that vacancy for these properties is typically running between 6.7 and 7.5 percent and that, as the number of units increases, so does the vacancy rate. Since the subject apartment building contains 130 units, it is probable that the vacancy rate for the subject property would fall between 6.7 percent as demonstrated by Apartment Building A (120 units) and 7.3 percent as demonstrated by Apartment Building B (150 units). It is reasonable to conclude that the vacancy rate for a comparable apartment building with 130 units should be approximately 7 percent. The deduction for vacancy for the subject property would therefore be 7 percent of the potential gross income.

The property deduction for vacancy can be as high as 50–60 percent for old hotels and motels or as low as about 1–3 percent for new, well-located, and well-managed office complexes. As buildings get older, the vacancy rate tends to increase. Physical condition, as well as functional and economic obsolescence, normally cause older buildings to be less desirable and less useful. The economic principles of supply and demand, change, competition, and substitution confirm this observation.

Collection Loss

Collection loss is simply the loss that results from the failure of tenants to pay the rent. The two major factors to consider in collection loss are the comparison with comparable properties and the tenants in the subject property. Consider the following example taken from the operating statements of two comparable properties.

Apartment	Rents Receivable	Rent Collected	Bad Checks and Noncollectible	Collection Loss (%)
A	$76,555	$75,680	$ 875	1.14
B	97,406	96,370	1,036	1.06

By comparing the above information from the operating statements, it can be seen that the collection loss is about 1 percent. The collection loss percentage is calculated by adding the amount of rent collected to the amount of rent uncollected and by dividing the noncollectibles by the total. The collection loss (1.14 percent) for Apartment Building A is calculated by dividing $875 (the noncollectibles) by $76,555 (the rents receivable). The rents receivable total does not consider those apartments which are vacant. Only the apartments that are occupied and that are expected to produce rent are considered.

Miscellaneous Income

The two preceding sections have demonstrated a vacancy and collection loss of 8 percent (vacancy, 7 percent; collection loss, 1 percent). After subtracting this total from the potential gross income, any miscellaneous income generated from the operation of the property must be added. Miscellaneous income may come from several sources other than actual rent, including parking, resale of utilities (gas, water, electricity), coin-operated laundry, and clubroom rent. As exemplified here, miscellaneous income is often referred to as *service income*.

The following example shows how effective gross income is calculated.

Potential gross income	$12,500
Less vacancy and collection loss (8%)	1,000
Effective gross income from rents	$11,500
Plus miscellaneous income (e.g., parking)	750
Effective gross income	$12,250

Net Income Estimates

Net income is the income remaining after the allowance for vacancy and collection loss and after the operating expenses are subtracted from potential gross income plus miscellaneous expenses.

	Potential gross income
minus	Vacancy and collection loss
plus	Miscellaneous income
equals	Effective gross income
minus	Operating expenses
equals	Net income

Thus, when proper annual expenses are deducted from annual effective gross income, the result is annual net income (before discount, recapture, and taxes). This is the amount that will be used with proper capitalization rates and procedures to arrive at a value conclusion.

Operating Expenses

After the effective gross income for the property has been estimated, the operating expenses must be analyzed. Understanding and analysis of an owner's operating statement are essential in order to determine correctly the proper and improper expenses related to the operation of the subject property.

As previously indicated, the income and expenses shown by an accountant on an operating statement prepared for income tax purposes cannot be taken for use in the income approach to value without careful analysis and determination regarding their propriety. The economic rent may or may not coincide with the stated income. In the case of expenses, only the reasonable and typical expenses necessary to support and maintain the income-producing capability of the property should be allowed.

The following discussion of expenses departs from traditional appraisal theory by eliminating the "fixed expense" classification. The reason for this is that no property expense is truly fixed and that those items which have been traditionally treated as fixed (taxes and insurance) are currently subject to fluctuations, as are other operating expenses. Therefore, insurance will be treated as an operating expense, and taxes will be included as a part of the capitalization rate.

Expenses for real estate, which are considered in the income approach to value, may be classified as (1) operating expenses and (2) reserves for replacement.

Operating expenses are ordinary and typical expenses that are necessary to keep the property functional and rented competitively with other properties in the area. *Reserves for replacement* include annual charges for items that have fast depreciation (short-lived) and that must be replaced before the end of the lease period or before the building reaches the end of its useful life.

Operating expenses vary from property to property, depending on type of occupancy, use type, and quality of management. In analyzing the operating expenses for a property, the operating statements from comparable properties must be reviewed and the following considered.

• Does the expense amount appear to be typical for the property in question, and is the amount substantiated by expense statements of comparable properties?
• Do the expenses tend to appear infrequently?
• Do the expenses appear to indicate typical management?
• Do the expenses indicate a specific weakness of the property in question (physical deterioration, functional obsolescence, or economic obsolescence)?
• Are the various reported expenses consistent as they relate to each other (maintenance, age, and reserves for replacement)?
• Is the ratio of expenses to gross income comparable to those for competitive properties?

These questions must be considered in analyzing expense items on an owner's operating statement, for it should be kept in mind that a prediction is being made of the stabilized annual net income that the property is expected to produce assuming competent management and a typical year. Specific expenses to be considered are considered under the categories of proper and improper expenses.

Proper Expenses. The following categories are proper expenses related to the operation of a property: (1) management, (2) salaries, (3) utilities, (4) supplies and materials, (5) repairs and maintenance, (6) property taxes, (7) insurance, (8) miscellaneous, and (9) reserves for replacement.

Management. Management is a proper expense for every income-producing property regardless of whether it is owner- or tenant-occupied and whether an actual management fee is paid or not. Management is usually stated as a percentage of effective gross income and varies depending on the geographic area and property type. The charge for management typically ranges between 3 and 10 percent of the rent collected. The rate for the subject property must be determined on the basis of the conditions in the area and the typical charge for management for comparable properties. Included in the management charge may be accounting expenses, office expenses, rent collections, advertising, and coordination between management and owners relating to all matters, including financial and personal management of the property. These may entail a management fee paid to a professional management firm. Such a fee is not to be confused with the salary of an on-site building manager, whose salary would be included in the expense category "salaries."

Salaries. This category consists of the salaries and fringe benefits that are included in the compensation of employees necessary to maintain the property and to provide the operational activities necessary to keep the property rented. Employees in this category would include resident and on-site managers, maintenance men, gardeners, elevator operators, security men, and other employees who may be needed in order to keep the property physically, functionally, and economically competitive. Expenses for the above management staff include salaries, vacations, sick leave, annual leave, holidays, social security, health insurance, unemployment insurance, and the rent on apartments provided for the employees who live on the property.

Utilities. Included in this category are gas, water, electricity, sewer charge, fuel, telephone, and trash removal. Since utilities fluctuate from time to time, a careful review of expenses of comparable properties must be made in order to determine reasonable and typical utility expenses.

Supplies and Materials. In this category are expendable items used in the day-to-day operation of the property, such as office supplies, light bulbs, grass seed, fuses, and fertilizer.

Repairs and Maintenance. This category includes expenses necessary to keep the property operating and covers the repair of such items as the roof, water heaters, cooling systems, broken glass, and painting. This category should not be confused with reserves for replacement. Expenses in the category "reserves for replacement" are anticipated, predetermined expenses, with an annual charge set up for replacement. Repairs and maintenance are normal maintenance expenses necessitated by the physical use of the property.

Property Taxes. Property taxes may be considered an expense item in the income approach. However, in appraisal procedures for assessment purposes, a preferable way of handling this item is to use an effective tax rate as part of the capitalization rate (see the section entitled "Effective Tax Rate" in chap. 11).

Insurance. This is a proper expense item that should be checked to ensure that the insurance coverage is adequate and that the expense charged is only for one year. (Many insurance premiums cover more than one year; in such cases, annual proration is necessary.)

Miscellaneous. Items in this category should be small ones that do not justify listing and amount to only a small percentage of the effective gross income. These items vary widely from property to property and should be examined in detail where the total is substantiated.

Reserves for Replacement. Expense items in this category may be compared to items that are depreciated in the cost approach as short-lived items. Those parts of a building that normally must be replaced before the building reaches the end of its economic life should have an annual expense charge as a reserve for replacement. If a property is under lease for twenty-five years, for example, it is reasonable to expect such items as carpeting and air conditioning to wear out before the end of the lease. Therefore, a reserves-for-replacement category is set aside annually to provide for the eventual replacement of these items. Replacement items that may be included in this category are the roof, water heaters, heating and air-conditioning systems, elevators, floor coverings, stoves, dishwashers, and refrigerators. The amount to be set aside for any specific item is calculated in the following manner:

1. Estimate the economic life of the item.
2. Estimate the replacement cost new.
3. Calculate the percentage per year by dividing 100 percent by the economic life of the item.
4. Multiply the percentage per year by the replacement cost new, to arrive at the yearly charge.

For example, a small retail store has a remaining economic life of forty years. The roof has an economic life of twenty years, and the cost of the roof is $3,000. The annual percentage can be calculated as follows:

$$\frac{100 \text{ percent}}{20 \text{ years}} = 5 \text{ percent each year.}$$

The annual percentage is then multiplied by the cost of

the roof, to determine the proper revenue for the re-placement charge for the roof:

Cost of roof	$ 3,000
Cost percentage	× 0.05
Annual reserve for roof	$150.00

Improper Expenses. Since the income approach relies on an accurate estimate of net income that the property will produce, it is important to estimate accurately all expenses that will be deducted from the effective gross income. There are several items often found in an owner's operating statement that are *not* proper expense charges in the income approach. Following is an explanation of some of these improper expenses.

Depreciation. Since depreciation will be considered in the income approach as recapture and handled as part of the capitalization rate, this charge is not proper. Depreciation is ordinarily set up on operating statements for income tax purposes and will not be the same as the recapture provision in the capitalization rate.

Debt Service. Debt service normally includes both the interest and the principal payments required to amortize the loan on the property. This item is also considered in the capitalization rate in the form of recapture and discount rates. Again, the rate used by the assessor may or may not be synonymous with the debt service found on the owner's operating statement.

Income Taxes. The income tax shown on the owner's operating statement is not a legitimate operating expense in the income approach, since the tax is based not on the property value but upon the personal income of the individual owner. Different owners may be in different tax brackets, but the appraisal is based on the market value of the property.

Capital Improvements. Capital improvements include additions to the property that may be made at any point in time and are not necessary to maintain the level of income at any given point. Capital improvements ordinarily result in an increase in the total value of the property, in the economic life of the property, or in the income of the property, or in all three. Therefore, these expenditures are not considered annual charges and should not be deducted from the effective gross income.

Owner's Business Expenses. The owner's business expenses that are not necessary for maintaining the rent produced by the property are not proper expenses. Even though this type of expense may be permitted for income tax reporting, they are considered personal expenses and not related to the income produced by rental property.

In determining proper and improper expenses for a property, the assessor must compare the current expenses with past years' expenses, compare the current expenses with those shown on statements of comparable properties, and interview the owner, manager, and/or accountant regarding expense items in question.

RECONSTRUCTING THE INCOME AND EXPENSE STATEMENT

Shown below is an example of an owner's operating statement for a ten-unit apartment building, the Colony Key Apartments. The rent is $140 per unit per month, for a potential gross income of $16,800. The actual rent of $140 per unit per month is supported by rentals of several comparable apartment properties in the area. Economic rent, therefore, is judged to be $140 per unit per month. The owner's statement shows an income received of $15,875. The difference between the potential gross income of $16,800 and the actual rent collected is the vacancy and collection loss of $925. Therefore, the effective gross income of this property is $15,875. The items listed in the owner's operating statement are typical, and each will be discussed individually with the recommendation as to the method of treatment by the appraiser.

Owner's Statement of Income and Expenses
Colony Key Apartments
December 31, 19＿

Rental income	$15,875	
Total income		$15,875
Real estate taxes	$ 2,125	
Mortgage amortization payment	2,376	
Interest on mortgage	1,499	
Insurance (3-year premium)	975	
Miscellaneous repairs	919	
New roof	2,000	
3 refrigerators	900	
1 stove	180	
Utilities (gas, electricity)	301	
Advertising	400	
Water	298	
Paint two units	253	
Depreciation	1,500	
Concrete patio	647	
Exterior painting	453	
Lawn care	447	
Exterminator	277	
Total expenses		$15,550
Net income		$ 325

Reconstructed Income and Expense Statement
Colony Key Apartments
December 31, 19＿

Potential gross income ($140 economic rent × 10 units × 12 months)		$16,800
Less vacancy and collection loss		925
Effective gross income		$15,875

	Expenses	
	Dollars	*Ratio*
Insurance	$ 325	0.020
Miscellaneous repairs	920	0.058
Management ($15,875 × 6%)	953	0.060
Utilities (gas, electricity)	360	0.023
Advertising	400	0.025
Water	300	0.019
Lawn care	450	0.028
Exterminator	275	0.017
New roof ($2,000 ÷ 10-year life)	200	0.013

Stoves (10 units × $180 = $1,800; divide by 10 years)	$ 180	0.011
Refrigerators (10 units × $300 = $3,000; divide by 10 years)	300	0.019
Interior painting (10 units × $125 = $1,250; divide by 4 years)	312	0.020
Exterior painting ($450 ÷ 3 years)	150	0.010
Heating system ($4,000 ÷ 15 years)	267	0.017
Water heaters (10 units × $120 = $1,200; divide by 15 years)	80	0.005
	$5,472	0.345

Effective gross income	$15,875
Less operating expenses	5,472
Net income (before discount, recapture, and taxes)	$10,403

The following discussion will explain how each item in the Colony Key Apartments income and expenses should be treated. The assessor's reconstructed income and expense statement shows the results of analysis and conclusions by the assessor regarding the expenses. The items are discussed in the order in which they appear on the owner's statement.

Real Estate Taxes. As discussed previously, real estate taxes may be taken as an expense, or a provision for taxes may be made in the capitalization rate. Since the appraisal is likely to affect the resulting assessment, real estate taxes should be removed as an expense item and included later in the effective tax rate.

Mortgage Amortization Payment. The mortgage amortization payment should never be included as an expense in the income approach. As will be seen in chapter 11, the capitalization rate for improved property always includes a provision for recapture of capital.

Interest on Mortgage. This item is never included as an expense and is also accounted for in the capitalization rate.

Insurance. It is necessary to prorate the three-year premium and to include only one year. One-third of the premium should be taken as an expense for this year's operating statement.

Miscellaneous Repairs. These include such items as equipment repairs, plumbing, broken glass, light bulbs, and other miscellaneous items.

Management. This item did not appear on the owner's statement but is a necessary and proper expense for this type of property. Since management is typically 6 percent of the effective gross income of comparable properties in the area, this figure is used in the reconstructed statement.

New Roof. The new roof should be set up in the reserve-for-replacement category. As previously explained, the annual charge is derived by estimating the economic life of the item.

Refrigerators. This is another item that should be set up as reserve for replacement. If three refrigerators cost $900, one refrigerator costs $300; if one refrigerator costs $300 and the apartment complex has ten units, the total cost of refrigerators for the complex would be 10 × $300, or $3,000. Assuming a ten-year life, the annual charge under the reserve-for-replacement category would be 10 percent of $3,000, or $300.

Stove. The stove would also be a part of the reserve for replacement. Assuming an economic life of ten years, the annual charge would be arrived at as with the refrigerators.

Utilities. Utilities are a proper expense in the operation of the property.

Advertising. Advertising is also an allowable expense.

Water. Water is simply an itemization of a utility.

Paint Two Units. This was classified as interior painting in the reconstructed statement and is treated as reserve for replacement: if two units can be painted for $250, ten units can be painted for $1,250; assuming that the paint will last four years, 25 percent of the $1,250 is the appropriate annual charge for interior painting.

Depreciation. Depreciation is not applicable, since it is a provision taken care of in the capitalization rate. Also, the depreciation shown on the owner's statement for income tax purposes may have no relationship to the remaining economic life of the property. Since future income is the reason an income property has value, past depreciation is of little concern. The remaining economic life of the property will determine the duration of the future income.

Concrete Patio. This is a capital improvement and should not be included as an annual expense in the income approach.

Exterior Painting. As interior painting, this item is set up under the reserve for replacement. The $150 figure assumes a three-year life for the exterior paint, or one-third of the total cost annually.

Lawn Care. This is a proper maintenance expense.

Extermination. This is also a proper maintenance expense.

Since this owner's statement does not include any mention of heating, air conditioning, or hot-water heaters, a reserve for replacement category should also be included as an expense item in the annual expense statement. The annual charge for the heating system is based on a total cost of $4,000 for the system and a remaining economic life of fifteen years. The annual expense for water heaters is based on an individual cost of $120 per heater, or $1,200 for the ten units. Economic life of the heaters is fifteen years.

The reconstructed expense statement shows a total annual expense of $5,472. This amount represents the proper expense figure to deduct from the effective gross income to arrive at a net income figure for the property. In this case the potential gross income is $16,800, and the actual rent collected is $15,875. This indicates a vacancy and collection loss of $925, or about 5.5 percent of potential gross income. Assuming that this is a typical vacancy and collection loss, the following calculations are indicated.

Potential gross income	$16,800
Less vacancy and collection loss (5.5%) . . .	925
Effective gross income	$15,875
Less expenses	5,472
Net income	$10,403

Operating Expense Ratios. It is both necessary and desirable that ratios of expenses to income be developed.

These ratios, when used properly, can provide a quick check on the expense figures for comparable properties and can be developed for extensive use in mass appraisal work. A commonly misunderstood point relating to expense ratios is whether to use potential gross income and then calculate the expense as a ratio of effective gross income. As a practical matter, the only difference would be vacancy and collection loss, plus the question of whether to include miscellaneous income. If properties are highly comparable, the vacancy and collection loss percentages will be similar, making the question of potential gross income academic. In any case, miscellaneous income should not be included when either potential gross income or effective gross income is used as the basis for establishing expense ratios. The assessor must be aware of the danger of comparing an expense ratio developed using potential gross income with an expense ratio using effective gross income where the vacancy and collection loss is high.

In the Colony Key Apartments illustration, the ratios are based on effective gross income. The percentage of effective gross income used to pay expenses is calculated by dividing the total expenses by the effective gross income. When the total expense of $5,472 is divided by the effective gross income of $15,875, the resulting expense ratio is 0.345, or 34.5 percent. In other words, the expense necessary to keep the property operating amounts to 34.5 percent of the effective gross income.

Each item of expense can be compared in the same manner. The ratios shown in the reconstructed expense statement are calculated individually by dividing each expense amount by the effective gross income. By having the individual expenses calculated as a percentage of effective gross income, one can quickly identify those expenses which appear to be out of line with the expenses of other comparable properties. The dollar amount may differ from one apartment to another, but the percentages represented by the expense should be reasonably comparable from one property to another of the same type.

The following table shows the typical range of operating expenses for various types of property. The ratios are not to be adopted for use in a particular jurisdiction without careful verification by the assessor. Investigation and analysis may show these expense ratios to be as follows:

Type of Property	Expense-Ratio Range (%)
Shopping centers	20–30
Office space	25–35
High-rise office buildings	25–35
Retail stores	20–30
Apartments, high-rise	30–40
Apartments, garden	25–40
Warehouses	15–25

These ratios do not include taxes. All other normal and typical expenses are included. It must be realized, however, that leases differ and, while some landlords are responsible for certain expenses, others are not. It should also be noted that higher rent scales tend to produce lower expense ratios. This is especially true when occupancy can be maintained at a high level.

Operating ratios vary widely from property to property and from area to area. Among the factors that affect operating ratios are (1) terms of the lease, (2) type of property, (3) age and condition of the property, (4) type of tenants, (5) management, and (6) geographical area.

Summary

The steps for arriving at net income before discount, recapture, and taxes are the following: (1) estimate potential gross income, (2) deduct for vacancy and collection loss, (3) add miscellaneous income, (4) determine operating expenses, and (5) deduct operating expenses. Following is a step-by-step delineation of the processes thus far described.

Gross Income Estimates

Potential gross income is economic rent for the property at 100 percent occupancy. From such sources as buyers and sellers, commercial property managers, realtors, and public records, rental market data must be collected.
1. Leases—ordinarily detail the terms and other factors reflecting considerations between tenant and owner.
2. Types of leases—month to month, short term, long term, percentage, graduated, renewal.
3. Lease considerations—date, name of owner and tenant, reference, legal description, term, amount of rent, owner's and tenant's responsibilities, right to sublease, option to renew, tenant improvements, security, termination, special provisions.
4. Types of rent—contract, excess, percentage, minimum, overage, economic.
5. Rental units of comparison—square foot, room, apartment, space, percentage of gross business income, gross leasable area (GLA), net leasable area (NLA).

Effective Gross Income Estimates

Effective gross income is potential gross income less vacancy and collection loss, plus appropriate miscellaneous income.
1. Vacancy—a necessary deduction, since property will not remain fully rented for entire period of life; determined by study of comparable properties and analysis of their rental histories.
2. Collection loss—the loss resulting from the failure of tenants to pay the rent.
3. Miscellaneous income—income from sources other than actual rent (parking, resale of utilities).

Net Income Estimates

Net income is the income remaining after the allowance for vacancy and collection loss and after subtraction of operating expenses from potential gross income plus miscellaneous expenses.

1. Operating expenses—thorough analysis necessary to determine proper and improper expenses; include operating expenses, reserves for replacement.

2. Proper expenses—include management, salaries, utilities, supplies, materials, repairs and maintenance, property taxes, insurance, miscellaneous, reserves for replacement.

3. Improper expenses—include depreciation, debt service, income taxes, capital improvements, owner's business expenses.

4. Operating expense ratios—provide a quick check on the expense figures for comparable properties.

11 The Income Approach: Capitalization Formulas and Rates

Capitalization is the process of converting a series of anticipated future payments (income) into present value. It relates net income produced by a property to the property value. The capitalization process, or the income approach, restates market value by converting the future benefits of property ownership into an expression of present worth.

As exemplified in chapter 9, the normal goals of the investor are twofold: (1) a return *on* the investment and (2) a return *of* the investment. With income-producing property, the return on the investment depends on the difference between the property income and all expenses for the same period, and the return of the investment depends on the resale value of the property. In considering the income of a property that is being appraised, the *quantity,* the *quality,* and the *durability* of income must be considered. In analyzing the quantity, the assessor is concerned with how much income the property can produce; when he is analyzing the quality, concern is with the responsibility of the tenants and their financial rating. When the durability of the income is considered, the concern is with the length of time the income will be received.

A rate that indicates the return required to attract investment capital is the connection between the future income and a value indication. For this reason, the selection of rates is of paramount importance in the capitalization process.

The following definitions will serve as a useful reference for this chapter.

- *Capitalization rate*—A rate used for converting property income into property value.
- *Discount rate*—The rate of return on a real estate investment. It reflects the compensation necessary to attract investors to give up liquidity, defer consumption, and assume the risks of investing. It is the rate of return required on total property investment to meet investment requirements. It is the weighted average of the mortgage interest rate and the equity rate, weighted by the proportions of total investment represented by mortgage(s) and equity. It is often called *interest rate.*
- *Recapture rate*—The rate of return of a real estate investment; the annual dollar requirement for returning to the investor a sum equal to the property value (improvements only) at the end of a given period of time.
- *Overall rate*—The direct relationship between annual net income and sale price or value; includes the proper provision for discount and recapture.
- *Yield rate*—The rate of return on equity capital; used in reference to return on equity investments as opposed to interest on mortgage loans.
- *Interest rate*—The rate on borrowed money; the loan or borrowing rate.
- *Effective tax rate*—The rate expressing the ratio between the property value and the current tax bill; the official tax rate of the taxing jurisdiction multiplied by the assessment ratio.

Basic Formulas

When a rate is used to convert income from property into the property value, the capitalization process is taking place. The rate used, therefore, is called the capitalization rate. In the following example, I = income, R = rate, and V = value:

$$V = \frac{I}{R} .$$

Assume that the net income from a retail-store property is $9,600 per year and that the proper capitalization rate is 12 percent. Using the formula $V = I \div R$ and the information provided, a property value of $80,000 is indicated:

$$\frac{\$9,600 \text{ (income)}}{0.12 \text{ (rate)}} = \$80,000 \text{ (value)} .$$

This illustrates the basic capitalization formula for value.

The relationship between the value of a property and the net income is expressed as a rate, or percentage; that is,

$$R = \frac{I}{V} .$$

For example, if a property with an annual net income of $9,600 sells for $80,000, the rate is 12 percent:

$$\frac{\$9,600 \text{ (income)}}{\$80,000 \text{ (value)}} = 0.12 \text{ (rate)} .$$

The rate of 0.12, or 12 percent, expresses the relationship between the net income and the property value: the annual net income for this property is 12 percent of the property value.

If the capitalization rate and property value are known, the net income necessary to produce a specified rate can be found by multiplying the rate by the value. For example, if the buyer of a small retail store has just purchased a property for $80,000 and wants a rate of 12 percent, the annual net rent that must be charged can be calculated as follows:

$$0.12 \text{ (rate)} \times \$80,000 \text{ (value)} = \$9,600 \text{ (income)} ,$$

that is,

$$I = R \times V .$$

The buyer must charge a net rent of \$9,600 annually (or \$800 per month) to realize a rate of 12 percent on his \$80,000 investment.

Knowledge of the three formulas is basic to the proper use of the income approach. The three capitalization formulas can be developed by making a mental picture of three blocks showing the letters I, R, V. If the block representing the unknown factors is covered, the relative positions of the two remaining blocks reveal the proper relationship. Assume that the rate, R, is unknown. If the R block is covered, the I block remains over the V block. This suggests the formula $R = I \div V$. When the V block is covered, I remains over R. If we cover I, R and V remain.

The formulas demonstrate that the property income, the capitalization rate, and the property value are all related to one another. A change in any one of the three factors will change the other two. It should be apparent also that, as the income goes up, the value increases. The following sections of this chapter and chapter 12 discuss the selection of rates and the methods and techniques of capitalization.

Selection of Rates

The understanding and proper selection of rates used in the income approach are necessary if valid estimates of value are to be made. A small difference in the capitalization rate will result in estimates differing by thousands of dollars. For example:

$$\frac{\$24,000 \text{ (net income)}}{0.12 \text{ (capitalization rate)}} = \$200,000 \text{ (value)} ;$$

$$\frac{\$24{,}000 \text{ (net income)}}{0.13 \text{ (capitalization rate)}} = \$184{,}615 \text{ (value)}.$$

Changing the capitalization rate by 1 percent, from 12 to 13 percent, causes the value indication to change by more than $15,000.

The three component parts of a capitalization rate are

- Discount rate
- Recapture rate
- Effective tax rate

When the property being appraised is vacant land, only the discount rate and the effective tax rate are used to obtain the proper capitalization rate. They are also used to apply to land in the building and land residual techniques (see chap. 12). The recapture rate is not used with land, since land is a nonwasting asset with recapture accomplished at the time of resale. When the property consists of improvements to the land, the proper building improvement capitalization rate is the sum of the discount rate, the recapture rate, and the effective tax rate. The recapture rate reflects the fact that improvements depreciate.

Land Only		Building Only	
Discount rate	9.0%	Discount rate	9.0%
Effective tax rate	2.5	Recapture rate	3.0
Capitalization rate	11.5%	Effective tax rate	2.5
		Capitalization rate	14.5%

Discount Rate

There are two reliable methods by which the discount rate can be developed for use in the income approach: the band-of-investment method and the market comparison method.

Band-of-Investment Method. The band-of-investment method of selecting a discount rate includes consideration of the interest rate paid by the investor on the first mortgage, the interest rates paid by the investor on additional mortgages, and the anticipated yield that the investor expects to receive on his equity in the property. This method considers the actual mortgage rates and terms prevailing for the type of property and for the area in question and therefore reflects the local market. In developing a discount rate by the band-of-investment method, information should be collected covering the following:

• The percentage of value (loan-value ratio) that lending institutions lend on the first mortgage for properties of this type, and the rate of interest; the same information on additional mortgages.
• The yield rate based on the equity requirements of the owner in the project. The yield rate should be the rate of return necessary to attract investors to this type of investment property. (The equity yield rate tends to be somewhat higher than the interest rates on first mortgages for prime investment properties. For investment properties with a higher risk, the yield rate may be considerably higher.)

The following example demonstrates the band-of-investment method in a typical appraisal situation. It has been determined that a first mortgage can be secured in the amount of $150,000 on a $200,000 apartment property. The prevailing interest rate for a mortgage on this type of property is 9.5 percent. An additional $20,000 may be borrowed on a second mortgage at an interest rate of 10 percent. The balance of the project represents the owner's equity and the owner's demand of a yield rate of 14 percent on this type of property. From this example, the first mortgage of $150,000 represents 75 percent of the total project cost of $200,000, and $20,000 on the second mortgage represents 10 percent of the total cost. If the first and second mortgages cover 85 percent, the owner's equity is 15 percent of the property value.

	Loan-Value Ratio (1)	Rate (2)	Weighted Average [(1) × (2)] (3)
First mortgage	0.75	0.095	0.07125
Second mortgage ...	0.10	0.10	0.01000
Equity mortgage	0.15	0.14	0.02100
Total	1.00	...	0.10225 (10.225%)

This procedure actually weights the prevailing interest and equity rates on the basis of the relative percentage of money invested in the property. The total weighted rates give an indicated discount rate for 100 percent of the property value in question. The proper discount rate for the property exemplified is 10.225 percent.

Market Comparison Method. This is a second method used in selecting the proper discount rate and is appropriate when comparable information from competitive properties can be obtained. It is very reliable because it directly reflects the discount rate indicated by actual investments in the income-producing property neighborhood. In theory the market comparison method is quite simple, since it involves only dividing the net income after recapture and after real estate taxes for a comparable property by its sale price. The formula used is "income divided by value equals rate." The result is the discount rate for the property under analysis.

For example, Property A recently sold for $120,000. The net income after recapture and taxes is calculated to be $12,500. By using the formula "income divided by value equals rate," a discount rate of 10.4 percent can be calculated for this property.

Property A sale price		$120,000
Net income before discount, recapture, and taxes		$ 17,900
Recapture	$3,000	
Taxes	2,400	
		$ 5,400
Net income after recapture and taxes		$ 12,500

Discount rate ($12,500 ÷ $120,000) = 10.4%

By doing the same analysis on other comparable properties, a range of discount rates can be established that should justify the appropriate discount rate for the property in question. The following example demonstrates how the market comparison method is used to select an appropriate discount rate.

Property	Sale	Net Income after Recapture and Taxes	Discount Rate (%)
A	$120,000	$12,500	10.4
B	150,000	15,200	10.1
C	110,000	11,250	10.2

The range of discount rates above is from 10.1 to 10.4 percent. By comparing the discount rate indicated by market comparison with the discount rate selected by the band-of-investment method in the previous example, it can be concluded that the proper discount rate for this type of property is 10.25 percent.

Interest and discount rates are normally expressed in whole numbers and quarters of a percent—for example, 10.25 percent and 10.50 percent. They may also be expressed as whole numbers and tenths and even twentieths of a percent—as in 10.10 percent, 10.20 percent, 10.05 percent, or 10.15 percent. The local custom and accuracy of rate information will decide such matters. The examples given represent selection of a discount rate to the nearest quarter of a percent.

Recapture of Capital Invested in Improvements

A real estate investor is interested in a return on his investment (discount) and a return of his investment. Recapture is the provision for returning to the investor a sum of money equal to the improvement value at the end of a given period of time. The investor is entitled to recover only the portion of his investment in the building during its economic life, since the land is a nonwasting asset and will have a residual value at the end of the building life. The rate for recapture is the second part of the total capitalization rate and may be selected by two methods: the economic-life method and the market comparison method.

Economic-Life Method. The economic-life method requires that a judgment be made as to the number of years the building will continue to produce income and, in effect, add value to the land. This judgment will be influenced by the actions of investors and lenders, which will determine how long investors are willing to allow their capital to be tied up in a particular project and how long lenders are willing to make mortgage commitments for the properties in question.

For example, assume that a study of comparable properties and information obtained from investors and lenders indicate that the remaining economic life of the subject building is twenty-five years. The indicated annual recapture rate for the building can be found by dividing 1 by 25 years:

$$\frac{1}{25 \text{ years}} = 0.04 \text{ per year}.$$

This simply means that 4 percent of the building value should be recovered each year on a straight-line basis; in other words, lenders will lend money and investors will invest equity money in this type of property for twenty-five years. It also means that, on the basis of experience with comparable properties, twenty-five years appears to be the typical recovery period for capital invested in the building.

Market Comparison Method. The second method used to select the proper recapture rate is similar to the method used to select the discount rate: net income after taxes and discount is divided by the building value to give a percentage.

Sale price	$150,000
Land value	$ 50,000
Discount rate	10%
Net income before recapture but after taxes	$ 17,000

By using the formula "rate times value equals income," the income necessary to satisfy a discount rate of 10 percent can be found:

$$\$150,000 \times 10 \text{ percent} = \$15,000 \, .$$

If $15,000 of the net income is discount, the remainder of the income represents recapture. Therefore, the recapture rate can be found by using the formula "income divided by value equals rate." Only the building value is used.

$$\frac{\$2,000}{\$100,000} = 0.02 \, .$$

The recapture rate is 2 percent.

Effective Tax Rate

The effective tax rate is the third component of the total capitalization rate. It is determined by multiplying the level of assessment for the property by the local current tax rate. In chapter 10, it was indicated that property taxes could be considered an expense item but that it was preferable appraisal practice to develop an effective tax rate. Consideration needs to be given to the tax rate structure prior to reaching this conclusion.

The local tax rate structure may vary from one taxing jurisdiction to another. Some jurisdictions refer to the rate as dollars per hundred, while others use millage or dollars per thousand. The assessment ratio will also differ, depending on the jurisdiction and possibly the class of property under assessment. When full-value assessments are referred to, the assessed value is theoretically equal to the market value. When the assessment is computed using a percentage, the result is a fractional assessment.

An *assessment ratio* is the ratio of assessed value to full market value. An assessment ratio can be demonstrated as follows: a new retail-store building just sold for $100,000; if the assessment is $40,000, the assessment ratio can be calculated by dividing the assessed value of $40,000 by the sale price of $100,000. The resulting ratio is 40 percent ($40,000 ÷ $100,000).

In considering the income and expenses of a property, a decision must be made regarding the property taxes. When property is valued for ad valorem tax purposes, taxes should not be considered an expense item. Since any deduction from gross income directly affects the indicated property value through the income approach, only typical and reasonable expenses can be used. It might be questioned how a typical and reasonable figure for taxes can be found when taxes are normally based on the property value itself. Furthermore, taxes are assessed annually on the basis of the property value, the level of assessment, and the current tax rate or millage. What figures should be used if the property is new and must be assessed for the first time, if taxes have increased rapidly for the past few years, or if the property is not equitably assessed?

When the income approach is used to determine the property value for tax purposes, the practice of using property taxes as an expense item is based on a preconceived value and discredits the whole approach. Since taxes are often the largest single expense, this practice leaves the final value conclusion subject to considerable error. The problem can be resolved by developing an effective tax rate and by including the rate in the capitalization rate for the property under appraisal.

The effective tax rate for a property expresses the relationship between the property value and the tax bill. For example, a properly assessed retail-store building with a value of $125,000 has a tax bill of $3,000. The effective tax rate is 2.4 percent:

$$\frac{\$3,000 \text{ (tax bill)}}{\$125,000 \text{ (property value)}} = 0.024 \ .$$

This demonstrates that owners of equitably assessed property will pay 2.4 percent of the property value in taxes this year.

Using the same figures, we may arrive at the rate 2.4 percent by multiplying the level of assessment by the tax rate. Assuming that commercial property is assessed at 40 percent of market value and that the tax rate is $6 per hundred, or 0.06, we have

$$0.40 \times 0.06 = 0.024 .$$

The effective tax rate can be developed for any class of property in a jurisdiction by multiplying the appropriate level of assessment by the current tax rate expressed as a decimal or a percentage. The resulting value conclusion is not prejudiced by a predetermined value judgment as it is when taxes are included as an expense item. When the same information is used for a given property, the result will be the same regardless of whether the taxes are subtracted from gross income as an expense or are included in the capitalization rate as an effective tax rate. This assumes that the taxes are based on a correct assessment, that the same tax rate is used, and that the same land and building values are used.

Table 11.1 presents an example demonstrating the validity of treating the real estate tax expense as an effective tax rate. The example in column 1 is a building residual technique problem worked with an effective tax rate included as part of the capitalization rate for both land and building. The example in column 2 is the same problem with real estate taxes as a deduction from effective gross income and assumes that the tax of $2,833 is the result of a proper assessment. This method prejudices the results, since an assumption must be made regarding the value before a determination can be made that $2,833 is a reasonable and proper figure for taxes. The difference of $3 between the two examples is due to rounding in the mathematical process.

Table 11.1

Proof of Effective Tax Rate

(Land Value, $30,000; Discount Rate, 9.0%; Recapture Rate, 2.5%; Tax Rate, 2.3%)

	Using Effective Tax Rate (1)	Using Taxes as Expenses (2)
Effective gross income	$ 25,000	$ 25,000
Less operating expenses (35%)	8,750	8,750 (35%)
Less real estate taxes.................	0	2,833 ($123,188 × 0.023)
Net income before recapture	$ 16,250	$ 13,417
Less net income imputable to land ($30,000 × 0.113)	3,390	2,700 ($30,000 × 0.09)
Income imputable to building	$ 12,860	$ 10,717
Building value ($12,860 ÷ 0.138)	$ 93,188	$ 93,191 ($10,717 ÷ 0.115)
Plus land value	30,000	30,000
Property value	$123,188	$123,191

As previously discussed, the discount rate, the recapture rate, and the effective tax rate comprise the elements of the capitalization rate for the income approach. Using as an example a property having a value of $85,000, of which $65,000 is building value and $20,000 land value, application of appropriate rates can indicate the total net income required to satisfy the investment and the component dollar totals of the net income.

$85,000 (property value) × 0.1025 (discount rate)	$ 8,712.50
$65,000 (building value) × 0.0200 (recapture rate)....	1,300.00
$85,000 (property value) × 0.0200 (effective tax rate) .	1,700.00
Total net income required	$11,712.50

Overall Capitalization Rate

The direct relationship between net income and the sale price or value can be expressed by an overall rate. This rate includes a provision for discount as well as recapture, even though land and building values are not separated. The overall rate is a weighted rate, in that the recapture rate is weighted by the land-to-building ratio. The result is a rate that is somewhat less than the rate for buildings but higher than the rate for land alone. When net income is derived from vacant land, the overall rate and the discount rate are the same. Although this is not a universal practice, when the overall rate is used the effective tax rate can be added to the overall rate and taxes not included as an expense.

The overall capitalization rate, then, expresses the relationship between the net income from the property before recapture but after taxes and the property value. For example, using the formula $R = I \div V$, if the value of a property is $90,000 and the net income before recapture but after taxes is $10,800, the overall capitalization rate is 12 percent:

$$\frac{\$10,800 \text{ (income)}}{\$90,000 \text{ (value)}} = 0.12 \text{ (rate)} .$$

Direct Capitalization. The overall rate is used in direct capitalization of both vacant land and improved property. *Direct capitalization* is the simplest of the five methods of capitalization (see chap. 12) and is very reliable when overall rates are selected from similar sale properties. To continue with the previous example, the net income is divided by the overall rate ($V = I \div R$):

$$\frac{\$9,000 \text{ (net income)}}{0.12 \text{ (overall rate)}} = \$75,000 \text{ (value)} .$$

As the following example illustrates, the net income used does not include taxes, since taxes have been subtracted. In actual practice, the dollar amount subtracted for taxes probably would be based on the most current tax bill with the knowledge of future increases.

The following sales then might be considered:

Sale	Sale Price	Net Income before Recapture and Taxes	Overall Rate (%)
1	$100,000	$11,500	11.5
2	75,000	9,000	12.0
3	120,000	14,000	11.7

The range of overall rates indicated from these three sales is 11.5–12 percent. In appraisal practice, the most comparable sale of the three would be selected and used as an overall rate to capitalize the income of the subject property into a value estimate. If the subject property has a net income before recapture of $10,500, and if sale 2 is the most comparable, the proper capitalization rate would be 12 percent *plus* the effective tax rate of, for example, 1.5 percent, for a total capitalization rate of 13.5 percent. The property value is then calculated as follows:

$$\frac{\$10,500 \text{ (income)}}{0.135 \text{ (rate)}} = \$77,778 \text{ (value)} .$$

If considerable sales data of this nature were consistently available, appropriate overall rates could be developed for all types of properties, and other methods of capitalization would be of little importance. Unfortunately, such reliable, verified sales data usually are not plentiful. Caution should be exercised in using this capitalization method. The comparability of the sale properties to the subject property must be analyzed internally, and there must be very similar land-to-building ratios in the sale properties and the subject properties.

Land-to-Building Ratio. In using the direct capitalization method, the overall rates developed from improved properties must never be used for vacant land. The overall rate for improved property includes recapture; the rate for land does not. Table 11.2 demonstrates the weighting effect of the land-to-building ratio on the overall rate.

The overall rate in this example falls exactly between the rate for land (11 percent) and the rate for building (15 percent). This is the case because half the property value is land and half is building. Since the land-to-building ratio is 1, the overall rate is the average of the two rates.

Table 11.2

Weighting Effect of Land-to-Building Ratio on Overall Rate
(Discount Rate, 9%; Recapture Rate, 4%; Effective Tax Rate, 2%)

Capitalization rate for land (9% + 2%)	11%
Capitalization rate for building (9% + 4% + 2%)	15%
Income to land ($100,000 × 0.11)	$ 11,000
Income to building	15,000
Net income before discount, recapture, and taxes	$ 26,000
Building value ($15,000 ÷ 0.15)	$100,000
Land value	100,000
Total value	$200,000
Overall rate demonstrated ($26,000 ÷ $200,000)	13%

The results can be proved as follows:

50% land value × 11% rate for land	5.5%
50% building value × 15% rate for building	7.5
Overall rate	13.0%

As the ratio of land to building is reduced, the overall rate will increase because of the recapture requirement of the improvements. When the land-to-building ratio changes from 1 to ⅓, the overall rate changes as follows:

25% land value × 11% rate for land	2.75%
75% building value × 15% rate for building	11.25
Overall rate	14.00%

In the case of vacant land, the overall rate and the land rate are the same, since no recapture provision is necessary.

100% land value × 11% rate for land	11%
Zero building value × 15% rate for building	0
Overall rate	11%

The following example shows that, even though two properties may have the same sale price, the ratio of land to building will affect the overall rate demonstrated by the property even when the discount rate and the rate of recapture are the same. Therefore, overall rates for improved properties must be selected from properties having comparable land-to-building ratios.

	Sale A	Sale B
Sale price	$200,000	$200,000
Land value	$100,000	$ 50,000
Building value	$100,000	$150,000
Discount rate	10%	10%
Recapture rate (20 years)	5%	5%
Discount on land and building	$ 20,000	$ 20,000
Recapture dollars	5,000	7,500
Total net income required	$ 25,000	$ 27,500
Overall rate	12.50%	13.75%

It should be noted that, as the ratio of building value to the total property increases, more net income is necessary to satisfy the additional recapture requirement.

Other Factors Affecting Overall Rate. In addition to land-to-building ratios, other factors affecting overall rates in direct capitalization include income-and-expense ratios, the remaining economic life of the buildings, the correlation of sale price with market value, and the period of time in which the sale and the income are established.

Income-and-Expense Ratios. The income-and-expense ratios for the sale properties should be similar to ratios for the property under appraisal. The following example shows that two sales with comparable gross incomes and resulting identical gross rent multipliers have substantially different overall capitalization rates due to a difference in the ratio of expenses.

	Property A	Property B
Gross income	$ 50,000	$ 50,000
Expenses	15,000 (30%)	20,000 (40%)
Net income	$ 35,000	$ 30,000
Sale price	$310,000	$310,000
Gross rent multiplier	6.2	6.2
Overall rate	11.29%	9.7%

This example illustrates the danger in using the gross rent multiplier without regard for operating expenses when the properties are not comparable with respect to income-and-expense ratios.

Remaining Economic Life. The remaining economic life of the improvements must be comparable between the sale properties and the subject property. The following illustration shows how a change in the recapture rate affects the overall rate.

Table 11.3
Effect of Change in Recapture Rate on Overall Rate
(Building Value, 80%; Land Value 20%)

	Estimated Remaining Economic Life (Years)			
	25	*30*	*40*	*50*
Annual recapture rate ...	4.0%	3.3%	2.5%	2.0%
Discount rate	9.0	9.0	9.0	9.0
Building capitalization rate	13.0%	12.3%	11.5%	11.0%
Building component of overall rate	10.4%	9.84%	9.2%	8.8%
Land component of over-all rate (20% of total value at 9% discount rate)	1.8	1.8	1.8	1.8
Overall rate	12.2%	11.64%	11.0%	10.6%

This example illustrates the following:

- As the remaining building life increases, the recapture rate decreases.
- The remaining economic life and resulting recapture rate cause a weighting of the overall rate based on the land-to-building ratio. The weighting results in a higher overall rate as the ratio of building to land increases.
- As the remaining economic life decreases, the overall rate increases (a shorter recapture period requires a higher annual recapture percentage).

Correlation of Sale Price with Market Value. The sales used in developing the overall rate must be verified, and the sale price must represent market value for the property. The following example demonstrates the effect on the overall rate of a sale in which an uninformed buyer pays more than market value for a property.

Discount Rate, 9%; Recapture Rate, 2%; Effective Tax Rate, 2%

Property value	$100,000
Net income before discount, recapture, and taxes	$ 12,000
Overall rate (12,000 ÷ $100,000)	12%
Land value	$ 50,000

Assume that an uninformed buyer pays $120,000 for the property, believing that the land is worth $60,000 and the building $60,000. The overall rate then becomes 10 percent: $12,000 ÷ $120,000 = 0.10.

Rent and Sale. The following illustration demonstrates that, when the rent and the sale price are not negotiated during the same period of time, the relationship between the two may not reflect the proper overall capitalization rate for other properties. The net income and the sale price used to develop the overall rate must represent the market for the same period of time. For example, a property that sold two years ago and is not rented might, on the basis of a recently negotiated lease, indicate an overall rate as follows:

Sale price (2 years ago)	$200,000
Net income (based on new lease)	$ 30,000
Overall capitalization rate ($30,000 ÷ $200,000)	15%

Assume that the net income was $25,000 at the time of sale based on the belief that $25,000 was market rent. The overall rate indicated is therefore 12.5 percent: $25,000 ÷ $200,000 = 0.125.

Summary

This chapter has dealt with the sixth step in the income approach to value: selection of the proper capitalization rate. An understanding of the capitalization rate and its components is essential to utilization of the capitalization methods and techniques described in the following chapter. Knowledge of the development of the discount rate, the recapture rate, and the effective tax rate is primary to the understanding of income-producing property as an investment. To reach a final value conclusion in the income approach, future income and the value indication must be linked, and the link is the capitalization rate. The capitalization rate and formulas can be summarized as follows:

Basic Formulas

There are three basic capitalization formulas for arriving at income, value, and rate.
1. $V = I \div R$—value equals income divided by rate.
2. $R = I \div V$—rate equals income divided by value.
3. $I = R \times V$—income equals rate times value.

Discount Rate

The discount rate is the first component of a capitalization rate and is the rate of return on a real estate investment. It can be developed by two methods.
1. Band-of-investment method—includes consideration of the interest rate paid by the investor on the first mortgage, the interest rates paid on additional mortgages, and the anticipated yield on equity.
2. Market comparison method—involves dividing the net income after recapture and after real estate taxes for a comparable property by its sale price.

Recapture Rate

Recapture is the provision for returning to the investor a sum of money equal to the improvement value at the end of a given period of time. It may be selected by two methods.
1. Economic-life method—requires a judgment as to the number of years the building will produce income and add value to the land.
2. Market comparison method—obtains rate by dividing net income after discount and taxes by the building value.

Effective Tax Rate

The effective tax rate is the third component of a capitalization rate. It may be determined in two ways.

1. Relationship between property value and tax bill—tax bill is divided by property value.

2. Relationship between level of assessment and tax rate —level of assessment is multiplied by tax rate.

Overall Capitalization Rate

The overall capitalization rate gives the direct relationship between the sale price or value and net income; it is used in direct capitalization and is affected by a number of factors.

1. Direct capitalization—the simplest of the methods of capitalization; reliable under certain circumstances.

2. Land-to-building ratio—the ratio of land to building affects the overall rate although sales have same sale price, recapture rate, and discount rate.

3. Other factors affecting overall rate—income-and-expense ratios, remaining economic life of improvements, and correlation of sale price with market value.

12 The Income Approach: Capitalization Procedures

The final steps in the income approach to value are the determination of the appropriate capitalization procedures (methods and techniques) and the subsequent capitalization of net income into an estimated value. The five methods of capitalization discussed in this chapter are the straight-line, sinking-fund, annuity, mortgage-equity, and direct methods. The first three methods are typically employed with the traditional residual techniques—land residual, building residual, and property residual.

In making a decision as to which method to use, it should once again be kept in mind that real estate is an investment and that the expectations of the investor are of prime importance.

The Income Stream

Investments in real estate are expected to produce income payments as well as property reversion. In other words, the owner of income-producing property anticipates receiving income for the lease period and also getting back the property at the end of the lease (*reversion,* which is the return of the rights in real estate to the grantor, e.g., lessor).

In determining which capitalization procedures to use,

the following should be considered relative to the income stream: quantity, quality, durability, and shape. The first three considerations were discussed in chapter 11: quantity refers to the amount of rent, quality to the credit rating of the tenants, and durability to the length of time rent will be paid. To this can be added the shape of the income stream—whether the payments are declining, increasing, or level.

Listed below are the ways in which an investor realizes his investment, depending on the shape and duration of the income stream.

1. *Level perpetual series*—The owner of the land expects equal periodic payments (rent) as long as the land is owned. Since land is a nonwasting asset and is expected to last indefinitely, the income from land is assumed to be perpetual.

2. *Level terminal series*—The word "terminal" implies that the rent payments will stop after the building reaches the end of its economic life. The owner of improved property expects equal periodic payments as long as the building lasts and is leased to a quality tenant.

3. *Declining terminal series*—The owner of improved property expects declining periodic payments terminating at the end of the lease or when the building has no remaining economic life. The decision as to whether the income stream is level or declining is influenced by the type of property, the financial strength of the tenant, and the terms and length of the lease.

4. *Single future-income payment*—The owner expects to get the property back at the end of the lease and then "cash out," or sell. Also, an investor may buy property "to hold" and sell at some future date, hoping for appreciation and profit from the single future-income payment.

Combinations of income streams and reversions may be undertaken. For example, a property under lease to a quality tenant would be expected to produce a level terminal series of rent payments (item 2 above) and a single future-income payment reversion (item 4) at the end of the lease period. This type of income would probably call for the annuity capitalization method and the land, building, or property residual techniques. Another example would be the combination of items 3 and 4. If the income is declining and is expected to terminate and if a reversion is anticipated at some time in the future, the method of capitalization to be used would typically be straight line.

Chart 12.1 shows the shape and duration of income streams with the corresponding appropriate capitalization procedures.

Chart 12.1

Capitalization Procedures for Different Income
Stream Characteristics

Income Stream Characteristics	*Application Indicated*
Appraisal Date	
LEVEL PERPETUAL	Direct capitalization of land
— — — — — Infinity	
LEVEL TERMINAL	1. Annuity capitalization with land, building, and property residual techniques
———Economic life———	2. Sinking-fund capitalization with land, building, and property residual techniques 3. Mortgage-equity capitalization
DECLINING TERMINAL	Straight-line capitalization with land, building, and property residual techniques
Economic life	
SINGLE FUTURE PAYMENT	1. Straight-line, sinking-fund, and annuity capitalization with property residual techniques (reversion of the land)
(Future income)	2. Value of the investment land

Selection of Capitalization Methods

The method of capitalization selected has a dramatic effect on the value produced by the income approach. The choice of the method should never be based on the predetermined idea of a low or high value but rather should depend on the character of the income produced by the property.

The three capitalization methods discussed in this section are the straight-line, sinking-fund, and annuity methods. Since direct and mortgage-equity capitalization methods are unique in many respects, they are discussed at the end of the chapter as alternate methods (see also chap. 11 for direct capitalization and the overall rate).

Straight-Line Capitalization

This method is appropriate under the following set of circumstances: (1) the tenant ranks financially average or poor on a scale of good, average, poor; (2) the lease is month to month or short term; (3) the income is likely to decline over the economic life of the improvement; (4) the building will be recaptured in equal amounts over its economic life; (5) the discount will be received each year on the remaining balance of the investment.

The following example explains what happens to the investment and the income when straight-line capitalization is used. Assume a property with a building value of $150,000 and land value of $50,000. The discount rate is 9 percent and the recapture rate 2.5 percent. Real estate taxes have been accounted for. The net income required is demonstrated in table 12.1.

This example demonstrates three characteristics of properties that are correctly appraised using straight-line capitalization: (1) income decreases as the property gets older, (2) recapture is received in equal amounts (straight

Table 12.1

Straight-Line Capitalization Method

	Value (1)	Rate (2)	Income [(1) × (2)] (3)
Land	$ 50,000	0.09	$ 4,500 Discount
Building	150,000	0.09	13,500 Discount
Building	150,000	0.025	3,750 Recapture
Net income ...	...	...	$21,750

Building (no land)		$150,000
Discount 9%	$13,500	
Recapture 2.5%	3,750	− 3,750
First-year income	$17,250	
Building (end of first year)		$146,250
Discount 9%	$13,163	
Recapture 2.5%	3,750	− 3,750
Second-year income	$16,913	
Building (end of second year)		$142,500
Discount 9%	$12,825	
Recapture 2.5%	3,750	− 3,750
Third-year income	$16,575	
Building (end of third year)		$138,750
Discount 9%	$12,488	
Recapture 2.5%	3,750	− 3,750
Fourth-year income	$16,238	
Building (end of fourth year)		$135,000
Discount 9%	$12,150	
Recapture 2.5%	3,750	− 3,750
Fifth-year income	$15,900	
Building (end of fifth year)		$131,250

line) over the life of the building, and (3) discount is received on the balance of the investment.

When the straight-line capitalization method is used, the three residual techniques may be employed. The rate for land includes the discount rate and the effective tax rate. The rate for building includes the total rate for land plus the recapture rate.

Rate for Land		Rate for Buildings	
Discount rate	9%	Discount rate	9%
Effective tax rate	2	Effective tax rate	2
Capitalization rate	11%	Recapture rate	3
		Capitalization rate	14%

Sinking-Fund Capitalization

The sinking-fund method of capitalization produces a mathematical result somewhat higher than the straight-line method as a result of the treatment of the recapture provision and a projected level net income stream. In this method it is assumed that, as the recapture is received, the amount is invested in a sinking fund at a safe rate (rate of return that a deposit can earn with minimum risk). A *sinking fund* is an account which can be used as a provision for the recapture of an asset and which accumulates interest on a compound basis for the periodic deposits made to the account. Since the recapture "grows" because of the periodic deposits and the compounded interest earned, the recapture rate required to recover the investment over a given period of time is less than the recapture rate for straight-line capitalization.

The example shown in table 12.2 will help to explain what happens to the investment and the income when the sinking-fund method is used. Assume that a property is purchased for $200,000 and that the building is worth $150,000. If the discount rate is 9 percent and the recapture period is forty years, the net income required is $18,969.

As demonstrated in this example, the sinking-fund capitalization method should be used under the following circumstances: (1) the income is constant (level), (2) the recapture is invested at a safe rate in a sinking fund, and (3) discount is received each year on the total original investment in the depreciating asset.

This method of capitalization with a built-in 3 percent safe rate is sometimes called the Hoskold method of capitalization. Critics of the method assert that the assumption regarding the investment of the recapture amount in a sinking fund is unrealistic and not typical of real estate investors. The method is gaining acceptance,

Table 12.2
Sinking-Fund Capitalization Method

	Value (1)	Rate (2)	Income [(1) × (2)] (3)
Land......................	$ 50,000	0.09	$ 4,500 Discount
Building	150,000	0.09	13,500 Discount
Building	150,000	0.006462	969 Recapture
Net income	...	...	$18,969

Sinking-fund deposit: $150,000 × 0.006462 = $969

Year	Income	9% Discount	Sinking- Fund Deposit	Interest	Accumu- lation	Remaining Building Investment
0	...	...	...	...	...	$150,000
1	$14,469	$13,500	$969	$ 0	$ 969	149,031
2	14,469	13,500	969	58	1,996	148,004
3	14,469	13,500	969	120	3,085	146,915
4	14,469	13,500	969	185	4,239	145,761
5	14,469	13,500	969	254	5,462	144,538
· ·	· · · ·	· · ·	· · · ·	· · ·	· · ·	· · · · ·
40			Continues through year 40			

Notes to Table 12.2

1. The recapture rate is taken from the sinking-fund table for 6 percent and forty years. Since 6 percent is believed to be a safe rate and the recapture rate represents forty years of remaining life, the factor has both of these considerations built in. See the compound interest tables in the Appendix.

2. The recapture amount for the second year includes $969 plus the interest earned on $969 in the sinking fund for one year at 6 percent. The interest on $969

at 6 percent for one year is $58.14 and is rounded to $58 for this example. The total recapture through the second year is, therefore, $969 (the sinking-fund deposit for the first year) plus $58 (the sinking-fund interest) plus the sinking-fund deposit for the second year ($969), or $1,996.

3. The recapture amount through the third year includes three deposits of $969 plus interest of $58 the second year and $120 the third year.

however, and is currently the best-known method for use with mineral properties. The methodology closely corresponds to the conditions that seem to exist when investments are made in mineral deposits: as the mineral deposit is depleted, the recapture provision should provide a return of the the investment, enabling the investor to buy another mineral property when it is depleted.

As demonstrated later in the chapter, the sinking-fund method of capitalization can be used with the land, building, and property residual techniques.

Annuity Capitalization

The annuity capitalization method produces a higher result than the sinking-fund method and a substantially higher result than straight-line capitalization. For example, assume that a property is purchased for $200,000, that the building is valued at $150,000, the discount rate is 9 percent, and the recapture period is forty years. The income required for the building is $13,944.

$150,000 (value) ÷ 10.7574 (factor) = $13,944 (income).

The first year's income requirement in this example is calculated by using the Inwood coefficient found on the 9 percent table for 40 years (10.7574). The Inwood coefficient is the present worth of 1 per period (col. 5 of compound interest tables).

Table 12.3
Annuity Capitalization Method

Year	Income (1)	Discount (2)	Recapture [(1) − (2)] (3)	Remaining Building Investment (4)
0	...	...	...	$150,000
1	$13,944	$13,500	$444	149,556
2	13,944	13,460	484	149,072
3	13,944	13,416	528	148,544
4	13,944	13,369	575	147,969
5	13,944	13,317	627	147,342
. . . .				
40	Continues through year 40			

When a factor or coefficient is used instead of a rate to compute value, the following formula is used: value = income × factor. If V = value, I = income, and F = factor, the three formulas derived from this relationship are $V = I \times F$, $I = V \div F$, and $F = V \div I$.

The following conclusions can be made regarding annuity capitalization: (1) the income stream is level; (2) the discount amount decreases, since the discount is on the remaining building value; and (3) the recapture rate increases by the amount that the discount decreases.

The annuity capitalization method may be selected if the following circumstances are assumed: (1) the property is in a prime location, (2) the improvements are modern and appropriate for the land, (3) the property is leased under a long-term lease at economic or market rent, (4) the lease provisions are favorable to the landlord, and (5) the tenant is financially sound. Like the sinking-fund and straight-line methods, the annuity method may be used with all three residual techniques.

Summary of Methods Selection

A summary of the results of the three capitalization methods reveals the following.

Straight-line method—lowest value

Sinking-fund method—midrange value

Annuity method—highest value

Chart 12.2 summarizes the behavior of the income stream with respect to income, discount, and recapture,

Chart 12.2

Income Stream Behavior and the Selection of Capitalization Methods

Straight-Line	Sinking-Fund	Annuity

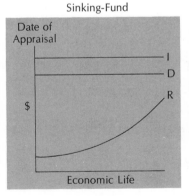 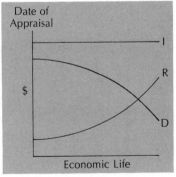

1. Income decreases as property age increases.
2. Recapture is received in equal amounts during the economic life of the improvement.
3. Discount is received on the balance of the investment.

1. Income remains constant over time.
2. Recapture is invested at a safe rate in a sinking fund.
3. Discount is received each year on the total original investment in the depreciating asset.

1. Income remains constant over time.
2. Discount based on remaining life of improvement and decreases over time.
3. Recapture increases by the amount that discount decreases.

together with assumptions made when selecting the straight-line, sinking-fund, or annuity method.

Selection of Capitalization Techniques

There are three residual techniques commonly used in the income approach to value: (1) building residual technique, (2) land residual technique, and (3) property residual technique. The use of the term *residual* implies that, after income requirements are satisfied for the known parts of the property, the residual, or remaining, income is processed into an indication of value for the unknown part.

The selection of the proper technique will be based upon the information available and the type of property being appraised. For example, if the subject property is improved with an old building and the land value can be reasonably determined from comparable sales, the building residual technique will probably be selected. Simply stated, if the building value is known, the land residual technique typically will be used; conversely, if the land value is known, the building residual technique will be employed. When neither the land nor the building value can be estimated, the property residual technique is likely to be used.

Building Residual Technique

This technique is commonly used when the land value is known and can be well documented with sales of comparable land. The technique is especially useful for old buildings where cost and depreciation are difficult to support in the cost approach to value. Of course, the technique can also be used to check the value indicated by the cost approach on new buildings. To process a building residual technique, the following must be known: (1) the net income, (2) the land value, (3) the proper discount rate, (4) the proper recapture rate, and (5) the effective tax rate.

Table 12.4 shows the building residual technique using straight-line, sinking-fund, and annuity methods of capitalization. Note that the result of the straight-line example is somewhat lower than the results of the sinking-fund and annuity methods.

Land Residual Technique

The land residual technique is ordinarily used when the building value is known and when there are no unimproved land sales to support the land value. In order for the technique to be valid, the building must be new and it must represent the highest and best use of the land. This residual technique is used typically with all three capitalization methods. Information necessary to process a land residual technique problem includes (1) the net income, (2) the building value, (3) the proper discount rate, (4) the proper recapture rate, and (5) the effective tax rate.

Table 12.5 demonstrates the land residual technique using all three capitalization methods.

Property Residual Technique

The property residual technique is normally used when neither land nor building value can be estimated reliably. This technique, demonstrated in table 12.6, treats the net income directly, relating the income to the total property value without giving consideration to separation of land or building from the total property value. In annuity

Table 12.4

Examples of Building Residual Technique

Straight-Line Capitalization

Net income before recapture and real estate taxes	$10,000
Income to land ($40,000 × 0.11 [0.09 discount + 0.02 effective tax rate])	4,400
Income attributable to building	$ 5,600

Capitalization rate:

Discount rate	9%	
Recapture (33 years)	3	
Effective tax rate	2	
Total	14%	
Building value ($5,600 ÷ 0.14)		$40,000
Plus land value		40,000
Property value		$80,000

Sinking-Fund Capitalization

Net income before recapture and real estate taxes	$10,000
Income to land ($40,000 × 0.11 [0.09 discount + 0.02 effective tax rate])	4,400
Income attributable to building	$ 5,600

Capitalization rate:

Discount rate	0.0900	
Recapture (factor for 6% sinking fund, 33 years)	0.01027	
Effective tax rate	0.02000	
Total	0.12027	
Building value ($5,600 ÷ 0.12027)		$46,562
Plus land value		40,000
Property value		$86,562

Annuity Capitalization

Net income before recapture and real estate taxes	$10,000
Income to land ($40,000 × 0.11 [0.09 discount + 0.02 effective tax rate])	4,400
Income attributable to building	$ 5,600

Capitalization rate:

Inwood factor at 9% discount for 33 years .	10.464	
Reciprocal of Inwood factor 10.464		0.09556
Partial payment factor	0.09556	
Effective tax rate	0.02000	
Total	0.11556	
Building value ($5,600 ÷ 0.11556)		$48,460
Plus land value		40,000
Property value		$88,460

Note to Table 12.4

The Inwood factor is the present worth of 1 per period, found in column 5 of the compound interest tables. Since the partial payment factor in column 6 is the reciprocal of the Inwood factor, the partial payment factor can be used as a rate and added to the tax rate when the annuity capitalization method is used. If 1 is divided by the Inwood factor for 9 percent and thirty-three years (10.464), the resulting reciprocal is the partial payment factor (0.09556).

Table 12.5
Examples of Land Residual Technique

Straight-Line Capitalization

Net income before recapture and real estate taxes		$10,000
Capitalization rate:		
Discount rate	9%	
Recapture (33-year life)	3	
Effective tax rate	2	
Total	14%	
Income attributable to building ($40,000 × 0.14)		5,600
Income attributable to land		$ 4,400
Land value ($4,400 ÷ 0.11 [0.09 discount + 0.02 effective tax rate])		$40,000
Plus building value		40,000
Property value		$80,000

Sinking-Fund Capitalization

Net income before recapture and real estate taxes		$10,000
Capitalization rate:		
Discount rate	0.09000	
Recapture (6% sinking fund, 33 years)	0.01027	
Effective tax rate	0.02000	
Total	0.12027	
Income attributable to building ($46,562 × 0.12027)		5,600
Income attributable to land		$ 4,400
Land value ($4,400 ÷ 0.11 [0.09 discount + 0.02 effective tax rate])		$40,000
Building value		46,562
Property value		$86,562

Annuity Capitalization

Net income before recapture and real estate taxes			$10,000
Capitalization rate:			
Inwood factor at 9% discount for 33 years		10.464	
Reciprocal of Inwood factor 10.464		0.09556	
Partial payment factor	0.09556		
Effective tax rate	0.02000		
Total	0.11556		
Income attributable to building ($48,460 × 0.11556)			5,600
Income attributable to land			$ 4,400
Land value ($4,400 ÷ 0.11 [0.09 discount + 0.02 effective tax rate])			$40,000
Plus building value			48,460
Property value			$88,459

Table 12.6

Examples of the Property Residual Technique

Straight-Line Capitalization

Net income before recapture and real estate taxes	$10,000.00
Reversion ($40,000 × 0.0582 [9% for 33 years])	2,328.00
Net income (10,000 − $46.56 [$2,328 × 0.02 effective tax rate = $46.56])	9,953.44
$71,096 ($9,953.44 [net income] ÷ 0.14) + $2,328 (reversion)	$73,424.00

Proof:

$73,424 × 0.02 = $1,468.48

Net income before recapture and taxes	$10,000.00
Taxes	1,468.48
Net income before recapture	$ 8,531.52

$71,096 ($8,531.52 ÷ 0.12) + $2,328 (reversion) $73,424.00

Sinking-Fund Capitalization

Net income before recapture and real estates taxes ...	$10,000.00
Reversion ($40,000 × 0.0582 [9% for 33 years])	2,328.00
Net income ($10,000 − $46.56 [$2,328 × 0.02 effective tax rate = $46.56])	9,953.44

Capitalization rate:

Discount rate	0.09000
Recapture (factor for 6% sinking fund, 33 years)	0.01027
Effective tax rate	0.02000
Total	0.12027

$82,759 ($9,953.44 ÷ 0.12027) + $2,328 (reversion) .. $85,087.00

Proof:

$85,087 × 0.02 = $1,701.74

Net income before recapture and taxes	$10,000.00
Taxes	1,701.74
Net income before recapture	$ 8,298.26

$82,759 ($8,298.26 ÷ 0.10027) + $2,328 (reversion) .. $85,087.00

Annuity Capitalization

Net income before recapture and real estate taxes	$10,000.00
Reversion ($40,000 × 0.0582 [9% for 33 years])	2,328.00
Net income adjusted for tax on reversion ($10,000 − $46.56 [$2,328 × 0.02 = $46.56])	9,953.44

Capitalization rate:

Inwood factor for 9% and 33 years 10.464	
Convert 10.464 to rate (reciprocal)	0.09556
Effective tax rate	0.02000
Total	0.11556

$86,132 ($9,953.44 ÷ 0.11556) + $2,328 (reversion) .. $88,460.00

---

capitalization the total net income before recapture is capitalized using the reciprocal of the appropriate Inwood factor. The partial payment factor can be used as a rate and added to the effective tax rate for the total capitalization rate. The land is assumed to have value at the end of the lease period, and the present worth of the land reversion can be calculated by discounting the anticipated land value at the end of the lease period to present worth using the "present worth of 1" column.

Alternate Capitalization Methods

There are two other capitalization methods which do not employ the residual techniques and which are rather specific with respect to their application: mortgage-equity capitalization and direct capitalization. Direct capitalization was covered extensively in chapter 11 and will be touched on only briefly in this section.

Mortgage-Equity Capitalization

The mortgage-equity method of capitalization has gained increasing acceptance over the years. The method takes various forms, from a relatively simple band of investment using the mortgage constant to a more sophisticated computation which considers that the yield to an equity position in a real estate investment will result from a series of cash-flow dividends during the term of the investment and growth or enhancement due to mortgage amortization to the extent that it exceeds any loss in the value of the property as a whole at the end of the investment period.

The basic form of the method is a band of investment

that selects an overall rate by using the mortgage constant (annual total debt service, including payments of interest and amortization expressed as a percentage of the amount of the loan) and the equity rate as the key ingredients. The following is an example:

80% first mortgage (9.5% interest, 25 years)	10.483%	8.386%
20% equity money	12.500	2.500
Overall rate	...	10.886%

The simple mortgage-equity band of investment is based on the investor's consideration that his annual recapture will be the amortization payments in the debt service. Each payment in a typical mortgage is composed of (1) interest on the outstanding balance of the debt and (2) repayment of a portion of the debt or borrowed amount.

In the above example, the current policy of lending institutions is to lend 80 percent of appraised value for properties that have the qualities of the one under appraisal for a period of twenty-five years at an interest rate of 9.5 percent calling for monthly payments.

Reference to the appropriate *monthly* compound interest table (partial payment—9.5 percent interest for twenty-five years) indicates a monthly constant of 0.008736, which is multiplied by 12 to produce the annual mortgage constant of 10.483 percent.

The remaining 20 percent of purchase price will come from the equity pocket of the investor, who needs a return of 12.5 percent to attract him to this investment, and market analysis indicates that this is an attainable rate of return. If a $100,000 property were the subject of this analysis, the following would be the annual net income requirement:

$80,000 (mortgage) × 10.483 percent

= $8,386 (total annual debt service);

$20,000 (equity) × 12.500 percent

= $2,500 (annual equity requirement;

Net income to satisfy this situation = $10,886.

This may be expressed more simply:

$100,000 (value) × 10.886 percent (overall rate)

= $10,886 (net income requirement).

If the normal real estate appraisal assignment were presented, the net income before recapture of $10,886 would be capitalized by the overall rate of 10.886 percent to render a value indication of $100,000. If a capitalization problem were presented so that the net income before recapture and before real estate taxes was calculated to be $12,886 and the overall rate was 10.886 percent, the effective tax rate of, for instance, 2 percent would be added for a total overall rate of 12.886 percent applied to the income of $12,886 for a value indication of $100,000. There is no consideration in this basic form of mortgage-equity capitalization of possible growth of the equity position in the investment.

Consider the situation in which a $100,000 property is purchased using an $80,000 first mortgage and $20,000 equity money. The property is held by the investor for ten years. During this time adequate net income is received to make monthly mortgage payments and provide an acceptable annual return on the equity investment. In addition, the value of the property during the ten-year ownership period either decreases, remains the same, or increases. It is reasonable to assume that investment in real estate during inflationary periods provides growth or capital gain in addition to periodic income (return *on* the investment).

Assume that the value of this property at the end of ten years remains at $100,000 and that the property is sold for this price. In the meantime the mortgage is being amortized, so that the balance is 75 percent of the original loan, or $60,000. What has happened to the equity position in the investment?

	Creation of Investment	Resale (Ten Years)
Mortgage balance ..	$ 80,000	$ 60,000
Equity position	20,000	40,000
Property value	$100,000	$100,000

The equity position in the investment has increased from $20,000 to $40,000, a result which the investor obviously considers in his investment decision. If the property value increases significantly to a level more than $100,000, the equity position is further enhanced. If there is a decrease in property value to $80,000, the equity position is not changed from the $20,000 level.

The more sophisticated forms of the mortgage-equity method of capitalization, therefore, take the potential change in equity position into consideration in the capitalization process. The Ellwood application, for instance, considers the following six items: (1) interest rate of loan, (2) term of loan, (3) ratio of loan to value, (4) anticipated term of ownership (holding period), (5) equity yield rate, and (6) anticipated property value change (appreciation or depreciation). Proved formulas (sometimes precomputed) affording the correct overall rate have been devised by Ellwood and others, reflecting the added effect of mortgage amortization and changes in equity position in an investment. The mechanics and complete theory of these forms are outside the scope of this text. However, an abbreviated example is as follows. Assume the following information:

Net income	$30,000	Ratio of loan	75%
Effective tax rate	2%	Holding period	19 years
Interest rate	9.5%	Equity yield rate	14%
Term of loan	25 years	Value change	0

The proper overall rate can be calculated to be 10.7299 percent. The effective tax rate of 2 percent is added, for a total overall rate of 12.7299 percent. Using the formula

$V = I \div R$, we have

$$\frac{\$30,000}{12.7299 \text{ percent}} = \$235,666 .$$

Direct Capitalization

Direct capitalization is the method used to convert net income from the property into an indication of property value using an overall rate developed from the market. The method does not consider the land separate from the building as do the land and building residual techniques.

An example of direct capitalization of land under the following assumptions is as follows:

Land Sale	Annual Rent (Net, Net, Net)	Rate Indicated
1. $80,000	$8,000	0.10
2. $60,000	6,000	0.10
3. $72,500	7,000	0.0965

If the land being appraised is leased for $7,750, direct capitalization could be used to produce a value of $77,500 based on an overall rate of 10 percent.

$$\frac{\$7,750 \text{ (income)}}{0.10 \text{ (rate)}} = \$77,500 \text{ (value)} .$$

Direct capitalization of improved property can be used in the same manner as in the example shown for land. The overall rate, however, must be developed from sales of improved properties that are highly comparable to the subject property. An important point to remember is that in all cases the subject property must be comparable in all respects to the sale properties; if it is not, the overall rate will be affected. This is discussed in depth in chapter 11.

DEMONSTRATION PROBLEM: NEIGHBORHOOD SHOPPING CENTER

The subject property is a shopping center with a 50,000-square-foot building that is twelve years old. The leases are short term, average $3 per square foot, and are mostly with local tenants. The vacancy and collection loss for comparable properties is about 6 percent. The owner has submitted the following expense statement.

Neighborhood Shopping Center
(Statement of Expenses, January 1–December 31)

Utilities	$ 16,920
Insurance (3 years)	2,100
Mortgage payment	87,560
Maintenance	4,406
Management	4,259
Real estate taxes	14,678
New roof (15-year life)	17,000
Painting (exterior every 4 years)	3,700
Advertising	1,876
Total expenses	$152,499

Lenders are typically willing to make first mortgages at 9 percent on 75 percent of the property value, second mortgages at 12 percent on 10 percent of the property. The 15 percent equity can be attracted at a rate of 14 percent. The remaining economic life for this type of property is fifteen years. The tax rate in the jurisdiction is $60 per $1,000 of assessed value, and commercial property is assessed at 40 percent. The land value, on the basis of comparable sales, is $150,000 ($1 per square foot × 150,000 square feet). On the basis of this information, the proper procedure would be that shown below.

Potential gross income (50,000 square feet × $3)			$150,000
Less vacancy and collection loss (6%)			9,000
Effective gross income			$141,000
Operating expenses:			
Insurance		$ 700	
Management		4,300	
Utilities		17,000	
Maintenance		4,400	
Advertising		1,900	
Roof reserve ($17,000 ÷ 15 years)		1,133	
Painting reserve ($3,700 ÷ 4 years)		925	
Heating and air conditioning ($15,000 ÷ 15 years)		1,000	
Painting (interior) reserve ($4,900 ÷ 3 years)		1,633	
Parking lot reserve ($30,000 ÷ 10 years) ...		3,000	
Total		$35,991	$ 35,991
Net income before discount, recapture, and taxes			$105,009

The capitalization method and technique must now be selected. Since the land value is known and the building appears to represent the highest and best use for the land, the building residual technique is judged appropriate. The straight-line method of capitalization should be used because of the short-term leases, the local tenants, and the age of the improvements. Therefore, we have the following:

Net income before discount, recapture, and taxes $105,009
Discount rate (by band of investment):
    75% first mortgage 0.0675
    10% second mortgage 0.0120
    15% equity at 14% 0.0210
                                       0.1005

Discount rate (rounded) .... 10 %
Effective tax rate (0.40 × 0.06) 2.4
Recapture rate (100% ÷ 25 years)..... 4
Rate for building 16.4
Rate for land (10% + 2.4%) 12.4
Income to land ($150,000 × 0.124) 18,600
Income residual to building .... $ 86,409

Building value ($86,409 ÷ 0.164) $526,884
Land value 150,000
Property value $676,884

Rounded to $677,000

Summary

The income approach to value is complete with the capitalization of net income into value by means of the appropriate capitalization procedures. The assessor must be familiar not only with the capitalization methods and techniques but also with the shape of the income stream and its effect upon the applicability of the various procedures. Following is a summary of the important aspects of the final steps in the income approach.

Income Stream

There are four ways in which an investor realizes his investment.
1. Level perpetual series—equal periodic payments.
2. Level terminal series—payments terminate after building reaches end of economic life.

3. Declining terminal series—declining periodic payments terminating when building reaches end of economic life.

4. Single future-income payment—single payment resulting from sale of property.

Capitalization Methods

The three capitalization methods employed with the residual techniques are the straight-line, sinking-fund, and annuity methods.

1. Straight-line method—discount rate applied to land value or income attributable to building; capitalization rate applied to building value or income attributable to building; effective tax rate applied with both rates.

2. Sinking-fund method—as recapture is received, the amount is invested in a sinking fund at a safe rate.

3. Annuity method—implies a level income received from an investment in a series of periodic payments that comprise return on and a partial return of capital.

Capitalization Techniques

The three techniques used in the income approach are the building residual, land residual, and property residual techniques.

1. Building residual—typically used when the land value is known and can be well documented.

2. Land residual—ordinarily used when the building value is known and when no unimproved land sales are available to support the land value.

3. Property residual—normally used when neither land nor building value can be reliably estimated.

Alternate Capitalization Methods

There are two methods that do not employ residual techniques: mortgage-equity and direct capitalization.

1. Mortgage-equity capitalization—takes various forms, from a simple band of investment to a computation which

considers that yield to an equity position will result from a series of cash-flow dividends during the term of the investment and growth due to mortgage amortization.

2. Direct capitalization—converts net income from the property into an indication of property value by using an overall rate developed from the market.

13 The Mass Appraisal Process

Mass appraisal is the process of valuing a universe of properties as of a given date, in a uniform order, utilizing standard methodology, employing a common reference for data, and allowing for statistical testing. As the vehicle of property tax assessment, the mass appraisal process has been the object of much misunderstanding and criticism. It is criticized as representing an arbitrary assigning of values to conglomerations of properties by an assessor from an unknowledgeable position and without the benefit of visitation. This misconception stems, in part, from labeling as "appraisals" the interim value adjustments made between reappraisal cycles. Clearly such adjustments are made with the intent of promoting equalization among and between property classes and represent attempts to satisfy statutory requirements.

The mass appraisal process does not warrant this criticism. The assessor's office has, in recent years, served as a leading source of property-related data. The professional assessor has knowledge of all valuation techniques and uses these techniques accurately. The modern mass appraisal system is producing value estimates within tolerances not thought possible ten years ago. Data in an assessment office are applied not to a few properties but to thousands, which puts the assessor in the position of developing what would otherwise be cost-prohibitive appraisal systems. The cost of such systems can be allocated over the thousands of properties that the assessor must re-value periodically. As a result of this economy of scale, assessment administrators are rapidly developing superior valuation systems, when contrasted to individual appraisal application.

Mass appraisal typically is governed by two jurisdictional parameters—legal and budgetary. As a result of these two major constraints, distortion and inequities tend to occur. It is therefore necessary to standardize techniques and procedures into a rational, equitable, and comprehensive system so that proper, objective policies can be achieved. Legal limitations set forth the policy objectives toward which the process operates, in addition to establishing the authority under which the appraisals are made. In addition, law usually dictates the procedure, purpose, and degree of sophistication found in the mass appraisal process. Budgetary limitations, on the other hand, depend on reality. The size of the jurisdiction, the importance given to policy objectives, and executive and political support of the process and effort define the feasibility of the appraisal techniques and organizational structures.

In previous chapters of this text, the appraisal process, the three approaches to value, and data collection and analysis have been dealt with in many cases with reference to their function and application to individual appraisals. Although it has been pointed out that the theories and techniques are as appropriate to mass appraisal as to individual appraisals, this chapter will demonstrate the special function which is the assessor's: a methodology varying considerably from that of the individual appraiser.

Establishing a Need for the Mass Appraisal Process

Property tax administrators agree that carrying over the "fee appraisal" techniques to the assessment field would provide an overabundance of information and be of questionable cost effectiveness to the taxpaying public, if budgets permitted. The benefits derived by the taxpayer would not justify the cost.

An effective mass appraisal provides a good valuation estimate quickly obtained and evidencing reasonable substantiation on forms or appraisal records that can be discussed with concerned taxpayers if the need arises. More important, a well-organized assessor's office is capable of responding to volatile real estate market conditions in periods of spiraling inflation, such as were experienced in the 1960s and 1970s. In periods of inflation the property tax can become extremely regressive if the assessor is unable to respond to value changes in the real estate market. Underlying most recent property tax legislation in this country is an unmistakable legislative intent to assure the taxpayer equality and fair treatment with respect to the property tax.

Figure 13.1 demonstrates the results of a relatively unsophisticated study of property values in a moderate-sized community. It demonstrates that although the general trend in property values is to increase, the rate of increase is directly related to location and socioeconomic conditions. Area A is an elite residential neighborhood characterized by newer, larger homes whose residents have an average annual income in excess of $20,000. Area B, on the other hand, is a transitional area of the city characterized by older, smaller homes, many of which are occupied by retired residents and residents with limited incomes. In addition, the incidence of unemployment for nonretired heads of households in this area is about five times that of Area A. The average selling price of a residence in Area A in the base year was $35,000, and value has increased over time on the average at the rate of $6,000 per year, resulting in an average value of $65,000 today. Area B residences had an average selling price of $12,000 in the base year, and value increased at the rate of

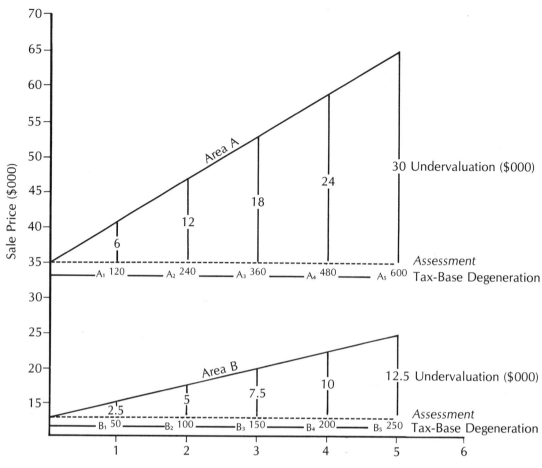

Fig. 13.1.—Demonstration of property tax regressivity. Note: 2 percent effective tax rate.

only $2,500 per year, resulting in a current value of $25,000 on the average. The dotted line in the figure represents the assessment. A measure of property tax regressivity is demonstrated in calculating $A_1 - B_1$, $A_2 - B_2$, and so forth. In year 5, for example, $A_5 - B_5 = \$600 - \$250 = \$350$. In other words, the lack of ability to respond to value change over time would result in tax avoidance of, on the average, $600 in Area A and $250 in Area B. The disparity between the dollars of tax avoidance—$600 in Area A as opposed to $250 in Area B—represents a shift in the tax burden from Area A to Area B, a fact which the aforementioned neighborhood evaluations make untenable. Only by revaluation can inequities of this type be controlled. Mass appraisal techniques provide a viable solution.

Statistics and Mass Appraisal

Although a technical treatment of the subject of statistics is beyond the scope of this chapter, it is necessary for the assessor to have a working knowledge of descriptive statistics, specifically measures of central tendency and measures of variability, in order to work effectively within the mass appraisal process.

In simple terms, descriptive statistics provide techniques for ordering data in meaningful ways, for condensing data with the objective of finding single values that typify the mass, and for determining measures of variability in the data mass and thereby allowing for evaluation of the reliability of calculated statistics.

The sales prices of twenty hypothetical properties are listed below. These sales will be referred to throughout this portion of the chapter.

$30,000	$27,600	$32,700	$29,700
$29,100	$27,000	$28,500	$28,500
$25,100	$28,700	$28,400	$28,700
$28,400	$28,000	$28,500	$31,500
$28,200	$27,700	$29,000	$28,900

Ordering Data: Arrays and Frequency Distributions

Among the easiest concepts in the analysis of mass data are the array and the frequency distribution. An array is merely a technique of arranging data, on an individual basis, in ascending or descending order based on magnitude. The twenty hypothetical sales might be arrayed in ascending order.

$25,100	$28,200	$28,500	$29,100
$27,000	$28,400	$28,700	$29,700
$27,600	$28,400	$28,700	$30,000
$27,700	$28,500	$28,900	$31,500
$28,000	$28,500	$29,000	$32,700

The frequency distribution condenses mass data into a more easily interpreted form. The following general rules apply to the formation of a frequency distribution: (1) determination of the range of the data, (2) division of the range into a workable number of class intervals of the same size, and (3) determination of the number of observations falling into each interval by using a tally or score sheet. A frequency distribution of our twenty hypothetical sales using $1,000 intervals is as follows:

Class Interval	Tally	Frequency
Less than 27,000	|	1
27,000–27,999	|||	3
28,000–28,999	⊪⊪ ⊪⊪	10
29,000–29,999	|||	3
30,000–30,999	|	1
31,000–31,999	|	1
32,000 and over	|	1

As the number of observations of sales increases, and if no bias exists, the sales can be expected to cluster about a central point referred to as a point of central tendency. If, in addition, the sales tend to array themselves graphically in a bell-shaped manner about the point of central tendency, it can be said that they represent a normal distribution. The importance of the concept of a normal distribution will become clear in this section.

Measures of Central Tendency

"Central tendency" refers to the tendency of the samples to cluster about a central point or representative value in a frequency distribution. Once the data have been organized into frequency distributions, they are ready for statistical analysis and a determination of the one value that best characterizes the entire frequency distribution. The measures of central tendency are the mean, the median, and the mode.

Mode. The mode is the simplest statistical measure of central tendency. It is defined as the most recurring or most frequently encountered value in a frequency distribution. In reference to the frequency distribution of the twenty hypothetical sales, the interval containing the largest number of sales is $28,500. This interval is said to be the modal interval.

Median. The median is the midpoint of the frequency distribution. It is the point above which and below which 50 percent of the values lie. If the number of samples appearing in the array is even, the median value is obtained by summing the middle two values and dividing by 2. The median in our example is $28,500.

Mean. The most common and well-understood measure of central tendency is the mean, or arithmetic average. It is calculated by dividing the sum of the individual values by the number of values involved. All observations enter into the calculation; therefore, the mean, unlike the mode and the median, is dramatically affected by extreme values at either the high or the low end. The mean of the hypothetical sales is $28,700.

Measures of Variability

The mean, median, and mode supply a single number that substitutes for the entire set of measurements from which they are derived. No single value indicator can be meaningfully interpreted, however, without some indication of the spread, or scatter, about that value. Variability relates to the scattering of the values of a frequency distribution from the measure of central tendency. The three most common measures of dispersion or data variability encountered in the assessment field are the range, the average absolute deviation, and the standard deviation.

Range. The range is the difference in value between the largest and smallest item. For the twenty sales, the range is equal to $32,700 minus $25,100, or $7,600. Although easily calculated (being dependent on only two items), the range is very much affected by extreme values. If a sale of $50,000 were introduced into our hypothetical sales, the range would react very strongly: $50,000 − $25,100 = $24,900.

Average Absolute Deviation. The average absolute deviation is the sum of the *absolute* (sign ignored) differences between the individual observations and the average of those observations, divided by the number of observations. (The absolute value of a quantity is the magnitude of the quantity irrespective of sign; e.g., if $X = -5$, the absolute value of X is 5.) It is important to note that the average absolute deviation can be calculated with respect to either median or mean. Column 5 of table 13.1 illustrates the calculation of the average absolute deviation from the mean sale price. In working with assessment-ratio data, however, it is probably preferable to calculate the average absolute deviation with respect to the median assessment/sale price ratio. This is partly because the median tends to provide a more stable measure of central tendency than the mean. It should also be noted that, for technical reasons, the average absolute deviation about the median is always less than or equal to the average absolute deviation about the mean.

The Standard Deviation. The standard deviation is another highly useful measure of variability. Technically,

Table 13.1

Calculation of Variance, Standard Deviation, and Average Absolute
Deviation from the Mean

Sale No. (1)	Sale Price ($000) (2)	Deviation from Mean ($000) (3)	Deviation Squared ($000) (4)	Absolute Deviation from the Mean ($000) (5)
1	25.1	−3.6	12.96	3.6
2	27.0	−1.7	2.89	1.7
3	27.6	−1.1	1.21	1.1
4	27.7	−1.2	1.44	1.2
5	28.0	−0.7	0.49	0.7
6	28.2	−0.5	0.25	0.5
7	28.4	−0.3	0.09	0.3
8	28.4	−0.3	0.09	0.3
9	28.5	−0.2	0.04	0.2
10	28.5	−0.2	0.04	0.2
11	28.5	−0.2	0.04	0.2
12	28.7	. . .	. . .	. . .
13	28.7	. . .	. . .	. . .
14	28.9	0.2	0.04	0.2
15	29.0	0.3	0.09	0.3
16	29.1	0.4	0.16	0.4
17	29.7	1.0	1.00	1.0
18	30.0	1.3	1.69	1.3
19	31.5	2.8	7.84	2.8
20	32.7	4.0	16.00	4.0
Total	574.2	0.0	46.36	20.0
Average	28.7	. . .	2.32	1.0

Mean, 28.7; median, 28.5
Variance, 2.32; standard deviation, $\sqrt{2.32} = 1.52$
Average absolute deviation, 1.0

the standard deviation is the square root of the average squared deviation from the mean. In other words, the deviations from the mean are squared, summed, and divided by the number of observations.[1] The result is the average squared deviation from the mean—a term referred to as *variance*. The standard deviation is the square root of the variance. Column 4 of table 13.1 illustrates the

1. In the generally used definitions of the variance and standard deviation, for technical reasons, the sum of the squared deviations is divided by the number of observations minus 1. The calculations in this chapter, however, will utilize the number of observations as the divisor.

procedures for calculating the variance and standard deviation. For our twenty sale properties, the variance is 2.32 and the standard deviation is 1.52.

The standard deviation has the important feature of utility in further statistical analyses. Both the source and the validity of this characteristic are derived from the normal distribution. The standard deviation satisfies the following relationships, provided that the data are normally distributed: (1) 68.26 percent of all values observed will be included in a band represented by the mean plus and minus 1 standard deviation; (2) 95.46 percent of all values observed will be included in a band represented by the mean plus and minus 2 standard deviations; and (3) 99.73 percent of all values observed will be included in a band represented by the mean plus and minus 3 standard deviations. It is important to bear in mind that these relationships depend on the assumption of a normal distribution.

A simple illustration will demonstrate what this means and what application there is to the mass appraisal process. Assume a hypothetical area characterized by a reasonable amount of homogeneity in relation to location, building, characteristics, and socioeconomic factors. Also assume the following:

• A sample of two hundred sales is collected, evidencing no bias and demonstrating a symmetrical pattern across a frequency distribution.
• The average selling price is $25.42 per square foot.
• The standard deviation of the sales sample is $0.72.

Knowing the above facts, the assessor is able to make inferences about unsold properties based on his knowledge of sales. For example, he is 99.73 percent confident, on the basis of knowledge of the relationship of the standard deviation to a normal distribution, that the value per square foot of an unsold property in the area should fall within the band represented by the mean, $25.42, plus or

minus $2.16 ($0.72 × 3), that is, between $23.26 and
$27.58. Similarly, he can be 95.46 percent confident that
the value falls in the band $23.96–26.86.

Measures of Relative Variability

Comparison of average absolute deviation and standard
deviation between two or more data sets is often very misleading. For example, if the average absolute deviation
from the median for one set of data is calculated to be
$2,500 and for another set is calculated to be $2,600, it
does not necessarily follow that both sets of data demonstrate like levels of relative variability. The $2,500 figure
might come from a sales sample of mostly $25,000 homes,
while the $2,600 figure comes from a sales sample of
mostly $50,000 homes. Clearly, relative variability is
greater in the first sales sample than in the second.

To make valid comparisons, it is necessary to convert
absolute measures of variability to relative measures. This
is accomplished by dividing absolute measures by the av-
erages or norms from which they are calculated.

Coefficient of Dispersion. The coefficient of dispersion is
the average absolute deviation from the mean or median
divided by the mean or median. In general, the coefficient
of dispersion is calculated about the median, and the term
"coefficient of dispersion" is taken to mean the average
absolute percentage deviation from the median. This is
not always the case, however. For this reason, it is helpful
to specify "coefficient of dispersion about the median" or
"coefficient of dispersion about the mean," whichever is
intended.

The coefficient of dispersion has long been accepted as
one of the prime indicators of the quality inherent in a
mass appraisal system. It has the advantage of being easily
understood, easy to compute, and not overly sensitive to
the effects of very low or very high values. As the average

absolute deviation from the mean (or median), it can be interpreted readily regardless of whether the data are normally distributed. Although, because of varying jurisdictional problems, no definite value can be stipulated as to the ideal coefficient of dispersion, most tax administrators feel comfortable with a coefficient in the 10–20 percent range.

Coefficient of Variation. The coefficient of variation is the standard deviation divided by the mean.[2] It is therefore the square root of the average squared deviation from the mean expressed as a percentage of the mean. Interpretation of the coefficient of variation, in contrast to the coefficient of dispersion, depends upon normal probability tables. If the data are in fact normally distributed, the coefficient of variation provides a more complete and useful description of relative variability than does the coefficient of dispersion. If, on the other hand, the data do not approximate a normal distribution, reliance on the coefficient of variation as a measure of relative variability will be somewhat misleading.

The Ratio Study

The assessor has a statutorily mandated purpose—that of valuing all property uniformly and equitably. It is both the assessor's responsibility and his duty to ensure that all assessed values on the rolls represent current market value. A comprehensive real estate market transaction program

2. The coefficient of variation has occasionally been termed the "coefficient of dispersion." This has led to a confusion of terminology as well as of concepts. Statistics books are uniform in referring to the standard deviation divided by the mean as the coefficient of variation, and the usage is followed here. As a general rule, "dispersion" in statistics implies that absolute differences have been computed, while "variation" implies that differences have been squared.

is therefore necessary. The findings of such programs typically are promulgated in the form of sales-ratio studies. Fulfillment of the obligation to make property assessments uniform and equitable compels the assessor to stay on top of local real estate market conditions, periodically reappraising areas in need of appraisal. Real estate is ever changing; the concept of "carrying over" last year's value nurtures inequities. The sales-ratio study functions as the assessor's yardstick in evaluating what is being done right, what is being done wrong, and what reappraisal activity is necessary.

Ratio analyses conducted at the state board of equalization level, the state agency level, and the local level demonstrate little commonality in purpose or function. State boards, being concerned primarily with interjurisdictional equalization, are interested in the development of average weighted ratios by jurisdiction. Little attention is focused on inconsistencies that may exist among individual properties. More breadth is found in studies conducted by state agencies responsible for monitoring assessment standards and functioning in an advisory capacity to the local level. In these studies, attempts typically are made to discover dispersion in assessment levels between and among property classes and areas within taxing jurisdictions.

Sales-ratio analyses conducted on the local level, on the other hand, contrast dramatically. On this level the purpose is closely aligned to the assessor's legal responsibility—making competent original assessments.

A ratio is a result of division. In sales-ratio analysis, the numerator is the amount in dollars for which a sale property is assessed. The denominator is the selling price of the property. The ratio of assessment to sale price for any sale property is expressed as follows:

$$\frac{\text{Assessed value}}{\text{Selling price}} = \text{Ratio} .$$

For example, if a residence sells for \$50,000 and is assessed (at the time of sale) for $10,000, the ratio of assessment to selling price is 0.20:

$$\frac{\$10,000}{\$50,000} = 0.20 \ .$$

Naturally, the first step involved in ratio-study development consists of the discovery, collection, and qualification of sales data, which have been covered in chapter 6. Suffice it to reiterate that the sales must be identified, the selling price and terms of sale ascertained, and the character of the transaction investigated. It is then necessary to equate each bona fide sale to its assessed value and property characteristics.

Use of Assessment/Sale Price Ratios

When sales data have been collected, the sales associated with assessment data, and the ratios of assessment to sale price developed, the primary concern becomes sample representativity. A common test of representativity is the comparative study of sale property characteristics and population characteristics. To illustrate, a sales sample of two hundred sales from a residential neighborhood is assumed. The left half of figure 13.2 is a histogram representing these sales. The horizontal axis measures square footage of living area in increments of 100 square feet, while the vertical axis measures the ratio of the number of sales in each class interval to the total number of sales in the sample. The right half of figure 13.2 reflects the same information for the entire neighborhood. An analysis of figure 13.2 reveals that the sample underrepresents both small and large homes in the neighborhood. Similar comparisons can be drawn for property characteristics, such as effective age, number of baths, and other physical features.

This approach serves two other significant purposes: (1) it provides for a quick statistical analysis of neighborhoods,

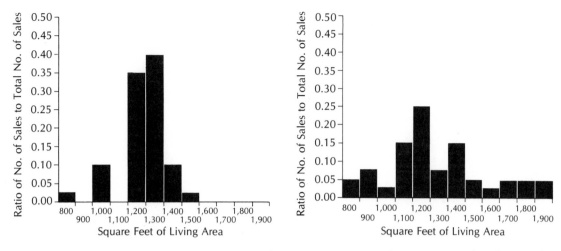

Fig. 13.2.—Square-footage comparison between sample of 200 sales (*left*) and the neighborhood (*right*).

and (2) it provides for identification of voids that may exist in sales information, thereby alerting the assessor to the need to give certain property types special consideration as exceptions. A drawback of this approach lies in the fact that the type of analysis required is very time-consuming and laborious. It may be impractical in the absence of an automated system.

Once the necessary statistical assumptions are satisfied, the next step is the utilization of sales ratios in detecting common areas of assessment inequities. Areas commonly exhibiting assessment bias include value ranges, age, and location. The assessor should investigate (1) whether lower-priced properties and higher-priced properties are treated equally, (2) whether there is assessment bias against newer homes, (3) whether the assessment presently on the tax roll discriminates by location, and (4) whether the present assessment indicates significant differences in assessment quality in respect to property type. Graphing provides insight into areas of bias of this type. Figure 13.3, a scatter diagram relating assessment/sale price ratios to selling price, is an example. The selling price is represented along the horizontal axis, while the ratio of assessment to selling price is plotted along the vertical axis. The indi-

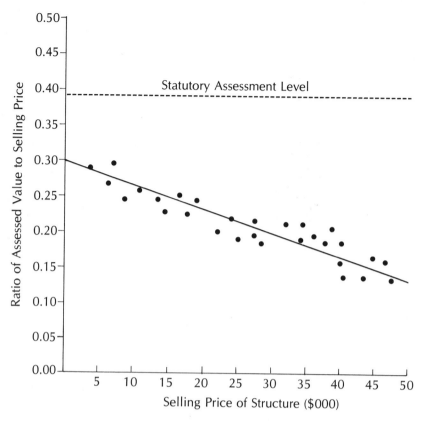

Fig. 13.3.—Linear correlation of assessment/sale price ratio with selling price.

vidual sales are then plotted to create a scatter diagram. This example illustrates that assessment bias exists between higher-valued properties and lower-valued properties. The tendency is to underassess the more valuable properties.

Mass Appraisal Techniques

The Boundary Problem

The assessor's vehicle in the analysis function is sales-ratio analysis. It is doubtful that an assessor would fail to discover a recognizable pattern as he analyzed sales ratios. However, the assessor faces a dilemma—the boundary problem. Geographical areas usually show distinct patterns of overassessment and underassessment, but upon what criteria will lines be drawn defining the geographical area in question? Which properties will be included in the reappraisal, and which might not be reappraised this year? Regardless of where the lines are drawn, there is always property on the other side.

Depending upon whether the program is conducted at the state level or the local level, the problem of boundaries varies. State programs generally address the problem of interjurisdictional equalization; therefore, the boundaries dealt with are legally defined as political subdivisions. All properties within the subdivision are typically appraised. On the local level, the problems are intensified.

One obvious solution to the boundary problem is simply not to draw boundaries but instead to revalue the entire jurisdiction annually. This solution, however, may not be viable. Although progress in revaluation has been significant in recent years, the annual reappraisal still has serious cost and methodological constraints. Where boundaries must be drawn, knowledgeable assessment administrators advocate drawing them in such a way as to maximize homogeneity. In this respect, rivers, terrain, lakes, freeways, major thoroughfares, railroad tracks, and centers of blocks are logical dividing points.

Data Collection

Before data collection commences, a data collection form must be developed. An example of a residential data collection form is illustrated in figure 13.4. A prime requisite in form design should be a high degree of correlation between the sequence of data elements on the form and the sequence in which the appraiser inspects and measures the property. If and when computerization takes place, foresight in form design will minimize conversion costs. Note that section 006 of the data collection form

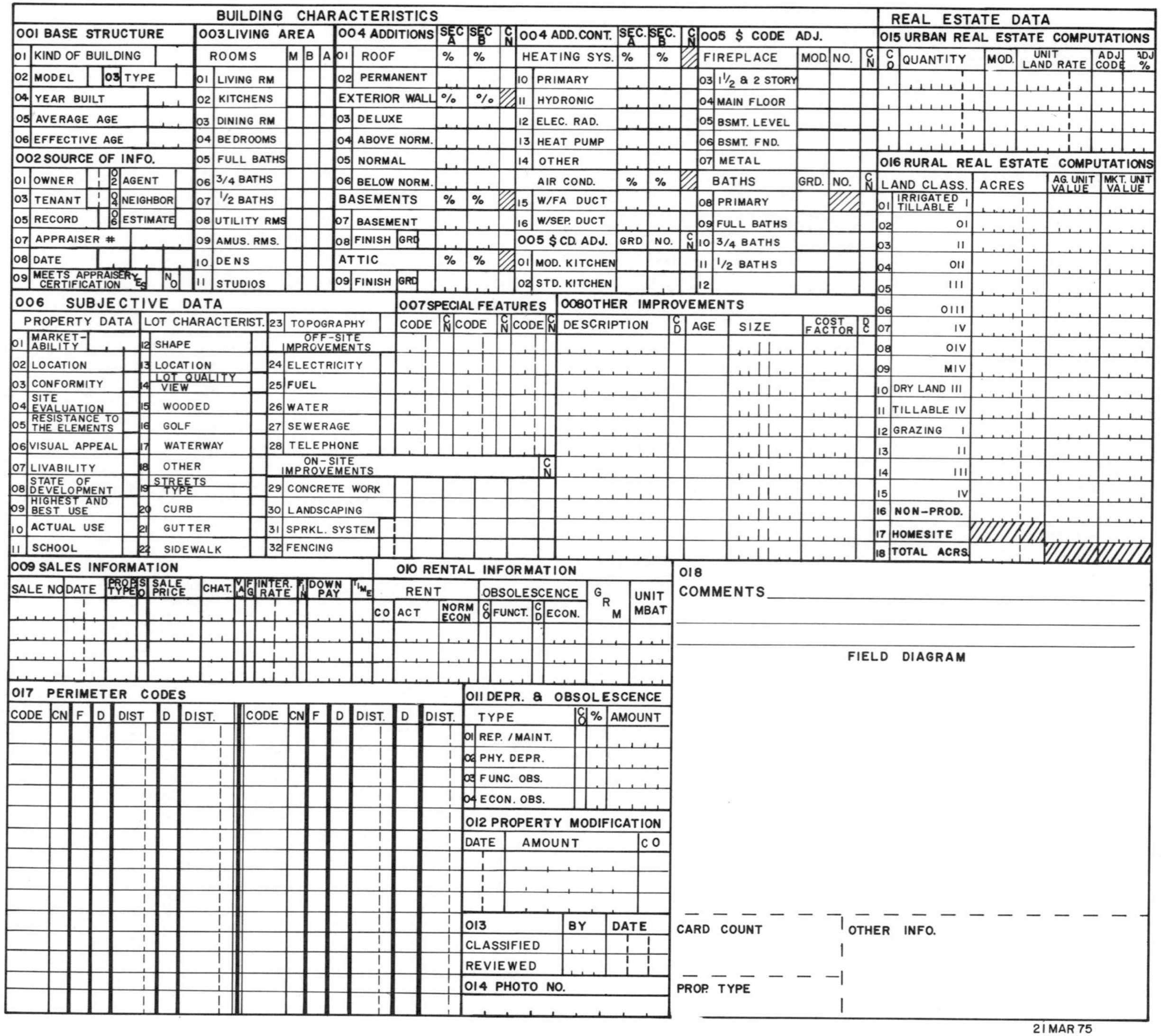

Fig. 13.4.—A sample data collection form

refers to "subjective data." Data of this type are all too often missing or of limited use in the assessor's data collection program, in part as a result of the historical reliance upon the cost approach by the assessment profession. Consideration of subjective data is, however, inherently part of the cost approach, as much so as many of the data thought to be essential. Subjective data provide the vehicle necessary for effective determination of functional or economic obsolescence and assist in site evaluation.

In order to promote uniformity, once the data elements have been defined, preparation of a field manual or an appraiser's instruction manual is of prime importance. The purpose of such a manual is to minimize conflicting views of field appraisers. In the preparation of the manual, every attempt should be made to be as graphic as possible, and illustrations and photographs should be used. The possibility of automation of the system at a later date makes it important to choose variable coding schemes compatible with computerization. An illustrative excerpt from an instruction manual is shown in exhibit 13.1. Reference is made to the form illustrated in figure 13.4.

The sum total of data collected and stored is often referred to as the *data base*.

Exhibit 13.1
Section 003. Living Area

003 LIVING AREA			
ROOMS	M	B	A
01 LIVING RM			
02 KITCHENS			
03 DINING RM			
04 BEDROOMS			
05 FULL BATHS			
06 3/4 BATHS			
07 1/2 BATHS			
08 UTILITY RMS			
09 AMUS. RMS.			
10 DENS			
11 STUDIOS			

The Living Area section of the input form provides spaces for eleven possible room types to be coded according to their location in the house. If the appraiser is unable to enter the building, a reliable room estimate can be made based on similar homes in the area which were inspected inside and by an exterior inspection of windows, door placement, and vent stacks.

Location

Each room will be marked according to its location in three areas of the building:

> *Main living area* (col. 1): This area includes all one-story portions of the structure.
> *Basement area* (col. 2): This area includes rooms located below the main living area or in basement residences.

Attic area (col. 3): This area includes rooms located in the second story of the structure.

Rooms

Spaces have been provided on the input form for eleven types of rooms to be marked. Rooms that do not fall into one of these categories should not be coded. For example, an art studio or a kitchen nook would not be marked on the input form.

Mark

Mark the number of each type of room under the column corresponding to the building area in which the rooms are located. Where no room of a type exists, leave the space blank.

01. Living Rooms

Usually the largest room in the house, the living room is used for social entertainment and family relaxation. This room is normally near the front entrance.

02. Kitchens

The kitchen is usually used for meal preparation and informal family dining. It may include cabinet and closet storage, counter space, cooking stoves and ovens, and sink and dishwashing facilities.

03. Dining Rooms

The dining room is a separate room set apart from other rooms for the purpose of formal dining. It may have three perimeter partitions, with a possible abbreviated fourth perimeter partitioning entry to the living room. One of the perimeters may have a door or archway access to the kitchen or hallway.

04. Bedrooms

A bedroom is an independent area enclosed for sleeping purposes and having a reach-in or walk-in closet. Rooms designed as bedrooms but used for other purposes will be marked as bedrooms.

05. Full Bath

A full bath includes water closet, lavatory, and bathtub with or without shower. It may have more than one of these items.

06. ¾ Bath

A ¾ bath includes water closet, lavatory, and shower stall instead of bathtub.

07. ½ Bath

A ½ bath includes water closet and lavatory with neither bathtub nor shower stall. (Note: Lavatories [sinks] may be located outside the room itself but must be in the immediate vicinity. A room having only a sink or a shower stall or a water closet is not considered a bath.)

08. Utility Rooms

A utility room is a finished laundry room with appropriate plumbing and wiring.

09. Amusement Rooms

This conveniently arranged room, often referred to as a "family" room, is intended for family entertainment. It may contain a fireplace, bookshelves, seating furniture, game tables, and stereo or television. The room may be part of the original design or an addition to the home. This room is not to be confused with some modern kitchen eating areas which are not designed for the diversified uses of an amusement room.

10. Dens

This is a separate room designed for quiet privacy and has no clothes closets. Offices, studies, and libraries without closets will be marked as dens. Do not mark rooms used for dens that were designed as bedrooms.

11. Studios

This is a room having the eating, sleeping, and living areas in the same room. It is also called an "efficiency apartment."

Cost Approach

The cost approach to value traditionally has played an important role in the mass appraisal process. This is because residential buildings comprise the bulk of the valuation work load in most assessment jurisdictions, and prior to computer applications the cost approach, better than any other, lent itself to the assembly-line techniques inherent in the process.

Those critics advocating the abolition of the cost approach are challenged to generate better values by using the comparative sales or income approach, given the assignment of appraising a small rural community where (1) the economic conditions are stagnant, (2) relatively few property conveyances take place each year, and (3) a high degree of heterogeneity exists. These conditions are not uncommon in the less densely populated parts of the United States and are characteristic of many farming communities today.

It is imperative, however, that cost manuals be kept current, and this is not a small task. A common technique utilized is the development of indexes. As an illustration, assume that a cost manual has six residential quality classes and that thirty recently constructed homes falling in quality class 3 have been identified. Through interviews with the builders, the actual building costs including profit, and net of personalty, are ascertained. An appraisal, utilizing the cost manual, is then made of each home and replacement cost new (RCN) (based on the cost manual) is determined. The ratio of actual cost of construction (including profit) to RCN appraised value is then determined. The results are displayed in table 13.2. On

Table 13.2

Example Demonstrating Development of Cost Indexes

Property No.	RCN	Cost	Cost/RCN (%)	Property No.	RCN	Cost	Cost/RCN (%)
1	31,818	35,000	110	16	31,609	37,500	115
2	26,667	29,600	111	17	28,261	32,500	115
3	27,027	30,000	111	18	28,696	33,000	115
4	27,027	30,000	111	19	31,304	36,000	115
5	28,125	31,500	112	20	30,870	35,500	115
6	27,009	30,250	112	21	32,672	37,900	116
7	28,319	32,000	113	22	28,103	32,600	116
8	24,336	27,500	113	23	29,487	34,500	117
9	26,404	30,100	114	24	33,333	39,000	117
10	26,096	29,750	114	25	29,915	35,000	117
11	31,304	36,000	115	26	31,356	37,000	118
12	23,478	27,000	115	27	26,017	30,700	118
13	26,304	30,250	115	28	31,933	38,000	119
14	25,652	29,500	115	29	31,513	37,500	119
15	22,609	26,000	115	30	32,083	38,500	120

Mean, 115%; median, 115%; mode, 115%

Range, 110%–120%

Average absolute deviation, 1.87%

Variance, 6.33%; standard deviation, 2.52%

Coefficient of dispersion, 1.87 ÷ 115 = 1.6%

Coefficient of variation, 2.52 ÷ 115 = 2.2%

the basis of the statistics presented in this table, application of a factor of 115 percent would appear to relate RCN developed through use of the cost manual with the construction market. Similar computations will adjust the remaining residential building qualities. If a commercially published cost manual is used, similar indexes for location may be required.

Application of costing tables can be a costly and laborious task if it is clerically accomplished. In addition, because it is a very tedious job, the incidence of clerical error is high. The computational process can be automated, however, and cost values generated quite inexpensively. Such computations have proved effective economically and in terms of enhanced accuracy.

Comparative Sales Approach

As indicated in chapter 6, the comparative sales approach rests on the principle of substitution. It is apparent, however, that substitutability is not easily discerned in real estate. A prospective buyer is faced with a high degree of uniqueness when viewing real estate ventures. Very few properties have an exact substitute. Variations in locational attributes, size, age, and quality are the rule, not the exception. It is the appraiser's responsibility to identify value-affecting departures from similarity and to compensate or adjust to approximate likeness. The assimilation function requires the appraiser to reference his representative sales to make such determinations as whether Property X is more valuable than Property Y because it is 200 square feet larger, or whether Property A is less valuable than Property B because it is twenty years older.

Ideally, the assessor's comparative sales information consists of a representative distribution of all properties and exact comparables of all unsold property. Given these conditions, the assessor would have to consider only time and conditions of sale to arrive at his market estimate.

Disparities between the selling prices of two or more totally identical properties selling at the same point in time and under the same conditions would be attributed to the whims of the marketplace.

This does not realistically describe the situation encountered in practice, however enviable it may be. All comparables differ to some degree from the universe of similar unsold properties. When these differences are in such characteristics as age, quality, size, and so on, a translation in terms of dollars is required to make valid market estimates. The qualified assessor defines, measures, and (using judgment) evaluates differences and similarities, attaching dollars to them.

How does an assessor decide which differences in characteristics are relevant and what value should be attached to them? The judgment function referred to need not be intuitive in nature; that is, it need not be done without the benefit of pencil and paper or in the assessor's head. The assimilation function referred to has been quantitatively defined in the field of mathematics and is known as *multivariate analysis*.

To lay the necessary groundwork for future discussion, the mathematical concept of correlation should be introduced at this point. As an illustration, the question as to whether the real estate market responds to differences in size might be asked. To answer this question, the following example might be considered: a hypothetical homogeneous neighborhood consisting of three hundred homes ranging from five to ten years old, thirty of which have been sold recently. As a first step, the thirty sales are plotted on a scatter diagram as shown in figure 13.5, where square footage is plotted along the X-axis and the selling price along the Y-axis. (The axis scales have been omitted intentionally in the scatter diagram because they lack relevancy.) If we analyze the scatter diagram, it is apparent that square footage plays an important part in the decision of the buyer. The best estimate of market

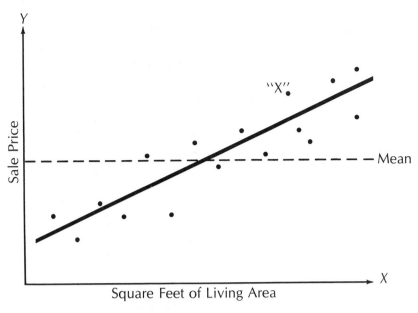

Fig. 13.5.—Scatter diagram

response is represented by the line drawn through the points of the scatter diagram.

Through visual observations of the points in the scatter diagram, the tendency for the selling price to increase as square footage increases is easily discernible, and it is possible to draw a line through the points. However, an infinite number of lines may be drawn to approximate the relationship between sale price and square footage. Although it is possible to inspect the points in a scatter diagram visually and approximate a line of best fit, mathematics fortunately provides a technique for fitting a line to the points—*least squares.* While a technical discussion of least squares is beyond the scope of this text, a simple illustration will give a rudimentary understanding. For illustrative purposes, a single observation, "X," appearing in figure 13.5 has been extracted and is presented in figure 13.6 with the constructed line and the mean of the thirty sales. In this illustration, *A* corresponds to the variance. By making the analysis two-dimensional—that is by looking at square footage and its relationship to selling price—it has been determined that square footage plays an important part in explaining selling price. The measure of this contribution is given by B in figure 13.6. The letter C represents the residual variation, or the amount of variation remaining unexplained after the line has been constructed, and demonstrates the principle underlying a least-squares line. A least-squares line, then, is the line that best approximates all points, or minimizes the residual variation.

Once the data elements to which the market is responding are defined, the assessor must attach dollars to the variation between the comparable sales and the properties under appraisal.

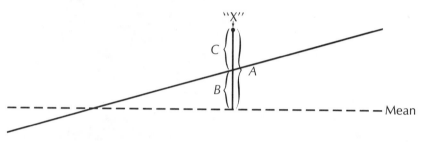

Fig. 13.6.—Illustration of explained and unexplained variation. A = Failure of the mean to provide an accurate estimate of the observation = Total variation; B = Contribution of the fitted line in explaining total variance = Explained variation; C = Inability of the fitted line to explain variation = Unexplained variation.

Aggregation. Because all properties have to be appraised in the mass appraisal process, a group of comparables may be used to value thousands of properties. This necessitates organizing sales into meaningful groups based on value indicators. This process, called aggregation, is nothing more than a classification of properties into sets characterized by comparability. The goal of aggregation is to approximate a condition whereby any given member of a set is a substitute for any other member. A practical limitation to creating groups covering all unsold properties, however, is the representativity of the sales base in respect to the universe of unsold properties. Obviously, if this limitation did not apply, a one-to-one relationship would exist, a highly unlikely occurrence. This limitation means that the aggregation groups must be fairly broad, and, within the groupings, appraisal judgment must come into play.

As an illustration, assume that an aggregation group is defined as follows: single-family residences, located in geographical area 10, with one bath, built in 1918. When the sales base is sorted, there is a good probability that the group parameter and age are too restrictive and that no sales fall within the defined group. In this case, if the age parameter were broadened to "built prior to 1925," the problem might be solved.

Given that there exists a sufficient number of sales within the group and that they are representative, the grouping of sales into aggregation groups narrows the assessor's task to an exercise in judgment within the groupings. This technique ensures a certain degree of uniformity but is subject to the use of sound judgment on the part of the assessor.

The computer can function as a valuable tool for the assessor in forming aggregation groups. The organization (e.g., sorting) and tabulation of sales are a time-consuming ordeal, and the computer affords an excellent solution. Through automation, the appraiser has at his disposal an efficient, economical solution to the iteration problem encountered when attempting to maximize grouping effectiveness. It can also provide economical assistance to the appraiser in the application of the analytical techniques previously discussed.

Multiple Regression Analysis. In addition to providing the assessor with techniques for determining the response of the market to data elements, mathematics provides a quantitative technique that is helpful in measuring the magnitude of market response in dollars. This technique is referred to as regression analysis. Regression analysis can be used to relate the characteristics of sale properties to their sale price, allowing the generation of an equation that would apply to the type of property for which the sales are representative.

In the preceding section, the least-squares concept of fitting a line to a set of data points in a scatter diagram was introduced. When most of the points in the scatter diagram fall close to a line so constructed, the two data elements are said to be highly correlated. If two data elements are correlated and if an increase in one data element results in an increase in the other (e.g., if an increase in square footage brings about an increase in selling price), the data elements are said to be positively correlated. If, on the other hand, an increase in one data element brings about a decrease in the other (e.g., an increase in age brings about a decrease in selling price), the data elements are said to be negatively correlated. The degree of correlation is measured by a mathematical measure known as the *coefficient of correlation*. The coefficient of correlation will fall between -1 and $+1$, where -1 indicates perfect negative correlation and $+1$ indicates perfect positive correlation. A correlation coefficient of zero indicates that the data elements are not correlated at all, and they are said to be independent.

When two data elements are highly correlated, it is possible to predict one from our knowledge of the other. For example, in figure 13.5 it is obvious that a high positive correlation exists between square footage of living area and selling price. Simple linear regression provides us a method with which to measure the market's response in dollars to changes in square footage. Selling price is said to be dependent upon square footage.

Obviously, size is not the only property characteristic affecting selling price. Characteristics like age, number of bedrooms, number of baths, and so on, all contribute to value in the buyer's mind. When the dependent variable, selling price, is regressed on more than one variable, we are looking at multiple linear regression. The mathematical equation for such a regression is given by

$$Y' = A + B_1X_1 + B_2X_2 + B_3X_3 + \ldots + B_n X_n + E,$$

where A is a constant in the regression equation and represents a residual portion of the estimate not accounted for by a coefficient; B_1 through B_n represent the amount of variability in the estimate accounted for by the various independent variables; and E equates to the residual variation, C, as illustrated in figure 13.6.

An illustration will be of assistance in demonstrating the application of a regression equation to unsold properties. For purposes of this illustration, assume that an analysis of five hundred sales results in the following regression equation when selling price is regressed on square footage (X_1), age (X_2), and number of baths (X_3):

$$Y = \$5,000 + 18.49X_1 - 425X_2 + 750X_3.$$

Further assume that an estimate is desired of the probable selling price of a residence that has 900 square feet of living area, is 12 years old, and has one bath. The following computation is an example of the application of the regression equation to estimate probable selling price:

$$\begin{aligned}
Y' &= \$5,000 + \$12.49(900) - \$425(12) + \$750(1) \\
&= \$5,000 + \$11,241 - \$5,100 + \$750 \\
&= \$11,891.
\end{aligned}$$

In simple terms, the preceding regression can be interpreted as follows: the estimated selling price of a residence is equal to $5,000, plus $12.49 per square foot of living area, less $425 for each year of age, plus $750 for each bath in the residence. The coefficients in a regression equation are meaningful only in relation to the whole regression equation.

In regression we have a sophisticated application of the market approach. The intuitive nature of the conventional comparative sales approach is improved through application of mathematical formulas. The regression technique is capable of working with volumes of data far surpassing human limitations when linked to a computer. The use of regression techniques coupled with computers underlies many of the most cost-effective and efficient mass appraisal systems in current application.

Income Approach

The income approach to value traditionally has played a less significant role in mass appraisal than the cost and comparative sales approaches. This stems from some common misconceptions about the income approach in mass appraisal, namely, (1) the income approach is too complicated for use in mass appraisal; (2) information is not available for its use; and (3) the income approach is not necessary. Successful use of the income valuation methods and techniques hinges on the ability of the assessor to discern trends in income and expenses of comparable types of properties. The generation of "normalized" rents and expense ratios and the selection of appropriate capitalization rates require the capability of selecting sample data, summarizing them, and proceeding accurately by inference to the larger universe of properties. In this regard, measures of central tendency and dispersion can be important tools for the assessor.

In considering the income approach for mass appraisal, the first step is to delineate the areas of the jurisdiction covered by commercial, industrial, and multifamily properties. Information must be gathered from owners, managers, and tenants for all properties in the delineated areas and this information in turn separated by property type and geographic area. Analysis of these data typically will consist of the development of a range of economic rent for each property type and geographic area, development of typical ratios for vacancy and collection loss and operating expenses, and development of capitalization rates for use on various property types in different areas and by age and condition of the building.

The data may then be compiled in tables and posted on ownership maps. The data will include the rental unit of comparison, the actual rent, economic rent, the vacancy and collection loss ratio and occupancy factor for selected "benchmark" properties, and the proper capitalization rate for the benchmark properties. Tables may show proper net capitalization rates for properties of various ages and with different discount and tax rates and may also extend the rental units of comparison to potential gross income. Forms that are set up to accommodate various residual techniques should be used. Finally, a review of the properties should be undertaken after these steps have been completed.

In order to use the income approach successfully in mass appraisal, the assessor must take all necessary steps for a complete data program, carefully analyze the acquired data, and properly apply the capitalization procedures.

Computer Application in Mass Appraisal

Throughout this chapter, reference has been made to automation and its applicability to various mass appraisal aspects. An attempt to enumerate all the applications of electronic data processing that are of interest to the assessor would be beyond the scope of this text; therefore the discussion will be confined to three broad categories: the computational area, the analytical area, and the reporting and tabulating area.

Computation Function

An obvious and cost-effective application of the computer in the assessor's office is the computation of replacement cost new (RCN) in the appraisal function. Figure 13.4 is a sample data collection form compatible with computer processing. The data elements, or building and property characteristics pertaining to each property, are collected and inputted into the computer, where a set of instructions (a program) designed specifically to satisfy the user (assessor) computes RCN or RCNLD and outputs the appraisal record for appraisal review and value finalization. The application of costing tables with computation by manual techniques is a very costly and often tedious operation, with a high incidence of error if costly audit procedures are not inherent in the process. As an illustrative time comparison of this process with the manual computational procedure, one taxing jurisdiction had the following experience with automated appraisal. An average of 45 minutes per finished residential appraisal was being expended in preaudit procedures (checks for logical content error), cost table lookup, manual computation, and postaudit procedures (final checks for transposition and so on) under the manual system. The computer-generated appraisals were processed at the rate of 800 per hour. This example is for illustrative purposes only, and it should be emphasized that conditions and factors vary significantly from one taxing jurisdiction to another.

Some taxing jurisdictions, recognizing the importance of the comparative sales approach in the appraisal process, have incorporated a second value indicator into their appraisal estimates utilizing multiple regression analysis (MRA). Such applications take advantage of the information collected in the field and processed through the cost system, substituting regression coefficients, the incremental dollar value of property characteristics as reflected in market sales activity, in the computational procedure. MRA has proved to be a cost-effective, efficient, and accurate technique of mass appraisal when properly implemented; however, it is one of literally hundreds of computer applications in property tax administration. In addition to the computational power and speed of a computer in the actual appraisal function, computers provide an efficient and economical solution to trending or factoring in the value-update process occurring between reappraisal cycles.

Analytical Function

Computer analytical capabilities in the assessment function have opened doors heretofore closed because of the cost-prohibitive nature of many forms of assessment-related data analysis. For example, MRA, while not complicated in concept, requires extremely complex mathematics, making utilization of a computer a necessity if a large number of property characteristics is to be considered in the modeling process.

Computer utilization has had a positive effect on assessment quality. Sales-ratio analysis and other statistical analyses are accomplished more efficiently and accurately where computer capabilities exist. The precision inherent in statistical data analysis is a function of the ability to cope financially and intellectually with the complexities of the analyses and the iterative processes often required.

Reporting and Tabulating Function

The potential of computers in the areas of reporting and tabulating is limited only by the foresight of those who design the electronic data processing system. A brief summary and description of some of the more important reports and tabulations follow.

Roll and Notice Preparation. Compared with the alternatives of posting machines, typing, and addressographing, the computer is a cost-effective and accurate means of producing the roll and notice preparation. Rolls can be computer-generated. For example, a computer can generate an assessment roll for a moderate-sized taxing jurisdiction in less than a day. Computer-generated documents may include, but are not limited to, assessment rolls, tax rolls, valuation notices, tax notices, and delinquency notices.

Sales Listings. The computer can be an indispensable tool to the appraiser in providing sales listings in any order of sort and format desired. For example, it can produce sales listings by neighborhood, by property type, by value range, by building size or age, and by type of wall construction. In the market analysis process, the computer gives valuable assistance to the iterative processing needed in the formation of aggregation groups.

Specialized Listings. Some commonly computer-generated listings include tax abatement listings, which provide auditing and inquiry capability; name-address-parcel identification listings, which again provide inquiry capability; new construction listings, which are beneficial to planning groups and in projections; and assessment change listings, which are valuable in projecting and budgeting consideration.

Summary

The mass appraisal of real property requires organization and effective implementation of the components of appraisal. Reappraisal priorities should be determined through analysis of sales and assessment/sale price ratios; boundaries must be determined; maps must be kept current; parcel identification procedures must be developed; data must be collected and maintained; and values must be determined through application of one or more of the three approaches to value.

Modern assessment agencies are emphasizing a systems approach to mass appraisal. This approach utilizes statistics to aid assessment personnel in the analysis of data.

Furthermore, the approach emphasizes the use of the computer to store and manipulate data and to assist assessment personnel in the valuation process. The advent of statistics and automation has led to the more effective use of the three valuation approaches. Value indications employing cost, income, and comparative sales are developed jointly and used dynamically to determine and support better-quality assessments. The assessor is given great flexibility in the use of these three valuation techniques.

Appendix

Compound Interest Tables

There are six compound interest tables in this Appendix. They are as follows.

Column	Name	Meaning
1	Amount of 1	Future worth of $1 with interest
2	Amount of 1 per Period	Future worth of $1 per period with interest
3	Sinking-Fund Factor	Accumulation to $1
4	Present Worth of 1	Reversion factor
5	Present Worth of 1 per Period	Ordinary annuity coefficient (Inwood factor)
6	Partial Payment	Amount to amortize $1

The tables show interest rates from 3 to 30 percent. Columns 1, 2, and 6 give factors that produce future values; columns 3, 4, and 5 give factors that produce present values. The tables are constructed by either adding or subtracting compound interest and are similar to those used by banks, savings and loan officials, realtors, and others in the field of real estate finance. The tables in this Appendix are for annual payments; however, factors are shown for 8 percent based on monthly, quarterly, and semiannual payments. The effect of the method of payment on the interest added or subtracted can be seen by carefully examining the tables. Thus, $1,200 deposited at the beginning of the year will earn interest on the full amount for twelve months, while $1,200 deposited during the year or $100 monthly will earn less interest.

Column 1: Amount of 1

This series of factors shows the amount to which $1 will grow at a given interest rate in a given number of years. The table is constructed by adding compound interest to the single deposit.

Example:

$1 is deposited at the beginning of the year and allowed to earn interest at 7 percent for three years.

Beginning of Year	Deposit	Interest Rate	Interest Earned	End of Year
First year	$1.00	0.07	$0.07	$1.07
Second year	1.07	0.07	0.0749	1.1449
Third year	1.1449	0.07	0.0801	1.2250

This shows that $1 at 7 percent will grow to $1.225 in three years and (from the table) to $1.967 in ten years. To calculate the amount to which any given number of dollars deposited will grow, simply multiply the number of dollars deposited by the factor for the selected interest rate and number of years: $20 deposited for ten years will grow to $39.34 ($20 × 1.967 = $39.34). The factors in this column are reciprocals of the factors in column 4, Present Worth of 1.

Column 2: Amount of 1 per Period

This series shows the amount to which $1 deposited each year will grow at a given rate of interest in a given number of years. The table is based on payments made at the end of the year along with the annual deposit.

Example:

$1 is deposited at the end of each year and allowed to earn interest at 7 percent.

End of Year	Total	Interest Rate	Interest Earned
First year	$1.00	0.07	$0.07
Second year	$2.07 ($1.07 + $1.00)	0.07	0.1449
Third year	$3.2149 ($2.2149 + $1.00)	0.07	0.2250

This shows that $1 deposited at the end of each year at 7 percent will grow to $3.2149 by the end of three years or (from the table) to $13.8164 in ten years. To calculate the amount to which any given number of dollars deposited annually will grow, simply multiply the number of dollars deposited by the factor for the selected interest rate and number of years: $20 per year deposited at the end of each year for ten years at 7 percent will grow to $276.33 ($20 × 13.8164 = $276.33). The factors in this column are reciprocals of the factors in column 3, Sinking-Fund Factor.

Column 3: Sinking-Fund Factor

This factor shows the annual deposit required to accumulate $1 at a given rate of interest in a given number of years.

Example:

An investor wants the sum of $100 to be available in three years. If the interest rate is 7 percent, the uniform annual deposit necessary to accrue $100 including interest is $31.11.

End of Year	Total	Interest Rate	Interest Earned
First year	$ 31.11	0.07	*
Second year	64.40	0.07	$2.18
Third year	100.00	...	4.51

* Since the deposit is made at the end of each year, no interest is earned until the second year.

This shows that $31.11 deposited each year at the end of the year for three years at 7 percent will grow to $100. From the table, $7.24 will grow to $100 in ten years. To calculate the annual deposit necessary to accumulate a given number of dollars, simply multiply the amount of the desired accumulation by the sinking-fund factor for the selected interest rate and number of years: the annual deposit necessary to accumulate $750 in ten years is $54.28 ($750 × 0.072378 = $54.28). The factors in this column are reciprocals of the factors in column 2, Amount of 1 per Period.

Column 4: Present Worth of 1

This factor shows the present worth of money to be collected after a given number of years at a given interest rate.

Example:

An investor wishes to know what he needs to pay for the right to receive $100 three years from today, assuming 7 percent interest on his money. From column 4 of the 7 percent annual table for three years, the factor is 0.816298. The present worth of $100 at 7 percent in three years is $81.63 ($100 × 0.816298 = $81.63). The "present worth of 1" factor is the reciprocal of column 1, Amount of 1.

Column 5: Present Worth of 1 per Period

This table shows the present value of the right to receive $1 per period for a given number of periods at a stated interest rate. This table is constructed by subtracting compound interest.

Example:

An investor wishes to know what he would pay today for the right to receive $100 each year for three years, assuming 7 percent interest on the money. From column 5 of the 7 percent annual table for three years, the factor is 2.624316. The present worth of 1 per period of $100 each year at 7 percent for three years is $262.43 ($100 ×

2.624316 = $262.43). These factors are the reciprocals of column 6, Partial Payment.

Column 6: Partial Payment

This table shows the amount required per period to amortize principal and interest on an investment or loan in a given number of periods at a given interest rate.

Example:

An investor wishes to know what to pay per year to pay off a $1,000 loan in three years at 7 percent interest. From column 6 of the 7 percent table for three years, the factor is 0.381052. The periodic payment per year for three years at 7 percent necessary to pay off a $1,000 loan is $381.05 ($1,000 × 0.381052 = $381.05 per year). The factors in this table are reciprocals of column 5, Present Worth of 1 per Period.

3% Annual Table

Years	1 Amount of 1	2 Amount of 1 per Period	3 Sinking-Fund Factor	4 Present Worth of 1	5 Present Worth of 1 per Period	6 Partial Payment
1	1.030 000	1.000 000	1.000 000	.970 874	.970 874	1.030 000
2	1.060 900	2.030 000	.492 611	.942 596	1.913 470	.522 611
3	1.092 727	3.090 900	.323 530	.915 142	2.828 611	.353 530
4	1.125 509	4.183 627	.239 027	.888 487	3.717 098	.269 027
5	1.159 274	5.309 136	.188 355	.862 609	4.579 707	.218 355
6	1.194 052	6.468 410	.154 598	.837 484	5.417 191	.184 598
7	1.229 874	7.662 462	.130 506	.813 092	6.230 283	.160 506
8	1.266 770	8.892 336	.112 456	.789 409	7.019 692	.142 456
9	1.304 773	10.159 106	.098 434	.766 417	7.786 109	.128 434
10	1.343 916	11.463 879	.087 231	.744 094	8.530 203	.117 231
11	1.384 234	12.807 796	.078 077	.722 421	9.252 624	.108 077
12	1.425 761	14.192 030	.070 462	.701 380	9.954 004	.100 462
13	1.468 534	15.617 790	.064 030	.680 951	10.634 955	.094 030
14	1.512 590	17.086 324	.058 526	.661 118	11.296 073	.088 526
15	1.557 967	18.598 914	.053 767	.641 862	11.937 935	.083 767
16	1.604 706	20.156 881	.049 611	.623 167	12.561 102	.079 611
17	1.652 848	21.761 588	.045 953	.605 016	13.166 118	.075 953
18	1.702 433	23.414 435	.042 709	.587 395	13.753 513	.072 709
19	1.753 506	25.116 868	.039 814	.570 286	14.323 799	.069 814
20	1.806 111	26.870 374	.037 216	.553 676	14.877 475	.067 216
21	1.860 295	28.676 486	.034 872	.537 549	15.415 024	.064 872
22	1.916 103	30.536 780	.032 747	.521 893	15.936 917	.062 747
23	1.973 587	32.452 884	.030 814	.506 692	16.443 608	.060 814
24	2.032 794	34.426 470	.029 047	.491 934	16.935 542	.059 047
25	2.093 778	36.459 264	.027 428	.477 606	17.413 148	.057 428
26	2.156 591	38.553 042	.025 938	.463 695	17.876 842	.055 938
27	2.221 289	40.709 634	.024 564	.450 189	18.327 031	.054 564
28	2.287 928	42.930 923	.023 293	.437 077	18.764 108	.053 293
29	2.356 566	45.218 850	.022 115	.424 346	19.188 455	.052 115
30	2.427 262	47.575 416	.021 019	.411 987	19.600 441	.051 019
31	2.500 080	50.002 678	.019 999	.399 987	20.000 428	.049 999
32	2.575 083	52.502 759	.019 047	.388 337	20.388 766	.049 047
33	2.652 335	55.077 841	.018 156	.377 026	20.765 792	.048 156
34	2.731 905	57.730 177	.017 322	.366 045	21.131 837	.047 322
35	2.813 862	60.462 082	.016 539	.355 383	21.487 220	.046 539
36	2.898 278	63.275 944	.015 804	.345 032	21.832 252	.045 804
37	2.985 227	66.174 223	.015 112	.334 983	22.167 235	.045 112
38	3.074 783	69.159 449	.014 459	.325 226	22.492 462	.044 459
39	3.167 027	72.234 233	.013 844	.315 754	22.808 215	.043 844
40	3.262 038	75.401 260	.013 262	.306 557	23.114 772	.043 262
41	3.359 899	78.663 298	.012 712	.297 628	23.412 400	.042 712
42	3.460 696	82.023 196	.012 192	.288 959	23.701 359	.042 192
43	3.564 517	85.483 892	.011 698	.280 543	23.981 902	.041 698
44	3.671 452	89.048 409	.011 230	.272 372	24.254 274	.041 230
45	3.781 596	92.719 861	.010 785	.264 439	24.518 713	.040 785
46	3.895 044	96.501 457	.010 363	.256 737	24.775 449	.040 363
47	4.011 895	100.396 501	.009 961	.249 259	25.024 708	.039 961
48	4.132 252	104.408 396	.009 578	.241 999	25.266 707	.039 578
49	4.256 219	108.540 648	.009 213	.234 950	25.501 657	.039 213
50	4.383 906	112.796 867	.008 865	.228 107	25.729 764	.038 865
51	4.515 423	117.180 773	.008 534	.221 463	25.951 227	.038 534
52	4.650 886	121.697 197	.008 217	.215 013	26.166 240	.038 217
53	4.790 412	126.347 082	.007 915	.208 750	26.374 990	.037 915
54	4.934 125	131.137 495	.007 626	.202 670	26.577 660	.037 626
55	5.082 149	136.071 620	.007 349	.196 767	26.774 428	.037 349
56	5.234 613	141.153 768	.007 084	.191 036	26.965 464	.037 084
57	5.391 651	146.388 381	.006 831	.185 472	27.150 936	.036 831
58	5.553 401	151.780 033	.006 588	.180 070	27.331 005	.036 588
59	5.720 003	157.333 434	.006 356	.174 825	27.505 831	.036 356
60	5.891 603	163.053 437	.006 133	.169 733	27.675 564	.036 133

$$S^n = (1+i)^n \qquad S_{\overline{n}|} = \frac{S^n - 1}{i} \qquad \frac{1}{S_{\overline{n}|}} = \frac{i}{S^n - 1} \qquad V^n = \frac{1}{S^n} \qquad A_{\overline{n}|} = \frac{1 - 1/S^n}{i} \qquad \frac{1}{A_{\overline{n}|}} = \frac{i}{1 - 1/S^n}$$

318

3¼%
Annual
Table

Years	1 Amount of 1	2 Amount of 1 per Period	3 Sinking- Fund Factor	4 Present Worth of 1	5 Present Worth of 1 per Period	6 Partial Payment
1	1.032 500	1.000 000	1.000 000	.968 523	.968 523	1.032 500
2	1.066 056	2.032 500	.492 005	.938 037	1.906 560	.524 505
3	1.100 703	3.098 556	.322 731	.908 510	2.815 070	.355 231
4	1.136 476	4.199 259	.238 137	.879 913	3.694 983	.270 637
5	1.173 411	5.335 735	.187 416	.852 216	4.547 199	.219 916
6	1.211 547	6.509 147	.153 630	.825 391	5.372 590	.186 130
7	1.250 923	7.720 694	.129 522	.799 410	6.172 000	.162 022
8	1.291 578	8.971 616	.111 463	.774 247	6.946 247	.143 963
9	1.333 554	10.263 194	.097 436	.749 876	7.696 123	.129 936
10	1.376 894	11.596 748	.086 231	.726 272	8.422 395	.118 731
11	1.421 643	12.973 642	.077 079	.703 411	9.125 806	.109 579
12	1.467 847	14.395 285	.069 467	.681 270	9.807 076	.101 967
13	1.515 552	15.863 132	.063 039	.659 826	10.466 902	.095 539
14	1.564 807	17.378 684	.057 542	.639 056	11.105 958	.090 042
15	1.615 663	18.943 491	.052 789	.618 941	11.724 899	.085 289
16	1.668 173	20.559 155	.048 640	.599 458	12.324 358	.081 140
17	1.722 388	22.227 327	.044 990	.580 589	12.904 947	.077 490
18	1.778 366	23.949 715	.041 754	.562 314	13.467 261	.074 254
19	1.836 163	25.728 081	.038 868	.544 614	14.011 875	.071 368
20	1.895 838	27.564 244	.036 279	.527 471	14.539 346	.068 779
21	1.957 453	29.460 082	.033 944	.510 868	15.050 214	.066 444
22	2.021 070	31.417 534	.031 829	.494 787	15.545 002	.064 329
23	2.086 755	33.438 604	.029 906	.479 213	16.024 215	.062 406
24	2.154 574	35.525 359	.028 149	.464 129	16.488 343	.060 649
25	2.224 598	37.679 933	.026 539	.449 519	16.937 863	.059 039
26	2.296 897	39.904 531	.025 060	.435 370	17.373 233	.057 560
27	2.371 546	42.201 428	.023 696	.421 666	17.794 899	.056 196
28	2.448 622	44.572 975	.022 435	.408 393	18.203 292	.054 935
29	2.528 202	47.021 596	.021 267	.395 538	18.598 830	.053 767
30	2.610 368	49.549 798	.020 182	.383 088	18.981 917	.052 682
31	2.695 205	52.160 167	.019 172	.371 029	19.352 947	.051 672
32	2.782 800	54.855 372	.018 230	.359 350	19.712 297	.050 730
33	2.873 241	57.638 172	.017 350	.348 039	20.060 336	.049 850
34	2.966 621	60.511 412	.016 526	.337 084	20.397 420	.049 026
35	3.063 036	63.478 033	.015 753	.326 473	20.723 893	.048 253
36	3.162 585	66.541 069	.015 028	.316 197	21.040 090	.047 528
37	3.265 369	69.703 654	.014 346	.306 244	21.346 335	.046 846
38	3.371 493	72.969 023	.013 704	.296 604	21.642 939	.046 204
39	3.481 067	76.340 516	.013 099	.287 268	21.930 207	.045 599
40	3.594 201	79.821 583	.012 528	.278 226	22.208 433	.045 028
41	3.711 013	83.415 784	.011 988	.269 468	22.477 901	.044 488
42	3.831 621	87.126 797	.011 478	.260 986	22.738 888	.043 978
43	3.956 149	90.958 418	.010 994	.252 771	22.991 659	.043 494
44	4.084 723	94.914 566	.010 536	.244 815	23.236 473	.043 036
45	4.217 477	98.999 290	.010 101	.237 109	23.473 582	.042 601
46	4.354 545	103.216 767	.009 688	.229 645	23.703 227	.042 188
47	4.496 068	107.571 312	.009 296	.222 417	23.925 644	.041 796
48	4.642 190	112.067 379	.008 923	.215 416	24.141 059	.041 423
49	4.793 061	116.709 569	.008 568	.208 635	24.349 694	.041 068
50	4.948 835	121.502 630	.008 230	.202 068	24.551 762	.040 730
51	5.109 673	126.451 466	.007 908	.195 707	24.747 469	.040 408
52	5.275 737	131.561 138	.007 601	.189 547	24.937 016	.040 101
53	5.447 198	136.836 875	.007 308	.183 581	25.120 597	.039 808
54	5.624 232	142.284 074	.007 028	.177 802	25.298 399	.039 528
55	5.807 020	147.908 306	.006 761	.172 205	25.470 604	.039 261
56	5.995 748	153.715 326	.006 506	.166 785	25.637 389	.039 006
57	6.190 610	159.711 074	.006 261	.161 535	25.798 924	.038 761
58	6.391 805	165.901 684	.006 028	.156 450	25.955 374	.038 528
59	6.599 538	172.293 489	.005 804	.151 526	26.106 900	.038 304
60	6.814 023	178.893 027	.005 590	.146 756	26.253 656	.038 090

$$S^n = (1+i)^n \qquad S_{\overline{n}|} = \frac{S^n - 1}{i} \qquad \frac{1}{S_{\overline{n}|}} = \frac{i}{S^n - 1} \qquad V^n = \frac{1}{S^n} \qquad A_{\overline{n}|} = \frac{1 - 1/S^n}{i} \qquad \frac{1}{A_{\overline{n}|}} = \frac{i}{1 - 1/S^n}$$

319

3½%
Annual
Table

Years	1 Amount of 1	2 Amount of 1 per Period	3 Sinking- Fund Factor	4 Present Worth of 1	5 Present Worth of 1 per Period	6 Partial Payment
1	1.035 000	1.000 000	1.000 000	.966 184	.966 184	1.035 000
2	1.071 225	2.035 000	.491 400	.933 511	1.899 694	.526 400
3	1.108 718	3.106 225	.321 934	.901 943	2.801 637	.356 934
4	1.147 523	4.214 943	.237 251	.871 442	3.673 079	.272 251
5	1.187 686	5.362 466	.186 481	.841 973	4.515 052	.221 481
6	1.229 255	6.550 152	.152 668	.813 501	5.328 553	.187 668
7	1.272 279	7.779 408	.128 544	.785 991	6.114 544	.163 544
8	1.316 809	9.051 687	.110 477	.759 412	6.873 956	.145 477
9	1.362 897	10.368 496	.096 446	.733 731	7.607 687	.131 446
10	1.410 599	11.731 393	.085 241	.708 919	8.316 605	.120 241
11	1.459 970	13.141 992	.076 092	.684 946	9.001 551	.111 092
12	1.511 069	14.601 962	.068 484	.661 783	9.663 334	.103 484
13	1.563 956	16.113 030	.062 062	.639 404	10.302 738	.097 062
14	1.618 695	17.676 986	.056 571	.617 782	10.920 520	.091 571
15	1.675 349	19.295 681	.051 825	.596 891	11.517 411	.086 825
16	1.733 986	20.971 030	.047 685	.576 706	12.094 117	.082 685
17	1.794 676	22.705 016	.044 043	.557 204	12.651 321	.079 043
18	1.857 489	24.499 691	.040 817	.538 361	13.189 682	.075 817
19	1.922 501	26.357 180	.037 940	.520 156	13.709 837	.072 940
20	1.989 789	28.279 682	.035 361	.502 566	14.212 403	.070 361
21	2.059 431	30.269 471	.033 037	.485 571	14.697 974	.068 037
22	2.131 512	32.328 902	.030 932	.469 151	15.167 125	.065 932
23	2.206 114	34.460 414	.029 019	.453 286	15.620 410	.064 019
24	2.283 328	36.666 528	.027 273	.437 957	16.058 368	.062 273
25	2.363 245	38.949 857	.025 674	.423 147	16.481 515	.060 674
26	2.445 959	41.313 102	.024 205	.408 838	16.890 352	.059 205
27	2.531 567	43.759 060	.022 852	.395 012	17.285 365	.057 852
28	2.620 172	46.290 627	.021 603	.381 654	17.667 019	.056 603
29	2.711 878	48.910 799	.020 445	.368 748	18.035 767	.055 445
30	2.806 794	51.622 677	.019 371	.356 278	18.392 045	.054 371
31	2.905 031	54.429 471	.018 372	.344 230	18.736 276	.053 372
32	3.006 708	57.334 502	.017 442	.332 590	19.068 865	.052 442
33	3.111 942	60.341 210	.016 572	.321 343	19.390 208	.051 572
34	3.220 860	63.453 152	.015 760	.310 476	19.700 684	.050 760
35	3.333 590	66.674 013	.014 998	.299 977	20.000 661	.049 998
36	3.450 266	70.007 603	.014 284	.289 833	20 290 494	.049 284
37	3.571 025	73.457 869	.013 613	.280 032	20.570 525	.048 613
38	3.696 011	77.028 895	.012 982	.270 562	20.841 087	.047 982
39	3.825 372	80.724 906	.012 388	.261 413	21.102 500	.047 388
40	3.959 260	84.550 278	.011 827	.252 572	21.355 072	.046 827
41	4.097 834	88.509 537	.011 298	.244 031	21.599 104	.046 298
42	4.241 258	92.607 371	.010 798	.235 779	21.834 883	.045 798
43	4.389 702	96.848 629	.010 325	.227 806	22.062 689	.045 325
44	4.543 342	101.238 331	.009 878	.220 102	22.282 791	.044 878
45	4.702 359	105.781 673	.009 453	.212 659	22.495 450	.044 453
46	4.866 941	110.484 031	.009 051	.205 468	22.700 918	.044 051
47	5.037 284	115.350 973	.008 669	.198 520	22.899 438	.043 669
48	5.213 589	120 388 257	.008 306	.191 806	23.091 244	.043 306
49	5.396 065	125.601 846	.007 962	.185 320	23.276 564	.042 962
50	5.584 927	130.997 910	.007 634	.179 053	23.455 618	.042 634
51	5.780 399	136.582 837	.007 322	.172 998	23.628 616	.042 322
52	5.982 713	142.363 236	.007 024	.167 148	23.795 765	.042 024
53	6.192 108	148.345 950	.006 741	.161 496	23.957 260	.041 741
54	6.408 832	154.538 058	.006 471	.156 035	24.113 295	.041 471
55	6.633 141	160.946 890	.006 213	.150 758	24.264 053	.041 213
56	6.865 301	167.580 031	.005 967	.145 660	24.409 713	.040 967
57	7.105 587	174.445 332	.005 732	.140 734	24.550 448	.040 732
58	7.354 282	181.550 919	.005 508	.135 975	24.686 423	.040 508
59	7.661 682	188.905 201	.005 294	.131 377	24.817 800	.040 294
60	7.878 091	196.516 883	.005 089	.126 934	24.944 734	.040 089

$$S^n = (1+i)^n \quad S_{\overline{n}|} = \frac{S^n - 1}{i} \quad \frac{1}{S_{\overline{n}|}} = \frac{i}{S^n - 1} \quad V^n = \frac{1}{S^n} \quad A_{\overline{n}|} = \frac{1 - 1/S^n}{i} \quad \frac{1}{A_{\overline{n}|}} = \frac{i}{1 - 1/S^n}$$

Years	1 Amount of 1	2 Amount of 1 per Period	3 Sinking- Fund Factor	4 Present Worth of 1	5 Present Worth of 1 per Period	6 Partial Payment
1	1.037 500	1.000 000	1.000 000	.963 855	.963 855	1.037 500
2	1.076 406	2.037 500	.490 798	.929 017	1.892 873	.528 298
3	1.116 771	3.113 906	.321 140	.895 438	2.788 311	.358 640
4	1.158 650	4.230 678	.236 369	.863 073	3.651 384	.273 869
5	1.202 100	5.389 328	.185 552	.831 878	4.483 262	.223 052
6	1.247 179	6.591 428	.151 712	.801 810	5.285 072	.189 212
7	1.293 948	7.838 607	.127 574	.772 829	6.057 900	.165 074
8	1.342 471	9.132 554	.109 498	.744 895	6.802 796	.146 998
9	1.392 813	10.475 025	.095 465	.717 971	7.520 767	.132 965
10	1.445 044	11.867 838	.084 261	.692 020	8.212 787	.121 761
11	1.499 233	13.312 882	.075 115	.667 008	8.879 795	.112 615
12	1.555 454	14.812 116	.067 512	.642 899	9.522 694	.105 012
13	1.613 784	16.367 570	.061 096	.619 662	10.142 356	.098 596
14	1.674 301	17.981 354	.055 613	.597 264	10.739 620	.093 113
15	1.737 087	19.655 654	.050 876	.575 676	11.315 296	.088 376
16	1.802 228	21.392 742	.046 745	.554 869	11.870 165	.084 245
17	1.869 811	23.194 969	.043 113	.534 813	12.404 978	.080 613
18	1.939 929	25.064 781	.039 897	.515 483	12.920 461	.077 397
19	2.012 677	27.004 710	.037 031	.496 851	13.417 312	.074 531
20	2.088 152	29.017 387	.034 462	.478 892	13.896 204	.071 962
21	2.166 458	31.105 539	.032 149	.461 583	14.357 787	.069 649
22	2.247 700	33.271 996	.030 055	.444 899	14.802 686	.067 555
23	2.331 989	35.519 696	.028 153	.428 819	15.231 505	.065 653
24	2.419 438	37.851 685	.026 419	.413 319	15.644 824	.063 919
25	2.510 167	40.271 123	.024 832	.398 380	16.043 204	.062 332
26	2.604 298	42.781 290	.023 375	.383 981	16.427 185	.060 875
27	2.701 960	45.385 588	.022 033	.370 102	16.797 286	.059 533
28	2.803 283	48.087 548	.020 795	.356 725	17.154 011	.058 295
29	2.908 406	50.890 831	.019 650	.343 831	17.497 842	.057 150
30	3.017 471	53.799 237	.018 588	.331 403	17.829 245	.056 088
31	3.130 627	56.816 709	.017 600	.319 425	18.148 670	.055 100
32	3.248 025	59.947 335	.016 681	.307 879	18.456 549	.054 181
33	3.369 826	63.195 360	.015 824	.296 751	18.753 301	.053 324
34	3.496 194	66.565 186	.015 023	.286 025	19.039 326	.052 523
35	3.627 302	70.061 381	.014 273	.275 687	19.315 013	.051 773
36	3.763 326	73.688 682	.013 571	.265 722	19.580 735	.051 071
37	3.904 450	77.452 008	.012 911	.256 118	19.836 853	.050 411
38	4.050 867	81.356 458	.012 292	.246 861	20.083 714	.049 792
39	4.202 775	85.407 326	.011 709	.237 938	20.321 652	.049 209
40	4.360 379	89.610 100	.011 159	.229 338	20.550 990	.048 659
41	4.523 893	93.970 479	.010 642	.221 049	20.772 039	.048 142
42	4.693 539	98.494 372	.010 153	.213 059	20.985 097	.047 653
43	4.869 547	103.187 911	.009 691	.205 358	21.190 455	.047 191
44	5.052 155	108.057 458	.009 254	.197 935	21.388 391	.046 754
45	5.241 610	113.109 612	.008 841	.190 781	21.579 172	.046 341
46	5.438 171	118.351 223	.008 449	.183 885	21.763 057	.045 949
47	5.642 102	123.789 394	.008 078	.177 239	21.940 296	.045 578
48	5.853 681	129.431 496	.007 726	.170 833	22.111 129	.045 226
49	6.073 194	135.285 177	.007 392	.164 658	22.275 787	.044 892
50	6.300 939	141.358 371	.007 074	.158 707	22.434 493	.044 574
51	6.537 224	147.659 310	.006 772	.152 970	22.587 463	.044 272
52	6.782 370	154.196 534	.006 485	.147 441	22.734 904	.043 985
53	7.036 709	160.978 904	.006 212	.142 112	22.877 016	.043 712
54	7.300 585	168.015 613	.005 952	.136 975	23.013 992	.043 452
55	7.574 357	175.316 198	.005 704	.132 024	23.146 016	.043 204
56	7.858 396	182.890 556	.005 468	.127 252	23.273 268	.042 968
57	8.153 086	190.748 952	.005 242	.122 653	23.395 921	.042 742
58	8.458 826	198.902 037	.005 028	.118 220	23.514 141	.042 528
59	8.776 032	207.360 864	.004 823	.113 947	23.628 088	.042 323
60	9.105 134	216.136 896	.004 627	.109 828	23.737 916	.042 127

$$S^n = (1+i)^n \quad S_{\overline{n}|} = \frac{S^n-1}{i} \quad \frac{1}{S_{\overline{n}|}} = \frac{i}{S^n-1} \quad V^n = \frac{1}{S^n} \quad A_{\overline{n}|} = \frac{1-1/S^n}{i} \quad \frac{1}{A_{\overline{n}|}} = \frac{i}{1-1/S^n}$$

	1	2	3	4	5	6
Years	Amount of 1	Amount of 1 per Period	Sinking-Fund Factor	Present Worth of 1	Present Worth of 1 per Period	Partial Payment
1	1.040 000	1.000 000	1.000 000	.961 538	.961 538	1.040 000
2	1.081 600	2.040 000	.490 196	.924 556	1.886 095	.530 196
3	1.124 864	3.121 600	.320 349	.888 996	2.775 091	.360 349
4	1.169 859	4.246 464	.235 490	.854 804	3.629 895	.275 490
5	1.216 653	5.416 323	.184 627	.821 927	4.451 822	.224 627
6	1.265 319	6.632 975	.150 762	.790 315	5.242 137	.190 762
7	1.315 932	7.898 294	.126 610	.759 918	6.002 055	.166 610
8	1.368 569	9.214 226	.108 528	.730 690	6.732 745	.148 528
9	1.423 312	10.582 795	.094 493	.702 587	7.435 332	.134 493
10	1.480 244	12.006 107	.083 291	.675 564	8.110 896	.123 291
11	1.539 454	13.486 351	.074 149	.649 581	8.760 477	.114 149
12	1.601 032	15.025 805	.066 552	.624 597	9.385 074	.106 552
13	1.665 074	16.626 838	.060 144	.600 574	9.985 648	.100 144
14	1.731 676	18.291 911	.054 669	.577 475	10.563 123	.094 669
15	1.800 944	20.023 588	.049 941	.555 265	11.118 387	.089 941
16	1.872 981	21.824 531	.045 820	.533 908	11.652 296	.085 820
17	1.947 900	23.697 512	.042 199	.513 373	12.165 669	.082 199
18	2.025 817	25.645 413	.038 993	.493 628	12.659 297	.078 993
19	2.106 849	27.671 229	.036 139	.474 642	13.133 939	.076 139
20	2.191 123	29.778 079	.033 582	.456 387	13.590 326	.073 582
21	2.278 768	31.969 202	.031 280	.438 834	14.029 160	.071 280
22	2.369 919	34.247 970	.029 199	.421 955	14.451 115	.069 199
23	2.464 716	36.617 889	.027 309	.405 726	14.856 842	.067 309
24	2.563 304	39.082 604	.025 587	.390 121	15.246 963.	.065 587
25	2.665 836	41.645 908	.024 012	.375 117	15.622 080	.064 012
26	2.772 470	44.311 745	.022 567	.360 689	15.982 769	.062 567
27	2.883 369	47.084 214	.021 239	.346 817	16.329 586	.061 239
28	2.998 703	49.967 583	.020 013	.333 477	16.663 063	.060 013
29	3.118 651	52.966 286	.018 880	.320 651	16.983 715	.058 880
30	3.243 398	56.084 938	.017 830	.308 319	17.292 033	.057 830
31	3.373 133	59.328 335	.016 855	.296 460	17.588 494	.056 855
32	3.508 059	62.701 469	.015 949	.285 058	17.873 551	.055 949
33	3.648 381	66.209 527	.015 104	.274 094	18.147 646	.055 104
34	3.794 316	69.857 909	.014 315	.263 552	18.411 198	.054 315
35	3.946 089	73.652 225	.013 577	.253 415	18.664 613	.053 577
36	4.103 933	77.598 314	.012 887	.243 669	18.908 282	.052 887
37	4.268 090	81.702 246	.012 240	.234 297	19.142 579	.052 240
38	4.438 813	85.970 336	.011 632	.225 285	19.367 864	.051 632
39	4.616 366	90.409 150	.011 061	.216 621	19.584 485	.051 061
40	4.801 021	95.025 516	.010 523	.208 289	19.792 774	.050 523
41	4.993 061	99.826 536	.010 017	.200 278	19.993 052	.050 017
42	5.192 784	104.819 598	.009 540	.192 575	20.185 627	.049 540
43	5.400 495	110.012 382	.009 090	.185 168	20.370 795	.049 090
44	5.616 515	115.412 877	.008 665	.178 046	20.548 841	.048 665
45	5.841 176	121.029 392	.008 262	.171 198	20.720 040	.048 262
46	6.074 823	126.870 568	.007 882	.164 614	20.884 654	.047 882
47	6.317 816	132.945 390	.007 522	.158 283	21.042 936	.047 522
48	6.570 528	139.263 206	.007 181	.152 195	21.195 131	.047 181
49	6.833 349	145.833 734	.006 857	.146 341	21.341 472	.046 857
50	7.106 683	152.667 084	.006 550	.140 713	21.482 185	.046 550
51	7.390 951	159.773 767	.006 259	.135 301	21.617 485	.046 259
52	7.686 589	167.164 718	.005 982	.130 097	21.747 582	.045 982
53	7.994 052	174.851 306	.005 719	.125 093	21.872 675	.045 719
54	8.313 814	182.845 359	.005 469	.120 282	21.992 957	.045 469
55	8.646 367	191.159 173	.005 231	.115 656	22.108 612	.045 231
56	8.992 222	199.805 540	.005 005	.111 207	22.219 819	.045 005
57	9.351 910	208.797 762	.004 789	.106 930	22.326 749	.044 789
58	9.725 987	218.149 672	.004 584	.102 817	22.429 567	.044 584
59	10.115 026	227.875 659	.004 388	.098 863	22.528 430	.044 388
60	10.519 627	237.990 685	.004 202	.095 060	22.623 490	.044 202

$$S^n = (1+i)^n \quad S_{\overline{n}|} = \frac{S^n - 1}{i} \quad \frac{1}{S_{\overline{n}|}} = \frac{i}{S^n - 1} \quad V^n = \frac{1}{S^n} \quad A_{\overline{n}|} = \frac{1 - 1/S^n}{i} \quad \frac{1}{A_{\overline{n}|}} = \frac{i}{1 - 1/S^n}$$

4¼%
Annual
Table

Years	1 Amount of 1	2 Amount of 1 per Period	3 Sinking- Fund Factor	4 Present Worth of 1	5 Present Worth of 1 per Period	6 Partial Payment
1	1.042 500	1.000 000	1.000 000	.959 233	.959 233	1.042 500
2	1.086 806	2.042 500	.489 596	.920 127	1.879 360	.532 096
3	1.132 996	3.129 306	.319 560	.882 616	2.761 976	.362 060
4	1.181 148	4.262 302	.234 615	.846 634	3.608 610	.277 115
5	1.231 347	5.443 450	.183 707	.812 119	4.420 729	.226 207
6	1.283 679	6.674 796	.149 817	.779 011	5.199 740	.192 317
7	1.338 235	7.958 475	.125 652	.747 253	5.946 993	.168 152
8	1.395 110	9.296 710	.107 565	.716 789	6.663 782	.150 065
9	1.454 402	10.691 820	.093 529	.687 568	7.351 350	.136 029
10	1.516 214	12.146 223	.082 330	.659 537	8.010 887	.124 830
11	1.580 654	13.662 437	.073 193	.632 650	8.643 537	.115 693
12	1.647 831	15.243 091	.065 603	.606 858	9.250 395	.108 103
13	1.717 864	16.890 922	.059 203	.582 118	9.832 513	.101 703
14	1.790 873	18.608 786	.053 738	.558 387	10.390 900	.096 238
15	1.866 986	20.399 660	.049 020	.535 623	10.926 523	.091 520
16	1.946 332	22.266 645	.044 910	.513 787	11.440 309	.087 410
17	2.029 052	24.212 978	.041 300	.492 841	11.933 151	.083 800
18	2.115 286	26.242 029	.038 107	.472 749	12.405 900	.080 607
19	2.205 186	28.357 316	.035 264	.453 477	12.859 376	.077 764
20	2.298 906	30.562 501	.032 720	.434 989	13.294 366	.075 220
21	2.396 610	32.861 408	.030 431	.417 256	13.711 622	.072 931
22	2.498 466	35.258 018	.028 362	.400 246	14.111 868	.070 862
23	2.604 651	37.756 483	.026 486	.383 929	14.495 796	.068 986
24	2.715 348	40.361 134	.024 776	.368 277	14.864 073	.067 276
25	2.830 750	43.076 482	.023 215	.353 263	15.217 336	.065 715
26	2.951 057	45.907 233	.021 783	.338 862	15.556 198	.064 283
27	3.076 477	48.858 290	.020 467	.325 047	15.881 245	.062 967
28	3.207 228	51.934 767	.019 255	.311 796	16.193 041	.061 755
29	3.343 535	55.141 995	.018 135	.299 085	16.492 125	.060 635
30	3.485 635	58.485 530	.017 098	.286 892	16.779 017	.059 598
31	3.633 775	61.971 165	.016 137	.275 196	17.054 213	.058 637
32	3.788 210	65.604 939	.015 243	.263 977	17.318 190	.057 743
33	3.949 209	69.393 149	.014 411	.253 215	17.571 405	.056 911
34	4.117 050	73.342 358	.013 635	.242 892	17.814 298	.056 135
35	4.292 025	77.459 408	.012 910	.232 990	18.047 288	.055 410
36	4.474 436	81.751 433	.012 232	.223 492	18.270 780	.054 732
37	4.664 599	86.225 869	.011 597	.214 381	18.485 160	.054 097
38	4.862 845	90.890 468	.011 002	.205 641	18.690 801	.053 502
39	5.069 516	95.753 313	.010 444	.197 257	18.888 059	.052 944
40	5.284 970	100.822 829	.009 918	.189 216	19.077 275	.052 418
41	5.509 581	106.107 799	.009 424	.181 502	19.258 777	.051 924
42	5.743 739	111.617 381	.008 959	.174 103	19.432 879	.051 459
43	5.987 848	117.361 119	.008 521	.167 005	19.599 884	.051 021
44	6.242 331	123.348 967	.008 107	.160 197	19.760 081	.050 607
45	6.507 630	129.591 298	.007 717	.153 666	19.913 747	.050 217
46	6.784 204	136.098 928	.007 348	.147 401	20.061 148	.049 848
47	7.072 533	142.883 133	.006 999	.141 392	20.202 540	.049 499
48	7.373 116	149.955 666	.006 669	.135 628	20.338 168	.049 169
49	7.686 473	157.328 782	.006 356	.130 099	20.468 266	.048 856
50	8.013 148	165.015 255	.006 060	.124 795	20.593 061	.048 560
51	8.353 707	173.028 403	.005 779	.119 707	20.712 769	.048 279
52	8.708 740	181.382 110	.005 513	.114 827	20.827 596	.048 013
53	9.078 861	190.090 850	.005 261	.110 146	20.937 742	.047 761
54	9.464 713	199.169 711	.005 021	.105 656	21.043 397	.047 521
55	9.866 963	208.634 424	.004 793	.101 348	21.144 746	.047 293
56	10.286 309	218.501 387	.004 577	.097 217	21.241 962	.047 077
57	10.723 477	228.787 696	.004 371	.093 253	21.335 216	.046 871
58	11.179 225	239.511 173	.004 175	.089 452	21.424 667	.046 675
59	11.654 342	250.690 398	.003 989	.085 805	21.510 472	.046 489
60	12.149 651	262.344 740	.003 812	.082 307	21.592 779	.046 312

$$S^n = (1+i)^n \qquad S_{\overline{n}|} = \frac{S^n - 1}{i} \qquad \frac{1}{S_{\overline{n}|}} = \frac{i}{S^n - 1} \qquad V^n = \frac{1}{S^n} \qquad A_{\overline{n}|} = \frac{1 - 1/S^n}{i} \qquad \frac{1}{A_{\overline{n}|}} = \frac{i}{1 - 1/S^n}$$

Years	1 Amount of 1	2 Amount of 1 per Period	3 Sinking- Fund Factor	4 Present Worth of 1	5 Present Worth of 1 per Period	6 Partial Payment
1	1.045 000	1.000 000	1.000 000	.956 938	.956 938	1.045 000
2	1.092 025	2.045 000	.488 998	.915 730	1.872 668	.533 998
3	1.141 166	3.137 025	.318 773	.876 297	2.748 964	.363 773
4	1.192 519	4.278 191	.233 744	.838 561	3.587 526	.278 744
5	1.246 182	5.470 710	.182 792	.802 451	4.389 977	.227 792
6	1.302 260	6.716 892	.148 878	.767 896	5.157 872	.193 878
7	1.360 862	8.019 152	.124 701	.734 828	5.892 701	.169 701
8	1.422 101	9.380 014	.106 610	.703 185	6.595 886	.151 610
9	1.486 095	10.802 114	.092 574	.672 904	7.268 790	.137 574
10	1.552 969	12.288 209	.081 379	.643 928	7.912 718	.126 379
11	1.622 853	13.841 179	.072 248	.616 199	8.528 917	.117 248
12	1.695 881	15.464 032	.064 666	.589 664	9.118 581	.019 666
13	1.772 196	17.159 913	.058 275	.564 272	9.682 852	.013 275
14	1.851 945	18.932 109	.052 820	.539 973	10.222 825	.097 820
15	1.935 282	20.784 054	.048 114	.516 720	10.739 546	.093 114
16	2.022 370	22.719 337	.044 015	.494 469	11.234 015	.089 015
17	2.113 377	24.741 707	.040 418	.473 176	11.707 191	.085 418
18	2.208 479	26.855 084	.037 237	.452 800	12.159 992	.082 237
19	2.307 860	29.063 562	.034 407	.433 302	12.593 294	.079 407
20	2.411 714	31.371 423	.031 876	.414 643	13.007 936	.076 876
21	2.520 241	33.783 137	.029 601	.396 787	13.404 724	.074 601
22	2.633 652	36.303 378	.027 546	.379 701	13.784 425	.072 546
23	2.752 166	38.937 030	.025 682	.363 350	14.147 775	.070 682
24	2.876 014	41.689 196	.023 987	.347 703	14.495 478	.068 987
25	3.005 434	44.565 210	.022 439	.332 731	14.828 209	.067 439
26	3.140 679	47.570 645	.021 021	.318 402	15.146 611	.066 021
27	3.282 010	50.711 324	.019 719	.304 691	15.451 303	.064 719
28	3.429 700	53.993 333	.018 521	.291 571	15.742 874	.063 521
29	3.584 036	57.423 033	.017 415	.279 015	16.021 889	.062 415
30	3.745 318	61.007 070	.016 392	.267 000	16.288 889	.061 392
31	3.913 857	64.752 388	.015 443	.255 502	16.544 391	.060 443
32	4.089 981	68.666 245	.014 563	.244 500	16.788 891	.059 563
33	4.274 030	72.756 226	.013 745	.233 971	17.022 862	.058 745
34	4.466 362	77.030 256	.012 982	.233 896	17.246 758	.057 982
35	4.667 348	81.496 618	.012 270	.214 254	17.461 012	.057 270
36	4.877 378	86.163 966	.011 606	.205 028	17.666 041	.056 606
37	5.096 860	91.041 344	.010 984	.196 199	17.862 240	.055 984
38	5.326 219	96.138 205	.010 402	.187 750	18.049 990	.055 402
39	5.565 899	101.464 424	.009 856	.179 665	18.229 656	.054 856
40	5.816 365	107.030 323	.009 343	.171 929	18.401 584	.054 343
41	6.078 101	112.846 688	.008 862	.164 525	18.566 109	.053 862
42	6.351 615	118.924 789	.008 409	.157 440	18.723 550	.053 409
43	6.637 438	125.276 404	.007 982	.150 661	18.874 210	.052 982
44	6.936 123	131.913 842	.007 581	.144 173	19.018 383	.052 581
45	7.248 248	138.849 965	.007 202	.137 964	19.156 347	.052 202
46	7.574 420	146.098 214	.006 845	.132 023	19.288 371	.051 845
47	7.915 268	153.672 633	.006 507	.126 338	19.414 709	.051 507
48	8.271 456	161.587 902	.006 189	.120 898	19.535 607	.051 189
49	8.643 671	169.859 357	.005 887	.115 692	19.651 298	.050 887
50	9.032 636	178.503 028	.005 602	.110 710	19.762 008	.050 602
51	9.439 105	187.535 665	.005 332	.105 942	19.867 950	.050 332
52	9.863 865	196.974 769	.005 077	.101 380	19.969 330	.050 077
53	10.307 739	206.838 634	.004 835	.097 014	20.066 345	.049 835
54	10.771 587	217.146 373	.004 605	.092 837	20.159 181	.049 605
55	11.256 308	227.917 959	.004 388	.088 839	20.248 021	.049 388
56	11.762 842	239.174 268	.004 181	.085 013	20.333 034	.049 181
57	12.292 170	250.937 110	.003 985	.081 353	20.414 387	.048 985
58	12.845 318	263.229 280	.003 799	.077 849	20.492 236	.048 799
59	13.423 357	276.074 597	.003 622	.074 497	20.566 733	.048 622
60	14.027 408	289.497 954	.003 454	.071 289	20.638 022	.048 454

$$S^n = (1+i)^n \quad S_{\overline{n}|} = \frac{S^n - 1}{i} \quad \frac{1}{S_{\overline{n}|}} = \frac{i}{S^n - 1} \quad V^n = \frac{1}{S^n} \quad A_{\overline{n}|} = \frac{1 - 1/S^n}{i} \quad \frac{1}{A_{\overline{n}|}} = \frac{i}{1 - 1/S^n}$$

4¾%
Annual
Table

	1	2	3	4	5	6
Years	Amount of 1	Amount of 1 per Period	Sinking-Fund Factor	Present Worth of 1	Present Worth of 1 per Period	Partial Payment
1	1.047 500	1.000 000	1.000 000	.954 654	.954 654	1.047 500
2	1.097 256	2.047 500	.488 400	.911 364	1.866 018	.535 900
3	1.149 376	3.144 756	.317 990	.870 037	2.736 055	.365 490
4	1.203 971	4.294 132	.232 876	.830 585	3.566 640	.280 376
5	1.261 160	5.498 103	.181 881	.792 921	4.359 561	.229 381
6	1.321 065	6.759 263	.147 945	.756 965	5.116 526	.195 445
7	1.383 816	8.080 328	.123 757	.722 640	5.839 166	.171 257
8	1.449 547	9.464 144	.105 662	.689 871	6.529 036	.153 162
9	1.518 400	10.913 691	.091 628	.658 588	7.187 624	.139 128
10	1.590 524	12.432 091	.080 437	.628 723	7.816 348	.127 937
11	1.666 074	14.022 615	.071 313	.600 213	8.416 561	.118 813
12	1.745 213	15.688 690	.063 740	.572 996	8.989 557	.111 240
13	1.828 110	17.433 902	.057 360	.547 013	9.536 570	.104 860
14	1.914 946	19.262 013	.051 916	.522 208	10.058 778	.099 416
15	2.005 906	21.176 958	.047 221	.498 528	10.557 306	.094 721
16	2.101 186	23.182 864	.043 135	.475 922	11.033 228	.090 635
17	2.200 992	25.284 050	.039 551	.454 341	11.487 568	.087 051
18	2.305 540	27.485 042	.036 383	.433 738	11.921 306	.083 883
19	2.415 053	29.790 582	.033 568	.414 070	12.335 376	.081 068
20	2.529 768	32.205 635	.031 050	.395 293	12.730 669	.078 550
21	2.649 932	34.735 402	.028 789	.377 368	13.108 037	.076 289
22	2.775 803	37.385 334	.026 748	.360 256	13.468 293	.074 248
23	2.907 654	40.161 137	.024 900	.343 920	13.812 213	.072 400
24	3.045 768	43.068 791	.023 219	.328 324	14.140 538	.070 719
25	3.190 442	46.114 559	.021 685	.313 436	14.453 974	.069 185
26	3.341 988	49.305 000	.020 282	.299 223	14.753 197	.067 782
27	3.500 732	52.646 988	.018 994	.285 655	15.038 852	.066 494
28	3.667 017	56.147 720	.017 810	.272 701	15.311 553	.065 310
29	3.841 200	59.814 736	.016 718	.260 335	15.571 888	.064 218
30	4.023 657	63.655 936	.015 709	.248 530	15.820 418	.063 209
31	4.214 781	67.679 593	.014 776	.237 260	16.057 679	.062 276
32	4.414 983	71.894 374	.013 909	.226 501	16.284 180	.061 409
33	4.624 694	76.309 357	.013 105	.216 231	16.500 410	.060 605
34	4.844 367	80.934 051	.012 356	.206 425	16.706 836	.059 856
35	5.074 475	85.778 419	.011 658	.197 065	16.903 901	.059 158
36	5.315 512	90.852 894	.011 007	.188 129	17.092 029	.058 507
37	5.567 999	96.168 406	.010 398	.179 598	17.271 627	.057 898
38	5.832 479	101.736 405	.009 829	.171 454	17.443 081	.057 329
39	6.109 522	107.568 884	.009 296	.163 679	17.606 759	.056 796
40	6.399 724	113.678 406	.008 797	.156 257	17.763 016	.056 297
41	6.703 711	120.078 131	.008 328	.149 171	17.912 187	.055 828
42	7.022 137	126.781 842	.007 888	.142 407	18.054 594	.055 388
43	7.355 689	133.803 980	.007 474	.135 949	18.190 543	.054 974
44	7.705 084	141.159 669	.007 084	.129 784	18.320 328	.054 584
45	8.071 076	148.864 753	.006 718	.123 899	18.444 227	.054 218
46	8.454 452	156.935 829	.006 372	.118 281	18.562 508	.053 872
47	8.856 038	165.390 280	.006 046	.112 917	18.675 425	.053 546
48	9.276 700	174.246 319	.005 739	.107 797	18.783 222	.053 239
49	9.717 343	183.523 019	.005 449	.102 909	18.886 131	.052 949
50	10.178 917	193.240 362	.005 175	.098 242	18.984 373	.052 675
51	10.662 416	203.419 279	.004 916	.093 787	19.078 160	.052 416
52	11.168 881	214.081 695	.004 671	.089 534	19.167 695	.052 171
53	11.699 402	225.250 576	.004 440	.085 474	19.253 169	.051 940
54	12.255 124	236.949 978	.004 220	.081 599	19.334 768	.051 720
55	12.837 242	249.205 102	.004 013	.077 898	19.412 666	.051 513
56	13.447 011	262.042 344	.003 816	.074 366	19.487 032	.051 316
57	14.085 744	275.489 356	.003 630	.070 994	19.558 026	.051 130
58	14.754 817	289.575 100	.003 453	.067 774	19.625 801	.050 953
59	15.455 671	304.329 917	.003 286	.064 701	19.690 502	.050 786
60	16.189 815	319.785 589	.003 127	.061 767	19.752 269	.050 627

$$S^n = (1+i)^n \quad S_{\overline{n}|} = \frac{S^n - 1}{i} \quad \frac{1}{S_{\overline{n}|}} = \frac{i}{S^n - 1} \quad V^n = \frac{1}{S^n} \quad A_{\overline{n}|} = \frac{1 - 1/S^n}{i} \quad \frac{1}{A_{\overline{n}|}} = \frac{i}{1 - 1/S^n}$$

5%
Annual
Table

Years	1 Amount of 1	2 Amount of 1 per Period	3 Sinking-Fund Factor	4 Present Worth of 1	5 Present Worth of 1 per Period	6 Partial Payment
1	1.050 000	1.000 000	1.000 000	.952 381	.952 381	1.050 000
2	1.102 500	2.050 000	.487 805	.907 029	1.859 410	.537 805
3	1.157 625	3.152 500	.317 209	.863 838	2.723 248	.367 209
4	1.215 506	4.310 125	.232 012	.822 702	3.545 951	.282 012
5	1.276 282	5.525 631	.180 975	.783 526	4.329 477	.230 975
6	1.340 096	6.801 913	.147 017	.746 215	5.075 692	.197 017
7	1.407 100	8.142 008	.122 820	.710 681	5.786 373	.172 820
8	1.477 455	9.549 109	.104 722	.676 839	6.463 213	.154 722
9	1.551 328	11.026 564	.090 690	.644 609	7.107 822	.140 690
10	1.628 895	12.577 893	.079 505	.613 913	7.721 735	.129 505
11	1.710 339	14.206 787	.070 389	.584 679	8.306 414	.120 389
12	1.795 856	15.917 127	.062 825	.556 837	8.863 252	.112 825
13	1.885 649	17.712 983	.056 456	.530 321	9.393 573	.106 456
14	1.979 932	19.598 632	.051 024	.505 068	9.898 641	.101 024
15	2.078 928	21.578 564	.046 342	.481 017	10.379 658	.096 342
16	2.182 875	23.657 492	.042 270	.458 112	10.837 770	.092 270
17	2.292 018	25.840 366	.038 699	.436 297	11.274 066	.088 699
18	2.406 619	28.132 385	.035 546	.415 521	11.689 587	.085 546
19	2.526 950	30.539 004	.032 745	.395 734	12.085 321	.082 745
20	2.653 298	33.065 954	.030 243	.376 889	12.462 210	.080 243
21	2.785 963	35.719 252	.027 996	.358 942	12.821 153	.077 996
22	2.925 261	38.505 214	.025 971	.341 850	13.163 003	.075 971
23	3.071 524	41.430 475	.024 137	.325 571	13.488 574	.074 137
24	3.225 100	44.501 999	.022 471	.310 068	13.798 642	.072 471
25	3.386 355	47.727 099	.020 952	.295 303	14.093 945	.070 952
26	3.555 673	51.113 454	.019 564	.281 241	14.375 185	.069 564
27	3.733 456	54.669 126	.018 292	.267 848	14.643 034	.068 292
28	3.920 129	58.402 583	.017 123	.255 094	14.898 127	.067 123
29	4.116 136	62.322 712	.016 046	.242 946	15.141 074	.066 046
30	4.321 942	66.438 848	.015 051	.231 377	15.372 451	.065 051
31	4.538 039	70.760 790	.014 132	.220 359	15.592 811	.064 132
32	4.764 941	75.298 829	.013 280	.209 866	15.802 677	.063 280
33	5.003 189	80.063 771	.012 490	.199 873	16.002 549	.062 490
34	5.253 348	85.066 959	.011 755	.190 355	16.192 904	.061 755
35	5.516 015	90.320 307	.011 072	.181 290	16.374 194	.061 072
36	5.791 816	95.836 323	.010 434	.172 657	16.546 852	.060 434
37	6.081 407	101.628 139	.009 840	.164 436	16.711 287	.059 840
38	6.385 477	107.709 546	.009 284	.156 605	16.867 893	.059 284
39	6.704 751	114.095 023	.008 765	.149 148	17.017 041	.058 765
40	7.039 989	120.799 774	.008 278	.142 046	17.159 086	.058 278
41	7.391 988	127.839 763	.007 822	.135 282	17.294 368	.057 822
42	7.761 588	135.231 751	.007 395	.128 840	17.423 208	.057 395
43	8.149 667	142.993 339	.006 993	.122 704	17.545 912	.056 993
44	8.557 150	151.143 006	.006 616	.116 861	17.662 773	.056 616
45	8.985 008	159.700 156	.006 262	.111 297	17.774 070	.056 262
46	9.434 258	168.685 164	.005 928	.105 997	17.880 066	.055 928
47	9.905 971	178.119 422	.005 614	.100 949	17.981 016	.055 614
48	10.401 270	188.025 393	.005 318	.096 142	18.077 158	.055 318
49	10.921 333	198.426 663	.005 040	.091 564	18.168 722	.055 040
50	11.467 400	209.347 996	.004 777	.087 204	18.255 925	.054 777
51	12.040 770	220.815 396	.004 529	.083 051	18.338 977	.054 529
52	12.642 808	232.856 165	.004 294	.079 096	18.418 073	.054 294
53	13.274 949	245.498 974	.004 073	.075 330	18.493 403	.054 073
54	13.938 696	258.773 922	.003 864	.071 743	18.565 146	.053 864
55	14.635 631	272.712 618	.003 667	.068 326	18.633 472	.053 667
56	15.367 412	287.348 249	.003 480	.065 073	18.698 545	.053 480
57	16.135 783	302.715 662	.003 303	.061 974	18.760 519	.053 303
58	16.942 572	318.851 445	.003 136	.059 023	18.819 542	.053 136
59	17.789 701	335.794 017	.002 978	.056 212	18.875 754	.052 978
60	18.679 186	353.583 718	.002 828	.053 536	18.929 290	.052 828

$$S^n = (1+i)^n \qquad S_{\overline{n}|} = \frac{S^n - 1}{i} \qquad \frac{1}{S_{\overline{n}|}} = \frac{i}{S^n - 1} \qquad V^n = \frac{1}{S^n} \qquad A_{\overline{n}|} = \frac{1 - 1/S^n}{i} \qquad \frac{1}{A_{\overline{n}|}} = \frac{i}{1 - 1/S^n}$$

326

5¼%
Annual
Table

Years	1 Amount of 1	2 Amount of 1 per Period	3 Sinking-Fund Factor	4 Present Worth of 1	5 Present Worth of 1 per Period	6 Partial Payment
1	1.052 500	1.000 000	1.000 000	.950 119	.950 119	1.052 500
2	1.107 756	2.052 500	.487 211	.902 726	1.852 844	.539 711
3	1.165 913	3.160 256	.316 430	.857 697	2.710 541	.368 930
4	1.227 124	4.326 170	.231 151	.814 914	3.525 455	.283 651
5	1.291 548	5.553 294	.180 073	.774 265	4.299 719	.232 573
6	1.359 354	6.844 842	.146 095	.735 643	5.035 363	.198 595
7	1.430 720	8.204 196	.121 889	.698 949	5.734 311	.174 389
8	1.505 833	9.634 916	.103 789	.664 084	6.398 396	.156 289
9	1.584 889	11.140 749	.089 761	.630 959	7.029 355	.142 261
10	1.668 096	12.725 638	.078 582	.599 486	7.628 840	.131 082
11	1.755 671	14.393 734	.069 475	.569 583	8.198 423	.121 975
12	1.847 844	16.149 405	.061 922	.541 171	8.739 595	.114 422
13	1.944 856	17.997 249	.055 564	.514 177	9.253 772	.108 064
14	2.046 961	19.942 105	.050 145	.488 529	9.742 301	.102 645
15	2.154 426	21.989 065	.045 477	.464 161	10.206 462	.097 977
16	2.267 533	24.143 491	.041 419	.441 008	10.647 469	.093 919
17	2.386 579	26.411 025	.037 863	.419 010	11.066 479	.090 363
18	2.511 874	28.797 603	.034 725	.398 109	11.464 588	.087 225
19	2.643 748	31.309 478	.031 939	.378 251	11.842 839	.084 439
20	2.782 544	33.953 225	.029 452	.359 383	12.202 223	.081 952
21	2.928 628	36.735 769	.027 221	.341 457	12.543 679	.079 721
22	3.082 381	39.664 397	.025 212	.324 425	12.868 104	.077 712
23	3.244 206	42.746 778	.023 394	.308 242	13.176 346	.075 894
24	3.414 527	45.990 984	.021 743	.292 866	13.469 212	.074 243
25	3.593 789	49.405 511	.020 241	.278 258	13.747 470	.072 741
26	3.782 463	52.999 300	.018 868	.264 378	14.011 848	.071 368
27	3.981 043	56.781 763	.017 611	.251 190	14.263 038	.070 111
28	4.190 047	60.762 806	.016 457	.238 661	14.501 699	.068 957
29	4.410 025	64.952 853	.015 396	.226 756	14.728 455	.067 896
30	4.641 551	69.362 878	.014 417	.215 445	14.943 901	.066 917
31	4.885 233	74.004 429	.013 513	.204 699	15.148 599	.066 013
32	5.141 707	78.889 662	.012 676	.194 488	15.343 087	.065 176
33	5.411 647	84.031 369	.011 900	.184 787	15.527 874	.064 400
34	5.695 758	89.443 016	.011 180	.175 569	15.703 443	.063 680
35	5.994 786	95.138 774	.010 511	.166 812	15.870 255	.063 011
36	6.309 512	101.133 560	.009 888	.158 491	16.028 745	.062 388
37	6.640 761	107.443 071	.009 307	.150 585	16.179 331	.061 807
38	6.989 401	114.083 833	.008 765	.143 074	16.322 404	.061 265
38	7.356 345	121.073 234	.008 259	.135 937	16.458 341	.060 759
40	7.742 553	128.429 579	.007 786	.129 156	16.587 498	.060 286
41	8.149 037	136.172 132	.007 344	.122 714	16.710 212	.059 844
42	8.576 861	144.321 169	.006 929	.116 593	16.826 804	.059 429
43	9.027 147	152.898 030	.006 540	.110 777	16.937 581	.059 040
44	9.501 072	161.925 176	.006 176	.105 251	17.042 833	.058 676
45	9.999 878	171.426 248	.005 833	.100 001	17.142 834	.058 333
46	10.524 872	181.426 126	.005 512	.095 013	17.237 847	.058 012
47	11.077 427	191.950 998	.005 210	.090 274	17.328 121	.057 710
48	11.658 992	203.028 425	.004 925	.085 771	17.413 891	.057 425
49	12.271 089	214.687 418	.004 658	.081 492	17.495 384	.057 158
50	12.915 322	226.958 507	.004 406	.077 427	17.572 811	.056 906
51	13.593 376	239.873 829	.004 169	.073 565	17.646 376	.056 669
52	14.307 028	253.467 205	.003 945	.069 896	17.716 272	.056 445
53	15.058 147	267.774 233	.003 734	.066 409	17.782 681	.056 234
54	15.848 700	282.832 380	.003 536	.063 097	17.845 778	.056 036
55	16.680 757	298.681 080	.003 348	.059 949	17.905 727	.055 848
56	17.556 496	315.361 837	.003 171	.056 959	17.962 686	.055 671
57	18.478 212	332.918 333	.003 004	.054 118	18.016 804	.055 504
58	19.448 319	351.396 546	.002 846	.051 418	18.068 222	.055 346
59	20.469 355	370.844 864	.002 697	.048 854	18.117 076	.055 197
60	21.543 997	391.314 220	.002 555	.046 417	18.163 493	.055 055

$S^n = (1+i)^n$	$S_{\overline{n}|} = \dfrac{S^n - 1}{i}$	$\dfrac{1}{S_{\overline{n}|}} = \dfrac{i}{S^n - 1}$	$V^n = \dfrac{1}{S^n}$	$A_{\overline{n}|} = \dfrac{1 - 1/S^n}{i}$	$\dfrac{1}{A_{\overline{n}|}} = \dfrac{i}{1 - 1/S^n}$

327

5½%
Annual
Table

Years	1 Amount of 1	2 Amount of 1 per Period	3 Sinking- Fund Factor	4 Present Worth of 1	5 Present Worth of 1 per Period	6 Partial Payment
1	1.055 000	1.000 000	1.000 000	.947 867	.947 867	1.055 000
2	1.113 025	2.055 000	.486 618	.898 452	1.846 320	.541 618
3	1.174 241	3.168 025	.315 654	.851 614	2.697 933	.370 654
4	1.238 825	4.342 266	.230 294	.807 217	3.505 150	.285 294
5	1.306 960	5.581 091	.179 176	.765 134	4.270 284	.234 176
6	1.378 843	6.888 051	.145 179	.725 246	4.995 530	.200 179
7	1.454 679	8.266 894	.120 964	.687 437	5.682 967	.175 964
8	1.534 687	9.721 573	.102 864	.651 599	6.334 566	.157 864
9	1.619 094	11.256 260	.088 839	.617 629	6.952 195	.143 839
10	1.708 144	12.875 354	.077 668	.585 431	7.537 626	.132 668
11	1.802 092	14.583 498	.068 571	.554 911	8.092 536	.123 571
12	1.901 207	16.385 591	.061 029	.525 982	8.618 518	.116 029
13	2.005 774	18.286 798	.054 684	.498 561	9.117 079	.109 684
14	2.116 091	20.292 572	.049 279	.472 569	9.589 648	.104 279
15	2.232 476	22.408 663	.044 626	.447 933	10.037 581	.099 626
16	2.355 263	24.641 140	.040 583	.424 581	10.462 162	.095 583
17	2.484 802	26.996 403	.037 042	.402 447	10.864 609	.092 042
18	2.621 466	29.481 205	.033 920	.381 466	11.246 074	.088 920
19	2.765 647	32.102 671	.031 150	.361 579	11.607 654	.086 150
20	2.917 757	34.868 318	.028 679	.342 729	11.950 382	.083 679
21	3.078 234	37.786 076	.026 465	.324 862	12.275 244	.081 465
22	3.247 537	40.864 310	.024 471	.307 926	12.583 170	.079 471
23	3.426 152	44.111 847	.022 670	.291 873	12.875 042	.077 670
24	3.614 590	47.537 998	.021 036	.276 657	13.151 699	.076 036
25	3.813 392	51.152 588	.019 549	.262 234	13.413 933	.074 549
26	4.023 129	54.965 981	.018 193	.248 563	13.662 495	.073 193
27	4.244 401	58.989 109	.016 952	.235 605	13.898 100	.071 952
28	4.477 843	63.233 510	.015 814	.223 322	14.121 422	.070 814
29	4.724 124	67.711 354	.014 769	.211 679	14.333 101	.069 769
30	4.983 951	72.435 478	.013 805	.200 644	14.533 745	.068 805
31	5.258 069	77.419 429	.012 917	.190 184	14.723 929	.067 917
32	5.547 262	82.677 498	.012 095	.180 269	14.904 198	.067 095
33	5.852 362	88.224 760	.011 335	.170 871	15.075 069	.066 335
34	6.174 242	94.077 122	.010 630	.161 963	15.237 033	.065 630
35	6.513 825	100.251 364	.009 975	.153 520	15.390 552	.064 975
36	6.872 085	106.765 189	.009 366	.145 516	15.536 068	.064 366
37	7.250 050	113.637 274	.008 800	.137 930	15.673 999	.063 800
38	7.648 803	120.887 324	.008 272	.130 739	15.804 738	.063 272
39	8.069 487	128.536 127	.007 780	.123 924	15.928 662	.062 780
40	8.513 309	136.605 614	.007 320	.117 463	16.046 125	.062 320
41	8.981 541	145.118 923	.006 891	.111 339	16.157 464	.061 891
42	9.475 525	154.100 464	.006 489	.105 535	16.262 999	.061 489
43	9.996 679	163.575 989	.006 113	.100 033	16.363 032	.061 113
44	10.546 497	173.572 669	.005 761	.094 818	16.457 851	.060 761
45	11.126 554	184.119 165	.005 431	.089 875	16.547 726	.060 431
46	11.738 515	195.245 719	.005 122	.085 190	16.632 915	.060 122
47	12.384 133	206.984 234	.004 831	.080 748	16.713 664	.059 831
48	13.065 260	219.368 367	.004 559	.076 539	16.790 203	.059 559
49	13.783 849	232.433 627	.004 302	.072 549	16.862 751	.059 302
50	14.541 961	246.217 476	.004 061	.068 767	16.931 518	.059 061
51	15.341 769	260.759 438	.003 835	.065 182	16.996 699	.058 835
52	16.185 566	276.101 207	.003 622	.061 783	17.058 483	.058 622
53	17.075 773	292.286 773	.003 421	.058 563	17.117 045	.058 421
54	18.014 940	309.362 546	.003 232	.055 509	17.172 555	.058 232
55	19.005 762	327.377 486	.003 055	.052 616	17.225 170	.058 055
56	20.051 079	346.383 247	.002 887	.049 873	17.275 043	.057 887
57	21.153 888	366.434 326	.002 729	.047 273	17.322 316	.057 729
58	22.317 352	387.588 214	.002 580	.044 808	17.367 124	.057 580
59	23.544 806	409.905 566	.002 440	.042 472	17.409 596	.057 440
60	24.839 770	433.450 372	.002 307	.040 258	17.449 854	.057 307

	$S^n=(1+i)^n$	$S_{\overline{n}\rvert}=\dfrac{S^n-1}{i}$	$\dfrac{1}{S_{\overline{n}\rvert}}=\dfrac{i}{S^n-1}$	$V^n=\dfrac{1}{S^n}$	$A_{\overline{n}\rvert}=\dfrac{1-1/S^n}{i}$	$\dfrac{1}{A_{\overline{n}\rvert}}=\dfrac{i}{1-1/S^n}$

5¾%
Annual
Table

Years	1 Amount of 1	2 Amount of 1 per Period	3 Sinking-Fund Factor	4 Present Worth of 1	5 Present Worth of 1 per Period	6 Partial Payment
1	1.057 500	1.000 000	1.000 000	.945 626	.945 626	1.057 500
2	1.118 306	2.057 500	.486 027	.894 209	1.839 836	.543 527
3	1.182 609	3.175 806	.314 881	.845 588	2.685 424	.372 381
4	1.250 609	4.358 415	.229 441	.799 611	3.485 035	.286 941
5	1.322 519	5.609 024	.178 284	.756 133	4.241 167	.235 784
6	1.398 564	6.931 543	.144 268	.715 019	4.956 187	.201 768
7	1.478 981	8.330 107	.120 046	.676 141	5.632 328	.177 546
8	1.564 023	9.809 088	.101 946	.639 377	6.271 705	.159 446
9	1.653 954	11.373 110	.087 927	.604 612	6.876 317	.145 427
10	1.749 056	13.027 064	.076 763	.571 737	7.448 054	.134 263
11	1.849 627	14.776 120	.067 677	.540 650	7.988 703	.125 177
12	1.955 980	16.625 747	.060 148	.511 253	8.499 956	.117 648
13	2.068 449	18.581 728	.053 816	.483 454	8.983 410	.111 316
14	2.187 385	20.650 177	.048 426	.457 167	9.440 576	.105 926
15	2.313 160	22.837 562	.043 788	.432 309	9.872 886	.101 288
16	2.446 167	25.150 722	.039 760	.408 803	10.281 688	.097 260
17	2.586 821	27.596 888	.036 236	.386 575	10.668 263	.093 736
18	2.735 563	30.183 710	.033 130	.365 555	11.033 819	.090 630
19	2.892 858	32.919 273	.030 377	.345 679	11.379 498	.087 877
20	3.059 198	35.812 131	.027 923	.326 883	11.706 381	.085 423
21	3.235 101	38.871 329	.025 726	.309 109	12.015 490	.083 226
22	3.421 120	42.106 430	.023 749	.292 302	12.307 792	.081 249
23	3.617 834	45.527 550	.021 965	.276 408	12.584 200	.079 465
24	3.825 860	49.145 384	.020 348	.261 379	12.845 580	.077 848
25	4.045 846	52.971 243	.018 878	.247 167	13.092 747	.076 378
26	4.278 483	57.017 090	.017 539	.233 728	13.326 474	.075 039
27	4.524 495	61.295 573	.016 314	.221 019	13.547 494	.073 814
28	4.784 654	65.820 068	.015 193	.209 002	13.756 495	.072 693
29	5.059 772	70.604 722	.014 163	.197 637	13.954 132	.071 663
30	5.350 708	75.664 493	.013 216	.186 891	14.141 024	.070 716
31	5.658 374	81.015 202	.012 343	.176 729	14.317 753	.069 843
32	5.983 731	86.673 576	.011 538	.167 120	14.484 873	.069 038
33	6.327 795	92.657 307	.010 792	.158 033	14.642 906	.068 292
34	6.691 643	98.985 102	.010 103	.149 440	14.792 346	.067 603
35	7.076 413	105.676 745	.009 463	.141 315	14.933 660	.066 963
36	7.483 307	112.753 158	.008 869	.133 631	15.067 291	.066 369
37	7.913 597	120.236 464	.008 317	.126 365	15.193 656	.065 817
38	8.368 629	128.150 061	.007 803	.119 494	15.313 150	.065 303
39	8.849 825	136.518 690	.007 325	.112 997	15.426 146	.064 825
40	9.358 690	145.368 514	.006 879	.106 853	15.532 999	.064 379
41	9.896 814	154.727 204	.006 463	.101 043	15.634 041	.063 963
42	10.465 881	164.624 018	.006 074	.095 549	15.729 590	.063 574
43	11.067 669	175.089 899	.005 711	.090 353	15.819 943	.063 211
44	11.704 060	186.157 568	.005 372	.085 440	15.905 384	.062 872
45	12.377 044	197.861 628	.005 054	.080 795	15.986 178	.062 554
46	13.088 724	210.238 672	.004 756	.076 402	16.062 580	.062 256
47	13.841 325	223.327 396	.004 478	.072 247	16.134 828	.061 978
48	14.637 201	237.168 721	.004 216	.068 319	16.203 147	.061 716
49	15.478 841	251.805 922	.003 971	.064 604	16.267 751	.061 471
50	16.368 874	267.284 763	.003 741	.061 092	16.328 842	.061 241
51	17.310 084	283.653 637	.003 525	.057 770	16.386 612	.061 025
52	18.305 414	300.963 721	.003 323	.054 629	16.441 241	.060 823
53	19.357 975	319.269 135	.003 132	.051 658	16.492 899	.060 632
54	20.471 059	338.627 110	.002 953	.048 849	16.541 749	.060 453
55	21.648 145	359.098 169	.002 785	.046 193	16.587 942	.060 285
56	22.892 913	380.746 314	.002 626	.043 682	16.631 624	.060 126
57	24.209 256	403.639 227	.002 477	.041 307	16.672 930	.059 977
58	25.601 288	427.848 482	.002 337	.039 061	16.711 991	.059 837
59	27.073 362	453.449 770	.002 205	.036 937	16.748 927	.059 705
60	28.630 080	480.523 132	.002 081	.034 928	16.783 856	.059 581

$$S^n = (1+i)^n \quad\Big|\quad S_{\overline{n}|} = \frac{S^n - 1}{i} \quad\Big|\quad \frac{1}{S_{\overline{n}|}} = \frac{i}{S^n - 1} \quad\Big|\quad V^n = \frac{1}{S^n} \quad\Big|\quad A_{\overline{n}|} = \frac{1 - 1/S^n}{i} \quad\Big|\quad \frac{1}{A_{\overline{n}|}} = \frac{i}{1 - 1/S^n}$$

6% Annual Table

Years	1 Amount of 1	2 Amount of 1 per Period	3 Sinking- Fund Factor	4 Present Worth of 1	5 Present Worth of 1 per Period	6 Partial Payment
1	1.060 000	1.000 000	1.000 000	.943 396	.943 396	1.060 000
2	1.123 600	2.060 000	.485 437	.889 996	1.833 393	.545 437
3	1.191 016	3.183 600	.314 110	.839 619	2.673 012	.374 110
4	1.262 477	4.374 616	.228 591	.792 094	3.465 106	.288 591
5	1.338 226	5.637 093	.177 396	.747 258	4.212 364	.237 396
6	1.418 519	6.975 319	.143 363	.704 961	4.917 324	.203 363
7	1.503 630	8.393 838	.119 135	.665 057	5.582 381	.179 135
8	1.593 848	9.897 468	.101 036	.627 412	6.209 794	.161 036
9	1.689 479	11.491 316	.087 022	.591 898	6.801 692	.147 022
10	1.790 848	13.180 795	.075 868	.558 395	7.360 087	.135 868
11	1.898 299	14.971 643	.066 793	.526 788	7.886 875	.126 793
12	2.012 196	16.869 941	.059 277	.496 969	8.383 844	.119 277
13	2.132 928	18.882 138	.052 960	.468 839	8.852 683	.112 960
14	2.260 904	21.015 066	.047 585	.442 301	9.294 984	.107 585
15	2.396 558	23.275 970	.042 963	.417 265	9.712 249	.102 963
16	2.540 352	25.672 528	.038 952	.393 646	10.105 895	.098 952
17	2.692 773	28.212 880	.035 445	.371 364	10.477 260	.095 445
18	2.854 339	30.905 653	.032 357	.350 344	10.827 603	.092 357
19	3.025 600	33.759 992	.029 621	.330 513	11.158 116	.089 621
20	3.207 135	36.785 591	.027 185	.311 805	11.469 921	.087 185
21	3.399 564	39.992 727	.025 005	.294 155	11.764 077	.085 005
22	3.603 537	43.392 290	.023 046	.277 505	12.041 582	.083 046
23	3.819 750	46.995 828	.021 278	.261 797	12.303 379	.081 278
24	4.048 935	50.815 577	.019 679	.246 979	12.550 358	.079 679
25	4.291 871	54.864 512	.018 227	.232 999	12.783 356	.078 227
26	4.549 383	59.156 383	.016 904	.219 810	13.003 166	.076 904
27	4.822 346	63.705 766	.015 697	.207 368	13.210 534	.075 697
28	5.111 687	68.528 112	.014 593	.195 630	13.406 164	.074 593
29	5.418 388	73.639 798	.013 580	.184 557	13.590 721	.073 580
30	5.743 491	79.058 186	.012 649	.174 110	13.764 831	.072 649
31	6.088 101	84.801 677	.011 792	.164 255	13.929 086	.071 792
32	6.453 387	90.889 778	.011 002	.154 957	14.084 043	.071 002
33	6.840 590	97.343 165	.010 273	.146 186	14.230 230	.070 273
34	7.251 025	104.183 755	.009 598	.137 912	14.368 141	.069 598
35	7.686 087	111.434 780	.008 974	.130 105	14.498 246	.068 974
36	8.147 252	119.120 867	.008 395	.122 741	14.620 987	.068 395
37	8.636 087	127.268 119	.007 857	.115 793	14.736 780	.067 857
38	9.154 252	135.904 206	.007 358	.109 239	14.846 019	.067 358
39	9.703 507	145.058 458	.006 894	.103 056	14.949 075	.066 894
40	10.285 718	154.761 966	.006 462	.097 222	15.046 297	.066 462
41	10.902 861	165.047 684	.006 059	.091 719	15.138 016	.066 059
42	11.557 033	175.950 545	.005 683	.086 527	15.224 543	.065 683
43	12.250 455	187.507 577	.005 333	.081 630	15.306 173	.065 333
44	12.985 482	199.758 032	.005 006	.077 009	15.383 182	.065 006
45	13.764 611	212.743 514	.004 700	.072 650	15.455 832	.064 700
46	14.590 487	226.508 125	.004 415	.068 538	15.524 370	.064 415
47	15.465 917	241.098 612	.004 148	.064 658	15.589 028	.064 148
48	16.393 872	256.564 529	.003 898	.060 998	15.650 027	.063 898
49	17.377 504	272.958 401	.003 664	.057 546	15.707 572	.063 664
50	18.420 154	290.335 905	.003 444	.054 288	15.761 861	.063 444
51	19.525 364	308.756 059	.003 239	.051 215	15.813 076	.063 239
52	20.696 885	328.281 422	.003 046	.048 316	15.861 393	.063 046
53	21.938 698	348.978 308	.002 866	.045 582	15.906 974	.062 866
54	23.255 020	370.917 006	.002 696	.043 001	15.949 976	.062 696
55	24.650 322	394.172 027	.002 537	.040 567	15.990 543	.062 537
56	26.129 341	418.822 348	.002 388	.038 271	16.028 814	.062 388
57	27.697 101	444.951 689	.002 247	.036 105	16.064 919	.062 247
58	29.358 927	472.648 790	.002 116	.034 061	16.098 980	.062 116
59	31.120 463	502.007 718	.001 992	.032 133	16.131 113	.061 992
60	32.987 691	533.128 181	.001 876	.030 314	16.161 428	.061 876

$$S^n = (1+i)^n \qquad S_{\overline{n}|} = \frac{S^n - 1}{i} \qquad \frac{1}{S_{\overline{n}|}} = \frac{i}{S^n - 1} \qquad V^n = \frac{1}{S^n} \qquad A_{\overline{n}|} = \frac{1 - 1/S^n}{i} \qquad \frac{1}{A_{\overline{n}|}} = \frac{i}{1 - 1/S^n}$$

6¼%
Annual
Table

Years	1 Amount of 1	2 Amount of 1 per Period	3 Sinking- Fund Factor	4 Present Worth of 1	5 Present Worth of 1 per Period	6 Partial Payment
1	1.062 500	1.000 000	1.000 000	.941 176	.941 176	1.062 500
2	1.128 906	2.062 500	.484 848	.885 813	1.826 990	.547 348
3	1.199 463	3.191 406	.313 341	.833 706	2.660 696	.375 841
4	1.274 429	4.390 869	.227 745	.784 665	3.445 361	.290 245
5	1.354 081	5.665 298	.176 513	.738 508	4.183 869	.239 013
6	1.438 711	7.019 380	.142 463	.695 067	4.878 936	.204 963
7	1.528 631	8.458 091	.118 230	.654 180	5.533 116	.180 730
8	1.624 170	9.986 722	.100 133	.615 699	6.148 815	.162 633
9	1.725 681	11.610 892	.086 126	.579 481	6.728 297	.148 626
10	1.833 536	13.336 572	.074 982	.545 394	7.273 691	.137 482
11	1.948 132	15.170 108	.065 919	.513 312	7.787 003	.128 419
12	2.069 890	17.118 240	.058 417	.483 118	8.270 121	.120 917
13	2.199 258	19.188 130	.052 116	.454 699	8.724 819	.114 616
14	2.336 712	21.387 388	.046 757	.427 952	9.152 771	.109 257
15	2.482 756	23.724 100	.042 151	.402 778	9.555 549	.104 651
16	2.637 928	26.206 856	.038 158	.379 085	9.934 635	.100 658
17	2.802 799	28.844 784	.034 668	.356 786	10.291 421	.097 168
18	2.977 974	31.647 583	.031 598	.335 799	10.627 220	.094 098
19	3.164 097	34.625 557	.028 880	.316 046	10.943 266	.091 380
20	3.361 853	37.789 655	.026 462	.297 455	11.240 721	.088 962
21	3.571 969	41.151 508	.024 300	.279 958	11.520 678	.086 800
22	3.795 217	44.723 477	.022 360	.263 490	11.784 168	.084 860
23	4.032 418	48.518 695	.020 611	.247 990	12.032 158	.083 111
24	4.284 445	52.551 113	.019 029	.233 402	12.265 560	.081 529
25	4.552 222	56.835 558	.017 595	.219 673	12.485 233	.080 095
26	4.836 736	61.387 780	.016 290	.206 751	12.691 984	.078 790
27	5.139 032	66.224 516	.015 100	.194 589	12.886 573	.077 600
28	5.460 222	71.363 549	.014 013	.183 143	13.069 716	.076 513
29	5.801 486	76.823 771	.013 017	.172 370	13.242 086	.075 517
30	6.164 079	82.625 256	.012 103	.162 230	13.404 316	.074 603
31	6.549 333	88.789 335	.011 263	.152 687	13.557 003	.073 763
32	6.958 667	95.338 668	.010 489	.143 706	13.700 709	.072 989
33	7.393 583	102.297 335	.009 775	.135 252	13.835 961	.072 275
34	7.855 682	109.690 918	.009 117	.127 296	13.963 258	.071 617
35	8.346 663	117.546 601	.008 507	.119 808	14.083 066	.071 007
36	8.868 329	125.893 263	.007 943	.112 761	14.195 827	.070 443
37	9.422 600	134.761 592	.007 421	.106 128	14.301 955	.069 921
38	10.011 512	144.184 192	.006 936	.099 885	14.401 840	.069 436
39	10.637 231	154.195 704	.006 485	.094 009	14.495 849	.068 985
40	11.302 058	164.832 935	.006 067	.088 479	14.584 329	.068 567
41	12.008 437	176.134 994	.005 677	.083 275	14.667 603	.068 177
42	12.758 964	188.143 431	.005 315	.078 376	14.745 980	.067 815
43	13.556 400	200.902 395	.004 978	.073 766	14.819 746	.067 478
44	14.403 675	214.458 795	.004 663	.069 427	14.889 172	.067 163
45	15.303 904	228.862 470	.004 369	.065 343	14.954 515	.066 869
46	16.260 398	244.166 374	.004 096	.061 499	15.016 014	.066 596
47	17.276 673	260.426 772	.003 840	.057 882	15.073 896	.066 340
48	18.356 465	277.703 445	.003 601	.054 477	15.128 372	.066 101
49	19.503 744	296.059 911	.003 378	.051 272	15.179 645	.065 878
50	20.722 728	315.563 655	.003 169	.048 256	15.227 901	.065 669
51	22.017 899	336.286 384	.002 974	.045 418	15.273 318	.065 474
52	23.394 018	358.304 283	.002 791	.042 746	15.316 064	.065 291
53	24.856 144	381.698 300	.002 620	.040 232	15.356 296	.065 120
54	26.409 653	406.554 444	.002 460	.037 865	15.394 161	.064 960
55	28.060 256	432.964 097	.002 310	.035 638	15.429 799	.064 810
56	29.814 022	461.024 353	.002 169	.033 541	15.463 340	.064 669
57	31.677 398	490.838 375	.002 037	.031 568	15.494 908	.064 537
58	33.657 236	522.515 773	.001 914	.029 711	15.524 619	.064 414
59	35.760 813	556.173 009	.001 798	.027 964	15.552 583	.064 298
60	37.995 864	591.933 822	.001 689	.026 319	15.578 902	.064 189

$$S^n = (1+i)^n \quad\Big|\quad S_{\overline{n}|} = \frac{S^n - 1}{i} \quad\Big|\quad \frac{1}{S_{\overline{n}|}} = \frac{i}{S^n - 1} \quad\Big|\quad V^n = \frac{1}{S^n} \quad\Big|\quad A_{\overline{n}|} = \frac{1 - 1/S^n}{i} \quad\Big|\quad \frac{1}{A_{\overline{n}|}} = \frac{i}{1 - 1/S^n}$$

331

6½% Annual Table

Years	1 Amount of 1	2 Amount of 1 per Period	3 Sinking- Fund Factor	4 Present Worth of 1	5 Present Worth of 1 per Period	6 Partial Payment
1	1.065 000	1.000 000	1.000 000	.938 967	.938 967	1.065 000
2	1.134 225	2.065 000	.484 262	.881 659	1.820 626	.549 262
3	1.207 950	3.199 225	.312 576	.827 849	2.648 476	.377 576
4	1.286 466	4.407 175	.226 903	.777 323	3.425 799	.291 903
5	1.370 087	5.693 641	.175 635	.729 881	4.155 679	.240 635
6	1.459 142	7.063 728	.141 568	.685 334	4.841 014	.206 568
7	1.553 987	8.522 870	117 331	.643 506	5.484 520	.182 331
8	1.654 996	10.076 856	.099 237	.604 231	6.088 751	.164 237
9	1.762 570	11.731 852	.085 238	.567 353	6.656 104	.150 238
10	1.877 137	13.494 423	.074 105	.532 726	7.188 830	.139 105
11	1.999 151	15.371 560	.065 055	.500 212	7.689 042	.130 055
12	2.129 096	17.370 711	.057 568	.469 683	8.158 725	.122 568
13	2.267 487	19.499 808	.051 283	.441 017	8.599 742	.116 283
14	2.414 874	21.767 295	.045 940	.414 100	9.013 842	.110 940
15	2.571 841	24.182 169	.041 353	.388 827	9.402 669	.106 353
16	2.739 011	26.754 010	.037 378	.365 095	9.767 764	.102 378
17	2.917 046	29.493 021	.033 906	.342 813	10.110 577	.098 906
18	3.106 654	32.410 067	.030 855	.321 890	10.432 466	.095 855
19	3.308 587	35.516 722	.028 156	.302 244	10.734 710	.093 156
20	3.523 645	38.825 309	.025 756	.283 797	11.018 507	.090 756
21	3.752 682	42.348 954	.023 613	.266 476	11.284 983	.088 613
22	3.996 606	46.101 636	.021 691	.250 212	11.535 196	.086 691
23	4.256 386	50.098 242	.019 961	.234 941	11.770 137	.084 961
24	4.533 051	54.354 628	.018 398	.220 602	11.990 739	.083 398
25	4.827 699	58.887 679	.016 981	.207 138	12.197 877	.081 981
26	5.141 500	63.715 378	.015 695	.194 496	12.392 373	.080 695
27	5.475 697	68.856 877	.014 523	.182 625	12.574 998	.079 523
28	5.831 617	74.332 574	.013 453	.171 479	12.746 477	.078 453
29	6.210 192	80.164 192	.012 474	.161 013	12.907 490	.077 474
30	6.614 366	86.374 864	.011 577	.151 186	13.058 676	.076 577
31	7.044 300	92.989 230	.010 754	.141 959	13.200 635	.075 754
32	7.502 179	100.033 530	.009 997	.133 295	13.333 929	.074 997
33	7.989 821	107.535 710	.009 299	.125 159	13.459 088	.074 299
34	8.509 159	115.525 531	.008 656	.117 520	13.576 609	.073 656
35	9.062 255	124.034 690	.008 062	.110 348	13.686 957	.073 062
36	9.651 301	133.096 945	.007 513	.103 613	13.790 570	.072 513
37	10.278 636	142.748 247	.007 005	.097 289	13.887 859	.072 005
38	10.946 747	153.026 883	.006 535	.091 351	13.979 210	.071 535
39	11.658 286	163.973 630	.006 099	.085 776	14.064 986	.071 099
40	12.416 075	175.631 916	.005 694	.080 541	14.145 527	.070 694
41	13.223 119	188.047 990	.005 318	.075 625	14.221 152	.070 318
42	14.082 622	201.271 110	.004 968	.071 010	14.292 161	.069 968
43	14.997 993	215.353 732	.004 644	.066 676	14.358 837	.069 644
44	15.972 862	230.351 725	.004 341	.062 606	14.421 443	.069 341
45	17.011 098	246.324 587	.004 060	.058 785	14.480 228	.069 060
46	18.116 820	263.335 685	.003 797	.055 197	14.535 426	.068 797
47	19.294 413	281.452 504	.003 553	.051 828	14.587 254	.068 553
48	20.548 550	300.746 917	.003 325	.048 665	14.635 919	.068 325
49	21.884 205	321.295 467	.003 112	.045 695	14.681 615	.068 112
50	23.306 679	343.179 672	.002 914	.042 906	14.724 521	.067 914
51	24.821 613	366.486 351	.002 729	.040 287	14.764 808	.067 729
52	26.435 018	391.307 963	.002 556	.037 829	14.802 637	.067 556
53	28.153 294	417.742 981	.002 394	.035 520	14.838 157	.067 394
54	29.983 258	445.896 275	.002 243	.033 352	14.871 509	.067 243
55	31.932 170	475.879 533	002 101	.031 316	14.902 825	.067 101
56	34.007 761	507.811 702	.001 969	.029 405	14.932 230	.066 969
57	36.218 265	541.819 463	.001 846	.027 610	14.959 840	.066 846
58	38.572 452	578.037 728	.001 730	.025 925	14.985 766	.066 730
59	41.079 662	616.610 180	.001 622	.024 343	15.010 109	.066 622
60	43.749 840	657.689 842	.001 520	.022 857	15.032 966	.066 520

$$S^n = (1+i)^n \qquad S_{\overline{n}|} = \frac{S^n - 1}{i} \qquad \frac{1}{S_{\overline{n}|}} = \frac{i}{S^n - 1} \qquad V^n = \frac{1}{S^n} \qquad A_{\overline{n}|} = \frac{1 - 1/S^n}{i} \qquad \frac{1}{A_{\overline{n}|}} = \frac{i}{1 - 1/S^n}$$

6¾%
Annual
Table

Years	1 Amount of 1	2 Amount of 1 per Period	3 Sinking- Fund Factor	4 Present Worth of 1	5 Present Worth of 1 per Period	6 Partial Payment
1	1.067 500	1.000 000	1.000 000	.936 768	.936 768	1.067 500
2	1.139 556	2.067 500	.483 676	.877 535	1.814 303	.551 176
3	1.216 476	3.207 056	.311 812	.822 046	2.636 349	.379 312
4	1.298 588	4.423 533	.226 064	.770 067	3.406 416	.293 564
5	1.386 243	5.722 121	.174 760	.721 374	4.127 790	.242 260
6	1.479 815	7.108 364	.140 679	.675 760	4.803 551	.208 179
7	1.579 702	8.588 179	.116 439	.633 031	5.436 581	.183 939
8	1.686 332	10.167 881	.098 349	.593 003	6.029 584	.165 849
9	1.800 159	11.854 213	.084 358	.555 506	6.585 091	.151 858
10	1.921 670	13.654 372	.073 237	.520 381	7.105 471	.140 737
11	2.051 383	15.576 042	.064 201	.487 476	7.592 947	.131 701
12	2.189 851	17.627 425	.056 730	.456 652	8.049 600	.124 230
13	2.337 666	19.817 276	.050 461	.427 777	8.477 377	.117 961
14	2.495 459	22.154 942	.045 137	.400 728	8.878 105	.112 637
15	2.663 902	24.650 401	.040 567	.375 389	9.253 494	.108 067
16	2.843 715	27.314 303	.036 611	.351 653	9.605 146	.104 111
17	3.035 666	30.158 019	.033 159	.329 417	9.934 563	.100 659
18	3.240 574	33.193 685	.030 126	.308 587	10.243 151	.097 626
19	3.459 312	36.434 259	.027 447	.289 075	10.532 225	.094 947
20	3.692 816	39.893 571	.025 067	.270 796	10.803 021	.092 567
21	3.942 081	43.586 387	.022 943	.253 673	11.056 695	.090 443
22	4.208 172	47.528 468	.021 040	.237 633	11.294 327	.088 540
23	4.492 223	51.736 640	.019 329	.222 607	11.516 934	.086 829
24	4.795 448	56.228 863	.017 784	.208 531	11.725 465	.085 284
25	5.119 141	61.024 311	.016 387	.195 345	11.920 811	.083 887
26	5.464 683	66.143 452	.015 119	.182 993	12.103 804	.082 619
27	5.833 549	71.608 135	.013 965	.171 422	12.275 226	.081 465
28	6.227 314	77.441 684	.012 913	.160 583	12.435 809	.080 413
29	6.647 657	83.668 998	.011 952	.150 429	12.586 238	.079 452
30	7.096 374	90.316 655	.011 072	.140 917	12.727 155	.078 572
31	7.575 380	97.413 030	.010 266	.132 007	12.859 162	.077 766
32	8.086 718	104.988 409	.009 525	.123 660	12.982 821	.077 025
33	8.632 571	113.075 127	.008 844	.115 840	13.098 662	.076 344
34	9.215 270	121.707 698	.008 216	.108 516	13.207 177	.075 716
35	9.837 300	130.922 967	.007 638	.101 654	13.308 831	.075 138
36	10.501 318	140.760 268	.007 104	.095 226	13.404 057	.074 604
37	11.210 157	151.261 586	.006 611	.089 205	13.493 262	.074 111
38	11.966 843	162.471 743	.006 155	.083 564	13.576 826	.073 655
39	12.774 605	174.438 586	.005 733	.078 280	13.655 107	.073 233
40	13.636 890	187.213 190	.005 342	.073 331	13.728 437	.072 842
41	14.557 380	200.850 080	.004 979	.068 694	13.797 131	.072 479
42	15.540 004	215.407 461	.004 642	.064 350	13.861 481	.072 142
43	16.588 954	230.947 464	.004 330	.060 281	13.921 762	.071 830
44	17.708 708	247.536 418	.004 040	.056 469	13.978 231	.071 540
45	18.904 046	265.245 127	.003 770	.052 899	14.031 130	.071 270
46	20.180 069	284.149 173	.003 519	.049 554	14.080 684	.071 019
47	21.542 224	304.329 242	.003 286	.046 420	14.127 104	.070 786
48	22.996 324	325.871 466	.003 069	.043 485	14.170 589	.070 569
49	24.548 576	348.867 789	.002 866	.040 736	14.211 325	.070 366
50	26.205 605	373.416 365	.002 678	.038 160	14.249 485	.070 178
51	27.974 483	399.621 970	.002 502	.035 747	14.285 232	.070 002
52	29.862 761	427.596 453	.002 339	.033 487	14.318 718	.069 839
53	31.878 497	457.459 213	.002 186	.031 369	14.350 087	.069 686
54	34.030 295	489.337 710	.002 044	.029 386	14.379 473	.069 544
55	36.327 340	523.368 006	.001 911	.027 527	14.407 000	.069 411
56	38.779 436	559.695 346	.001 787	.025 787	14.432 787	.069 287
57	41.397 048	598.474 782	.001 671	.024 156	14.456 944	.069 171
58	44.191 349	639.871 830	.001 563	.022 629	14.479 572	.069 063
59	47.174 265	684.063 178	.001 462	.021 198	14.500 770	.068 962
60	50.358 527	731.237 443	.001 368	.019 858	14.520 628	.068 868

$$S^n = (1+i)^n \qquad S_{\overline{n}|} = \frac{S^n - 1}{i} \qquad \frac{1}{S_{\overline{n}|}} = \frac{i}{S^n - 1} \qquad V^n = \frac{1}{S^n} \qquad A_{\overline{n}|} = \frac{1 - 1/S^n}{i} \qquad \frac{1}{A_{\overline{n}|}} = \frac{i}{1 - 1/S^n}$$

333

7% Annual Table

Years	1 Amount of 1	2 Amount of 1 per Period	3 Sinking- Fund Factor	4 Present Worth of 1	5 Present Worth of 1 per Period	6 Partial Payment
1	1.070 000	1.000 000	1.000 000	.934 579	.934 579	1.070 000
2	1.144 900	2.070 000	.483 092	.873 439	1.808 018	.553 092
3	1.225 043	3.214 900	.311 052	.816 298	2.624 316	.381 052
4	1.310 796	4.439 943	.225 228	.762 895	3.387 211	.295 228
5	1.402 552	5.750 739	.173 891	.712 986	4.100 197	.243 891
6	1.500 730	7.153 291	.139 796	.666 342	4.766 540	.209 796
7	1.605 781	8.654 021	.115 553	.622 750	5.389 289	.185 553
8	1.718 186	10.259 803	.097 468	.582 009	5.971 299	.167 468
9	1.838 459	11.977 989	.083 486	.543 934	6.515 232	.153 486
10	1.967 151	13.816 448	.072 378	.508 349	7.023 582	.142 378
11	2.104 852	15.783 599	.063 357	.475 093	7.498 674	.133 357
12	2.252 192	17.888 451	.055 902	.444 012	7.942 686	.125 902
13	2.409 845	20.140 643	.049 651	.414 964	8.357 651	.119 651
14	2.578 534	22.550 488	.044 345	.387 817	8.745 468	.114 345
15	2.759 032	25.129 022	.039 795	.362 446	9.107 914	.109 795
16	2.952 164	27.888 054	.035 858	.338 735	9.446 649	.105 858
17	3.158 815	30.840 217	.032 425	.316 574	9.763 223	.102 425
18	3.379 932	33.999 033	.029 413	.295 864	10.059 087	.099 413
19	3.616 528	37.378 965	.026 753	.276 508	10.335 595	.096 753
20	3.869 684	40.995 492	.024 393	.258 419	10.594 014	.094 393
21	4.140 562	44.865 177	.022 289	.241 513	10.835 527	.092 289
22	4.430 402	49.005 739	.020 406	.225 713	11.061 240	.090 406
23	4.740 530	53.436 141	.018 714	.210 947	11.272 187	.088 714
24	5.072 367	58.176 671	.017 189	.197 147	11.469 334	.087 189
25	5.427 433	63.249 038	.015 811	.184 249	11.653 583	.085 811
26	5.807 353	68.676 470	.014 561	.172 195	11.825 779	.084 561
27	6.213 868	74.483 823	.013 426	.160 930	11.986 709	.083 426
28	6.648 838	80.697 691	.012 392	.150 402	12.137 111	.082 392
29	7.114 257	87.346 529	.011 449	.140 563	12.277 674	.081 449
30	7.612 255	94.460 786	.010 586	.131 367	12.409 041	.080 586
31	8.145 113	102.073 041	.009 797	.122 773	12.531 814	.079 797
32	8.715 271	110.218 154	.009 073	.114 741	12.646 555	.079 073
33	9.325 340	118.933 425	.008 408	.107 235	12.753 790	.078 408
34	9.978 114	128.258 765	.007 797	.100 219	12.854 009	.077 797
35	10.676 581	138.236 878	.007 234	.093 663	12.947 672	.077 234
36	11.423 942	148.913 460	.006 715	.087 535	13.035 208	.076 715
37	12.223 618	160.337 402	.006 237	.081 809	13.117 017	.076 237
38	13.079 271	172.561 020	.005 795	.076 457	13.193 473	.075 795
39	13.994 820	185.640 292	.005 387	.071 455	13.264 928	.075 387
40	14.974 458	199.635 112	.005 009	.066 780	13.331 709	.075 009
41	16.022 670	214.609 570	.004 660	.062 412	13.394 120	.074 660
42	17.144 257	230.632 240	.004 336	.058 329	13.452 449	.074 336
43	18.344 355	247.776 496	.004 036	.054 513	13.506 962	.074 036
44	19.628 460	266.120 851	.003 758	.050 946	13.557 908	.073 758
45	21.002 452	285.749 311	.003 500	.047 613	13.605 522	.073 500
46	22.472 623	306.751 763	.003 260	.044 499	13.650 020	.073 260
47	24.045 707	329.224 386	.003 037	.041 587	13.691 608	.073 037
48	25.728 907	353.270 093	.002 831	.038 867	13.730 474	.072 831
49	27.529 930	378.999 000	.002 639	.036 324	13.766 799	.072 639
50	29.457 025	406.528 929	.002 460	.033 948	13.800 746	.072 460
51	31.519 017	435.985 955	.002 294	.031 727	13.832 473	.072 294
52	33.725 348	467.504 971	.002 139	.029 651	13.862 124	.072 139
53	36.086 122	501.230 319	.001 995	.027 711	13.889 836	.071 995
54	38.612 151	537.316 442	.001 861	.025 899	13.915 735	.071 861
55	41.315 001	575.928 593	.001 736	.024 204	13.939 939	.071 736
56	44.207 052	617.243 594	.001 620	.022 621	13.962 560	.071 620
57	47.301 545	661.450 646	.001 512	.021 141	13.983 701	.071 512
58	50.612 653	708.752 191	.001 411	.019 758	14.003 458	.071 411
59	54.155 539	759.364 844	.001 317	.018 465	14.021 924	.071 317
60	57.946 427	813.520 383	.001 229	.017 257	14.039 181	.071 229

$$S^n = (1+i)^n \qquad S_{\overline{n}|} = \frac{S^n - 1}{i} \qquad \frac{1}{S_{\overline{n}|}} = \frac{i}{S^n - 1} \qquad V^n = \frac{1}{S^n} \qquad A_{\overline{n}|} = \frac{1 - 1/S^n}{i} \qquad \frac{1}{A_{\overline{n}|}} = \frac{i}{1 - 1/S^n}$$

7¼%
Annual
Table

Years	1 Amount of 1	2 Amount of 1 per Period	3 Sinking- Fund Factor	4 Present Worth of 1	5 Present Worth of 1 per Period	6 Partial Payment
1	1.072 500	1.000 000	1.000 000	.932 401	.932 401	1.072 500
2	1.150 256	2.072 500	.482 509	.869 371	1.801 772	.555 009
3	1.233 650	3.222 756	.310 293	.810 603	2.612 375	.382 793
4	1.323 089	4.456 406	.224 396	.755 807	3.368 182	.296 896
5	1.419 013	5.779 496	.173 025	.704 715	4.072 897	.245 525
6	1.521 892	7.198 509	.138 918	.657 077	4.729 974	.211 418
7	1.632 229	8.720 401	.114 674	.612 659	5.342 633	.187 174
8	1.750 566	10.352 630	.096 594	.571 244	5.913 877	.169 094
9	1.877 482	12.103 196	.082 623	.532 628	6.446 505	.155 123
10	2.013 599	13.980 677	.071 527	.496 623	6.943 128	.144 027
11	2.159 585	15.994 276	.062 522	.463 052	7.406 180	.135 022
12	2.316 155	18.153 861	.055 085	.431 750	7.837 930	.127 585
13	2.484 076	20.470 016	.048 852	.402 564	8.240 495	.121 352
14	2.664 172	22.954 093	.043 565	.375 351	8.615 846	.116 065
15	2.857 324	25.618 264	.039 035	.349 978	8.965 824	.111 535
16	3.064 480	28.475 588	.035 118	.326 320	9.292 143	.107 618
17	3.286 655	31.540 069	.031 706	.304 261	9.596 404	.104 206
18	3.524 937	34.826 724	.028 714	.283 693	9.880 097	.101 214
19	3.780 495	38.351 661	.026 074	.264 516	10.144 612	.098 574
20	4.054 581	42.132 156	.023 735	.246 635	10.391 247	.096 235
21	4.348 538	46.186 738	.021 651	.229 962	10.621 209	.094 151
22	4.663 808	50.535 276	.019 788	.214 417	10.835 626	.092 288
23	5.001 934	55.199 084	.018 116	.199 923	11.035 549	.090 616
24	5.364 574	60.201 017	.016 611	.186 408	11.221 957	.089 111
25	5.753 505	65.565 591	.015 252	.173 807	11.395 764	.087 752
26	6.170 634	71.319 096	.014 021	.162 058	11.557 822	.086 521
27	6.618 005	77.489 731	.012 905	.151 103	11.708 925	.085 405
28	7.097 811	84.107 736	.011 890	.140 889	11.849 814	.084 390
29	7.612 402	91.205 547	.010 964	.131 365	11.981 178	.083 464
30	8.164 301	98.817 949	.010 120	.122 484	12.103 663	.082 620
31	8.756 213	106.982 251	.009 347	.114 205	12.217 867	.081 847
32	9.391 039	115.738 464	.008 640	.106 484	12.324 352	.081 140
33	10.071 889	125.129 503	.007 992	.099 286	12.423 638	.080 492
34	10.802 101	135.201 392	.007 396	.092 575	12.516 213	.079 896
35	11.585 253	146.003 492	.006 849	.086 317	12.602 529	.079 349
36	12.425 184	157.588 746	.006 346	.080 482	12.683 011	.078 846
37	13.326 010	170.013 930	.005 882	.075 041	12.758 052	.078 382
38	14.292 146	183.339 940	.005 454	.069 969	12.828 021	.077 954
39	15.328 326	197.632 085	.005 060	.065 239	12.893 259	.077 560
40	16.439 630	212.960 411	.004 696	.060 829	12.954 088	.077 196
41	17.631 503	229.400 041	.004 359	.056 717	13.010 805	.076 859
42	18.909 787	247.031 544	.004 048	.052 883	13.063 687	.076 548
43	20.280 747	265.941 331	.003 760	.049 308	13.112 995	.076 260
44	21.751 101	286.222 078	.003 494	.045 975	13.158 970	.075 994
45	23.328 055	307.973 178	.003 247	.042 867	13.201 837	.075 747
46	25.019 339	331.301 234	.003 018	.039 969	13.241 806	.075 518
47	26.833 242	356.320 573	.002 806	.037 267	13.279 073	.075 306
48	28.778 652	383.153 815	.002 610	.034 748	13.313 821	.075 110
49	30.865 104	411.932 466	.002 428	.032 399	13.346 220	.074 928
50	33.102 824	442.797 570	.002 258	.030 209	13.376 429	.074 758
51	35.502 779	475.900 394	.002 101	.028 167	13.404 596	.074 601
52	38.076 730	511.403 173	.001 955	.026 263	13.430 858	.074 455
53	40.837 293	549.479 903	.001 820	.024 487	13.455 346	.074 320
54	43.797 997	590.317 195	.001 694	.022 832	13.478 178	.074 194
55	46.973 351	634.115 192	.001 577	.021 289	13.499 467	.074 077
56	50.378 919	681.088 544	.001 468	.019 850	13.519 316	.073 968
57	54.031 391	731.467 463	.001 367	.018 508	13.537 824	.073 867
58	57.948 667	785.498 854	.001 273	.017 257	13.555 081	.073 773
59	62.149 945	843.447 521	.001 186	.016 090	13.571 171	.073 686
60	66.655 816	905.597 466	.001 104	.015 002	13.586 173	.073 604

$$S^n = (1+i)^n \quad S_{\overline{n}|} = \frac{S^n - 1}{i} \quad \frac{1}{S_{\overline{n}|}} = \frac{i}{S^n - 1} \quad V^n = \frac{1}{S^n} \quad A_{\overline{n}|} = \frac{1 - 1/S^n}{i} \quad \frac{1}{A_{\overline{n}|}} = \frac{i}{1 - 1/S^n}$$

7½%
Annual
Table

Years	1 Amount of 1	2 Amount of 1 per Period	3 Sinking- Fund Factor	4 Present Worth of 1	5 Present Worth of 1 per Period	6 Partial Payment
1	1.075 000	1.000 000	1.000 000	.930 233	.930 233	1.075 000
2	1.155 625	2.075 000	.481 928	.865 333	1.795 565	.556 928
3	1.242 297	3.230 625	.309 538	.804 961	2.600 526	.384 538
4	1.335 469	4.472 922	.223 568	.748 801	3.349 326	.298 568
5	1.435 629	5.808 391	.172 165	.696 559	4.045 885	.247 165
6	1.543 302	7.244 020	.138 045	.647 962	4.693 846	.213 045
7	1.659 049	8.787 322	.113 800	.602 755	5.296 601	.188 800
8	1.783 478	10.446 371	.095 727	.560 702	5.857 304	.170 727
9	1.917 239	12.229 849	.081 767	.521 583	6.378 887	.156 767
10	2.061 032	14.147 087	.070 686	.485 194	6.864 081	.145 686
11	2.215 609	16.208 119	.061 697	.451 343	7.315 424	.136 697
12	2.381 780	18.423 728	.054 278	.419 854	7.735 278	.129 278
13	2.560 413	20.805 508	.048 064	.390 562	8.125 840	.123 064
14	2.752 444	23.365 921	.042 797	.363 313	8.489 154	.117 797
15	2.958 877	26.118 365	.038 287	.337 966	8.827 120	.113 287
16	3.180 793	29.077 242	.034 391	.314 387	9.141 507	.109 391
17	3.419 353	32.258 035	.031 000	.292 453	9.433 960	.106 000
18	3.675 804	35.677 388	.028 029	.272 049	9.706 009	.103 029
19	3.951 489	39.353 192	.025 411	.253 069	9.959 078	.100 411
20	4.247 851	43.304 681	.023 092	.235 413	10.194 491	.098 092
21	4.566 440	47.552 532	.021 029	.218 989	10.413 480	.096 029
22	4.908 923	52.118 972	.019 187	.203 711	10.617 191	.094 187
23	5.277 092	57.027 895	.017 535	.189 498	10.806 689	.092 535
24	5.672 874	62.304 987	.016 050	.176 277	10.982 967	.091 050
25	6.098 340	67.977 862	.014 711	.163 979	11.146 946	.089 711
26	6.555 715	74.076 201	.013 500	.152 539	11.299 485	.088 500
27	7.047 394	80.631 916	.012 402	.141 896	11.441 381	.087 402
28	7.575 948	87.679 310	.011 405	.131 997	11.573 378	.086 405
29	8.144 144	95.255 258	.010 498	.122 788	11.696 165	.085 498
30	8.754 955	103.399 403	.009 671	.114 221	11.810 386	.084 671
31	9.411 577	112.154 358	.008 916	.106 252	11.916 638	.083 916
32	10.117 445	121.565 935	.008 226	.098 839	12.015 478	.083 226
33	10.876 253	131.683 380	.007 594	.091 943	12.107 421	.082 594
34	11.691 972	142.559 633	.007 015	.085 529	12.192 950	.082 015
35	12.568 870	154.251 606	.006 483	.079 562	12.272 511	.081 483
36	13.511 536	166.820 476	.005 994	.074 011	12.346 522	.080 994
37	14.524 901	180.332 012	.005 545	.068 847	12.415 370	.080 545
38	15.614 268	194.856 913	.005 132	.064 044	12.479 414	.080 132
39	16.785 339	210.471 181	.004 751	.059 576	12.538 989	.079 751
40	18.044 239	227.256 520	.004 400	.055 419	12.594 409	.079 400
41	19.397 557	245.300 759	.004 077	.051 553	12.645 962	.079 077
42	20.852 374	264.698 315	.003 778	.047 956	12.693 918	.078 778
43	22.416 302	285.550 689	.003 502	.044 610	12.738 528	.078 502
44	24.097 524	307.966 991	.003 247	.041 498	12.780 026	.078 247
45	25.904 839	332.064 515	.003 011	.038 603	12.818 629	.078 011
46	27.847 702	357.969 354	.002 794	.035 910	12.854 539	.077 794
47	29.936 279	385.817 055	.002 592	.033 404	12.887 943	.077 592
48	32.181 500	415.753 334	.002 405	.031 074	12.919 017	.077 405
49	34.595 113	447.934 835	.002 232	.028 906	12.947 922	.077 232
50	37.189 746	482.529 947	.002 072	.026 889	12.974 812	.077 072
51	39.978 977	519.719 693	.001 924	.025 013	12.999 825	.076 924
52	42.977 400	559.698 670	.001 787	.023 268	13.023 093	.076 787
53	46.200 705	602.676 070	.001 659	.021 645	13.044 737	.076 659
54	49.665 758	648.876 776	.001 541	.020 135	13.064 872	.076 541
55	53.390 690	698.542 534	.001 432	.018 730	13.083 602	.076 432
56	57.394 992	751.933 224	.001 330	.017 423	13.101 025	.076 330
57	61.699 616	809.328 216	.001 236	.016 208	13.117 233	.076 236
58	66.327 087	871.027 832	.001 148	.015 077	13.132 309	.076 148
59	71.301 619	937.354 919	.001 067	.014 025	13.146 334	.076 067
60	76.649 240	1008.656 538	.000 991	.013 046	13.159 381	.075 991

	$S^n = (1+i)^n$	$S_{\overline{n}|} = \dfrac{S^n - 1}{i}$	$\dfrac{1}{S_{\overline{n}|}} = \dfrac{i}{S^n - 1}$	$V^n = \dfrac{1}{S^n}$	$A_{\overline{n}|} = \dfrac{1 - 1/S^n}{i}$	$\dfrac{1}{A_{\overline{n}|}} = \dfrac{i}{1 - 1/S^n}$

336

Years	1 Amount of 1	2 Amount of 1 per Period	3 Sinking- Fund Factor	4 Present Worth of 1	5 Present Worth of 1 per Period	6 Partial Payment
1	1.077 500	1.000 000	1.000 000	.928 074	.928 074	1.077 500
2	1.161 006	2.077 500	.481 348	.861 322	1.789 396	.558 848
3	1.250 984	3.238 506	.308 784	.799 371	2.588 767	.386 284
4	1.347 936	4.489 490	.222 742	.741 875	3.330 642	.300 242
5	1.452 401	5.837 426	.171 308	.688 515	4.019 157	.248 808
6	1.564 962	7.289 827	.137 177	.638 993	4.658 151	.214 677
7	1.686 246	8.854 788	.112 933	.593 033	5.251 184	.190 433
8	1.816 930	10.541 034	.094 867	.550 379	5.801 563	.172 367
9	1.957 742	12.357 964	.080 919	.510 792	6.312 355	.158 419
10	2.109 467	14.315 707	.069 853	.474 053	6.786 409	.147 353
11	2.272 951	16.425 174	.060 882	.439 957	7.226 365	.138 382
12	2.449 105	18.698 125	.053 481	.408 312	7.634 678	.130 981
13	2.638 910	21.147 229	.047 288	.378 944	8.013 622	.124 788
14	2.843 426	23.786 140	.042 041	.351 688	8.365 310	.119 541
15	3.063 791	26.629 566	.037 552	.326 393	8.691 703	.115 052
16	3.301 235	29.693 357	.033 678	.302 917	8.994 620	.111 178
17	3.557 081	32.994 592	.030 308	.281 129	9.275 750	.107 808
18	3.832 755	36.551 673	.027 359	.260 909	9.536 659	.104 859
19	4.129 793	40.384 428	.024 762	.242 143	9.778 802	.102 262
20	4.449 852	44.514 221	.022 465	.224 727	10.003 528	.099 965
21	4.794 716	48.964 073	.020 423	.208 563	10.212 091	.097 923
22	5.166 306	53.758 788	.018 602	.193 562	10.405 653	.096 102
23	5.566 695	58.925 095	.016 971	.179 640	10.585 293	.094 471
24	5.998 114	64.491 789	.015 506	.166 719	10.752 012	.093 006
25	6.462 967	70.489 903	.014 186	.154 728	10.906 740	.091 686
26	6.963 847	76.952 870	.012 995	.143 599	11.050 338	.090 495
27	7.503 546	83.916 718	.011 917	.133 270	11.183 609	.089 417
28	8.085 070	91.420 264	.010 938	.123 685	11.307 293	.088 438
29	8.711 663	99.505 334	.010 050	.114 789	11.422 082	.087 550
30	9.386 817	108.216 997	.009 241	.106 532	11.528 614	.086 741
31	10.114 296	117.603 815	.008 503	.098 870	11.627 484	.086 003
32	10.898 154	127.718 110	.007 830	.091 759	11.719 243	.085 330
33	11.742 760	138.616 264	.007 214	.085 159	11.804 402	.084 714
34	12.652 824	150.359 024	.006 651	.079 034	11.883 436	.084 151
35	13.633 418	163.011 849	.006 135	.073 349	11.956 785	.083 635
36	14.690 008	176.645 267	.005 661	.068 073	12.024 858	.083 161
37	15.828 484	191.335 275	.005 226	.063 177	12.088 036	.082 726
38	17.055 191	207.163 759	.004 827	.058 633	12.146 669	.082 327
39	18.376 969	224.218 950	.004 460	.054 416	12.201 085	.081 960
40	19.801 184	242.595 919	.004 122	.050 502	12.251 587	.081 622
41	21.335 775	262.397 103	.003 811	.046 870	12.298 456	.081 311
42	22.989 298	283.732 878	.003 524	.043 499	12.341 955	.081 024
43	24.770 969	306.722 176	.003 260	.040 370	12.382 325	.080 760
44	26.690 719	331.493 145	.003 017	.037 466	12.419 791	.080 517
45	28.759 249	358.183 864	.002 792	.034 771	12.454 562	.080 292
46	30.988 091	386.943 113	.002 584	.032 270	12.486 833	.080 084
47	33.389 668	417.931 204	.002 393	.029 949	12.516 782	.079 893
48	35.977 368	451.320 873	.002 216	.027 795	12.544 577	.079 716
49	38.765 614	487.298 240	.002 052	.025 796	12.570 373	.079 552
50	41.769 949	526.063 854	.001 901	.023 941	12.594 314	.079 401
51	45.007 120	567.833 803	.001 761	.022 219	12.616 533	.079 261
52	48.495 171	612.840 922	.001 632	.020 621	12.637 153	.079 132
53	52.253 547	661.336 094	.001 512	.019 137	13.656 291	.079 012
54	56.303 197	713.589 641	.001 401	.017 761	12.674 052	.078 901
55	60.666 695	769.892 838	.001 299	.016 484	12.690 535	.078 799
56	65.368 364	830.559 533	.001 204	.015 298	12.705 833	.078 704
57	70.434 412	895.927 897	.001 116	.014 198	12.720 031	.078 616
58	75.893 079	966.362 309	.001 035	.013 176	12.733 207	.078 535
59	81.774 793	1042.255 388	.000 959	.012 229	12.745 436	.078 459
60	88.112 339	1124.030 180	.000 890	.011 349	12.756 785	.078 390

$$S^n=(1+i)^n \quad\bigg|\quad S_{\overline{n}|}=\frac{S^n-1}{i} \quad\bigg|\quad \frac{1}{S_{\overline{n}|}}=\frac{i}{S^n-1} \quad\bigg|\quad V^n=\frac{1}{S^n} \quad\bigg|\quad A_{\overline{n}|}=\frac{1-1/S^n}{i} \quad\bigg|\quad \frac{1}{A_{\overline{n}|}}=\frac{i}{1-1/S^n}$$

337

8%
Annual
Table

Effective Rate 8%;
Base 1.08

	1	2	3	4	5	6
Years	Amount of 1	Amount of 1 per Period	Sinking-Fund Factor	Present Worth of 1	Present Worth of 1 per Period	Partial Payment
1	1.080 000	1.000 000	1.000 000	.925 926	.925 926	1.080 000
2	1.166 400	2.080 000	.480 769	.857 339	1.783 265	.560 769
3	1.259 712	3.246 400	.308 034	.793 832	2.577 097	.388 034
4	1.360 489	4.506 112	.221 921	.735 030	3.312 127	.301 921
5	1.469 328	5.866 601	.170 456	.680 583	3.992 710	.250 456
6	1.586 874	7.335 929	.136 315	.630 170	4.622 880	.216 315
7	1.713 824	8.922 803	.112 072	.583 490	5.206 370	.192 072
8	1.850 930	10.636 628	.094 015	.540 269	5.746 639	.174 015
9	1.999 005	12.487 558	.080 080	.500 249	6.246 888	.160 080
10	2.158 925	14.486 562	.069 029	.463 193	6.710 081	.149 029
11	2.331 639	16.645 487	.060 076	.428 883	7.138 964	.140 076
12	2.518 170	18.977 126	.052 695	.397 114	7.536 078	.132 695
13	2.719 624	21.495 297	.046 522	.367 698	7.903 776	.126 522
14	2.937 194	24.214 920	.041 297	.340 461	8.244 237	.121 297
15	3.172 169	27.152 114	.036 830	.315 242	8.559 479	.116 830
16	3.425 943	30.324 283	.032 977	.291 890	8.851 369	.112 977
17	3.700 018	33.750 226	.029 629	.270 269	9.121 638	.109 629
18	3.996 019	37.450 244	.026 702	.250 249	9.371 887	.106 702
19	4.315 701	41.446 263	.024 128	.231 712	9.603 599	.104 128
20	4.660 957	45.761 964	.021 852	.214 548	9.818 147	.101 852
21	5.033 834	50.422 921	.019 832	.198 656	10.016 803	.099 832
22	5.436 540	55.456 755	.018 032	.183 941	10.200 744	.098 032
23	5.871 464	60.893 296	.016 422	.170 315	10.371 059	.096 422
24	6.341 181	66.764 759	.014 978	.157 699	10.528 758	.094 978
25	6.848 475	73.105 940	.013 679	.146 018	10.674 776	.093 679
26	7.396 353	79.954 415	.012 507	.135 202	10.809 978	.092 507
27	7.988 061	87.350 768	.011 448	.125 187	10.935 165	.091 448
28	8.627 106	95.338 830	.010 489	.115 914	11.051 078	.090 489
29	9.317 275	103.965 936	.009 619	.107 328	11.158 406	.089 619
30	10.062 657	113.283 211	.008 827	.099 377	11.257 783	.088 827
31	10.867 669	123.345 868	.008 107	.092 016	11.349 799	.088 107
32	11.737 083	134.213 537	.007 451	.085 200	11.434 999	.087 451
33	12.676 050	145.950 620	.006 852	.078 889	11.513 888	.086 852
34	13.690 134	158.626 670	.006 304	.073 045	11.586 934	.086 304
35	14.785 344	172.316 804	.005 803	.067 635	11.654 568	.085 803
36	15.968 172	187.102 148	.005 345	.062 625	11.717 193	.085 345
37	17.245 626	203.070 320	.004 924	.057 986	11.775 179	.084 924
38	18.625 276	220.315 945	.004 539	.053 690	11.828 869	.084 539
39	20.115 298	238.941 221	.004 185	.049 713	11.878 582	.084 185
40	21.724 521	259.056 519	.003 860	.046 031	11.924 613	.083 860
41	23.462 483	280.781 040	.003 561	.042 621	11.967 235	.083 561
42	25.339 482	304.243 523	.003 287	.039 464	12.006 699	.083 287
43	27.366 640	329.583 005	.003 034	.036 541	12.043 240	.083 034
44	29.555 972	356.949 646	.002 802	.033 834	12.077 074	.082 802
45	31.920 449	386.505 617	.002 587	.031 328	12.108 402	.082 587
46	34.474 085	418.426 067	.002 390	.029 007	12.137 409	.082 390
47	37.232 012	452.900 152	.002 208	.026 859	12.164 267	.082 208
48	40.210 573	490.132 164	.002 040	.024 869	12.189 136	.082 040
49	43.427 419	530.342 737	.001 886	.023 027	12.212 163	.081 886
50	46.901 613	573.770 156	.001 743	.021 321	12.233 485	.081 743
51	50.653 742	620.671 769	.001 611	.019 742	12.253 227	.081 611
52	54.706 041	671.325 510	.001 490	.018 280	12.271 506	.081 490
53	59.082 524	726.031 551	.001 377	.016 925	12.288 432	.081 377
54	63.809 126	785.114 075	.001 274	.015 672	12.304 103	.081 274
55	68.913 856	848.923 201	.001 178	.014 511	12.318 614	.081 178
56	74.426 965	917.837 058	.001 090	.013 436	12.332 050	.081 090
57	80.381 122	992.264 022	.001 008	.012 441	12.344 491	.081 008
58	86.811 612	1072.645 144	.000 932	.011 519	12.356 010	.080 932
59	93.756 540	1159.456 755	.000 862	.010 666	12.366 676	.080 862
60	101.257 064	1253.213 296	.000 798	.009 876	12.376 552	.080 798

$$S^n=(1+i)^n \quad S_{\overline{n}|}=\frac{S^n-1}{i} \quad \frac{1}{S_{\overline{n}|}}=\frac{i}{S^n-1} \quad V^n=\frac{1}{S^n} \quad A_{\overline{n}|}=\frac{1-1/S^n}{i} \quad \frac{1}{A_{\overline{n}|}}=\frac{i}{1-1/S^n}$$

8%
Monthly
Table

Effective Rate ⅔%;
Base 1.0066+

Months	1 Amount of 1	2 Amount of 1 per Period	3 Sinking- Fund Factor	4 Present Worth of 1	5 Present Worth of 1 per Period	6 Partial Payment
1	1.006 667	1.000 000	1.000 000	.993 377	.993 377	1.006 667
2	1.013 378	2.006 667	.498 339	.986 799	1.980 176	.505 006
3	1.020 134	3.020 044	.331 121	.980 264	2.960 440	.337 788
4	1.026 935	4.040 178	.247 514	.973 772	3.934 212	.254 181
5	1.033 781	5.067 113	.197 351	.967 323	4.901 535	.204 018
6	1.040 673	6.100 893	.163 910	.960 917	5.862 452	.170 577
7	1.047 610	7.141 566	.140 025	.954 553	6.817 005	.146 692
8	1.054 595	8.189 176	.122 112	.948 232	7.765 237	.128 779
9	1.061 625	9.243 771	.108 181	.941 952	8.707 189	.114 848
10	1.068 703	10.305 396	.097 037	.935 714	9.642 903	.103 703
11	1.075 827	11.374 099	.087 919	.929 517	10.572 420	.094 586
Years						
1	1.083 000	12.449 926	.080 322	.923 361	11.495 782	.086 988
2	1.172 888	25.933 190	.038 561	.852 596	22.110 544	.045 227
3	1.270 237	40.535 558	.024 670	.787 255	31.911 806	.031 336
4	1.375 666	56.349 915	.017 746	.726 921	40.961 913	.024 413
5	1.489 846	73.476 856	.013 610	.671 210	49.318 433	.020 276
6	1.613 502	92.025 325	.010 867	.619 770	57.034 522	.017 533
7	1.747 422	112.113 308	.008 920	.572 272	64.159 261	.015 586
8	1.892 457	133.868 583	.007 470	.528 414	70.737 970	.014 137
9	2.049 530	157.429 535	.006 352	.487 917	76.812 497	.013 019
10	2.219 640	182.946 035	.005 466	.450 523	82.421 481	.012 133
11	2.403 869	210.580 392	.004 749	.415 996	87.600 600	.011 415
12	2.603 389	240.508 387	.004 158	.384 115	92.382 800	010 825
13	2.819 469	272.920 390	.003 664	.354 677	96.798 498	.010 331
14	3.053 484	308.022 574	.003 247	.327 495	100.875 784	.009 913
15	3.306 921	346.038 222	.002 890	.302 396	104.640 592	.009 557
16	3.581 394	387.209 149	.002 583	.279 221	108.116 871	.009 249
17	3.878 648	431.797 244	.002 316	.257 822	111.326 733	.008 983
18	4.200 574	480.086 128	.002 083	.238 063	114.290 596	.008 750
19	4.549 220	532.382 966	.001 878	.219 818	117.027 313	.008 545
20	4.926 803	589.020 416	.001 698	.202 971	119.554 292	.008 364
21	5.335 725	650.358 746	.001 538	.187 416	121.887 606	.008 204
22	5.778 588	716.788 127	.001 395	.173 053	124.042 099	.008 062
23	6.258 207	788.731 114	.001 268	.159 790	126.031 475	.007 935
24	6.777 636	866.645 333	.001 154	.147 544	127.868 388	.007 821
25	7.340 176	951.026 395	.001 051	.136 237	129.564 523	.007 718
26	7.949 407	1042.411 042	.000 959	.125 796	131.130 668	.007 626
27	8.609 204	1141.380 571	.000 876	.116 155	132.576 786	.007 543
28	9.323 763	1248.564 521	.000 801	.107 253	133.912 076	.007 468
29	10.097 631	1364.644 687	.000 733	.099 033	135.145 031	.007 399
30	10.935 730	1490.359 449	.000 671	.091 443	136.283 494	.007 338
31	11.843 390	1626.508 474	.000 615	.084 435	137.334 707	.007 281
32	12.826 385	1773.957 801	.000 564	.077 964	138.305 357	.007 230
33	13.890 969	1933.645 350	.000 517	.071 989	139.201 617	.007 184
34	15.043 913	2106.586 886	.000 475	.066 472	140.029 190	.007 141
35	16.292 550	2293.882 485	.000 436	.061 378	140.793 338	.007 103
36	17.644 824	2496.723 526	.000 401	.056 674	141.498 923	.007 067
37	19.109 335	2716.400 273	.000 368	.052 330	142.150 433	.007 035
38	20.695 401	2954.310 082	.000 338	.048 320	142.752 013	.007 005
39	22.413 109	3211.966 288	.000 311	.044 617	143.307 488	.006 978
40	24.273 386	3491.007 831	.000 286	.041 197	143.820 392	.006 953
41	26.288 065	3793.209 686	.000 264	.038 040	144.293 988	.006 930
42	28.469 961	4120.494 145	.000 243	.035 125	144.731 289	.006 909
43	30.832 954	4474.943 053	.000 223	.032 433	145.135 075	.006 890
44	33.392 074	4858.811 045	.000 206	.029 947	145.507 916	.006 872
45	36.163 599	5274.539 891	.000 190	.027 652	145.852 183	.006 856
46	39.165 160	5724.774 027	.000 175	.025 533	146.170 065	.006 841
47	42.415 849	6212.377 374	.000 161	.023 576	146.463 586	.006 828
48	45.936 344	6740.451 558	.000 148	.021 769	146.734 612	.006 815
49	49.749 038	7312.355 639	.000 137	.020 101	146.984 866	.006 803
50	53.878 183	7931.727 477	.000 126	.018 560	147.215 942	.006 793

$$S^n = (1+i)^n \qquad S_{\overline{n}|} = \frac{S^n - 1}{i} \qquad \frac{1}{S_{\overline{n}|}} = \frac{i}{S^n - 1} \qquad V^n = \frac{1}{S^n} \qquad A_{\overline{n}|} = \frac{1 - 1/S^n}{i} \qquad \frac{1}{A_{\overline{n}|}} = \frac{i}{1 - 1/S^n}$$

339

8% Quarterly Table

**Effective Rate 2%;
Base 1.02**

	1	2	3	4	5	6
Quarters	Amount of 1	Amount of 1 per Period	Sinking-Fund Factor	Present Worth of 1	Present Worth of 1 per Period	Partial Payment
1	1.020 000	1.000 000	1.000 000	.980 392	.980 392	1.020 000
2	1.040 400	2.020 000	.495 050	.961 169	1.941 561	.515 050
3	1.061 208	3.060 400	.326 755	.942 322	2.883 883	.346 755
Years						
1	1.082 432	4.121 608	.242 624	.923 845	3.807 729	.262 624
2	1.171 659	8.582 969	.116 510	.853 490	7.325 481	.136 510
3	1.268 242	13.412 090	.074 560	.788 493	10.575 341	.094 560
4	1.372 786	18.639 285	.053 650	.728 446	13.577 709	.073 650
5	1.485 947	24.297 370	.041 157	.672 971	16.351 433	.061 157
6	1.608 437	30.421 862	.032 871	.621 721	18.913 926	.052 871
7	1.741 024	37.051 210	.026 990	.574 375	21.281 272	.046 990
8	1.884 541	44.227 030	.022 611	.530 633	23.468 335	.042 611
9	2.039 887	51.994 367	.019 233	.490 223	25.488 842	.039 233
10	2.208 040	60.401 983	.016 556	.452 890	27.355 479	.036 556
11	2.390 053	69.502 657	.014 388	.418 401	29.079 963	.034 388
12	2.587 070	79.353 519	.012 602	.386 538	30.673 120	.032 602
13	2.800 328	90.016 409	.011 109	.357 101	32.144 950	.031 109
14	3.031 165	101.558 264	.009 847	.329 906	33.504 694	.029 847
15	3.281 031	114.051 539	.008 768	.304 782	34.760 887	.028 768
16	3.551 493	127.574 662	.007 839	.281 572	35.921 415	.027 839
17	3.844 251	142.212 525	.007 032	.260 129	36.993 564	.027 032
18	4.161 140	158.057 019	.006 327	.240 319	37.984 063	.026 327
19	4.504 152	175.207 608	.005 708	.222 017	38.899 132	.025 708
20	4.875 439	193.771 958	.005 161	.205 110	39.744 514	.025 161
21	5.277 332	213.866 607	.004 676	.189 490	40.525 516	.024 676
22	5.712 354	235.617 701	.004 244	.175 059	41.247 041	.024 244
23	6.183 236	259.161 785	.003 859	.161 728	41.913 619	.023 859
24	6.692 933	284.646 659	.003 513	.149 411	42.529 434	.023 513
25	7.244 646	312.232 306	.003 203	.138 033	43.098 352	.023 203
26	7.841 838	342.091 897	.002 923	.127 521	43.623 944	.022 923
27	8.488 258	374.412 879	.002 671	.117 810	44.109 510	.022 671
28	9.187 963	409.398 150	.002 443	.108 838	44.558 097	.022 443
29	9.945 347	447.267 331	.002 236	.100 550	44.972 523	.022 236
30	10.765 163	488.258 152	.002 048	.092 892	45.355 389	.022 048
31	11.652 559	532.627 934	.001 877	.085 818	45.709 097	.021 877
32	12.613 104	580.655 213	.001 722	.079 283	46.035 869	.021 722
33	13.652 830	632.641 484	.001 581	.073 245	46.337 756	.021 581
34	14.778 262	688.913 096	.001 452	.067 667	46.616 652	.021 452
35	15.996 466	749.823 299	.001 334	.062 514	46.874 310	.021 334
36	17.315 089	815.754 461	.001 226	.057 753	47.112 345	.021 226
37	18.742 409	887.120 471	.001 127	.053 355	47.332 253	.021 127
38	20.287 387	964.369 336	.001 037	.049 292	47.535 414	.021 037
39	21.959 720	1047.985 991	.000 954	.045 538	47.723 104	.020 954
40	23.769 907	1138.495 348	.000 878	.042 070	47.896 500	.020 878
41	25.729 312	1236.465 587	.000 809	.038 866	48.056 691	.020 809
42	27.850 234	1342.511 724	.000 745	.035 906	48.204 683	.020 745
43	30.145 989	1457.299 473	.000 686	.033 172	48.341 405	.020 686
44	32.630 988	1581.549 425	.000 632	.030 646	48.467 714	.020 632
45	35.320 831	1716.041 568	.000 583	.028 312	48.584 405	.020 583
46	38.232 404	1861.620 189	.000 537	.026 156	48.692 209	.020 537
47	41.383 983	2019.199 170	.000 495	.024 164	48.791 803	.020 495
48	44.795 355	2189.767 727	.000 457	.022 324	48.883 813	.020 457
49	48.487 932	2374.396 619	.000 421	.020 624	48.968 816	.020 421
50	52.484 897	2574.244 869	.000 388	.019 053	49.047 345	.020 388

$$S^n = (1+i)^n \qquad S_{\overline{n}|} = \frac{S^n - 1}{i} \qquad \frac{1}{S_{\overline{n}|}} = \frac{i}{S^n - 1} \qquad V^n = \frac{1}{S^n} \qquad A_{\overline{n}|} = \frac{1 - 1/S^n}{i} \qquad \frac{1}{A_{\overline{n}|}} = \frac{i}{1 - 1/S^n}$$

8% Semi-annual Table

Effective Rate 4%;
Base 1.04

	1	2	3	4	5	6
Half-Years	Amount of 1	Amount of 1 per Period	Sinking-Fund Factor	Present Worth of 1	Present Worth of 1 per Period	Partial Payment
1	1.040 000	1.000 000	1.000 000	.961 538	.961 538	1.040 000
Years						
1	1.081 600	2.040 000	.490 196	.924 556	1.886 095	.530 196
2	1.169 859	4.246 464	.235 490	.854 804	3.629 895	.275 490
3	1.265 319	6.632 975	.150 762	.790 315	5.242 137	.190 762
4	1.368 569	9.214 226	.108 528	.730 690	6.732 745	.148 528
5	1.480 244	12.006 107	.083 291	.675 564	8.110 896	.123 291
6	1.601 032	15.025 805	.066 552	.624 597	9.385 074	.106 552
7	1.731 676	18.291 911	.054 669	.577 475	10.563 123	.094 669
8	1.872 981	21.824 531	.045 820	.533 908	11.652 296	.085 820
9	2.025 817	25.645 413	.038 993	.493 628	12.659 297	.078 993
10	2.191 123	29.778 079	.033 582	.456 387	13.590 326	.073 582
11	2.369 919	34.247 970	.029 199	.421 955	14.451 115	.069 199
12	2.563 304	39.082 604	.025 587	.390 121	15.246 963	.065 587
13	2.772 470	44.311 745	.022 567	.360 689	15.982 769	.062 567
14	2.998 703	49.967 583	.020 013	.333 477	16.663 063	.060 013
15	3.243 398	56.084 938	.017 830	.308 319	17.292 033	.057 830
16	3.508 059	62.701 469	.015 949	.285 058	17.873 551	.055 949
17	3.794 316	69.857 909	.014 316	.263 552	18.411 198	.054 315
18	4.103 933	77.598 314	.012 887	.243 669	18.908 282	.052 887
19	4.438 813	85.970 336	.011 632	.225 285	19.367 864	.051 632
20	4.801 021	95.025 516	.010 523	.208 289	19.792 774	.050 523
21	5.192 784	104.819 598	.009 540	.192 575	20.185 627	.049 540
22	5.616 515	115.412 877	.008 665	.178 046	20.548 841	.048 665
23	6.074 823	126.870 568	.007 882	.164 614	20.884 654	.047 882
24	6.570 528	139.263 206	.007 181	.152 195	21.195 131	.047 181
25	7.106 683	152.667 084	.006 550	.140 713	21.482 185	.046 550
26	7.686 589	167.164 718	.005 982	.130 097	21.747 582	.045 982
27	8.313 814	182.845 359	.005 469	.120 282	21.992 957	.045 469
28	8.992 222	199.805 540	.005 005	.111 207	22.219 819	.045 005
29	9.725 987	218.149 672	.004 584	.102 817	22.429 567	.044 584
30	10.519 627	237.990 685	.004 202	.095 060	22.623 490	.044 202
31	11.378 029	259.450 725	.003 854	.087 889	22.802 783	.043 854
32	12.306 476	282.661 904	.003 538	.081 258	22.968 549	.043 538
33	13.310 685	307.767 116	.003 249	.075 128	23.121 810	.043 249
34	14.396 836	334.920 912	.002 986	.069 460	23.263 507	.042 986
35	15.571 618	364.290 459	.002 745	.064 219	23.394 515	.042 745
36	16.842 262	396.056 560	.002 525	.059 374	23.515 639	.042 525
37	18.216 591	430.414 776	.002 323	.054 895	23.627 625	.042 323
38	19.703 065	467.576 621	.002 139	.050 754	23.731 162	.042 139
39	21.310 835	507.770 873	.001 969	.046 924	23.826 888	.041 969
40	23.049 799	551.244 977	.001 814	.043 384	23.915 392	.041 814
41	24.930 663	598.266 567	.001 671	.040 111	23.997 219	.041 671
42	26.965 005	649.125 119	.001 541	.037 085	24.072 872	.041 541
43	29.165 349	704.133 728	.001 420	.034 287	24.142 818	.041 420
44	31.545 242	763.631 041	.001 310	.031 701	24.207 487	.041 310
45	34.119 333	827.983 334	.001 208	.029 309	24.267 278	.041 208
46	36.903 471	897.586 774	.001 114	.027 098	24.322 557	.041 114
47	39.914 794	972.869 854	.001 028	.025 053	24.373 666	.041 028
48	43.171 841	1054.296 034	.000 949	.023 163	24.420 919	.040 949
49	46.694 664	1142.366 591	.000 875	.021 416	24.464 607	.040 875
50	50.504 948	1237.623 705	.000 808	.019 800	24.504 999	.040 808

$S^n = (1+i)^n$	$S_{\overline{n}} = \dfrac{S^n - 1}{i}$	$\dfrac{1}{S_{\overline{n}}} = \dfrac{i}{S^n - 1}$	$V^n = \dfrac{1}{S^n}$	$A_{\overline{n}} = \dfrac{1 - 1/S^n}{i}$	$\dfrac{1}{A_{\overline{n}}} = \dfrac{i}{1 - 1/S^n}$

8¼%
Annual
Table

Years	1 Amount of 1	2 Amount of 1 per Period	3 Sinking-Fund Factor	4 Present Worth of 1	5 Present Worth of 1 per Period	6 Partial Payment
1	1.082 500	1.000 000	1.000 000	.923 788	.923 788	1.082 500
2	1.171 806	2.082 500	.480 192	.853 383	1.777 171	.562 692
3	1.268 480	3.254 306	.307 285	.788 345	2.565 516	.389 785
4	1.373 130	4.522 787	.221 103	.728 263	3.293 779	.303 603
5	1.486 413	5.895 916	.169 609	.672 760	3.966 540	.252 109
6	1.609 042	7.382 330	.135 459	.621 488	4.588 027	.217 959
7	1.741 788	8.991 372	.111 218	.574 123	5.162 150	.193 718
8	1.885 486	10.733 160	.093 169	.530 367	5.692 517	.175 669
9	2.041 038	12.618 646	.079 248	.489 947	6.182 464	.161 748
10	2.209 424	14.659 684	.068 214	.452 607	6.635 071	.150 714
11	2.391 701	16.869 108	.059 280	.418 112	7.053 183	.141 780
12	2.589 017	19.260 809	.051 919	.386 247	7.439 430	.134 419
13	2.802 611	21.849 826	.045 767	.356 810	7.796 240	.128 267
14	3.033 826	24.652 436	.040 564	.329 617	8.125 857	.123 064
15	3.284 117	27.686 262	.036 119	.304 496	8.430 353	.118 619
16	3.555 056	30.970 379	.032 289	.281 289	8.711 642	.114 789
17	3.848 348	34.525 435	.028 964	.259 852	8.971 494	.111 464
18	4.165 837	38.373 784	.026 059	.240 048	9.211 542	.108 559
19	4.509 519	42.539 621	.023 507	.221 753	9.433 295	.106 007
20	4.881 554	47.049 140	.021 254	.204 853	9.638 148	.103 754
21	5.284 282	51.930 694	.019 256	.189 240	9.827 388	.101 756
22	5.720 236	57.214 976	.017 478	.174 818	10.002 206	.099 978
23	6.192 155	62.935 212	.015 889	.161 495	10.163 701	.098 389
24	6.703 008	69.127 366	.014 466	.149 187	10.312 888	.096 966
25	7.256 006	75.830 374	.013 187	.137 817	10.450 705	.095 687
26	7.854 626	83.086 380	.012 036	.127 314	10.578 018	.094 536
27	8.502 633	90.941 006	.010 996	.117 611	10.695 629	.093 496
28	9.204 100	99.443 639	.010 056	.108 647	10.804 276	.092 556
29	9.963 439	108.647 740	.009 204	.100 367	10.904 643	.091 704
30	10.785 422	118.611 178	.008 431	.092 718	10.997 361	.090 931
31	11.675 220	129.396 600	.007 728	.085 651	11.083 012	.090 228
32	12.638 425	141.071 820	.007 089	.079 124	11.162 136	.089 589
33	13.681 095	153.710 245	.006 506	.073 094	11.235 230	.089 006
34	14.809 786	167.391 340	.005 974	.067 523	11.302 752	.088 474
35	16.031 593	182.201 126	.005 488	.062 377	11.365 129	.087 988
36	17.354 199	198.232 719	.005 045	.057 623	11.422 752	.087 545
37	18.785 921	215.586 918	.004 639	.053 231	11.475 984	.087 139
38	20.335 759	234.372 839	.004 267	.049 174	11.525 158	.086 767
39	22.013 459	254.708 598	.003 926	.045 427	11.570 585	.086 426
40	23.829 570	276.722 058	.003 614	.041 965	11.612 549	.086 114
41	25.795 509	300.551 627	.003 327	.038 766	11.651 316	.085 827
42	27.923 639	326.347 137	.003 064	.035 812	11.687 128	.085 564
43	30.227 339	354.270 775	.002 823	.033 083	11.720 210	.085 323
44	32.721 094	384.498 114	.002 601	.030 561	11.750 772	.085 101
45	35.420 585	417.219 209	.002 397	.028 232	11.779 004	.084 897
46	38.342 783	452.639 793	.002 209	.026 081	11.805 085	.084 709
47	41.506 063	490.982 576	.002 037	.024 093	11.829 177	.084 537
48	44.930 313	532.488 639	.001 878	.022 257	11.851 434	.084 378
49	48.637 064	577.418 952	.001 732	.020 560	11.871 995	.084 232
50	52.649 621	626.056 015	.001 597	.018 993	11.890 988	.084 097
51	56.993 215	678.705 636	.001 473	.017 546	11.908 534	.083 973
52	61.695 155	735.698 851	.001 359	.016 209	11.924 743	.083 859
53	66.785 006	797.394 007	.001 254	.014 973	11.939 716	.083 754
54	72.294 768	864.179 012	.001 157	.013 832	11.953 548	.083 657
55	78.259 087	936.473 781	.001 068	.012 778	11.966 326	.083 568
56	84.715 462	1014.732 868	.000 985	.011 804	11.978 131	.083 485
57	91.704 487	1099.448 329	.000 910	.010 905	11.989 035	.083 410
58	99.270 107	1191.152 816	.000 840	.010 074	11.999 109	.083 340
59	107.459 891	1290.422 924	.000 775	.009 306	12.008 415	.083 275
60	116.325 332	1397.882 815	.000 715	.008 597	12.017 011	.083 215

| $S^n=(1+i)^n$ | $S_{\overline{n}|}=\dfrac{S^n-1}{i}$ | $\dfrac{1}{S_{\overline{n}|}}=\dfrac{i}{S^n-1}$ | $V^n=\dfrac{1}{S^n}$ | $A_{\overline{n}|}=\dfrac{1-1/S^n}{i}$ | $\dfrac{1}{A_{\overline{n}|}}=\dfrac{i}{1-1/S^n}$ |

342

8½% Annual Table

Years	1 Amount of 1	2 Amount of 1 per Period	3 Sinking-Fund Factor	4 Present Worth of 1	5 Present Worth of 1 per Period	6 Partial Payment
1	1.085 000	1.000 000	1.000 000	.921 659	.921 659	1.085 000
2	1.177 225	2.085 000	.479 616	.849 455	1.771 114	.564 616
3	1.277 289	3.262 225	.306 539	.782 908	2.554 022	.391 539
4	1.385 859	4.539 514	.220 288	.721 574	3.275 597	.305 288
5	1.503 657	5.925 373	.168 766	.665 045	3.940 642	.253 766
6	1.631 468	7.429 030	.134 607	.612 945	4.553 587	.219 607
7	1.770 142	9.060 497	.110 369	.564 926	5.118 514	.195 369
8	1.920 604	10.830 639	.092 331	.520 669	5.639 183	.177 331
9	2.083 856	12.751 244	.078 424	.479 880	6.119 063	.163 424
10	2.260 983	14.835 099	.067 408	.442 285	6.561 348	.152 408
11	2.453 167	17.096 083	.058 493	.407 636	6.968 984	.143 493
12	2.661 686	19.549 250	.051 153	.375 702	7.344 686	.136 153
13	2.887 930	22.210 936	.045 023	.346 269	7.690 955	.130 023
14	3.133 404	25.098 866	.039 842	.319 142	8.010 097	.124 842
15	3.399 743	28.232 269	.035 420	.294 140	8.304 237	.120 420
16	3.688 721	31.632 012	.031 614	.271 097	8.575 333	.116 614
17	4.002 262	35.320 733	.029 312	.249 859	8.825 192	.113 312
18	4.342 455	39.322 995	.025 430	.230 285	9.055 476	.110 430
19	4.711 563	43.665 450	.022 901	.212 244	9.267 720	.107 901
20	5.112 046	48.377 013	.020 671	.195 616	9.463 337	.105 671
21	5.546 570	53.489 059	.018 695	.180 292	9.643 628	.103 695
22	6.018 028	59.035 629	.016 939	.166 167	9.809 796	.101 939
23	6.529 561	65.053 658	.015 372	.153 150	9.962 945	.100 372
24	7.084 574	71.583 219	.013 970	.141 152	10.104 097	.098 970
25	7.686 762	78.667 792	.012 712	.130 094	10.234 191	.097 712
26	8.340 137	86.354 555	.011 580	.119 902	10.354 093	.096 580
27	9.049 049	94.694 692	.010 560	.110 509	10.464 602	.095 560
28	9.818 218	103.743 741	.009 639	.101 851	10.566 453	.094 639
29	10.652 766	113.561 959	.008 806	.093 872	10.660 326	.093 806
30	11.558 252	124.214 725	.008 051	.086 518	10.746 844	.093 051
31	12.540 703	135.772 977	.007 365	.079 740	10.826 584	.092 365
32	13.606 663	148.313 680	.006 742	.073 493	10.900 078	.091 742
33	14.763 229	161.920 343	.006 176	.067 736	10.967 813	.091 176
34	16.018 104	176.683 572	.005 660	.062 429	11.030 243	.090 660
35	17.379 642	192.701 675	.005 189	.057 539	11.087 781	.090 189
36	18.856 912	210.081 318	.004 760	.053 031	11.140 812	.089 760
37	20.459 750	228.938 230	.004 368	.048 876	11.189 689	.089 368
38	22.198 828	249.397 979	.004 010	.045 047	11.234 736	.089 010
39	24.085 729	271.596 808	.003 682	.041 518	11.276 255	.088 682
40	26.133 016	295.682 536	.003 382	.038 266	11.314 520	.088 382
41	28.354 322	321.815 552	.003 107	.035 268	11.349 788	.088 107
42	30.764 439	350.169 874	.002 856	.032 505	11.382 293	.087 856
43	33.379 417	380.934 313	.002 625	.029 959	11.412 252	.087 625
44	36.216 667	414.313 730	.002 414	.027 612	11.439 864	.087 414
45	39.295 084	450.530 397	.002 220	.025 448	11.465 312	.087 220
46	42.635 166	489.825 480	.002 042	.023 455	11.488 767	.087 042
47	46.259 155	532.460 646	.001 878	.021 617	11.510 384	.086 878
48	50.191 183	578.719 801	.001 728	.019 924	11.530 308	.086 728
49	54.457 434	628.910 984	.001 590	.018 363	11.548 671	.086 590
50	59.086 316	683.368 418	.001 463	.016 924	11.565 595	.086 463
51	64.108 652	742.454 733	.001 347	.015 599	11.581 914	.086 347
52	69.557 888	806.563 386	.001 240	.014 377	11.595 570	.086 240
53	75.470 308	876.121 273	.001 141	.013 250	11.608 821	.086 141
54	81.885 284	951.591 582	.001 051	.012 212	11.621 033	.086 051
55	88.845 534	1033.476 866	.000 968	.011 255	11.632 288	.085 968
56	96.397 404	1122.322 400	.000 891	.010 374	11.642 662	.085 891
57	104.591 183	1218.719 804	.000 821	.009 561	11.652 223	.085 821
58	113.481 434	1323.310 987	.000 756	.008 812	11.661 035	.085 756
59	123.127 356	1436.792 421	.000 696	.008 122	11.669 157	.085 696
60	133.593 181	1559.919 777	.000 641	.007 485	11.676 642	.085 641

$$S^n=(1+i)^n \quad S_{\overline{n}|}=\frac{S^n-1}{i} \quad \frac{1}{S_{\overline{n}|}}=\frac{i}{S^n-1} \quad V^n=\frac{1}{S^n} \quad A_{\overline{n}|}=\frac{1-1/S^n}{i} \quad \frac{1}{A_{\overline{n}|}}=\frac{i}{1-1/S^n}$$

8¾%
Annual
Table

	1	2	3	4	5	6
Years	Amount of 1	Amount of 1 per Period	Sinking-Fund Factor	Present Worth of 1	Present Worth of 1 per Period	Partial Payment
1	1.087 500	1.000 000	1.000 000	.919 540	.919 540	1.087 500
2	1.182 656	2.087 500	.479 042	.845 554	1.765 094	.566 542
3	1.286 139	3.270 156	.305 796	.777 521	2.542 616	.393 296
4	1.398 676	4.556 295	.219 477	.714 962	3.257 578	.306 977
5	1.521 060	5.954 971	.167 927	.657 436	3.915 014	.255 427
6	1.654 153	7.476 031	.133 761	.604 539	4.519 553	.221 261
7	1.798 891	9.130 183	.109 527	.555 898	5.075 451	.197 027
8	1.956 294	10.929 074	.091 499	.511 171	5.586 622	.178 999
9	2.127 470	12.885 368	.077 607	.470 042	6.056 664	.165 107
10	2.313 623	15.012 838	.066 610	.432 222	6.488 886	.154 110
11	2.516 065	17.326 461	.057 715	.397 446	6.886 332	.145 215
12	2.736 221	19.842 527	.050 397	.365 468	7.251 800	.137 897
13	2.975 640	22.578 748	.044 289	.336 062	7.587 862	.131 789
14	3.236 009	25.554 388	.039 132	.309 023	7.896 884	.126 632
15	3.519 160	28.790 397	.034 734	.284 159	8.181 043	.122 234
16	3.827 086	32.309 557	.030 951	.261 295	8.442 338	.118 451
17	4.161 956	36.136 643	.027 673	.240 272	8.682 610	.115 173
18	4.526 127	40.298 600	.024 815	.220 939	8.903 549	.112 315
19	4.922 164	44.824 727	.022 309	.203 163	9.106 712	.109 809
20	5.352 853	49.746 891	.020 102	.186 816	9.293 528	.107 602
21	5.821 228	55.099 744	.018 149	.171 785	9.465 313	.105 649
22	6.330 585	60.920 971	.016 415	.157 963	9.623 277	.103 915
23	6.884 511	67.251 556	.014 870	.145 254	9.768 530	.102 370
24	7.486 906	74.136 067	.013 489	.133 567	9.902 097	.100 989
25	8.142 010	81.622 973	.012 251	.122 820	10.024 917	.099 751
26	8.854 436	89.764 984	.011 140	.112 938	10.137 854	.098 640
27	9.629 199	98.619 420	.010 140	.103 851	10.241 705	.097 640
28	10.471 754	108.248 619	.009 238	.095 495	10.337 200	.096 738
29	11.388 033	118.720 373	.008 423	.087 811	10.425 012	.095 923
30	12.384 485	130.108 406	.007 686	.080 746	10.505 758	.095 186
31	13.468 128	142.492 891	.007 018	.074 249	10.580 007	.094 518
32	14.646 589	155.961 019	.006 412	.068 275	10.648 282	.093 912
33	15.928 166	170.607 608	.005 861	.062 782	10.711 064	.093 361
34	17.321 880	186.535 774	.005 361	.057 730	10.768 795	.092 861
35	18.837 545	203.857 654	.004 905	.053 085	10.821 880	.092 405
36	20.485 830	222.695 199	.004 490	.048 814	10.870 695	.091 990
37	22.278 340	243.181 029	.004 112	.044 887	10.915 581	.091 612
38	24.227 695	265.459 369	.003 767	.041 275	10.956 856	.091 267
39	26.347 618	289.687 064	.003 452	.037 954	10.994 810	.090 952
40	28.653 035	316.034 682	.003 164	.034 900	11.029 711	.090 664
41	31.160 175	344.687 716	.002 901	.032 092	11.061 803	.090 401
42	33.886 691	375.847 892	.002 661	.029 510	11.091 313	.090 161
43	36.851 776	409.734 582	.002 441	.027 136	11.118 449	.089 941
44	40.076 306	446.586 358	.002 239	.024 952	11.143 401	.089 739
45	43.582 983	486.662 664	.002 055	.022 945	11.166 346	.089 555
46	47.396 494	530.245 648	.001 886	.021 099	11.187 444	.089 386
47	51.543 687	577.642 142	.001 731	.019 401	11.206 846	.089 231
48	56.053 760	629.185 829	.001 589	.017 840	11.224 686	.089 089
49	60.958 464	685.239 589	.001 459	.016 405	11.241 090	.088 959
50	66.292 330	746.198 053	.001 340	.015 085	11.256 175	.088 840
51	72.092 909	812.490 383	.001 231	.013 871	11.270 046	.088 731
52	78.401 038	884.583 291	.001 130	.012 755	11.282 801	.088 630
53	85.261 129	962.984 329	.001 038	.011 729	11.294 529	.088 538
54	92.721 478	1048.245 458	.000 954	.010 785	11.305 314	.088 454
55	100.834 607	1140.966 936	.000 876	.009 917	11.315 232	.088 376
56	109.657 635	1241.801 543	.000 805	.009 119	11.324 351	.088 305
57	119.252 678	1351.459 178	.000 740	.008 386	11.332 737	.088 240
58	129.687 287	1470.711 856	.000 680	.007 711	11.340 447	.088 180
59	141.034 925	1600.399 143	.000 625	.007 090	11.347 538	.088 125
60	153.375 481	1741.434 068	.000 574	.006 520	11.354 058	.088 074
	$S^n=(1+i)^n$	$S_{\overline{n}|}=\dfrac{S^n-1}{i}$	$\dfrac{1}{S_{\overline{n}|}}=\dfrac{i}{S^n-1}$	$V^n=\dfrac{1}{S^n}$	$A_{\overline{n}|}=\dfrac{1-1/S^n}{i}$	$\dfrac{1}{A_{\overline{n}|}}=\dfrac{i}{1-1/S^n}$

344

9% Annual Table

Years	1 Amount of 1	2 Amount of 1 per Period	3 Sinking- Fund Factor	4 Present Worth of 1	5 Present Worth of 1 per Period	6 Partial Payment
1	1.090 000	1.000 000	1.000 000	.917 431	.917 431	1.090 000
2	1.188 100	2.090 000	.478 469	.841 680	1.759 111	.568 469
3	1.295 029	3.278 100	.305 055	.772 183	2.531 295	.395 055
4	1.411 582	4.573 129	.218 669	.708 425	3.239 720	.308 669
5	1.538 624	5.984 711	.167 092	.649 931	3.889 651	.257 092
6	1.677 100	7.523 335	.132 920	.596 267	4.485 919	.222 920
7	1.828 039	9.200 435	.108 691	.547 034	5.032 953	.198 691
8	1.992 563	11.028 474	.090 674	.501 866	5.534 819	.180 674
9	2.171 893	13.021 036	.076 799	.460 428	5.995 247	.166 799
10	2.367 364	15.192 930	.065 820	.422 411	6.417 658	.155 820
11	2.580 426	17.560 293	.056 947	.387 533	6.805 191	.146 947
12	2.812 665	20.140 720	.049 651	.355 535	7.160 725	.139 651
13	3.065 805	22.953 385	.043 567	.326 179	7.486 904	.133 567
14	3.341 727	26.019 189	.038 433	.299 246	7.786 150	.128 433
15	3.642 482	29.360 916	.034 059	.274 538	8.060 688	.124 059
16	3.970 306	33.003 399	.030 300	.251 870	8.312 558	.120 300
17	4.327 633	36.973 705	.027 046	.231 073	8.543 631	.117 046
18	4.717 120	41.301 338	.024 212	.211 994	8.755 625	.114 212
19	5.141 661	46.018 458	.021 730	.194 490	8.950 115	.111 730
20	5.604 411	51.160 120	.019 546	.178 431	9.128 546	.109 546
21	6.108 808	56.764 530	.017 617	.163 698	9.292 244	.107 617
22	6.658 600	62.873 338	.015 905	.150 182	9.442 425	.105 905
23	7.257 874	69.531 939	.014 382	.137 781	9.580 207	.104 382
24	7.911 083	76.789 813	.013 023	.126 405	9.706 612	.103 023
25	8.623 081	84.700 896	.011 806	.115 968	9.822 580	.101 806
26	9.399 158	93.323 977	.010 715	.106 393	9.928 972	.100 715
27	10.245 082	102.723 135	.009 735	.097 608	10.026 580	.099 735
28	11.167 140	112.968 217	.008 852	.089 548	10.116 128	.098 852
29	12.172 182	124.135 356	.008 056	.082 155	10.198 283	.098 056
30	13.267 678	136.307 539	.007 336	.075 371	10.273 654	.097 336
31	14.461 770	149.575 217	.006 686	.069 148	10.342 802	.096 686
32	15.763 329	164.036 987	.006 096	.063 438	10.406 240	.096 096
33	17.182 028	179.800 315	.005 562	.058 200	10.464 441	.095 562
34	18.728 411	196.982 344	.005 077	.053 395	10.517 835	.095 077
35	20.413 968	215.710 755	.004 636	.048 986	10.566 821	.094 636
36	22.251 225	236.124 723	.004 235	.044 941	10.611 763	.094 235
37	24.253 835	258.375 948	.003 870	.041 231	10.652 993	.093 870
38	26.436 680	282.629 783	.003 538	.037 826	10.690 820	.093 538
39	28.815 982	309.066 463	.003 236	.034 703	10.725 523	.093 236
40	31.409 420	337.882 445	.002 960	.031 838	10.757 360	.092 960
41	34.236 268	369.291 865	.002 708	.029 209	10.786 569	.092 708
42	37.317 532	403.528 133	.002 478	.026 797	10.813 366	.092 478
43	40.676 110	440.845 665	.002 268	.024 584	10.837 950	.092 268
44	44.336 960	481.521 775	.002 077	.022 555	10.860 505	.092 077
45	48.327 286	525.858 734	.001 902	.020 692	10.881 197	.091 902
46	52.676 742	574.186 021	.001 742	.018 984	10.900 181	.091 742
47	57.417 649	626.862 762	.001 595	.017 416	10.917 597	.091 595
48	62.585 237	684.280 411	.001 461	.015 978	10.933 575	.091 461
49	68.217 908	746.865 648	.001 339	.014 659	10.948 234	.091 339
50	74.357 520	815.083 556	.001 227	.013 449	10.961 683	.091 227
51	81.049 697	889.441 076	.001 124	.012 338	10.974 021	.091 124
52	88.344 170	970.490 773	.001 030	.011 319	10.985 340	.091 030
53	96.295 145	1058.834 943	.000 944	.010 385	10.995 725	.090 944
54	104.961 708	1155.130 088	.000 866	.009 527	11.005 252	.090 866
55	114.408 262	1260.091 796	.000 794	.008 741	11.013 993	.090 794
56	124.705 005	1374.500 057	.000 728	.008 019	11.022 012	.090 728
57	135.928 456	1499.205 063	.000 667	.007 357	11.029 369	.090 667
58	148.162 017	1635.133 518	.000 612	.006 749	11.036 118	.090 612
59	161.496 598	1783.295 535	.000 561	.006 192	11.042 310	.090 561
60	176.031 292	1944.792 133	.000 514	.005 681	11.047 991	.090 514

$$S^n = (1+i)^n \qquad S_{\overline{n}|} = \frac{S^n - 1}{i} \qquad \frac{1}{S_{\overline{n}|}} = \frac{i}{S^n - 1} \qquad V^n = \frac{1}{S^n} \qquad A_{\overline{n}|} = \frac{1 - 1/S^n}{i} \qquad \frac{1}{A_{\overline{n}|}} = \frac{i}{1 - 1/S^n}$$

345

	1	2	3	4	5	6
Years	Amount of 1	Amount of 1 per Period	Sinking-Fund Factor	Present Worth of 1	Present Worth of 1 per Period	Partial Payment
1	1.092 500	1.000 000	1.000 000	.915 332	.915 332	1.092 500
2	1.193 556	2.092 500	.477 897	.837 832	1.753 164	.570 397
3	1.303 960	3.286 056	.304 316	.766 895	2.520 059	.396 816
4	1.424 577	4.590 016	.217 864	.701 963	3.222 022	.310 364
5	1.556 350	6.014 593	.166 262	.642 529	3.864 551	.258 762
6	1.700 312	7.570 943	.132 084	.588 127	4.452 678	.224 584
7	1.857 591	9.271 255	.107 860	.538 332	4.991 010	.200 360
8	2.029 418	11.128 846	.089 857	.492 752	5.483 762	.182 357
9	2.217 139	13.158 264	.075 998	.451 032	5.934 793	.168 498
10	2.422 225	15.375 404	.065 039	.412 844	6.347 637	.157 539
11	2.646 281	17.797 629	.056 187	.377 889	6.725 526	.148 687
12	2.891 062	20.443 909	.048 914	.345 894	7.071 419	.141 414
13	3.158 485	23.334 971	.042 854	.316 608	7.388 027	.135 354
14	3.450 645	26.493 456	.037 745	.289 801	7.677 828	.130 245
15	3.769 829	29.944 100	.033 396	.265 264	7.943 092	.125 896
16	4.118 539	33.713 930	.029 661	.242 805	8.185 896	.122 161
17	4.499 503	37.832 468	.026 432	.222 247	8.408 143	.118 932
18	4.915 707	42.331 972	.023 623	.203 430	8.611 573	.116 123
19	5.370 410	47.247 679	.021 165	.186 206	8.797 778	.113 665
20	5.867 173	52.618 089	.019 005	.170 440	8.968 218	.111 505
21	6.409 887	58.485 262	.017 098	.156 009	9.124 227	.109 598
22	7.002 801	64.895 149	.015 409	.142 800	9.267 027	.107 909
23	7.650 560	71.897 951	.013 909	.130 709	9.397 736	.106 409
24	8.358 237	79.548 511	.012 571	.119 642	9.517 379	.105 071
25	9.131 374	87.906 748	.011 376	.109 513	9.626 891	.103 876
26	9.976 026	97.038 122	.010 305	.100 240	9.727 132	.102 805
27	10.898 809	107.014 149	.009 345	.091 753	9.818 885	.101 845
28	11.906 949	117.912 958	.008 481	.083 985	9.902 869	.100 981
29	13.008 341	129.819 906	.007 703	.076 874	9.979 743	.100 203
30	14.211 613	142.828 247	.007 001	.070 365	10.050 108	.099 501
31	15.526 187	157.039 860	.006 368	.064 407	10.114 516	.098 868
32	16.962 359	172.566 047	.005 795	.058 954	10.173 470	.098 295
33	18.531 378	189.528 407	.005 276	.053 963	10.227 432	.097 776
34	20.245 530	208.059 784	.004 806	.049 394	10.276 826	.097 306
35	22.118 242	228.305 315	.004 380	.045 212	10.322 037	.096 880
36	24.164 179	250.423 556	.003 993	.041 384	10.363 421	.096 493
37	26.399 365	274.587 735	.003 642	.037 880	10.401 301	.096 142
38	28.841 307	300.987 101	.003 322	.034 672	10.435 973	.095 822
39	31.509 128	329.828 407	.003 032	.031 737	10.467 710	.095 532
40	34.423 722	361.337 535	.002 767	.029 050	10.496 760	.095 267
41	37.607 916	395.761 257	.002 527	.026 590	10.523 350	.095 027
42	41.086 649	433.369 173	.002 308	.024 339	10.547 689	.094 808
43	44.887 164	474.455 822	.002 108	.022 278	10.569 967	.094 608
44	49.039 226	519.342 985	.001 926	.020 392	10.590 358	.094 426
45	53.575 355	568.382 212	.001 759	.018 665	10.609 024	.094 259
46	58.531 075	621.957 566	.001 608	.017 085	10.626 109	.094 108
47	63.945 199	680.488 641	.001 470	.015 638	10.641 747	.093 970
48	69.860 130	744.433 840	.001 343	.014 314	10.656 061	.093 843
49	76.322 192	814.293 970	.001 228	.013 102	10.669 164	.093 728
50	83.381 995	890.616 163	.001 123	.011 993	10.681 157	.093 623
51	91.094 830	973.998 158	.001 027	.010 978	10.692 134	.093 527
52	99.521 101	1065.092 987	.000 939	.010 048	10.702 182	.093 439
53	108.726 803	1164.614 089	.000 859	.009 197	10.711 380	.093 359
54	118.784 033	1273.340 892	.000 785	.008 419	10.719 798	.093 285
55	129.771 556	1392.124 924	.000 718	.007 706	10.727 504	.093 218
56	141.775 424	1521.896 480	.000 657	.007 053	10.734 558	.093 157
57	154.889 651	1663.671 904	.000 601	.006 456	10.741 014	.093 101
58	169.216 944	1818.561 555	.000 550	.005 910	10.746 924	.093 050
59	184.869 511	1987.778 499	.000 503	.005 409	10.752 333	.093 003
60	201.969 941	2172.648 011	.000 460	.004 951	10.757 284	.092 960

$$S^n = (1+i)^n \qquad S_{\overline{n}|} = \frac{S^n-1}{i} \qquad \frac{1}{S_{\overline{n}|}} = \frac{i}{S^n-1} \qquad V^n = \frac{1}{S^n} \qquad A_{\overline{n}|} = \frac{1-1/S^n}{i} \qquad \frac{1}{A_{\overline{n}|}} = \frac{i}{1-1/S^n}$$

9½% Annual Table

Years	1 Amount of 1	2 Amount of 1 per Period	3 Sinking-Fund Factor	4 Present Worth of 1	5 Present Worth of 1 per Period	6 Partial Payment
1	1.095 000	1.000 000	1.000 000	.913 242	.913 242	1.095 000
2	1.199 025	2.095 000	.477 327	.834 011	1.747 253	.572 327
3	1.312 932	3.294 025	.303 580	.761 654	2.508 907	.398 580
4	1.437 661	4.606 957	.217 063	.695 574	3.204 481	.312 063
5	1.574 239	6.044 618	.165 436	.635 228	3.839 709	.260 436
6	1.723 791	7.618 857	.131 253	.580 117	4.419 825	.226 253
7	1.887 552	9.342 648	.107 036	.529 787	4.949 612	.202 036
8	2.066 869	11.230 200	.089 046	.483 824	5.433 436	.184 046
9	2.263 222	13.297 069	.075 205	.441 848	5.875 284	.170 205
10	2.478 228	15.560 291	.064 266	.403 514	6.278 798	.159 266
11	2.713 659	18.038 518	.055 437	.368 506	6.647 304	.150 437
12	2.971 457	20.752 178	.048 188	.336 535	6.983 839	.143 188
13	3.253 745	23.723 634	.042 152	.307 338	7.291 178	.137 152
14	3.562 851	26.977 380	.037 068	.280 674	7.571 852	.132 068
15	3.901 322	30.540 231	.032 744	.256 323	7.828 175	.127 744
16	4.271 948	34.441 553	.029 035	.234 085	8.062 260	.124 035
17	4.677 783	38.713 500	.025 831	.213 777	8.276 037	.120 831
18	5.122 172	43.391 283	.023 046	.195 230	8.471 266	.118 046
19	5.608 778	48.513 454	.020 613	.178 292	8.649 558	.115 613
20	6.141 612	54.122 233	.018 477	.162 824	8.812 382	.113 477
21	6.725 065	60.263 845	.016 594	.148 697	8.961 080	.111 594
22	7.363 946	66.988 910	.014 928	.135 797	9.096 876	.109 928
23	8.063 521	74.352 856	.013 449	.124 015	9.220 892	.108 449
24	8.829 556	82.416 378	.012 134	.113 256	9.334 148	.107 134
25	9.668 364	91.245 934	.010 959	.103 430	9.437 578	.105 959
26	10.586 858	100.914 297	.009 909	.094 457	9.532 034	.104 909
27	11.592 610	111.501 156	.008 969	.086 262	9.618 296	.103 969
28	12.693 908	123.093 766	.008 124	.078 778	9.697 074	.103 124
29	13.899 829	135.787 673	.007 364	.071 943	9.769 018	.102 364
30	15.220 313	149.687 502	.006 681	.065 702	9.834 719	.101 681
31	16.666 242	164.907 815	.006 064	.060 002	9.894 721	.101 064
32	18.249 535	181.574 057	.005 507	.054 796	9.949 517	.100 507
33	19.983 241	199.823 593	.005 004	.050 042	9.999 559	.100 004
34	21.881 649	219.806 834	.004 549	.045 700	10.045 259	.099 549
35	23.960 406	241.688 483	.004 138	.041 736	10.086 995	.099 138
36	26.236 644	265.648 889	.003 764	.038 115	10.125 109	.098 764
37	28.729 126	291.885 534	.003 426	.034 808	10.159 917	.098 426
38	31.458 393	320.614 659	.003 119	.031 788	10.191 705	.098 119
39	34.446 940	352.073 052	.002 840	.029 030	10.220 735	.097 840
40	37.719 399	386.519 992	.002 587	.026 512	10.247 247	.097 587
41	41.302 742	424.239 391	.002 357	.024 211	10.271 458	.097 357
42	45.226 503	465.542 133	.002 148	.022 111	10.293 569	.097 148
43	49.523 020	510.768 636	.001 958	.020 193	10.313 762	.096 958
44	54.227 707	560.291 656	.001 785	.018 441	10.332 203	.096 785
45	59.379 340	614.519 364	.001 627	.016 841	10.349 043	.096 627
46	65.020 377	673.898 703	.001 484	.015 380	10.364 423	.096 484
47	71.197 313	738.919 080	.001 353	.014 045	10.378 469	.096.353
48	77.961 057	810.116 393	.001 234	.012 827	10.391 296	.096 234
49	85.367 358	888.077 450	.001 126	.011 714	10.403 010	.096 126
50	93.477 257	973.444 808	.001 027	.010 698	10.413 707	.096 027
51	102.357 596	1066.922 065	.000 937	.009 770	10.423 477	.095 937
52	112.081 568	1169.279 661	.000 855	.008 922	10.432 399	.095 855
53	122.729 317	1281.361 229	.000 780	.008 148	10.440 547	.095 780
54	134.388 602	1404.090 545	.000 712	.007 441	10.447 988	.095 712
55	147.155 519	1538.479 147	.000 650	.006 796	10.454 784	.095 650
56	161.135 293	1685.634 666	.000 593	.006 206	10.460 990	.095 593
57	176.443 146	1846.769 959	.000 541	.005 668	10.466 657	.095 541
58	193.205 245	2023.213 106	.000 494	.005 176	10.471 833	.095 494
59	211.559 743	2216.418 351	.000 451	.004 727	10.476 560	.095 451
60	231.657 919	2427.978 094	.000 412	.004 317	10.480 877	.095 412

$$S^n = (1+i)^n \qquad S_{\overline{n}|} = \frac{S^n - 1}{i} \qquad \frac{1}{S_{\overline{n}|}} = \frac{i}{S^n - 1} \qquad V^n = \frac{1}{S^n} \qquad A_{\overline{n}|} = \frac{1 - 1/S^n}{i} \qquad \frac{1}{A_{\overline{n}|}} = \frac{i}{1 - 1/S^n}$$

9¾%
Annual
Table

Years	1 Amount of 1	2 Amount of 1 per Period	3 Sinking- Fund Factor	4 Present Worth of 1	5 Present Worth of 1 per Period	6 Partial Payment
1	1.097 500	1.000 000	1.000 000	.911 162	.911 162	1.097 500
2	1.204 506	2.097 500	.476 758	.830 216	1.741 377	.574 258
3	1.321 946	3.302 006	.302 846	.756 461	2.497 838	.400 346
4	1.450 835	4.623 952	.216 265	.689 258	3.187 096	.313 765
5	1.592 292	6.074 787	.164 615	.628 026	3.815 122	.262 115
6	1.747 540	7.667 079	.130 428	.572 233	4.387 355	.227 928
7	1.917 925	9.414 619	.106 218	.521 397	4.908 752	.203 718
8	2.104 923	11.332 544	.088 241	.475 077	5.383 828	.185 741
9	2.310 153	13.437 468	.074 419	.432 872	5.816 700	.171 919
10	2.535 393	15.747 621	.063 502	.394 416	6.211 116	.161 002
11	2.782 594	18.283 014	.054 696	.359 377	6.570 493	.152 196
12	3.053 897	21.065 607	.047 471	.327 450	6.897 944	.144 971
13	3.351 652	24.119 504	.041 460	.298 360	7.196 304	.138 960
14	3.678 438	27.471 156	.036 402	.271 855	7.468 159	.133 902
15	4.037 085	31.149 594	.032 103	.247 703	7.715 862	.129 603
16	4.430 701	35.186 679	.028 420	.225 698	7.941 560	.125 920
17	4.862 695	39.617 380	.025 241	.205 647	8.147 207	.122 741
18	5.336 807	44.480 075	.022 482	.187 378	8.334 585	.119 982
19	5.857 146	49.816 882	.020 074	.170 732	8.505 317	.117 574
20	6.428 218	55.674 028	.017 962	.155 564	8.660 881	.115 462
21	7.054 969	62.102 246	.016 102	.141 744	8.802 625	.113 602
22	7.742 828	69.157 215	.014 460	.129 152	8.931 777	.111 960
23	8.497 754	76.900 043	.013 004	.117 678	9.049 455	.110 504
24	9.326 285	85.397 797	.011 710	.107 224	9.156 679	.109 210
25	10.235 598	94.724 083	.010 557	.097 698	9.254 377	.108 057
26	11.233 569	104.959 681	.009 527	.089 019	9.343 396	.107 027
27	12.328 842	116.193 249	.008 606	.081 111	9.424 506	.106 106
28	13.530 904	128.522 091	.007 781	.073 905	9.498 411	.105 281
29	14.850 167	142.052 995	.007 040	.067 339	9.565 751	.104 540
30	16.298 058	156.903 162	.006 373	.061 357	9.627 108	.103 873
31	17.887 119	173.201 221	.005 774	.055 906	9.683 014	.103 274
32	19.631 113	191.088 340	.005 233	.050 940	9.733 953	.102 733
33	21.545 147	210.719 453	.004 746	.046 414	9.780 368	.102 246
34	23.645 798	232.264 599	.004 305	.042 291	9.822 658	.101 805
35	25.951 264	255.910 398	.003 908	.038 534	9.861 192	.101 408
36	28.481 512	281.861 661	.003 548	.035 110	9.896 303	.101 048
37	31.258 459	310.343 173	.003 222	.031 991	9.928 294	.100 722
38	34.306 159	341.601 633	.002 927	.029 149	9.957 443	.100 427
39	37.651 010	375.907 792	.002 660	.026 560	9.984 003	.100 160
40	41.321 983	413.558 802	.002 418	.024 200	10.008 203	.099 918
41	45.350 877	454.880 785	.002 198	.022 050	10.030 253	.099 698
42	49.772 587	500.231 662	.001 999	.020 091	10.050 345	.099 499
43	54.625 414	550.004 249	.001 818	.018 306	10.068 651	.099 318
44	59.951 392	604.629 663	.001 654	.016 680	10.085 331	.099 154
45	65.796 653	664.581 055	.001 505	.015 198	10.100 530	.099 005
46	72.211 827	730.377 708	.001 369	.013 848	10.114 378	.098 869
47	79.252 480	802.589 534	.001 246	.012 618	10.126 996	.098 746
48	86.979 596	881.842 014	.001 134	.011 497	10.138 493	.098 634
49	95.460 107	968.821 610	.001 032	.010 476	10.148 968	.098 532
50	104.767 467	1064.281 717	.000 940	.009 545	10.158 513	.098 440
51	114.982 295	1169.049 185	.000 855	.008 697	10.167 210	.098 355
52	126.193 069	1284.031 480	.000 779	.007 924	10.175 135	.098 279
53	138.496 894	1410.224 549	.000 709	.007 220	10.182 355	.098 209
54	152.000 341	1548.721 443	.000 646	.006 579	10.188 934	.098 146
55	166.820 374	1700.721 784	.000 588	.005 994	10.194 928	.098 088
56	183.085 360	1867.542 158	.000 535	.005 462	10.200 390	.098 035
57	200.936 183	2050.627 518	.000 488	.004 977	10.205 367	.097 988
58	220.527 461	2251.563 701	.000 444	.004 535	10.209 902	.097 944
59	242.028 888	2472.091 162	.000 405	.004 132	10.214 033	.097 905
60	265.626 705	2714.120 050	.000 368	.003 765	10.217 798	.097 868

$$S^n = (1+i)^n \qquad S_{\overline{n}|} = \frac{S^n-1}{i} \qquad \frac{1}{S_{\overline{n}|}} = \frac{i}{S^n-1} \qquad V^n = \frac{1}{S^n} \qquad A_{\overline{n}|} = \frac{1-1/S^n}{i} \qquad \frac{1}{A_{\overline{n}|}} = \frac{i}{1-1/S^n}$$

348

10% Annual Table

Years	1 Amount of 1	2 Amount of 1 per Period	3 Sinking-Fund Factor	4 Present Worth of 1	5 Present Worth of 1 per Period	6 Partial Payment
1	1.100 000	1.000 000	1.000 000	.909 091	.909 091	1.100 000
2	1.210 000	2.100 000	.476 190	.826 446	1.735 537	.576 190
3	1.331 000	3.310 000	.302 115	.751 315	2.486 852	.402 115
4	1.464 100	4.641 000	.215 471	.683 013	3.169 865	.315 471
5	1.610 510	6.105 100	.163 797	.620 921	3.790 787	.263 797
6	1.771 561	7.715 610	.129 607	.564 474	4.355 261	.229 607
7	1.948 717	9.487 171	.105 405	.513 158	4.868 419	.205 405
8	2.143 589	11.435 888	.087 444	.466 507	5.334 926	.187 444
9	2.357 948	13.579 477	.073 641	.424 098	5.759 024	.173 641
10	2.593 742	15.937 425	.062 745	.385 543	6.144 567	.162 745
11	2.853 117	18.531 167	.053 963	.350 494	6.495 061	.153 963
12	3.138 428	21.384 284	.046 763	.318 631	6.813 692	.146 763
13	3.452 271	24.522 712	.040 779	.289 664	7.103 356	.140 779
14	3.797 498	27.974 983	.035 746	.263 331	7.366 687	.135 746
15	4.177 248	31.772 482	.031 474	.239 392	7.606 080	.131 474
16	4.594 973	35.949 730	.027 817	.217 629	7.823 709	.127 817
17	5.054 470	40.544 703	.024 664	.197 845	8.021 553	.124 664
18	5.559 917	45.599 173	.021 930	.179 859	8.201 412	.121 930
19	6.115 909	51.159 090	.019 547	.163 508	8.364 920	.119 547
20	6.727 500	57.274 999	.017 460	.148 644	8.513 564	.117 460
21	7.400 250	64.002 499	.015 624	.135 131	8.648 694	.115 624
22	8.140 275	71.402 749	.014 005	.122 846	8.771 540	.114 005
23	8.954 302	79.543 024	.012 572	.111 678	8.883 218	.112 572
24	9.849 733	88.497 327	.011 300	.101 526	8.984 744	.111 300
25	10.843 706	98.347 059	.010 168	.092 296	9.077 040	.110 168
26	11.918 177	109.181 765	.009 159	.083 905	9.160 945	.109 159
27	13.109 994	121.099 942	.008 258	.076 278	9.237 223	.108 258
28	14.420 994	134.209 936	.007 451	.069 343	9.306 567	.107 451
29	15.863 093	148.630 930	.006 728	.063 039	9.369 606	.106 728
30	17.449 402	164.494 023	.006 079	.057 309	9.426 914	.106 079
31	19.194 342	181.943 425	.005 496	.052 099	9.479 013	.105 496
32	21.113 777	201.137 767	.004 972	.047 362	9.526 376	.104 972
33	23.225 154	222.251 544	.004 499	.043 057	9.569 432	.104 499
34	25.547 670	245.476 699	.004 074	.039 143	9.608 575	.104 074
35	28.102 437	271.024 368	.003 690	.035 584	9.644 159	.103 690
36	30.912 681	299.126 805	.003 343	.032 349	9.676 508	.103 343
37	34.003 949	330.039 486	.003 030	.029 408	9.705 917	.103 030
38	37.404 343	364.043 434	.002 747	.026 735	9.732 651	.102 747
39	41.144 778	401.447 778	.002 491	.024 304	9.756 956	.102 491
40	45.259 256	442.592 556	.002 259	.022 095	9.779 051	.102 259
41	49.785 181	487.851 811	.002 050	.020 086	9.799 137	.102 050
42	54.763 699	537.636 992	.001 860	.018 260	9.817 397	.101 860
43	60.240 069	592.400 692	.001 688	.016 600	9.833 998	.101 688
44	66.264 076	652.640 761	.001 532	.015 091	9.849 089	.101 532
45	72.890 484	718.904 837	.001 391	.013 719	9.862 808	.101 391
46	80.179 532	791.795 321	.001 263	.012 472	9.875 280	.101 263
47	88.197 485	871.974 853	.001 147	.011 338	9.886 618	.101 147
48	97.017 234	960.172 338	.001 041	.010 307	9.896 926	.101 041
49	106.718 957	1057.189 572	.000 946	.009 370	9.906 296	.100 946
50	117.390 853	1163.908 529	.000 859	.008 519	9.914 814	.100 859
51	129.129 938	1281.299 382	.000 780	.007 744	9.922 559	.100 780
52	142.042 932	1410.429 320	.000 709	.007 040	9.929 599	.100 709
53	156.247 225	1552.472 252	.000 644	.006 400	9.935 999	.100 644
54	171.871 948	1708.719 477	.000 585	.005 818	9.941 817	.100 585
55	189.059 142	1880.591 425	.000 532	.005 289	9.947 106	.100 532
56	207.965 057	2069.650 567	.000 483	.004 809	9.951 915	.100 483
57	228.761 562	2277.615 624	.000 439	.004 371	9.956 286	.100 439
58	251.637 719	2506.377 186	.000 399	.003 974	9.960 260	.100 399
59	276.801 490	2758.014 905	.000 363	.003 613	9.963 873	.100 363
60	304.481 640	3034.816 395	.000 330	.003 284	9.967 157	.100 330

$$S^n = (1+i)^n \qquad S_{\overline{n}|} = \frac{S^n - 1}{i} \qquad \frac{1}{S_{\overline{n}|}} = \frac{i}{S^n - 1} \qquad V^n = \frac{1}{S^n} \qquad A_{\overline{n}|} = \frac{1 - 1/S^n}{i} \qquad \frac{1}{A_{\overline{n}|}} = \frac{i}{1 - 1/S^n}$$

10¼%
Annual
Table

Years	1 Amount of 1	2 Amount of 1 per Period	3 Sinking- Fund Factor	4 Present Worth of 1	5 Present Worth of 1 per Period	6 Partial Payment
1	1.102 500	1.000 000	1.000 000	.907 029	.907 029	1.102 500
2	1.215 506	2.102 500	.475 624	.822 702	1.729 732	.578 124
3	1.340 096	3.318 006	.301 386	.746 215	2.475 947	.403 886
4	1.477 455	4.658 102	.214 680	.676 839	3.152 787	.317 180
5	1.628 895	6.135 557	.162 984	.613 913	3.766 700	.265 484
6	1.795 856	7.764 452	.128 792	.556 837	4.323 537	.231 292
7	1.979 932	9.560 308	.104 599	.505 068	4.828 605	.207 099
8	2.182 875	11.540 240	.086 653	.458 112	5.286 717	.189 153
9	2.406 619	13.723 114	.072 870	.415 521	5.702 238	.175 370
10	2.653 298	16.129 734	.061 997	.376 889	6.079 127	.164 497
11	2.925 261	18.783 031	.053 240	.341 850	6.420 977	.155 740
12	3.225 100	21.708 292	.046 065	.310 068	6.731 045	.148 565
13	3.555 673	24.933 392	.040 107	.281 241	7.012 286	.142 607
14	3.920 129	28.489 065	.035 101	.255 094	7.267 379	.137 601
15	4.321 942	32.409 194	.030 855	.231 377	7.498 757	.133 355
16	4.764 941	36.731 136	.027 225	.209 866	7.708 623	.129 725
17	5.253 348	41.496 078	.024 099	.190 355	7.898 978	.126 599
18	5.791 816	46.749 426	.021 391	.172 657	8.071 635	.123 891
19	6.385 477	52.541 242	.019 033	.156 605	8.228 240	.121 533
20	7.039 989	58.926 719	.016 970	.142 046	8.370 286	.119 470
21	7.761 588	65.966 708	.015 159	.128 840	8.499 126	.117 659
22	8.557 150	73.728 295	.013 563	.116 861	8.615 987	.116 063
23	9.434 258	82.285 446	.012 153	.105 997	8.721 984	.114 653
24	10.401 270	91.719 704	.010 903	.096 142	8.818 126	.113 403
25	11.467 400	102.120 974	.009 792	.087 204	8.905 329	.112 292
26	12.642 808	113.588 373	.008 804	.079 096	8.984 426	.111 304
27	13.938 696	126.231 182	.007 922	.071 743	9.056 169	.110 422
28	15.367 412	140.169 878	.007 134	.065 073	9.121 241	.109 634
29	16.942 572	155.537 290	.006 429	.059 023	9.180 264	.108 929
30	18.679 186	172.479 862	.005 798	.053 536	9.233 800	.108 298
31	20.593 802	191.159 048	.005 231	.048 558	9.282 358	.107 731
32	22.704 667	211.752 851	.004 722	.044 044	9.326 402	.107 222
33	25.031 896	234.457 518	.004 265	.039 949	9.366 351	.106 765
34	27.597 665	259.489 414	.003 854	.036 235	9.402 586	.106 354
35	30.426 426	287.087 078	.003 483	.032 866	9.435 452	.105 983
36	33.545 134	317.513 504	.003 149	.029 811	9.465 263	.105 649
37	36.983 510	351.058 638	.002 849	.027 039	9.492 302	.105 349
38	40.774 320	388.042 148	.002 577	.024 525	9.516 827	.105 077
39	44.953 688	428.816 469	.002 332	.022 245	9.539 072	.104 832
40	49.561 441	473.770 157	.002 111	.020 177	9.559 249	.104 611
41	54.641 489	523.331 598	.001 911	.018 301	9.577 550	.104 411
42	60.242 241	577.973 087	.001 730	.016 600	9.594 150	.104 230
43	66.417 071	638.215 328	.001 567	.015 056	9.609 206	.104 067
44	73.224 821	704.632 399	.001 419	.013 657	9.622 863	.103 919
45	80.730 365	777.857 220	.001 286	.012 387	9.635 250	.103 786
46	89.005 227	858.587 585	.001 165	.011 235	9.646 485	.103 665
47	98.128 263	947.592 813	.001 055	.010 191	9.656 676	.103 555
48	108.186 410	1045.721 076	.000 956	.009 243	9.665 919	.103 456
49	119.275 517	1153.907 486	.000 867	.008 384	9.674 303	.103 367
50	131.501 258	1273.183 003	.000 785	.007 604	9.681 907	.103 285
51	144.980 137	1404.684 261	.000 712	.006 897	9.688 805	.103 212
52	159.840 601	1549.664 398	.000 645	.006 256	9.695 061	.103 145
53	176.224 262	1709.504 999	.000 585	.005 675	9.700 736	.103 085
54	194.287 249	1885.729 261	.000 530	.005 147	9.705 883	.103 030
55	214.201 692	2080.016 510	.000 481	.004 668	9.710 551	.102 981
56	236.157 366	2294.218 203	.000 436	.004 234	9.714 786	.102 936
57	260.363 496	2530.375 569	.000 395	.003 841	9.718 626	.102 895
58	287.050 754	2790.739 064	.000 358	.003 484	9.722 110	.102 858
59	316.473 456	3077.789 818	.000 325	.003 160	9.725 270	.102 825
60	348.911 986	3394.263 275	.000 295	.002 866	9.728 136	.102 795

$$S^n=(1+i)^n \quad\Big|\quad S_{\overline{n}|}=\frac{S^n-1}{i} \quad\Big|\quad \frac{1}{S_{\overline{n}|}}=\frac{i}{S^n-1} \quad\Big|\quad V^n=\frac{1}{S^n} \quad\Big|\quad A_{\overline{n}|}=\frac{1-1/S^n}{i} \quad\Big|\quad \frac{1}{A_{\overline{n}|}}=\frac{i}{1-1/S^n}$$

10½%
Annual
Table

Years	1 Amount of 1	2 Amount of 1 per Period	3 Sinking- Fund Factor	4 Present Worth of 1	5 Present Worth of 1 per Period	6 Partial Payment
1	1.105 000	1.000 000	1.000 000	.904 977	.904 977	1.105 000
2	1.221 025	2.105 000	.475 059	.818 984	1.723 961	.580 059
3	1.349 233	3.326 025	.300 659	.741 162	2.465 123	.405 659
4	1.490 902	4.675 258	.213 892	.670 735	3.135 858	.318 892
5	1.647 447	6.166 160	.162 175	.607 000	3.742 858	.267 175
6	1.820 429	7.813 606	.127 982	.549 321	4.292 179	.232 982
7	2.011 574	9.634 035	.103 799	.497 123	4.789 303	.208 799
8	2.222 789	11.645 609	.085 869	.449 885	5.239 188	.190 869
9	2.456 182	13.868 398	.072 106	.407 136	5.646 324	.177 106
10	2.714 081	16.324 579	.061 257	.368 449	6.014 773	.166 257
11	2.999 059	19.038 660	.052 525	.333 438	6.348 211	.157 525
12	3.313 961	22.037 720	.045 377	.301 754	6.649 964	.150 377
13	3.661 926	25.351 680	.039 445	.273 080	6.923 045	.144 445
14	4.046 429	29.013 607	.034 467	.247 132	7.170 176	.139 467
15	4.471 304	33.060 035	.030 248	.223 648	7.393 825	.135 248
16	4.940 791	37.531 339	.026 644	.202 397	7.596 221	.131 644
17	5.459 574	42.472 130	.023 545	.183 164	7.779 386	.128 545
18	6.032 829	47.931 703	.020 863	.165 760	7.945 146	.125 863
19	6.666 276	53.964 532	.018 531	.150 009	8.095 154	.123 531
20	7.366 235	60.630 808	.016 493	.135 755	8.230 909	.121 493
21	8.139 690	67.997 043	.014 707	.122 855	8.353 764	.119 707
22	8.994 357	76.136 732	.013 134	.111 181	8.464 945	.118 134
23	9.938 764	85.131 089	.011 747	.100 616	8.565 561	.116 747
24	10.982 335	95.069 854	.010 519	.091 055	8.656 616	.115 519
25	12.135 480	106.052 188	.009 429	.082 403	8.739 019	.114 429
26	13.409 705	118.187 668	.008 461	.074 573	8.813 592	.113 461
27	14.817 724	131.597 373	.007 599	.067 487	8.881 079	.112 599
28	16.373 585	146.415 097	.006 830	.061 074	8.942 153	.111 830
29	18.092 812	162.788 683	.006 143	.055 271	8.997 423	.111 143
30	19.992 557	180.881 494	.005 528	.050 019	9.047 442	.110 528
31	22.091 775	200.874 051	.004 978	.045 266	9.092 707	.109 978
32	24.411 412	222.965 827	.004 485	.040 964	9.133 672	.109 485
33	26.974 610	247.377 238	.004 042	.037 072	9.170 744	.109 042
34	29.806 944	274.351 848	.003 645	.033 549	9.204 293	.108 645
35	32.936 673	304.158 792	.003 288	.030 361	9.234 654	.108 288
36	36.395 024	337.095 466	.002 967	.027 476	9.262 131	.107 967
37	40.216 501	373.490 489	.002 677	.024 865	9.286 996	.107 677
38	44.439 234	413.706 991	.002 417	.022 503	9.309 499	.107 417
39	49.105 354	458.146 225	.002 183	.020 364	9.329 863	.107 183
40	54.261 416	507.251 579	.001 971	.018 429	9.348 292	.106 971
41	59.958 864	561.512 994	.001 781	.016 678	9.364 970	.106 781
42	66.254 545	621.471 859	.001 609	.015 093	9.380 064	.106 609
43	73.211 272	687.726 404	.001 454	.013 659	9.393 723	.106 454
44	80.898 456	760.937 676	.001 314	.012 361	9.406 084	.106 314
45	89.392 794	841.836 132	.001 188	.011 187	9.417 271	.106 188
46	98.779 037	931.228 926	.001 074	.010 124	9.427 394	.106 074
47	109.150 836	1030.007 963	.000 971	.009 162	9.436 556	.105 971
48	120.611 674	1139.158 800	.000 878	.008 291	9.444 847	.105 878
49	133.275 900	1259.770 473	.000 794	.007 503	9.452 350	.105 794
50	147.269 869	1393.046 373	.000 718	.006 790	9.459 140	.105 718
51	162.733 205	1540.316 242	.000 649	.006 145	9.465 285	.105 649
52	179.820 192	1703.049 448	.000 587	.005 561	9.470 847	.105 587
53	198.701 312	1882.869 640	.000 531	.005 033	9.475 879	.105 531
54	219.564 950	2081.570 952	.000 480	.004 554	9.480 434	.105 480
55	242.619 270	2301.135 902	.000 435	.004 122	9.484 555	.105 435
56	268.094 293	2543.755 172	.000 393	.003 730	9.488 285	.105 393
57	296.244 194	2811.849 465	.000 356	.003 376	9.491 661	.105 356
58	327.349 834	3108.093 659	.000 322	.003 055	9.494 716	.105 322
59	361.721 567	3435.443 493	.000 291	.002 765	9.497 480	.105 291
60	399.702 331	3797.165 059	.000 263	.002 502	9.499 982	.105 263

$$S^n = (1+i)^n \qquad S_{\overline{n}|} = \frac{S^n-1}{i} \qquad \frac{1}{S_{\overline{n}|}} = \frac{i}{S^n-1} \qquad V^n = \frac{1}{S^n} \qquad A_{\overline{n}|} = \frac{1-1/S^n}{i} \qquad \frac{1}{A_{\overline{n}|}} = \frac{i}{1-1/S^n}$$

10¾%
Annual
Table

Years	1 Amount of 1	2 Amount of 1 per Period	3 Sinking- Fund Factor	4 Present Worth of 1	5 Present Worth of 1 per Period	6 Partial Payment
1	1.107 500	1.000 000	1.000 000	.902 935	.902 935	1.107 500
2	1.226 556	2.107 500	.474 496	.815 291	1.718 225	.581 996
3	1.358 411	3.334 056	.299 935	.736 154	2.454 380	.407 435
4	1.504 440	4.692 467	.213 108	.664 699	3.119 079	.320 608
5	1.666 168	6.196 908	.161 371	.600 180	3.719 258	.268 871
6	1.845 281	7.863 075	.127 177	.541 923	4.261 181	.234 677
7	2.043 648	9.708 356	.103 004	.489 321	4.750 502	.210 504
8	2.263 340	11.752 004	.085 092	.441 825	5.192 327	.192 592
9	2.506 650	14.015 344	.071 350	.398 939	5.591 266	.178 850
10	2.776 114	16.521 994	.060 525	.360 216	5.951 482	.168 025
11	3.074 547	19.298 108	.051 819	.325 251	6.276 733	.159 319
12	3.405 060	22.372 655	.044 697	.293 681	6.570 414	.152 197
13	3.771 104	25.777 715	.038 793	.265 174	6.835 588	.146 293
14	4.176 498	29.548 820	.033 842	.239 435	7.075 023	.141 342
15	4.625 472	33.725 318	.029 651	.216 194	7.291 217	.137 151
16	5.122 710	38.350 789	.026 075	.195 209	7.486 426	.133 575
17	5.673 401	43.473 499	.023 003	.176 261	7.662 687	.130 503
18	6.283 292	49.146 900	.020 347	.159 152	7.821 840	.127 847
19	6.958 746	55.430 192	.018 041	.143 704	7.965 544	.125 541
20	7.706 811	62.388 938	.016 028	.129 755	8.095 299	.123 528
21	8.535 293	70.095 749	.014 266	.117 161	8.212 460	.121 766
22	9.452 837	78.631 042	.012 718	.105 788	8.318 248	.120 218
23	10.469 017	88.083 879	.011 353	.095 520	8.413 768	.118 853
24	11.594 436	98.552 895	.010 147	.086 248	8.500.016	.117 647
25	12.840 838	110.147 332	.009 079	.077 877	8.577 893	.116 579
26	14.221 228	122.988 170	.008 131	.070 317	8.648 210	.115 631
27	15.750 010	137.209 398	.007 288	.063 492	8.711 702	.114 788
38	17.443 136	152.959 408	.006 538	.057 329	8.769 031	.114 038
29	19.318 274	170.402 545	.005 868	.051 764	8.820 796	.113 368
30	21.394 988	189.720 818	.005 271	.046 740	8.867 536	.112 771
31	23.694 949	211.115 806	.004 737	.042 203	8.909 739	.112 237
32	26.242 156	234.810 756	.004 259	.038 107	8.947 845	.111 759
33	29.063 188	261.052 912	.003 831	.034 408	8.982 253	.111 331
34	32.187 481	290.116 100	.003 447	.031 068	9.013 321	.110 947
35	35.647 635	322.303 581	.003 103	.028 052	9.041 373	.110 603
36	39.479 756	357.951 215	.002 794	.025 329	9.066 703	.110 294
37	43.723 829	397.430 971	.002 516	.022 871	9.089 574	.110 016
38	48.424 141	441.154 801	.002 267	.020 651	9.110 225	.109 767
39	53.629 736	489.578 942	.002 043	.018 646	9.128 871	.109 543
40	59.394 933	543.208 678	.001 841	.016 836	9.145 707	.109 341
41	65.779 888	602.603 611	.001 659	.015 202	9.160 910	.109 159
42	72.851 226	668.383 499	.001 496	.013 727	9.174 636	.108 996
43	80.682 733	741.234 725	.001 349	.012 394	9.187 030	.108 849
44	89.356 127	821.917 458	.001 217	.011 191	9.198 222	.108 717
45	98.961 910	911.273 585	.001 097	.010 105	9.208 327	.108 597
46	109.600 316	1010.235 495	.000 990	.009 124	9.217 451	.108 490
47	121.382 350	1119.835 811	.000 893	.008 238	9.225 689	.108 393
48	134.430 952	1241.218 160	.000 806	.007 439	9.233 128	.108 306
49	148.882 280	1375.649 113	.000 727	.006 717	9.239 845	.108 227
50	164.887 125	1524.531 392	.000 656	.006 065	9.245 909	.108 156
51	182.612 491	1689.418 517	.000 592	.005 476	9.251 385	.108 092
52	202.243 333	1872.031 007	.000 534	.004 945	9.256 330	.108 034
53	223.984 492	2074.274 341	.000 482	.004 465	9.260 794	.107 982
54	248.062 824	2298.258 832	.000 435	.004 031	9.264 826	.107 935
55	274.729 578	2546.321 657	.000 393	.003 640	9.268 466	.107 893
56	304.263 008	2821.051 235	.000 354	.003 287	9.271 752	.107 854
57	336.971 281	3125.314 243	.000 320	.002 968	9.274 720	.107 820
58	373.195 694	3462.285 524	.000 289	.002 680	9.277 399	.107 789
59	413.314 231	3835.481 218	.000 261	.002 419	9.279 819	.107 761
60	457.745 511	4248.795 449	.000 235	.002 185	9.282 004	.107 735

$$S^n=(1+i)^n \qquad S_{\overline{n}|}=\frac{S^n-1}{i} \qquad \frac{1}{S_{\overline{n}|}}=\frac{i}{S^n-1} \qquad V^n=\frac{1}{S^n} \qquad A_{\overline{n}|}=\frac{1-1/S^n}{i} \qquad \frac{1}{A_{\overline{n}|}}=\frac{i}{1-1/S^n}$$

11% Annual Table

Years	1 Amount of 1	2 Amount of 1 per Period	3 Sinking- Fund Factor	4 Present Worth of 1	5 Present Worth of 1 per Period	6 Partial Payment
1	1.110 000	1.000 000	1.000 000	.900 901	.900 901	1.110 000
2	1.232 100	2.110 000	.473 934	.811 622	1.712 523	.583 934
3	1.367 631	3.342 100	.299 213	.731 191	2.443 715	.409 213
4	1.518 070	4.709 731	.212 326	.658 731	3.102 446	.322 326
5	1.685 058	6.227 801	.160 570	.593 451	3.695 897	.270 570
6	1.870 415	7.912 860	.126 377	.534 641	4.230 538	.236 377
7	2.076 160	9.783 274	.102 215	.481 658	4.712 196	.212 215
8	2.304 538	11.859 434	.084 321	.433 926	5.146 123	.194 321
9	2.558 037	14.163 972	.070 602	.390 925	5.537 048	..180 602
10	2.839 421	16.722 009	.059 801	.352 184	5.889 232	.169 801
11	3.151 757	19.561 430	.051 121	.317 283	6.206 515	.161 121
12	3.498 451	22.713 187	.044 027	.285 841	6.492 356	.154 027
13	3.883 280	26.211 638	.038 151	.257 514	6.749 870	.148 151
14	4.310 441	30.094 918	.033 228	.231 995	6.981 865	.143 228
15	4.784 589	34.405 359	.029 065	.209 004	7.190 870	.139 065
16	5.310 894	39.189 948	.025 517	.188 292	7.379 162	.135 517
17	5.895 093	44.500 843	.022 471	.169 633	7.548 794	.132 471
18	6.543 553	50.395 936	.019 843	.152 822	7.701 617	.129 843
19	7.263 344	56.939 488	.017 563	.137 678	7.839 294	.127 563
20	8.062 312	64.202 832	.015 576	.124 034	7.963 328	.125 576
21	8.949 166	72.265 144	.013 838	.111 742	8.075 070	.123 838
22	9.933 574	81.214 309	.012 313	.100 669	8.175 739	.122 313
23	11.026 267	91.147 884	.010 971	.090 693	8.266 432	.120 971
24	12.239 157	102.174 151	.009 787	.081 705	8.348 137	.119 787
25	13.585 464	114.413 307	.008 740	.073 608	8.421 745	.118 740
26	15.079 865	127.998 771	.007 813	.066 314	8.488 058	.117 813
27	16.738 650	143.078 636	.006 989	.059 742	8.547 800	.116 989
28	18.579 901	159.817 286	.006 257	.053 822	8.601 622	.116 257
29	20.623 691	178.397 187	.005 605	.048 488	8.650 110	.115 605
30	22.892 297	199.020 878	.005 025	.043 683	8.693 793	.115 025
31	25.410 449	221.913 174	.004 506	.039 354	8.733 146	.114 506
32	28.205 599	247.323 624	.004 043	.035 454	8.768 600	.114 043
33	31.308 214	275.529 222	.003 629	.031 940	8.800 541	.113 629
34	34.752 118	306.837 437	.003 259	.028 775	8.829 316	.113 259
35	38.574 851	341.589 555	.002 927	.025 924	8.855 240	.112 927
36	42.818 085	380.164 406	.002 630	.023 355	8.878 594	.112 630
37	47.528 074	422.982 490	.002 364	.021 040	8.899 635	.112 364
38	52.756 162	470.510 564	.002 125	.018 955	8.918 590	.112 125
39	58.559 340	523.266 726	.001 911	.017 077	8.935 666	.111 911
40	65.000 867	581.826 066	.001 719	.015 384	8.951 051	.111 719
41	72.150 963	646.826 934	.001 546	.013 860	8.964 911	.111 546
42	80.087 569	718.977 896	.001 391	.012 486	8.977 397	.111 391
43	88.897 201	799.065 465	.001 251	.011 249	8.988 646	.111 251
44	98.675 893	887.962 666	.001 126	.010 134	8.998 780	.111 126
45	109.530 242	986.638 559	.001 014	.009 130	9.007 910	.111 014
46	121.578 568	1096.168 801	.000 912	.008 225	9.016 135	.110 912
47	134.952 211	1217.747 369	.000 821	.007 410	9.023 545	.110 821
48	149.796 954	1352.699 580	.000 739	.006 676	9.030 221	.110 739
49	166.274 619	1502.496 533	.000 666	.006 014	9.036 235	.110 666
50	184.564 827	1668.771 152	.000 599	.005 418	9.041 653	.110 599
51	204.866 958	1853.335 979	.000 540	.004 881	9.046 534	.110 540
52	227.402 323	2058.202 937	.000 486	.004 397	9.050 932	.110 486
53	252.416 579	2285.605 260	.000 438	.003 962	9.054 894	.110 438
54	280.182 402	2538.021 838	.000 394	.003 569	9.058 463	.110 394
55	311.002 466	2818.204 240	.000 355	.003 215	9.061 678	.110 355
56	345.212 738	3129.206 707	.000 320	.002 897	9.064 575	.110 320
57	383.186 139	3474.419 445	.000 288	.002 610	9.067 185	.110 288
58	425.336 614	3857.605 583	.000 259	.002 351	9.069 536	.110 259
59	472.123 642	4282.942 198	.000 233	.002 118	9.071 654	.110 233
60	524.057 242	4755.065 839	.000 210	.001 908	9.073 562	.110 210

$$S^n = (1+i)^n \qquad S_{\overline{n}|} = \frac{S^n - 1}{i} \qquad \frac{1}{S_{\overline{n}|}} = \frac{i}{S^n - 1} \qquad V^n = \frac{1}{S^n} \qquad A_{\overline{n}|} = \frac{1 - 1/S^n}{i} \qquad \frac{1}{A_{\overline{n}|}} = \frac{i}{1 - 1/S^n}$$

11¼%
Annual
Table

Years	1 Amount of 1	2 Amount of 1 per Period	3 Sinking- Fund Factor	4 Present Worth of 1	5 Present Worth of 1 per Period	6 Partial Payment
1	1.112 500	1.000 000	1.000 000	.898 876	.898 876	1.112 500
2	1.237 656	2.112 500	.473 373	.807 979	1.706 855	.585 873
3	1.376 893	3.350 156	.298 494	.726 273	2.433 128	.410 994
4	1.531 793	4.727 049	.211 548	.652 830	3.085 958	.324 048
5	1.704 120	6.258 842	.159 774	.586 813	3.672 771	.272 274
6	1.895 833	7.962 962	.125 581	.527 473	4.200 244	.238 081
7	2.109 114	9.858 795	.101 432	.474 133	4.674 376	.213 932
8	2.346 390	11.967 909	.083 557	.426 187	5.100 563	.196 057
9	2.610 359	14.314 299	.069 860	.383 089	5.483 652	.182 360
10	2.904 024	16.924 657	.059 085	.344 350	5.828 002	.171 585
11	3.230 727	19.828 681	.050 432	.309 528	6.137 530	.162 932
12	3.594 183	23.059 408	.043 366	.278 227	6.415 757	.155 866
13	3.998 529	26.653 592	.037 518	.250 092	6.665 849	.150 018
14	4.448 364	30.652 121	.032 624	.224 802	6.890 651	.145 124
15	4.948 804	35.100 484	.028 490	.202 069	7.092 720	.140 990
16	5.505 545	40.049 289	.024 969	.181 635	7.274 355	.137 469
17	6.124 919	45.554 834	.021 952	.163 267	7.437 622	.134 452
18	6.813 972	51.679 752	.019 350	.146 757	7.584 380	.131 850
19	7.580 544	58.493 725	.017 096	.131 917	7.716 296	.129 596
20	8.433 355	66.074 269	.015 134	.118 577	7.834 873	.127 634
21	9.382 108	74.507 624	.013 421	.106 586	7.941 459	.125 921
22	10.437 595	83.889 731	.011 920	.095 808	8.037 267	.124 420
23	11.611 824	94.327 326	.010 601	.086 119	8.123 386	.123 101
24	12.918 154	105.939 150	.009 439	.077 410	8.200 796	.121 939
25	14.371 447	118.857 305	.008 413	.069 582	8.270 379	.120 913
26	15.988 235	133.228 752	.007 506	.062 546	8.332 925	.120 006
27	17.786 911	149.216 986	.006 702	.056 221	8.389 146	.119 202
28	19.787 938	167.003 897	.005 988	.050 536	8.439 681	.118 488
29	22.014 081	186.791 836	.005 354	.045 425	8.485 107	.117 854
30	24.490 666	208.805 917	.004 789	.040 832	8.525 939	.117 289
31	27.245 866	233.296 583	.004 286	.036 703	8.562 642	.116 786
32	30.311 025	260.542 448	.003 838	.032 991	8.595 633	.116 338
33	33.721 016	290.853 474	.003 438	.029 655	8.625 288	.115 938
34	37.514 630	324.574 489	.003 081	.026 656	8.651 944	.115 581
35	41.735 026	362.089 120	.002 762	.023 961	8.675 905	.115 262
36	46.430 216	403.824 145	.002 476	.021 538	8.697 443	.114 976
37	51.653 616	450.254 362	.002 221	.019 360	8.716 .802	.114 721
38	57.464 647	501.907 978	.001 992	.017 402	8.734 204	.114 492
39	63.929 420	559.372 625	.001 788	.015 642	8.749 847	.114 288
40	71.121 480	623.302 045	.001 604	.014 060	8.763 907	.114 104
41	79.122 647	694.423 525	.001 440	.012 639	8.776 546	.113 940
42	88.023 944	773.546 172	.001 293	.011 361	8.787 906	.113 793
43	97.926 638	861.570 116	.001 161	.010 212	8.798 118	.113 661
44	108.943 385	959.496 755	.001 042	.009 179	8.807 297	.113 542
45	121.199 516	1068.440 139	.000 936	.008 251	8.815 548	.113 436
46	134.834 461	1189.639 665	.000 841	.007 417	8.822 964	.113 341
47	150.003 338	1324.474 116	.000 755	.006 667	8.829 631	.113 255
48	166.878 714	1474.477 454	.000 678	.005 992	8.835 623	.113 178
49	185.652 569	1641.356 168	.000 609	.005 386	8.841 010	.113 109
50	206.538 483	1827.008 737	.000 547	.004 842	8.845 851	.113 047
51	229.774 062	2033.547 220	.000 492	.004 352	8.850 204	.112 992
52	255.623 644	2263.321 282	.000 442	.003 912	8.854 116	.112 942
53	284.381 304	2518.944 926	.000 397	.003 516	8.857 632	.112 897
54	316.374 201	3803.326 230	.000 357	.003 161	8.860 793	.112 857
55	351.966 299	3119.700 431	.000 321	.002 841	8.863 634	.112 821
56	391.562 507	3471.666 730	.000 288	.002 554	8.866 188	.112 788
57	435.613 289	3863.229 237	.000 259	.002 296	8.868 483	.112 759
58	484.619 784	4298.842 526	.000 233	.002 063	8.870 547	.112 733
59	539.139 510	4783.462 310	.000 209	.001 855	8.872 402	.112 709
60	599.792 705	5322.601 820	.000 188	.001 667	8.874 069	.112 688

$$S^n = (1+i)^n \quad S_{\overline{n}|} = \frac{S^n - 1}{i} \quad \frac{1}{S_{\overline{n}|}} = \frac{i}{S^n - 1} \quad V^n = \frac{1}{S^n} \quad A_{\overline{n}|} = \frac{1 - 1/S^n}{i} \quad \frac{1}{A_{\overline{n}|}} = \frac{i}{1 - 1/S^n}$$

11½% Annual Table

Years	1 Amount of 1	2 Amount of 1 per Period	3 Sinking- Fund Factor	4 Present Worth of 1	5 Present Worth of 1 per Period	6 Partial Payment
1	1.115 000	1.000 000	1.000 000	.896 861	.896 861	1.115 000
2	1.243 225	2.115 000	.472 813	.804 360	1.701 221	.587 813
3	1.386 196	3.358 225	.297 776	.721 399	2.422 619	.412 776
4	1.545 608	4.744 421	.210 774	.646 994	3.069 614	.325 774
5	1.723 353	6.290 029	.158 982	.580 264	3.649 878	.273 982
6	1.921 539	8.013 383	.124 791	.520 416	4.170 294	.239 791
7	2.142 516	9.934 922	.100 655	.466 741	4.637 035	.215 655
8	2.388 905	12.077 438	.082 799	.418 602	5.055 637	.197 799
9	2.663 629	14.466 343	.069 126	.375 428	5.431 064	.184 126
10	2.969 947	17.129 972	.058 377	.336 706	5.767 771	.173 377
11	3.311 491	20.099 919	.049 751	.301 979	6.069 750	.164 751
12	3.692 312	23.411 410	.042 714	.270 833	6.340 583	.157 714
13	4.116 928	27.103 722	.036 895	.242 900	6.583 482	.151 895
14	4.590 375	31.220 650	.032 030	.217 847	6.801 329	.147 030
15	5.118 268	35.811 025	.027 924	.195 379	6.996 708	.142 924
16	5.706 869	40.929 293	.024 432	.175 227	7.171 935	.139 432
17	6.363 159	46.636 161	.021 443	.157 155	7.329 090	.136 443
18	7.094 922	52.999 320	.018 868	.140 946	7.470 036	.133 868
19	7.910 838	60.094 242	.016 641	.126 409	7.596 445	.131 641
20	8.820 584	68.005 080	.014 705	.113 371	7.709 816	.129 705
21	9.834 951	76.825 664	.013 016	.101 678	7.811 494	.128 016
22	10.965 971	86.660 615	.011 539	.091 191	7.902 685	.126 539
23	12.227 057	97.626 586	.010 243	.081 786	7.984 471	.125 243
24	13.633 169	109.853 643	.009 103	.073 351	8.057 822	.124 103
25	15.200 983	123.486 812	.008 098	.065 785	8.123 607	.123 098
26	16.949 096	138.687 796	.007 210	.059 000	8.182 607	.122 210
27	18.898 243	155.636 892	.006 425	.052 915	8.235 522	.121 425
28	21.071 540	174.535 135	.005 730	.047 457	8.282 979	.120 730
29	23.494 768	195.606 675	.005 112	.042 563	8.325 542	.120 112
30	26.196 666	219.101 443	.004 564	.038 173	8.363 715	.119 564
31	29.209 282	245.298 109	.004 077	.034 236	8.397 951	.119 077
32	32.568 350	274.507 391	.003 643	.030 705	8.428 655	.118 643
33	36.313 710	307.075 741	.003 257	.027 538	8.456 193	.118 257
34	40.489 787	343.389 451	.002 912	.024 698	8.480 891	.117 912
35	45.146 112	383.879 238	.002 605	.022 150	8.503 041	.117 605
36	50.337 915	429.025 351	.002 331	.019 866	8.522 907	.117 331
37	56.126 776	479.363 266	.002 086	.017 817	8.540 723	.117 086
38	62.581 355	535.490 042	.001 867	.015 979	8.556 703	.116 867
39	69.778 211	598.071 396	.001 672	.014 331	8.571 034	.116 672
40	77.802 705	667.849 607	.001 497	.012 853	8.583 887	.116 497
41	86.750 016	745.652 312	.001 341	.011 527	8.595 414	.116 341
42	96.726 268	832.402 327	.001 201	.010 338	8.605 753	.116 201
43	107.849 788	929.128 595	.001 076	.009 272	8.615 025	.116 076
44	120.252 514	1036.978 384	.000 964	.008 316	8.623 341	.115 964
45	134.081 553	1157.230 898	.000 864	.007 458	8.630 799	.115 864
46	149.500 932	1291.312 451	.000 774	.006 689	8.637 488	.115 774
47	166.693 539	1440.813 383	.000 694	.005 999	8.643 487	.115 694
48	185.863 296	1607.506 922	.000 622	.005 380	8.648 867	.115 622
49	207.237 575	1793.370 218	.000 558	.004 825	8.653 692	.115 558
50	231.069 896	2000.607 793	.000 500	.004 328	8.658 020	.115 500
51	257.642 934	2231.677 689	.000 448	.003 881	8.661 901	.115 448
52	287.271 872	2489.320 623	.000 402	.003 481	8.665 382	.115 402
53	320.308 137	2776.592 495	.000 360	.003 122	8.668 504	.115 360
54	357.143 573	3096.900 632	.000 323	.002 800	8.671 304	.115 323
55	398.215 084	3454.044 205	.000 290	.002 511	8.673 816	.115 290
56	444.009 818	3852.259 288	.000 260	.002 252	8.676 068	.115 260
57	495.070 947	4296.269 106	.000 233	.002 020	8.678 088	.115 233
58	552.004 106	4791.340 053	.000 209	.001 812	8.679 899	.115 209
59	615.484 578	5343.344 159	.000 187	.001 625	8.681 524	.115 187
60	686.265 305	5958.828 738	.000 168	.001 457	8.682 981	.115 168

$S^n=(1+i)^n$	$S_{\overline{n}|}=\dfrac{S^n-1}{i}$	$\dfrac{1}{S_{\overline{n}|}}=\dfrac{i}{S^n-1}$	$V^n=\dfrac{1}{S^n}$	$A_{\overline{n}|}=\dfrac{1-1/S^n}{i}$	$\dfrac{1}{A_{\overline{n}|}}=\dfrac{i}{1-1/S^n}$

11¾%
Annual
Table

Years	1 Amount of 1	2 Amount of 1 per Period	3 Sinking- Fund Factor	4 Present Worth of 1	5 Present Worth of 1 per Period	6 Partial Payment
1	1.117 500	1.000 000	1.000 000	.894 855	.894 855	1.117 500
2	1.248 806	2.117 500	.472 255	.800 765	1.695 619	.589 755
3	1.395 541	3.366 306	.297 062	.716 568	2.412 187	.414 562
4	1.559 517	4.761 847	.210 003	.641 224	3.053 411	.327 503
5	1.742 760	6.321 364	.158 194	.573 802	3.627 214	.275 694
6	1.947 535	8.064 125	.124 006	.513 470	4.140 684	.241 506
7	2.176 370	10.011 659	.099 884	.459 481	4.600 164	.217 384
8	2.432 093	12.188 029	.082 048	.411 168	5.011 333	.199 548
9	2.717 864	14.620 123	.068 399	.367 936	5.379 269	.185 899
10	3.037 213	17.337 987	.057 677	.329 249	5.708 518	.175 177
11	3.394 086	20.375 200	.049 079	.294 630	6.003 148	.166 579
12	3.792 891	23.769 287	.042 071	.263 651	6.266 799	.159 571
13	4.238 556	27.562 178	.036 282	.235 929	6.502 728	.153 782
14	4.736 586	31.800 734	.031 446	.211 123	6.713 851	.148 946
15	5.293 135	36.537 320	.027 369	.188 924	6.902 775	.144 869
16	5.915 078	41.830 455	.023 906	.169 059	7.071 834	.141 406
17	6.610 100	47.745 533	.020 944	.151 284	7.233 118	.138 444
18	7.386 787	54.355 634	.018 397	.135 377	7.358 495	.135 897
19	8.254 734	61.742 420	.016 196	.121 143	7.479 637	.133 696
20	9.224 666	69.997 155	.014 286	.108 405	7.588 042	.131 786
21	10.308 564	79.221 821	.012 623	.097 007	7.685 049	.130 123
22	11.519 820	89.530 384	.011 169	.086 807	7.771 856	.128 669
23	12.873 399	101.050 205	.009 896	.077 680	7.849 536	.127 396
24	14.386 023	113.923 604	.008 778	.069 512	7.919 048	.126 278
25	16.076 381	128.309 627	.007 794	.062 203	7.981 251	.125 294
26	17.965 356	144.386 008	.006 926	.055 663	8.036 913	.124 426
27	20.076 285	162.351 364	.006 159	.049 810	8.086 723	.123 659
28	22.435 249	182.427 650	.005 482	.044 573	8.131 296	.122 982
29	25.071 391	204.862 898	.004 881	.039 886	8.171 182	.122 381
30	28.017 279	299.934 289	.004 349	.035 692	8.206 874	.121 849
31	31.309 309	257.951 568	.003 877	.031 939	8.238 814	.121 377
32	34.988 153	289.260 877	.003 457	.028 581	8.267 395	.120 957
33	39.099 261	324.249 030	.003 084	.025 576	8.292 971	.120 584
34	43.693 424	363.348 291	.002 752	.022 887	8.315 858	.120 252
35	48.827 402	407.041 715	.002 457	.020 480	8.336 338	.119 957
36	54.564 621	455.869 117	.002 194	.018 327	8.354 665	.119 694
37	60.975 964	510.433 738	.001 959	.016 400	8.371 065	.119 459
38	68.140 640	571.409 702	.001 750	.014 676	8.385 740	.119 250
39	76.147 165	639.550 343	.001 564	.013 132	8.398 873	.119 064
40	85.094 457	715.697 508	.001 397	.011 752	8.410 624	.118 897
41	95.093 056	800.791 965	.001 249	.010 516	8.421 140	.118 749
42	106.266 490	895.885 021	.001 116	.009 410	8.430 551	.118 616
43	118.752 803	1002.151 511	.000 998	.008 421	8.438 971	.118 498
44	132.706 257	1120.904 313	.000 892	.007 535	8.446 507	.118 392
45	148.299 242	1253.610 570	.000 798	.006 743	8.453 250	.118 298
46	165.724 403	1401.909 812	.000 713	.006 034	8.459 284	.118 213
47	185.197 020	1567.634 215	.000 638	.005 400	8.464 684	.118 138
48	206.957 670	1752.831 235	.000 571	.004 832	8.469 516	.118 071
49	231.275 196	1959.788 905	.000 510	.004 324	8.473 840	.118 010
50	258.450 032	2191.064 102	.000 456	.003 869	8.477 709	.117 956
51	288.817 911	2449.514 134	.000 408	.003 462	8.481 171	.117 908
52	322.754 015	2738.332 044	.000 365	.003 098	8.484 269	.117 865
53	360.677 612	3061.086 060	.000 327	.002 773	8.487 042	.117 827
54	403.057 231	3421.763 672	.000 292	.002 481	8.489 523	.117 792
55	450.416 456	3824.820 903	.000 261	.002 220	8.491 743	.117 761
56	503.340 390	4275.237 359	.000 234	.001 987	8.493 730	.117 734
57	562.482 885	4778.577 749	.000 209	.001 778	8.495 508	.117 709
58	628.574 625	5341.060 634	.000 187	.001 591	8.497 099	.117 687
59	702.432 143	5969.635 259	.000 168	.001 424	8.498 522	.117 668
60	784.967 920	6672.067 402	.000 150	.001 274	8.499 796	.117 650

$$S^n = (1+i)^n \qquad S_{\overline{n}|} = \frac{S^n - 1}{i} \qquad \frac{1}{S_{\overline{n}|}} = \frac{i}{S^n - 1} \qquad V^n = \frac{1}{S^n} \qquad A_{\overline{n}|} = \frac{1 - 1/S^n}{i} \qquad \frac{1}{A_{\overline{n}|}} = \frac{i}{1 - 1/S^n}$$

12% Annual Table

Years	1 Amount of 1	2 Amount of 1 per Period	3 Sinking- Fund Factor	4 Present Worth of 1	5 Present Worth of 1 per Period	6 Partial Payment
1	1.120 000	1.000 000	1.000 000	.892 857	.892 857	1.120 000
2	1.254 400	2.120 000	.471 698	.797 194	1.690 051	.591 698
3	1.404 928	3.374 400	.296 349	.711 780	2.401 831	.416 349
4	1.573 519	4.779 328	.209 234	.635 518	3.037 349	.329 234
5	1.762 342	6.352 847	.157 410	.567 427	3.604 776	.277 410
6	1.973 823	8.115 189	.123 226	.506 631	4.111 407	.243 226
7	2.210 681	10.089 012	.099 118	.452 349	4.563 757	.219 118
8	2.475 963	12.299 693	.081 303	.403 883	4.967 640	.201 303
9	2.773 079	14.775 656	.067 679	.360 610	5.328 250	.187 679
10	3.105 848	17.548 735	.056 984	.321 973	5.650 223	.176 984
11	3.478 550	20.654 583	.048 415	.287 476	5.937 699	.168 415
12	3.895 976	24.133 133	.041 437	.256 675	6.194 374	.161 437
13	4.363 493	28.029 109	.035 677	.229 174	6.423 548	.155 677
14	4.887 112	32.392 602	.030 871	.204 620	6.628 168	.150 871
15	5.473 566	37.279 715	.026 824	.182 696	6.810 864	.146 824
16	6.130 394	42.753 280	.023 390	.163 122	6.973 986	.143 390
17	6.866 041	48.883 674	.020 457	.145 644	7.119 630	.140 457
18	7.689 966	55.749 715	.017 937	.130 040	7.249 670	.137 937
19	8.612 762	63.439 681	.015 763	.116 107	7.365 777	.135 763
20	9.646 293	72.052 442	.013 879	.103 667	7.469 444	.133 879
21	10.803 848	81.698 736	.012 240	.092 560	7.562 003	.132 240
22	12.100 310	92.502 584	.010 811	.082 643	7.644 646	.130 811
23	13.552 347	104.602 894	.009 560	.073 788	7.718 434	.129 560
24	15.178 629	118.155 241	.008 463	.065 882	7.784 316	.128 463
25	17.000 064	133.333 870	.007 500	.058 823	7.843 139	.127 500
26	19.040 072	150.333 934	.006 652	.052 521	7.895 660	.126 652
27	21.324 881	169.374 007	.005 904	.046 894	7.942 554	.125 904
28	23.883 866	190.698 887	.005 244	.041 869	7.984 423	.125 244
29	26.749 930	214.582 754	.004 660	.037 383	8.021 806	.124 660
30	29.959 922	241.332 684	.004 144	.033 378	8.055 184	.124 144
31	33.555 113	271.292 606	.003 686	.029 802	8.084 986	.123 686
32	37.581 726	304.847 719	.003 280	.026 609	8.111 594	.123 280
33	42.091 533	342.429 446	.002 920	.023 758	8.135 352	.122 920
34	47.142 517	384.520 979	.002 601	.021 212	8.156 564	.122 601
35	52.799 620	431.663 496	.002 317	.018 940	8.175 504	.122 317
36	59.135 574	484.463 116	.002 064	.016 910	8.192 414	.122 064
37	66.231 843	543.598 690	.001 840	.015 098	8.207 513	.121 840
38	74.179 664	609.830 533	.001 640	.013 481	8.220 993	.121 640
39	83.081 224	684.010 197	.001 462	.012 036	8.233 030	.121 462
40	93.050 970	767.091 420	.001 304	.010 747	8.243 777	.121 304
41	104.217 087	860.142 391	.001 163	.009 595	8.253 372	.121 163
42	116.723 137	964.359 478	.001 037	.008 567	8.261 939	.121 037
43	130.729 914	1081.082 615	.000 925	.007 649	8.269 589	.120 925
44	146.417 503	1211.812 529	.000 825	.006 830	8.276 418	.120 825
45	163.987 604	1358.230 032	.000 736	.006 098	8.282 516	.120 736
46	183.666 116	1522.217 636	.000 657	.005 445	8.287 961	.120 657
47	205.706 050	1705.883 752	.000 586	.004 861	8.292 822	.120 586
48	230.390 776	1911.589 803	.000 523	.004 340	8.297 163	.120 523
49	258.037 669	2141.980 579	.000 467	.003 875	8.301 038	.120 467
50	289.002 190	2400.018 249	.000 417	.003 460	8.304 498	.120 417
51	323.682 453	2689.020 438	.000 372	.003 089	8.307 588	.120 372
52	362.524 347	3012.702 891	.000 332	.002 758	8.310 346	.120 332
53	406.027 269	3375.227 238	.000 296	.002 463	8.312 809	.120 296
54	454.750 541	3781.254 506	.000 264	.002 199	8.315 008	.120 264
55	509.320 606	4236.005 047	.000 236	.001 963	8.316 972	.120 236
56	570.439 078	4745.325 653	.000 211	.001 753	8.318 725	.120 211
57	638.891 768	5315.764 731	.000 188	.001 565	8.320 290	.120 188
58	715.558 780	5954.656 499	.000 168	.001 398	8.321 687	.120 168
59	801.425 833	6670.215 279	.000 150	.001 248	8.322 935	.120 150
60	897.596 933	7471.641 112	.000 134	.001 114	8.324 049	.120 134

$$S^n = (1+i)^n \quad S_{\overline{n}|} = \frac{S^n - 1}{i} \quad \frac{1}{S_{\overline{n}|}} = \frac{i}{S^n - 1} \quad V^n = \frac{1}{S^n} \quad A_{\overline{n}|} = \frac{1 - 1/S^n}{i} \quad \frac{1}{A_{\overline{n}|}} = \frac{i}{1 - 1/S^n}$$

357

12¼%
Annual
Table

Years	1 Amount of 1	2 Amount of 1 per Period	3 Sinking- Fund Factor	4 Present Worth of 1	5 Present Worth of 1 per Period	6 Partial Payment
1	1.122 500	1.000 000	1.000 000	.890 869	.890 869	1.122 500
2	1.260 006	2.122 500	.471 143	.793 647	1.684 515	.593 643
3	1.414 357	3.382 506	.295 639	.707 035	2.391 551	.418 139
4	1.587 616	4.796 863	.208 470	.629 875	3.021 426	.330 970
5	1.782 099	6.384 479	.156 630	.561 136	3.582 562	.279 130
6	2.000 406	8.166 578	.122 450	.499 899	4.082 461	.244 950
7	2.245 455	10.166 983	.098 358	.445 344	4.527 805	.220 858
8	2.520 524	12.412 439	.080 564	.396 743	4.924 547	.203 064
9	2.829 288	14.932 963	.066 966	.353 446	5.277 993	.189 466
10	3.175 876	17.762 251	.056 299	.314 874	5.592 867	.178 799
11	3.564 920	20.938 126	.047 760	.280 511	5.873 378	.170 260
12	4.001 623	24.503 047	.040 811	.249 899	6.123 277	.163 311
13	4.491 822	28.504 670	.035 082	.222 627	6.345 904	.157 582
14	5.042 070	32.996 492	.030 306	.198 331	6.544 235	.152 806
15	5.659 724	38.038 562	.026 289	.176 687	6.720 922	.148 789
16	6.353 040	43.698 286	.022 884	.157 405	6.878 327	.145 384
17	7.131 287	50.051 326	.019 979	.140 227	7.018 554	.142 479
18	8.004 870	57.182 614	.017 488	.124 924	7.143 478	.139 988
19	8.985 467	65.187 484	.015 340	.111 291	7.254 769	.137 840
20	10.086 186	74.172 951	.013 482	.099 145	7.353 914	.135 982
21	11.321 744	84.259 137	.011 868	.088 326	7.442 240	.134 368
22	12.708 658	95.580 882	.010 462	.078 687	7.520 926	.132 962
23	14.265 469	108.289 540	.009 235	.070 099	7.591 026	.131 735
24	16.012 989	122.555 008	.008 160	.062 449	7.653 475	.130 660
25	17.974 580	138.567 997	.007 217	.055 634	7.709 109	.129 717
26	20.176 466	156.542 576	.006 388	.049 563	7.758 672	.128 888
27	22.648 083	176.719 042	.005 659	.044 154	7.802 826	.128 159
28	25.422 473	199.367 125	.005 016	.039 335	7.842 161	.127 516
29	48.536 726	224.789 597	.004 449	.035 043	7.877 204	.126 949
30	32.032 475	253.326 323	.003 947	.031 218	7.908 422	.126 447
31	35.956 453	285.358 798	.003 504	.027 811	7.936 233	.126 004
32	40.361 118	321.315 250	.003 112	.024 776	7.961 010	.125 612
33	45.305 355	361.676 369	.002 765	.022 072	7.983 082	.125 265
34	50.855 261	406.981 724	.002 457	.019 664	8.002 746	.124 957
35	57.085 031	457.836 985	.002 184	.017 518	8.020 263	.124 684
36	64.077 947	514.922 016	.001 942	.015 606	8.035 869	.124 442
37	71.927 495	578.999 963	.001 727	.013 903	8.049 772	.124 227
38	80.738 614	650.927 458	.001 536	.012 386	8.062 158	.124 036
39	90.629 094	731.666 072	.001 367	.011 034	8.073 192	.123 867
40	101.731 158	822.295 165	.001 216	.009 830	8.083 022	.123 716
41	114.193 225	924.026 323	.001 082	.008 757	8.091 779	.123 582
42	128.181 895	1038.219 548	.000 963	.007 801	8.099 580	.123 463
43	143.884 177	1166.401 442	.000 837	.006 950	8.106 530	.123 357
44	161.509 988	1310.285 619	.000 763	.006 192	8.112 722	.123 263
45	181.294 962	1471.795 607	.000 679	.005 516	8.118 238	.123 179
46	203.503 595	1653.090 569	.000 605	.004 914	8.123 152	.123 105
47	228.432 785	1856.594 164	.000 539	.004 378	8.127 529	.123 039
48	256.415 801	2085.026 949	.000 480	.003 900	8.131 429	.122 980
49	287.826 737	2341.442 750	.000 427	.003 474	8.134 904	.122 927
50	323.085 512	2629.269 487	.000 380	.003 095	8.137 999	.122 880
51	362.663 487	2952.354 999	.000 339	.002 757	8.140 756	.122 839
52	407.089 765	3315.018 487	.000 302	.002 456	8.143 213	.122 802
53	456.958 261	3722.108 251	.000 269	.002 188	8.145 401	.122 769
54	512.935 648	4179.066 512	.000 239	.001 950	8.147 351	.122 739
55	575.770 265	4692.002 160	.000 213	.001 737	8.149 087	.122 713
56	646.302 122	5267.772 424	.000 190	.001 547	8.150 635	.122 690
57	725.474 132	5914.074 546	.000 169	.001 378	8.152 013	.122 669
58	814.344 713	6639.548 678	.000 151	.001 228	8.153 241	.122 651
59	914.101 940	7453.893 391	.000 134	.001 094	8.154 335	.122 634
60	1026.079 428	8367.995 332	.000 120	.000 975	8.155 310	.122 620

	$S^n = (1+i)^n$	$S_{\overline{n}\rvert} = \dfrac{S^n-1}{i}$	$\dfrac{1}{S_{\overline{n}\rvert}} = \dfrac{i}{S^n-1}$	$V^n = \dfrac{1}{S^n}$	$A_{\overline{n}\rvert} = \dfrac{1-1/S^n}{i}$	$\dfrac{1}{A_{\overline{n}\rvert}} = \dfrac{i}{1-1/S^n}$

358

12½% Annual Table

Years	1 Amount of 1	2 Amount of 1 per Period	3 Sinking-Fund Factor	4 Present Worth of 1	5 Present Worth of 1 per period	6 Partial Payment
1	1.125 000	1.000 000	1.000 000	.888 889	.888 889	1.125 000
2	1.265 625	2.125 000	.470 588	.790 123	1.679 012	.595 588
3	1.423 828	3.390 625	.294 931	.702 332	2.381 344	.419 931
4	1.601 807	4.814 453	.207 708	.624 295	3.005 639	.332 708
5	1.802 032	6.416 260	.155 854	.554 929	3.560 568	.280 854
6	2.027 287	8.218 292	.121 680	.493 270	4.053 839	.246 680
7	2.280 697	10.245 579	.097 603	.438 462	4.492 301	.222 603
8	2.565 785	12.526 276	.079 832	.389 744	4.882 045	.204 832
9	2.886 508	15.092 061	.066 260	.346 439	5.228 485	.191 260
10	3.247 321	17.978 568	.055 622	.307 946	5.536 431	.180 622
11	3.653 236	21.225 889	.047 112	.273 730	5.810 161	.172 112
12	4.109 891	24.879 125	.040 194	.243 315	6.053 476	.165 194
13	4.623 627	28.989 016	.034 496	.216 280	6.269 757	.159 496
14	5.201 580	33.612 643	.029 751	.192 249	6.462 006	.154 751
15	5.851 778	38.814 223	.025 764	.170 888	6.632 894	.150 764
16	6.583 250	44.666 001	.022 388	.151 901	6.784 795	.147 388
17	7.406 156	51.249 252	.019 512	.135 023	6.919 818	.144 512
18	8.331 926	58.655 408	.017 049	.120 020	7.039 838	.142 049
19	9.373 417	66.987 334	.014 928	.106 685	7.146 523	.139 928
20	10.545 094	76.360 751	.013 096	.094 831	7.241 353	.138 096
21	11.863 231	86.905 845	.011 507	.084 294	7.325 647	.136 507
22	13.346 134	98.769 075	.010 125	.074 928	7.400 575	.135 125
23	15.014 401	112.115 210	.008 919	.066 603	7.467 178	.133 919
24	16.891 201	127.129 611	.007 866	.059 202	7.526 381	.132 866
25	19.002 602	144.020 812	.006 943	.052 624	7.579 005	.131 943
26	21.377 927	163.023 414	.006 134	.046 777	7.625 782	.131 134
27	24.050 168	184.401 340	.005 423	.041 580	7.667 362	.130 423
28	27.056 438	208.451 508	.004 797	.036 960	7.704 322	.129 797
29	30.438 493	235.507 946	.004 246	.032 853	7.737 175	.129 246
30	34.243 305	265.946 440	.003 760	.029 203	7.766 378	.128 760
31	38.523 718	300.189 745	.003 331	.025 958	7.792 336	.128 331
32	43.339 183	338.713 463	.002 952	.023 074	7.815 410	.127 952
33	48.756 581	382.052 645	.002 617	.020 510	7.835 920	.127 617
34	54.851 153	430.809 226	.002 321	.018 231	7.854 151	.127 321
35	61.707 547	485.660 379	.002 059	.016 205	7.870 356	.127 059
36	69.420 991	547.367 927	.001 827	.014 405	7.884 761	.126 827
37	78.098 615	616.788 918	.001 621	.012 804	7.897 565	.126 621
38	87.860 942	694.887 532	.001 439	.011 382	7.908 947	.126 439
39	98.843 559	782.748 474	.001 278	.010 117	7.919 064	.126 278
40	111.199 004	881.592 033	.001 134	.008 993	7.928 057	.126 134
41	125.098 880	992.791 037	.001 007	.007 994	7.936 051	.126 007
42	140.736 240	1117.889 917	.000 895	.007 105	7.943 156	.125 895
43	158.328 270	1258.626 157	.000 795	.006 316	7.949 472	.125 795
44	178.119 303	1416.954 426	.000 706	.005 614	7.955 086	.125 706
45	200.384 216	1595.073 729	.000 627	.004 990	7.960 077	.125 627
46	225.432 243	1795.457 946	.000 557	.004 436	7.964 513	.125 557
47	253.611 274	2020.890 189	.000 495	.003 943	7.968 456	.125 495
48	285.312 683	2274.501 462	.000 440	.003 505	7.971 961	.125 440
49	320.976 768	2559.814 145	.000 391	.003 115	7.975 076	.125 391
50	361.098 864	2880.790 913	.000 347	.002 769	7.977 845	.125 347
51	406.236 222	3241.889 778	.000 308	.002 462	7.980 307	.125 308
52	457.015 750	3648.126 000	.000 274	.002 188	7.982 495	.125 274
53	514.142 719	4105.141 750	.000 244	.001 945	7.984 440	.125 244
54	578.410 559	4619.284 468	.000 216	.001 729	7.986 169	.125 216
55	650.711 878	5197.695 027	.000 192	.001 537	7.987 706	.125 192
56	732.050 863	5848.406 905	.000 171	.001 366	7.989 072	.125 171
57	823.557 221	6580.457 769	.000 152	.001 214	7.990 286	.125 152
58	926.501 874	7404.014 990	.000 135	.001 079	7.991 365	.125 135
59	1042.314 608	8330.516 863	.000 120	.000 959	7.992 325	.125 120
60	1172.603 934	9372.831 471	.000 107	.000 853	7.993 178	.125 107

$S^n=(1+i)^n$	$S_{\overline{n}|}=\dfrac{S^n-1}{i}$	$\dfrac{1}{S_{\overline{n}|}}=\dfrac{i}{S^n-1}$	$V^n=\dfrac{1}{S^n}$	$A_{\overline{n}|}=\dfrac{1-1/S^n}{i}$	$\dfrac{1}{A_{\overline{n}|}}=\dfrac{i}{1-1/S^n}$

12¾% Annual Table

Years	1 Amount of 1	2 Amount of 1 per Period	3 Sinking- Fund Factor	4 Present Worth of 1	5 Present Worth of 1 per Period	6 Partial Payment
1	1.127 500	1.000 000	1.000 000	.886 918	.886 918	1.127 500
2	1.271 256	2.127 500	.470 035	.786 623	1.673 541	.597 535
3	1.433 341	3.398 756	.294 225	.697 670	2.371 212	.421 725
4	1.616 092	4.832 098	.206 949	.618 776	2.989 988	.334 449
5	1.822 144	6.448 190	.155 082	.548 804	3.538 792	.282 582
6	2.054 468	8.270 334	.120 914	.486 744	4.025 536	.248 414
7	2.316 412	10.324 802	.096 854	.431 702	4.457 239	.224 354
8	2.661 755	12.641 214	.079 106	.382 884	4.840 123	.206 606
9	2.944 754	15.252 969	.065 561	.339 587	5.179 710	.193 061
10	3.320 210	18.197 723	.054 952	.301 186	5.480 896	.182 452
11	3.743 536	21.517 932	.046 473	.267 127	5.748 023	.173 973
12	4.220 837	25.261 469	.039 586	.236 920	5.984 943	.167 086
13	4.758 994	29.482 306	.033 919	.210 128	6.195 071	.161 419
14	5.365 766	34.241 300	.029 204	.186 367	6.381 438	.156 704
15	6.049 901	39.607 066	.025 248	.165 292	6.546 730	.152 748
16	6.821 263	45.656 966	.021 902	.146 600	6.693 330	.149 402
17	7.690 974	52.478 230	.019 056	.130 023	6.823 353	.146 556
18	8.671 574	60.169 204	.016 620	.115 319	6.938 672	.144 120
19	9.777 199	68.840 777	.014 526	.102 279	7.040 951	.142 026
20	11.023 792	78.617 977	.012 720	.090 713	7.131 664	.140 220
21	12.429 326	89.641 769	.011 156	.080 455	7.212 119	.138 656
22	14.014 065	102.071 094	.009 797	.071 357	7.283 475	.137 297
23	15.800 858	116.085 159	.008 614	.063 288	7.346 763	.136 114
24	17.815 467	131.886 016	.007 582	.056 131	7.402 894	.135 082
25	20.086 939	149.701 483	.006 680	.049 784	7.452 678	.134 180
26	22.648 024	169.788 423	.005 890	.044 154	7.496 832	.133 390
27	25.535 647	192.436 446	.005 197	.039 161	7.535 993	.132 697
28	28.791 442	217.972 093	.004 588	.034 733	7.570 725	.132 088
29	32.462 351	246.763 535	.004 052	.030 805	7.601 530	.131 552
30	36.601 300	279.225 886	.003 581	.027 321	7.628 852	.131 081
31	41.267 966	315.827 187	.003 166	.024 232	7.653 083	.130 666
32	46.529 632	357.095 153	.002 800	.021 492	7.674 575	.130 300
33	52.462 160	403.624 785	.002 478	.019 061	7.693 636	.129 978
34	59.151 085	456.086 945	.002 193	.016 906	7.710 542	.129 693
35	66.692 849	515.238 030	.001 941	.014 994	7.725 536	.129 441
36	75.196 187	581.930 879	.001 718	.013 299	7.738 835	.129 218
37	84.783 701	657.127 066	.001 522	.011 795	7.750 630	.129 022
38	95.593 623	741.910 767	.001 348	.010 461	7.761 091	.128 848
39	107.781 810	837.504 390	.001 194	.009 278	7.770 369	.128 694
40	121.523 990	945.286 200	.001 058	.008 229	7.778 597	.128 558
41	137.018 299	1066.810 190	.000 937	.007 298	7.785 896	.128 437
42	154.488 132	1203.828 490	.000 831	.006 473	7.792 369	.128 331
43	174.185 369	1358.316 622	.000 736	.005 741	7.798 110	.128 236
44	196.394 004	1532.501 991	.000 653	.005 092	7.803 202	.128 153
45	221.434 239	1728.895 995	.000 578	.004 516	7.807 718	.128 078
46	249.667 105	1950.330 235	.000 513	.004 005	7.811 723	.128 013
47	281.499 661	2199.997 339	.000 455	.003 552	7.815 275	.127 955
48	317.390 868	2481.497 000	.000 403	.003 151	7.818 426	.127 903
49	357.858 203	2798.887 868	.000 357	.002 794	7.821 220	.127 857
50	403.485 124	3156.746 071	.000 317	.002 478	7.823 699	.127 817
51	454.929 477	3560.231 195	.000 281	.002 198	7.825 897	.127 781
52	512.932 986	4015.160 672	.000 249	.001 950	7.827 846	.127 749
53	578.331 941	4528.093 658	.000 221	.001 729	7.829 576	.127 721
54	652.069 264	5106.425 599	.000 196	.001 534	7.831 109	.127 696
55	735.208 095	5758.494 863	.000 174	.001 360	7.832 469	.127 674
56	828.947 127	6493.702 959	.000 154	.001 206	7.833 676	.127 654
57	934.637 886	7322.650 086	.000 137	.001 070	7.834 746	.127 637
58	1053.804 216	8257.287 972	.000 121	.000 949	7.835 695	.127 621
59	1188.164 254	9311.092 188	.000 107	.000 842	7.836 536	.127 607
60	1339.655 196	10499.256 442	.000 095	.000 746	7.837 283	.127 595

$S^n=(1+i)^n$	$S_{\overline{n}\rceil}=\dfrac{S^n-1}{i}$	$\dfrac{1}{S_{\overline{n}\rceil}}=\dfrac{i}{S^n-1}$	$V^n=\dfrac{1}{S^n}$	$A_{\overline{n}\rceil}=\dfrac{1-1/S^n}{i}$	$\dfrac{1}{A_{\overline{n}\rceil}}=\dfrac{i}{1-1/S^n}$

13%
Annual
Table

Years	1 Amount of 1	2 Amount of 1 per Period	3 Sinking- Fund Factor	4 Present Worth of 1	5 Present Worth of 1 per Period	6 Partial Payment
1	1.130 000	1.000 000	1.000 000	.884 956	.884 956	1.130 000
2	1.276 900	2.130 000	.469 484	.783 147	1.668 102	.599 484
3	1.442 897	3.406 900	.293 522	.693 050	2.361 153	.423 522
4	1.630 474	4.849 797	.206 194	.613 319	2.974 471	.336 194
5	1.842 435	6.480 271	.154 315	.542 760	3.517 231	.284 315
6	2.081 952	8.322 706	.120 153	.480 319	3.997 550	.250 153
7	2.352 605	10.404 658	.096 111	.425 061	4.422 610	.226 111
8	2.658 444	13.757 263	.078 387	.376 160	4.798 770	.208 387
9	3.004 042	15.415 707	.064 869	.332 885	5.131 655	.194 869
10	3.394 567	18.419 749	.054 290	.294 588	5.426 243	.184 290
11	3.835 861	21.814 317	.045 841	.260 698	5.686 941	.175 841
12	4.334 523	25.650 178	.038 986	.230 706	5.917 647	.168 986
13	4.898 011	29.984 701	.033 350	.204 165	6.121 812	.163 350
14	5.534 753	34.882 712	.028 667	.180 677	6.302 488	.158 667
15	6.254 270	40.417 464	.024 742	.159 891	6.462 379	.154 742
16	7.067 326	46.671 735	.021 426	.141 496	6.603 875	.151 426
17	7.986 078	53.739 060	.018 608	.125 218	6.729 093	.148 608
18	9.024 268	61.725 138	.016 201	.110 812	6.839 905	.146 201
19	10.197 423	70.749 406	.014 134	.098 064	6.937 969	.144 134
20	11.523 088	80.946 829	.012 354	.086 782	7.024 752	.142 354
21	13.021 089	92.469 917	.010 814	.076 798	7.101 550	.140 814
22	14.713 831	105.491 006	.009 479	.067 963	7.169 513	.139 479
23	16.626 629	120.204 837	.008 319	.060 144	7.229 658	.138 319
24	18.788 091	136.831 465	.007 308	.053 225	7.282 883	.137 308
25	21.230 542	155.619 556	.006 426	.047 102	7.329 985	.136 426
26	23.990 513	176.850 098	.005 655	.041 683	7.371 668	.135 655
27	27.109 279	200.840 611	.004 979	.036 888	7.408 556	.134 979
28	30.633 486	227.949 890	.004 387	.032 644	7.441 200	.134 387
29	34.615 839	258.583 376	.003 867	.028 889	7.470 088	.133 867
30	39.115 898	293.199 215	.003 411	.025 565	7.495 653	.133 411
31	44.200 965	332.315 113	.003 009	.022 624	7.518 277	.133 009
32	49.947 090	376.516 078	.002 656	.020 021	7.538 299	.132 656
33	56.440 212	426.463 168	.002 345	.017 718	7.556 016	.132 345
34	63.777 439	482.903 380	.002 071	.015 680	7.571 696	.132 071
35	72.068 506	546.680 819	.001 829	.013 876	7.585 572	.131 829
36	81.437 412	618.749 325	.001 616	.012 279	7.597 851	.131 616
37	92.024 276	700.186 738	.001 428	.010 867	7.608 718	.131 428
38	103.987 432	792.211 014	.001 262	.009 617	7.618 334	.131 262
39	117.505 798	896.198 445	.001 116	.008 510	7.626 844	.131 116
40	132.781 552	1013.704 243	.000 986	.007 531	7.634 376	.130 986
41	150.043 153	1146.485 795	.000 872	.006 665	7.641 040	.130 872
42	169.548 763	1296.528 948	.000 771	.005 898	7.646 938	.130 771
43	191.590 103	1466.077 712	.000 682	.005 219	7.652 158	.130 682
44	216.496 816	1657.667 814	.000 603	.004 619	7.656 777	.130 603
45	244.641 402	1874.164 630	.000 534	.004 088	7.660 864	.130 534
46	276.444 784	2118.806 032	.000 472	.003 617	7.664 482	.130 472
47	312.382 606	2395.250 816	.000 417	.003 201	7.667 683	.130 417
48	352.992 345	2707.633 422	.000 369	.002 833	7.670 516	.130 369
49	398.881 350	3060.625 767	.000 327	.002 507	7.673 023	.130 327
50	450.735 925	3459.507 117	.000 289	.002 219	7.675 242	.130 289
51	509.331 595	3910.243 042	.000 256	.001 963	7.677 205	.130 256
52	575.544 703	4419.574 637	.000 226	.001 737	7.678 942	.130 226
53	650.365 514	4995.119 340	.000 200	.001 538	7.680 480	.130 200
54	734.913 031	5645.484 854	.000 177	.001 361	7.681 841	.130 177
55	830.451 725	6380.397 885	.000 157	.001 204	7.683 045	.130 157
56	938.410 449	7210.849 610	.000 139	.001 066	7.684 111	.130 139
57	1060.403 808	8149.260 060	.000 123	.000 943	7.685 054	.130 123
58	1198.256 303	9209.663 867	.000 109	.000 835	7.685 888	.130 109
59	1354.029 622	10407.920 170	.000 096	.000 739	7.686 627	.130 096
60	1530.053 473	11761.949 792	.000 085	.000 654	7.687 280	.130 085

$$S^n = (1+i)^n \qquad S_{\overline{n}|} = \frac{S^n-1}{i} \qquad \frac{1}{S_{\overline{n}|}} = \frac{i}{S^n-1} \qquad V^n = \frac{1}{S^n} \qquad A_{\overline{n}|} = \frac{1-1/S^n}{i} \qquad \frac{1}{A_{\overline{n}|}} = \frac{i}{1-1/S^n}$$

14%
Annual
Table

Years	1 Amount of 1	2 Amount of 1 per Period	3 Sinking- Fund Factor	4 Present Worth of 1	5 Present Worth of 1 per Period	6 Partial Payment
1	1.140 000	1.000 000	1.000 000	.877 193	.877 193	1.140 000
2	1.299 600	2.140 000	.467 290	.769 468	1.646 661	.607 290
3	1.481 544	3.439 600	.290 731	.674 972	2.321 632	.430 731
4	1.688 960	4.921 144	.203 205	.592 080	2.913 712	.343 205
5	1.925 415	6.610 104	.151 284	.519 369	3.433 081	.291 284
6	2.194 973	8.535 519	.117 157	.455 587	3.888 668	.257 157
7	2.502 269	10.730 491	.093 192	.399 637	4.288 305	.233 192
8	2.852 586	13.232 760	.075 570	.350 559	4.638 864	.215 570
9	3.251 949	16.085 347	.062 168	.307 508	4.946 372	.202 168
10	3.707 221	19.337 295	.051 714	.269 744	5.216 116	.191 714
11	4.226 232	23.044 516	.043 394	.236 617	5.452 733	.183 394
12	4.817 905	27.270 749	.036 669	.207 559	5.660 292	.176 669
13	5.492 411	32.088 654	.031 164	.182 069	5.842 362	.171 164
14	6.261 349	37.581 065	.026 609	.159 710	6.002 072	.166 609
15	7.137 938	43.842 414	.022 809	.140 096	6.142 168	.162 809
16	8.137 249	50.980 352	.019 615	.122 892	6.265 060	.159 615
17	9.276 464	59.117 601	.016 915	.107 800	6.372 859	.156 915
18	10.575 169	68.394 066	.014 621	.094 561	6.467 420	.154 621
19	12.055 693	78.969 235	.012 663	.082 948	6.550 369	.152 663
20	13.743 490	91.024 928	.010 986	.072 762	6.623 131	.150 986
21	15.667 578	104.768 418	.009 545	.063 826	6.686 957	.149 545
22	17.861 039	120.435 996	.008 303	.055 988	6.742 944	.148 303
23	20.361 585	138.297 035	.007 231	.049 112	6.792 056	.147 231
24	23.212 207	158.658 620	.006 303	.043 081	6.835 137	.146 303
25	26.461 916	181.870 827	.005 498	.037 790	6.872 927	.145 498
26	30.166 584	208.332 743	.004 800	.033 149	6.906 077	.144 800
27	34.389 906	238.499 327	.004 193	.029 078	6.935 155	.144 193
28	39.204 493	272.889 233	.003 664	.025 507	6.960 662	.143 664
29	44.693 122	312.093 725	.003 204	.022 375	6.983 037	.143 204
30	50.950 159	356.786 847	.002 803	.019 627	7.002 664	.142 803
31	58.083 181	407.737 006	.002 453	.017 217	7.019 881	.142 453
32	66.214 826	465.820 186	.002 147	.015 102	7.034 983	.142 147
33	75.484 902	532.035 012	.001 880	.013 248	7.048 231	.141 880
34	86.052 788	607.519 914	.001 646	.011 621	7.059 852	.141 646
35	98.100 178	693.572 702	.001 442	.010 194	7.070 045	.141 442
36	111.834 203	791.672 881	.001 263	.008 942	7.078 987	.141 263
37	127.490 992	903.507 084	.001 107	.007 844	7.086 831	.141 107
38	145.339 731	1030.998 076	.000 970	.006 880	7.093 711	.140 970
39	165.687 293	1176.337 806	.000 850	.006 035	7.099 747	.140 850
40	188.883 514	1342.025 099	.000 745	.005 294	7.105 041	.140 745
41	215.327 206	1530.908 613	.000 653	.004 644	7.109 685	.140 653
42	245.473 015	1746.235 819	.000 573	.004 074	7.113 759	.140 573
43	279.839 237	1991.708 833	.000 502	.003 573	7.117 332	.140 502
44	319.016 730	2271.548 070	.000 440	.003 135	7.120 467	.140 440
45	363.679 072	2590.564 800	.000 386	.002 750	7.123 217	.140 386
46	414.594 142	2954.243 872	.000 338	.002 412	7.125 629	.140 338
47	472.637 322	3368.838 014	.000 297	.002 116	7.127 744	.140 297
48	538.806 547	3841.475 336	.000 260	.001 856	7.129 600	.140 260
49	614.239 464	4380.281 883	.000 228	.001 628	7.131 228	.140 228
50	700.232 988	4994.521 346	.000 200	.001 428	7.132 656	.140 200
51	798.265 607	5694.754 335	.000 176	.001 253	7.133 909	.140 176
52	910.022 792	6493.019 941	.000 154	.001 099	7.135 008	.140 154
53	1037.425 983	7403.042 733	.000 135	.000 964	7.135 972	.140 135
54	1182.665 620	8440.468 716	.000 118	.000 846	7.136 818	.140 118
55	1348.238 807	9623.134 336	.000 104	.000 742	7.137 559	.140 104
56	1536.992 240	10971.373 143	.000 091	.000 651	7.138 210	.140 091
57	1752.171 154	12508.365 383	.000 080	.000 571	7.138 781	.140 080
58	1997.475 115	14260.536 537	.000 070	.000 501	7.139 281	.140 070
59	2277.121 631	16258.011 652	.000 062	.000 439	7.139 720	.140 062
60	2595.918 660	18535.133 283	.000 054	.000 385	7.140 106	.140 054

$$S^n = (1+i)^n \qquad S_{\overline{n}|} = \frac{S^n - 1}{i} \qquad \frac{1}{S_{\overline{n}|}} = \frac{i}{S^n - 1} \qquad V^n = \frac{1}{S^n} \qquad A_{\overline{n}|} = \frac{1 - 1/S^n}{i} \qquad \frac{1}{A_{\overline{n}|}} = \frac{i}{1 - 1/S^n}$$

15% Annual Table

Years	1 Amount of 1	2 Amount of 1 per Period	3 Sinking-Fund Factor	4 Present Worth of 1	5 Present Worth of 1 per Period	6 Partial Payment
1	1.150 000	1.000 000	1.000 000	.869 565	.869 565	1.150 000
2	1.322 500	2.150 000	.465 116	.756 144	1.625 709	.615 116
3	1.520 875	3.472 500	.287 977	.657 516	2.283 225	.437 977
4	1.749 006	4.993 375	.200 265	.571 753	2.854 978	.350 265
5	2.011 357	6.742 381	.148 316	.497 177	3.352 155	.298 316
6	2.313 061	8.753 738	.114 237	.432 328	3.784 483	.264 237
7	2.660 020	11.066 799	.090 360	.375 937	4.160 420	.240 360
8	3.059 023	13.726 819	.072 850	.326 902	4.487 322	.222 850
9	3.517 876	16.785 842	.059 574	.284 262	4.771 584	.209 574
10	4.045 558	20.303 718	.049 252	.247 185	5.018 769	.199 252
11	4.652 391	24.349 276	.041 069	.214 943	5.233 712	.191 069
12	5.350 250	29.001 667	.034 481	.186 907	5.420 619	.184 481
13	6.152 788	34.351 917	.029 110	.162 528	5.583 147	.179 110
14	7.075 706	40.504 705	.024 688	.141 329	5.724 476	.174 688
15	8.137 062	47.580 411	.021 017	.122 894	5.847 370	.171 017
16	9.357 621	55.717 472	.017 948	.106 865	5.954 235	.167 948
17	10.761 264	65.075 093	.015 367	.092 926	6.047 161	.165 367
18	12.375 454	75.836 357	.013 186	.080 805	6.127 966	.163 186
19	14.231 772	88.211 811	.011 336	.070 265	6.198 231	.161 336
20	16.366 537	102.443 583	.009 761	.061 100	6.259 331	.159 761
21	18.821 518	118.810 120	.008 417	.053 131	6.312 462	.158 417
22	21.644 746	137.631 638	.007 266	.046 201	6.358 663	.157 266
23	24.891 458	159.276 384	.006 278	.040 174	6.398 837	.156 278
24	28.625 176	184.167 841	.005 430	.034 934	6.433 771	.155 430
25	32.918 953	212.793 017	.004 699	.030 378	6.464 149	.154 699
26	37.856 796	245.711 970	.004 070	.026 415	6.490 564	.154 070
27	43.535 315	283.568 766	.003 526	.022 970	6.513 534	.153 526
28	50.065 612	327.104 080	.003 057	.019 974	6.533 508	.153 057
29	57.575 454	377.169 693	.002 651	.017 369	6.550 877	.152 651
30	66.211 772	434.745 146	.002 300	.015 103	6.565 980	.152 300
31	76.143 538	500.956 918	.001 996	.013 133	6.579 113	.151 996
32	87.565 068	577.100 456	.001 733	.011 420	6.590 533	.151 733
33	100.699 829	664.665 524	.001 505	.009 931	6.600 463	.151 505
34	115.804 803	765.365 353	.001 307	.008 635	6.609 099	.151 307
35	133.175 523	881.170 156	.001 135	.007 509	6.616 607	.151 135
36	153.151 852	1014.345 680	.000 986	.006 529	6.623 137	.150 986
37	176.124 630	1167.497 532	.000 857	.005 678	6.628 815	.150 857
38	202.543 324	1343.622 161	.000 744	.004 937	6.633 752	.150 744
39	232.924 823	1546.165 485	.000 647	.004 293	6.638 045	.150 647
40	267.863 546	1779.090 308	.000 562	.003 733	6.641 778	.150 562
41	308.043 078	2046.953 854	.000 489	.003 246	6.645 025	.150 489
42	354.249 540	2354.996 933	.000 425	.002 823	6.647 848	.150 425
43	407.386 971	2709.246 473	.000 369	.002 455	6.650 302	.150 369
44	468.495 017	3116.633 443	.000 321	.002 134	6.652 437	.150 321
45	538.769 269	3585.128 460	.000 279	.001 856	6.654 293	.150 279
46	619.584 659	4123.897 729	.000 242	.001 614	6.655 907	.150 242
47	712.522 358	4743.482 388	.000 211	.001 403	6.657 310	.150 211
48	819.400 712	5456.004 746	.000 183	.001 220	6.658 531	.150 183
49	942.310 819	6275.405 458	.000 159	.001 061	6.659 592	.150 159
50	1083.657 442	7217.716 277	.000 139	.000 923	6.660 515	.150 139
51	1246.206 058	8301.373 719	.000 120	.000 802	6.661 317	.150 120
52	1433.136 966	9547.579 777	.000 105	.000 698	6.662 015	.150 105
53	1648.107 511	10980.716 743	.000 091	.000 607	6.662 622	.150 091
54	1895.323 638	12628.824 255	.000 079	.000 528	6.663 149	.150 079
55	2179.622 184	14524.147 893	.000 069	.000 459	6.663 608	.150 069
56	2506.565 512	16703.770 077	.000 060	.000 399	6.664 007	.150 060
57	2882.550 338	19210.335 588	.000 052	.000 347	6.664 354	.150 052
58	3314.932 889	22092.885 926	.000 045	.000 302	6.664 656	.150 045
59	3812.172 822	25407.818 815	.000 039	.000 262	6.664 918	.150 039
60	4383.998 746	29219.991 638	.000 034	.000 228	6.665 146	.150 034

	$S^n = (1+i)^n$	$S_{\overline{n}|} = \dfrac{S^n - 1}{i}$	$\dfrac{1}{S_{\overline{n}|}} = \dfrac{i}{S^n - 1}$	$V^n = \dfrac{1}{S^n}$	$A_{\overline{n}|} = \dfrac{1 - 1/S^n}{i}$	$\dfrac{1}{A_{\overline{n}|}} = \dfrac{i}{1 - 1/S^n}$

363

16%
Annual
Table

Years	1 Amount of 1	2 Amount of 1 per Period	3 Sinking- Fund Factor	4 Present Worth of 1	5 Present Worth of 1. per Period	6 Partial Payment
1	1.160 000	1.000 000	1.000 000	.862 069	.862 069	1.160 000
2	1.345 600	2.160 000	.462 963	.743 163	1.605 232	.622 963
3	1.560 896	3.505 600	.285 258	.640 658	2.245 890	.445 258
4	1.810 639	5.066 496	.197 375	.552 291	2.798 181	.357 375
5	2.100 342	6.877 135	.145 409	.476 113	3.274 294	.305 409
6	2.436 396	8.977 477	.111 390	.410 442	3.684 736	.271 390
7	2.826 220	11.413 873	.087 613	.353 830	4.038 565	.247 613
8	3.278 415	14.240 093	.070 224	.305 025	4.343 591	.230 224
9	3.802 961	17.518 508	.057 082	.262 953	4.606 544	.217 082
10	4.411 435	21.321 469	.046 901	.226 684	4.833 227	.206 901
11	5.117 265	25.732 904	.038 861	.195 417	5.028 644	.198 861
12	5.936 027	30.850 169	.032 415	.168 463	5.197 107	.192 415
13	6.885 791	36.786 196	.027 184	.145 227	5.342 334	.187 184
14	7.987 518	43.671 987	.022 898	.125 195	5.467 529	.182 898
15	9.265 521	51.659 505	.019 358	.107 927	5.575 456	.179 358
16	10.748 004	60.925 026	.016 414	.093 041	5.668 497	.176 414
17	12.467 685	71.673 030	.013 952	.080 207	5.748 704	.173 952
18	14.462 514	84.140 715	.011 885	.069 144	5.817 848	.171 885
19	16.776 517	98.603 230	.010 142	.059 607	5.877 455	.170 142
20	19.460 759	115.379 747	.008 667	.051 385	5.928 841	.168 667
21	22.574 481	134.840 506	.007 416	.044 298	5.973 139	.167 416
22	26.186 398	157.414 987	.006 353	.038 188	6.011 326	.166 353
23	30.376 222	183.601 385	.005 447	.032 920	6.044 247	.165 447
24	35.236 417	213.977 607	.004 673	.028 380	6.072 627	.164 673
25	40.874 244	249.214 024	.004 013	.024 465	6.097 092	.164 013
26	47.414 123	290.088 267	.003 447	.021 091	6.118 183	.163 447
27	55.000 382	337.502 390	.002 963	.018 182	6.136 364	.162 963
28	63.800 444	392.502 773	.002 548	.015 674	6.152 038	.162 548
29	74.008 515	456.303 216	.002 192	.013 512	6.165 550	.162 192
30	85.849 877	530.311 731	.001 886	.011 648	6.177 198	.161 886
31	99.585 857	616.161 608	.001 623	.010 042	6.187 240	.161 623
32	115.519 594	715.747 465	.001 397	.008 657	6.195 897	.161 397
33	134.002 729	831.267 059	.001 203	.007 463	6.203 359	.161 203
34	155.443 166	965.269 789	.001 036	.006 433	6.209 792	.161 036
35	180.314 073	1120.712 955	.000 892	.005 546	6.215 338	.160 892
36	209.164 324	1301.027 028	.000 769	.004 781	6.220 119	.160 769
37	242.630 616	1510.191 352	.000 662	.004 121	6.224 241	.160 662
38	281.451 515	1752.821 968	.000 571	.003 553	6.227 794	.160 571
39	326.483 757	2034.273 483	.000 492	.003 063	6.230 857	.160 492
40	378.721 158	2360.757 241	.000 424	.002 640	6.233 497	.160 424
41	439.316 544	2739.478 399	.000 365	.002 276	6.235 773	.160 365
42	509.607 191	3178.794 943	.000 315	.001 962	6.237 736	.160 315
43	591.144 341	3688.402 134	.000 271	.001 692	6.239 427	.160 271
44	685.727 436	4279.546 475	.000 234	.001 458	6.240 886	.160 234
45	795.443 826	4965.273 911	.000 201	.001 257	6.242 143	.160 201
46	922.714 838	5760.717 737	.000 174	.001 084	6.243 227	.160 174
47	1070.349 212	6683.432 575	.000 150	.000 934	6.244 161	.160 150
48	1241.605 086	7753.781 787	.000 129	.000 805	6.244 966	.160 129
49	1440.261 900	8995.386 873	.000 111	.000 694	6.245 661	.160 111
50	1670.703 804	10435.648 773	.000 096	.000 599	6.246 259	.160 096
51	1938.016 412	12106.352 576	.000 083	.000 516	6.246 775	.160 083
52	2248.099 038	14044.368 988	.000 071	.000 445	6.247 220	.160 071
53	2607.794 884	16292.468 026	.000 061	.000 383	6.247 603	.160 061
54	3025.042 066	18900.262 911	.000 053	.000 331	6.247 934	.160 053
55	3509.048 796	21925.304 976	.000 046	.000 285	6.248 219	.160 046
56	4070.496 604	25434.353 773	.000 039	.000 246	6.248 465	.160 039
57	4721.776 060	29504.850 376	.000 034	.000 212	6.248 676	.160 034
58	5477.260 230	34226.626 436	.000 029	.000 183	6.248 859	.160 029
59	6353.621 867	39703.886 666	.000 025	.000 157	6.249 016	.160 025
60	7370.201 365	46057.508 533	.000 022	.000 136	6.249 152	.160 022

| $S^n=(1+i)^n$ | $S_{\overline{n}|}=\dfrac{S^n-1}{i}$ | $\dfrac{1}{S_{\overline{n}|}}=\dfrac{i}{S^n-1}$ | $V^n=\dfrac{1}{S^n}$ | $A_{\overline{n}|}=\dfrac{1-1/S^n}{i}$ | $\dfrac{1}{A_{\overline{n}|}}=\dfrac{i}{1-1/S^n}$ |

17%
Annual
Table

	1	2	3	4	5	6
Years	Amount of 1	Amount of 1 per Period	Sinking-Fund Factor	Present Worth of 1	Present Worth of 1 per Period	Partial Payment
1	1.170 000	1.000 000	1.000 000	.854 701	.854 701	1.170 000
2	1.368 900	2.170 000	.460 829	.730 514	1.585 214	.630 829
3	1.601 613	3.538 900	.282 574	.624 371	2.209 585	.452 574
4	1.873 887	5.140 513	.194 533	.533 650	2.743 235	.364 533
5	2.192 448	7.014 400	.142 564	.456 111	3.199 346	.312 564
6	2.565 164	9.206 848	.108 615	.389 839	3.589 185	.278 615
7	3.001 242	11.772 012	.084 947	.333 195	3.922 380	.254 947
8	3.511 453	14.773 255	.067 690	.284 782	4.207 163	.237 690
9	4.108 400	18.284 708	.054 691	.243 404	4.450 566	.224 691
10	4.806 828	22.393 108	.044 657	.208 037	4.658 604	.214 657
11	5.623 989	27.199 937	.036 765	.177 810	4.836 413	.206 765
12	6.580 067	32.823 926	.030 466	.151 974	4.988 387	.200 466
13	7.698 679	39.403 993	.025 378	.129 892	5.118 280	.195 378
14	9.007 454	47.102 672	.021 230	.111 019	5.229 299	.191 230
15	10.538 721	56.110 126	.017 822	.094 888	5.324 187	.187 822
16	12.330 304	66.648 848	.015 004	.081 101	5.405 288	.185 004
17	14.426 456	78.979 152	.012 662	.069 317	5.474 605	.182 662
18	16.878 953	93.405 608	.010 706	.059 245	5.533 851	.180 706
19	19.748 375	110.284 561	.009 067	.050 637	5.584 488	.179 067
20	23.105 599	130.032 936	.007 690	.043 280	5.627 767	.177 690
21	27.033 551	153.138 535	.006 530	.036 991	5.664 758	.176 530
22	31.629 255	180.172 086	.005 550	.031 616	5.696 375	.175 550
23	37.006 228	211.801 341	.004 721	.027 022	5.723 397	.174 721
24	43.297 287	248.807 569	.004 019	.023 096	5.746 493	.174 019
25	50.657 826	292.104 856	.003 423	.019 740	5.766 234	.173 423
26	59.269 656	342.762 681	.002 917	.016 872	5.783 106	.172 917
27	69.345 497	402.032 337	.002 487	.014 421	5.797 526	.172 487
28	81.134 232	471.377 835	.002 121	.012 325	5.809 851	.172 121
29	94.927 051	552.512 066	.001 810	.010 534	5.820 386	.171 810
30	111.064 650	647.439 118	.001 545	.009 004	5.829 390	.171 545
31	129.945 641	758.503 768	.001 318	.007 696	5.837 085	.171 318
32	152.036 399	888.449 408	.001 126	.006 577	5.843 663	.171 126
33	177.882 587	1040.485 808	.000 961	.005 622	5.849 284	.170 961
34	208.122 627	1218.368 395	.000 821	.004 805	5.854 089	.170 821
35	243.503 474	1426.491 022	.000 701	.004 107	5.858 196	.170 701
36	284.899 064	1669.994 496	.000 599	.003 510	5.861 706	.170 599
37	333.331 905	1954.893 560	.000 512	.003 000	5.864 706	.170 512
38	389.998 329	2288.225 465	.000 437	.002 564	5.867 270	.170 437
39	456.298 045	2678.223 794	.000 373	.002 192	5.869 461	.170 373
40	533.868 713	3134.521 839	.000 319	.001 873	5.871 335	.170 319
41	624.626 394	3668.390 552	.000 273	.001 601	5.872 936	.170 273
42	730.812 881	4293.016 946	.000 233	.001 368	5.874 304	.170 233
43	855.051 071	5023.829 827	.000 199	.001 170	5.875 473	.170 199
44	1000.409 753	5878.880 897	.000 170	.001 000	5.876 473	.170 170
45	1170.479 411	6879.290 650	.000 145	.000 854	5.877 327	.170 145
46	1369.460 910	8049.770 061	.000 124	.000 730	5.878 058	.170 124
47	1602.269 265	9419.230 971	.000 106	.000 624	5.878 682	.170 106
48	1874.655 040	11021.500 236	.000 091	.000 533	5.879 215	.170 091
49	2193.346 397	12896.155 276	.000 078	.000 456	5.879 671	.170 078
50	2566.215 284	15089.501 673	.000 066	.000 390	5.880 061	.170 066
51	3002.471 883	17655.716 957	.000 057	.000 333	5.880 394	.170 057
52	3512.892 103	20658.188 840	.000 048	.000 285	5.880 678	.170 048
53	4110.083 760	24171.080 943	.000 041	.000 243	5.880 922	.170 041
54	4808.798 000	28281.164 703	.000 035	.000 208	5.881 130	.170 035
55	5626.293 659	33089.962 703	.000 030	.000 178	5.881 307	.170 030
56	6582.763 582	38716.256 362	.000 026	.000 152	5.881 459	.170 026
57	7701.833 390	45299.019 944	.000 022	.000 130	5.881 589	.170 022
58	9011.145 067	53000.853 334	.000 019	.000 111	5.881 700	.170 019
59	10543.039 728	62011.998 401	.000 016	.000 095	5.881 795	.170 016
60	12335.356 482	72555.038 129	.000 014	.000 081	5.881 876	.170 014

$S^n = (1+i)^n$	$S_{\overline{n}} = \dfrac{S^n-1}{i}$	$\dfrac{1}{S_{\overline{n}}} = \dfrac{i}{S^n-1}$	$V^n = \dfrac{1}{S^n}$	$A_{\overline{n}} = \dfrac{1-1/S^n}{i}$	$\dfrac{1}{A_{\overline{n}}} = \dfrac{i}{1-1/S^n}$

18% Annual Table

Years	1 Amount of 1	2 Amount of 1 per Period	3 Sinking- Fund Factor	4 Present Worth of 1	5 Present Worth of 1 per Period	6 Partial Payment
1	1.180 000	1.000 000	1.000 000	.847 458	.847 458	1.180 000
2	1.392 400	2.180 000	.458 716	.718 184	1.565 642	.638 716
3	1.643 032	3.572 400	.279 924	.608 631	2.174 273	.459 924
4	1.938 778	5.215 432	.191 739	.515 789	2.690 062	.371 739
5	2.287 758	7.154 210	.139 778	.437 109	3.127 171	.319 778
6	2.699 554	9.441 968	.105 910	.370 432	3.497 603	.285 910
7	3.185 474	12.141 522	.082 362	.313 925	3.811 528	.262 362
8	3.758 859	15.326 996	.065 244	.266 038	4.077 566	.245 244
9	4.435 454	19.085 855	.052 395	.225 456	4.303 022	.232 395
10	5.233 836	23.521 309	.042 515	.191 064	4.494 086	.222 515
11	6.175 926	28.755 144	.034 776	.161 919	4.656 005	.214 776
12	7.287 593	34.931 070	.028 628	.137 220	4.793 225	.208 628
13	8.599 359	42.218 663	.023 686	.116 288	4.909 513	.203 686
14	10.147 244	50.818 022	.019 678	.098 549	5.008 062	.199 678
15	11.973 748	60.965 266	.016 403	.083 516	5.091 578	.196 403
16	14.129 023	72.939 014	.013 710	.070 776	5.162 354	.193 710
17	16.672 247	87.068 036	.011 485	.059 980	5.222 334	.191 485
18	19.673 251	103.740 283	.009 639	.050 830	5.273 164	.189 639
19	23.214 436	123.413 534	.008 103	.043 077	5.316 241	.188 103
20	27.393 035	146.627 970	.006 820	.036 506	5.352 746	.186 820
21	32.323 781	174.021 005	.005 746	.030 937	5.383 683	.185 746
22	38.142 061	206.344 785	.004 846	.026 218	5.409 901	.184 846
23	45.007 632	244.486 847	.004 090	.022 218	5.432 120	.184 090
24	53.109 006	289.494 479	.003 454	.018 829	5.450 949	.183 454
25	62.668 627	342.603 486	.002 919	.015 957	5.466 906	.182 919
26	73.948 980	405.272 113	.002 467	.013 523	5.480 429	.182 467
27	87.259 797	479.221 093	.002 087	.011 460	5.491 889	.182 087
28	102.966 560	566.480 890	.001 765	.009 712	5.501 601	.181 765
29	121.500 541	669.447 450	.001 494	.008 230	5.509 831	.181 494
30	143.370 638	790.947 991	.001 264	.006 975	5.516 806	.181 264
31	169.177 353	934.318 630	.001 070	.005 911	5.522 717	.181 070
32	199.629 277	1103.495 983	.000 906	.005 009	5.527 726	.180 906
33	235.562 547	1303.125 260	.000 767	.004 245	5.531 971	.180 767
34	277.963 805	1538.687 807	.000 650	.003 598	5.535 569	.180 650
35	327.997 290	1816.651 612	.000 550	.003 049	5.538 618	.180 550
36	387.036 802	2144.648 902	.000 466	.002 584	5.541 201	.180 466
37	456.703 427	2531.685 705	.000 395	.002 190	5.543 391	.180 395
38	538.910 044	2988.389 132	.000 335	.001 856	5.545 247	.180 335
39	635.913 852	3527.299 175	.000 284	.001 573	5.546 819	.180 284
40	750.378 345	4163.213 027	.000 240	.001 333	5.548 152	.180 240
41	885.446 447	4913.591 372	.000 204	.001 129	5.549 281	.180 204
42	1044.826 807	5799.037 819	.000 172	.000 957	5.550 238	.180 172
43	1232.895 633	6843.864 626	.000 146	.000 811	5.551 049	.180 146
44	1454.816 847	8076.760 259	.000 124	.000 687	5.551 737	.180 124
45	1716.683 879	9531.577 105	.000 105	.000 583	5.552 319	.180 105
46	2025.686 977	11248.260 984	.000 089	.000 494	5.552 813	.180 089
47	2390.310 633	13273.947 961	.000 075	.000 418	5.553 231	.180 075
48	2820.566 547	15664.258 594	.000 064	.000 355	5.553 586	.180 064
49	3328.268 525	18484.825 141	.000 054	.000 300	5.553 886	.180 054
50	3927.356 860	21813.093 666	.000 046	.000 255	5.554 141	.180 046
51	4634.281 095	25740.450 526	.000 039	.000 216	5.554 357	.180 039
52	5468.451 692	30374.731 621	.000 033	.000 183	5.554 540	.180 033
53	6452.772 996	35843.183 313	.000 028	.000 155	5.554 695	.180 028
54	7614.272 136	42295.956 309	.000 024	.000 131	5.554 826	.180 024
55	8984.841 120	49910.228 445	.000 020	.000 111	5.554 937	.180 020

$S^n = (1+i)^n$	$S_{\overline{n}|} = \dfrac{S^n - 1}{i}$	$\dfrac{1}{S_{\overline{n}|}} = \dfrac{i}{S^n - 1}$	$V^n = \dfrac{1}{S^n}$	$A_{\overline{n}|} = \dfrac{1 - 1/S^n}{i}$	$\dfrac{1}{A_{\overline{n}|}} = \dfrac{i}{1 - 1/S^n}$

Years	1 Amount of 1	2 Amount of 1 per Period	3 Sinking- Fund Factor	4 Present Worth of 1	5 Present Worth of 1 per Period	6 Partial Payment
1	1.190 000	1.000 000	1.000 000	.840 336	.840 336	1.190 000
2	1.416 100	2.190 000	.456 621	.706 165	1.546 501	.646 621
3	1.685 159	3.606 100	.277 308	.593 416	2.139 917	.467 308
4	2.005 339	5.291 259	.188 991	.498 669	2.638 586	.378 991
5	2.386 354	7.296 598	.137 050	.419 049	3.057 635	.327 050
6	2.839 761	9.682 952	.103 274	.352 142	3.409 777	.293 274
7	3.379 315	12.522 713	.079 855	.295 918	3.705 695	.269 855
8	4.021 385	15.902 028	.062 885	.248 671	3.954 366	.252 885
9	4.785 449	19.923 413	.050 192	.208 967	4.163 332	.240 192
10	5.694 684	24.708 862	.040 471	.175 602	4.338 935	.230 471
11	6.776 674	30.403 546	.032 891	.147 565	4.486 500	.222 891
12	8.064 242	37.180 220	.026 896	.124 004	4.610 504	.216 896
13	9.596 448	45.244 461	.022 102	.104 205	4.714 709	.212 102
14	11.419 773	54.840 909	.018 235	.087 567	4.802 277	.208 235
15	13.589 530	66.260 682	.015 092	.073 586	4.875 863	.205 092
16	16.171 540	79.850 211	.012 523	.061 837	4.937 700	.202 523
17	19.244 133	96.021 751	.010 414	.051 964	4.989 664	.200 414
18	22.900 518	115.265 884	.008 676	.043 667	5.033 331	.198 676
19	27.251 616	138.166 402	.007 238	.036 695	5.070 026	.197 238
20	32.429 423	165.418 018	.006 045	.030 836	5.100 862	.196 045
21	38.591 014	197.847 442	.005 054	.025 913	5.126 775	.195 054
22	45.923 307	236.438 456	.004 229	.021 775	5.148 550	.194 229
23	54.648 735	282.361 762	.003 542	.018 299	5.166 849	.193 542
24	65.031 994	337.010 497	.002 967	.015 377	5.182 226	.192 967
25	77.388 073	402.042 491	.002 487	.012 922	5.195 148	.192 487
26	92.091 807	479.430 565	.002 086	.010 859	5.206 007	.192 086
27	109.589 251	571.522 372	.001 750	.009 125	5.215 132	.191 750
28	130.411 208	681.111 623	.001 468	.007 668	5.222 800	.191 468
29	155.189 338	811.522 831	.001 232	.006 444	5.229 243	.191 232
30	184.675 312	966.712 169	.001 034	.005 415	5.234 658	.191 035
31	219.763 621	1151.387 481	.000 869	.004 550	5.239 209	.190 869
32	261.518 710	1371.151 103	.000 729	.003 824	5.243 033	.190 729
33	311.207 264	1632.669 812	.000 612	.003 213	5.246 246	.190 612
34	370.336 645	1943.877 077	.000 514	.002 700	5.248 946	.190 514
35	440.700 607	2314.213 721	.000 432	.002 269	5.251 215	.190 432
36	524.433 722	2754.914 328	.000 363	.001 907	5.253 122	.190 363
37	624.076 130	3279.348 051	.000 305	.001 602	5.254 724	.190 305
38	742.650 594	3903.424 180	.000 256	.001 347	5.256 071	.190 256
39	883.754 207	4646.074 775	.000 215	.001 132	5.257 202	.190 215
40	1051.667 507	5529.828 982	.000 181	.000 951	5.258 153	.190 181
41	1251.484 333	6581.496 488	.000 152	.000 799	5.258 952	.190 152
42	1489.266 356	7832.980 821	.000 128	.000 671	5.259 624	.190 128
43	1772.226 964	9322.247 177	.000 107	.000 564	5.260 188	.190 107
44	2108.950 087	11094.474 141	.000 090	.000 474	5.260 662	.190 090
45	2509.650 603	13203.424 228	.000 076	.000 398	5.261 061	.190 076
46	2986.484 218	15713.074 831	.000 064	.000 335	5.261 396	.190 064
47	3553.916 219	18699.559 049	.000 053	.000 281	5.261 677	.190 053
48	4229.160 301	22253.475 268	.000 045	.000 236	5.261 913	.190 045
49	5032.700 758	26482.635 569	.000 038	.000 199	5.262 112	.190 038
50	5988.913 902	31515.336 327	.000 032	.000 167	5.262 279	.190 032
51	7126.807 544	37504.250 230	.000 027	.000 140	5.262 419	.190 027
52	8480.900 977	44631.057 773	.000 022	.000 118	5.262 537	.190 022
53	10092.272 163	53111.958 750	.000 019	.000 099	5.262 636	.190 019
54	12009.803 873	63204.230 913	.000 016	.000 083	5.262 720	.190 016
55	14291.666 609	75214.034 786	.000 013	.000 070	5.262 790	.190 013

$$S^n=(1+i)^n \qquad S_{\overline{n}|}=\frac{S^n-1}{i} \qquad \frac{1}{S_{\overline{n}|}}=\frac{i}{S^n-1} \qquad V^n=\frac{1}{S^n} \qquad A_{\overline{n}|}=\frac{1-1/S^n}{i} \qquad \frac{1}{A_{\overline{n}|}}=\frac{i}{1-1/S^n}$$

20% Annual Table

Years	1 Amount of 1	2 Amount of 1 per Period	3 Sinking- Fund Factor	4 Present Worth of 1	5 Present Worth of 1 per Period	6 Partial Payment
1	1.200 000	1.000 000	1.000 000	.833 333	.833 333	1.200 000
2	1.440 000	2.200 000	.454 545	.694 444	1.527 778	.654 545
3	1.728 000	3.640 000	.274 725	.578 704	2.106 481	.474 725
4	2.073 600	5.368 000	.186 289	.482 253	2.588 735	.386 289
5	2.488 320	7.441 600	.134 380	.401 878	2.990 612	.334 380
6	2.985 984	9.929 920	.100 706	.334 898	3.325 510	.300 706
7	3.583 181	12.915 904	.077 424	.279 082	3.604 592	.277 424
8	4.299 817	16.499 085	.060 609	.232 568	3.837 160	.260 609
9	5.159 780	20.798 902	.048 079	.193 807	4.030 967	.248 079
10	6.191 736	25.958 682	.038 523	.161 506	4.192 472	.238 523
11	7.430 084	32.150 419	.031 104	.134 588	4.327 060	.231 104
12	8.916 100	39.580 502	.025 265	.112 157	4.439 217	.225 265
13	10.699 321	48.496 603	.020 620	.093 464	4.532 681	.220 620
14	12.839 185	59.195 923	.016 893	.077 887	4.610 567	.216 893
15	15.407 022	72.035 108	.013 882	.064 905	4.675 473	.213 882
16	18.488 426	87.442 129	.011 436	.054 088	4.729 561	.211 436
17	22.186 111	105.930 555	.009 440	.045 073	4.774 634	.209 440
18	26.623 333	128.116 666	.007 805	.037 561	4.812 195	.207 805
19	31.948 000	154.740 000	.006 462	.031 301	4.843 496	.206 462
20	38.337 600	186.688 000	.005 357	.026 084	4.869 580	.205 357
21	46.005 120	225.025 600	.004 444	.021 737	4.891 316	.204 444
22	55.206 144	271.030 719	.003 690	.018 114	4.909 430	.203 690
23	66.247 373	326.236 863	.003 065	.015 095	4.924 525	.203 065
24	79.496 847	392.484 236	.002 548	.012 579	4.937 104	.202 548
25	95.396 217	471.981 083	.002 119	.010 483	4.947 587	.202 119
26	114.475 460	567.377 300	.001 762	.008 735	4.956 323	.201 762
27	137.370 552	681.852 760	.001 467	.007 280	4.963 602	.201 467
28	164.844 662	819.223 312	.001 221	.006 066	4.969 668	.201 221
29	197.813 595	984.067 974	.001 016	.005 055	4.974 724	.201 016
30	237.376 314	1181.881 569	.000 846	.004 213	4.978 936	.200 846
31	284.851 577	1419.257 883	.000 705	.003 511	4.982 447	.200 705
32	341.821 892	1704.109 459	.000 587	.002 926	4.985 372	.200 587
33	410.186 270	2045.931 351	.000 489	.002 438	4.987 810	.200 489
34	492.223 524	2456.117 621	.000 407	.002 032	4.989 842	.200 407
35	590.668 229	2948.341 146	.000 339	.001 693	4.991 535	.200 339
36	708.801 875	3539.009 375	.000 283	.001 411	4.992 946	.200 283
37	850.562 250	4247.811 250	.000 235	.001 176	4.994 122	.200 235
38	1020.674 700	5098.373 500	.000 196	.000 980	4.995 101	.200 196
39	1224.809 640	6119.048 200	.000 163	.000 816	4.995 918	.200 163
40	1469.771 568	7343.857 840	.000 136	.000 680	4.996 598	.200 136
41	1763.725 882	8813.629 408	.000 113	.000 567	4.997 165	.200 113
42	2116.471 058	10577.355 289	.000 095	.000 472	4.997 638	.200 095
43	2539.765 269	12693.826 347	.000 079	.000 394	4.998 031	.200 079
44	3047.718 323	15233.591 617	.000 066	.000 328	4.998 359	.200 066
45	3657.261 988	18281.309 940	.000 055	.000 273	4.998 633	.200 055
46	4388.714 386	21938.571 928	.000 046	.000 228	4.998 861	.200 046
47	5266.457 263	26327.286 314	.000 038	.000 190	4.999 051	.200 038
48	6319.748 715	31593.743 576	.000 032	.000 158	4.999 209	.200 032
49	7583.698 458	37913.492 292	.000 026	.000 132	4.999 341	.200 026
50	9100.438 150	45497.190 750	.000 022	.000 110	4.999 451	.200 022
	$S^n = (1+i)^n$	$S_{\overline{n}|} = \dfrac{S^n - 1}{i}$	$\dfrac{1}{S_{\overline{n}|}} = \dfrac{i}{S^n - 1}$	$V^n = \dfrac{1}{S^n}$	$A_{\overline{n}|} = \dfrac{1 - 1/S^n}{i}$	$\dfrac{1}{A_{\overline{n}|}} = \dfrac{i}{1 - 1/S^n}$

368

21% Annual Table

	1	2	3	4	5	6
Years	Amount of 1	Amount of 1 per Period	Sinking-Fund Factor	Present Worth of 1	Present Worth of 1 per Period	Partial Payment
1	1.210 000	1.000 000	1.000 000	.826 446	.826 446	1.210 000
2	1.464 100	2.210 000	.452 489	.683 013	1.509 460	.662 489
3	1.771 561	3.674 100	.272 175	.564 474	2.073 934	.482 175
4	2.143 589	5.445 661	.183 632	.466 507	2.540 441	.393 632
5	2.593 742	7.589 250	.131 765	.385 543	2.925 984	.341 765
6	3.138 428	10.182 992	.098 203	.318 631	3.244 615	.308 203
7	3.797 498	13.321 421	.075 067	.263 331	3.507 946	.285 067
8	4.594 973	17.118 919	.058 415	.217 629	3.725 576	.268 415
9	5.559 917	21.713 892	.046 053	.179 859	3.905 434	.256 053
10	6.727 500	27.273 809	.036 665	.148 644	4.054 078	.246 665
11	8.140 275	34.001 309	.029 411	.122 846	4.176 924	.239 411
12	9.849 733	42.141 584	.023 730	.101 526	4.278 450	.233 730
13	11.918 177	51.991 317	.019 234	.083 905	4.362 355	.229 234
14	14.420 994	63.909 493	.015 647	.069 343	4.431 698	.225 647
15	17.449 402	78.330 487	.012 766	.057 309	4.489 007	.222 766
16	21.113 777	95.779 889	.010 441	.047 362	4.536 369	.220 441
17	25.547 670	116.893 666	.008 555	.039 143	4.575 512	.218 555
18	30.912 681	142.441 336	.007 020	.032 349	4.607 861	.217 020
19	37.404 343	173.354 016	.005 769	.026 735	4.634 596	.215 769
20	45.259 256	210.758 360	.004 745	.022 095	4.656 691	.214 745
21	54.763 699	256.017 615	.003 906	.018 260	4.674 951	.213 906
22	66.264 076	310.781 315	.003 218	.015 091	4.690 042	.213 218
23	80.179 532	377.045 391	.002 652	.012 472	4.702 514	.212 652
24	97.017 234	457.224 923	.002 187	.010 307	4.712 822	.212 187
25	117.390 853	554.242 157	.001 804	.008 519	4.721 340	.211 804
26	142.042 932	671.633 009	.001 489	.007 040	4.728 380	.211 489
27	171.871 948	813.675 941	.001 229	.005 818	4.734 199	.211 229
28	207.965 057	985.547 889	.001 015	.004 809	4.739 007	.211 015
29	251.637 719	1193.512 946	.000 838	.003 974	4.742 981	.210 838
30	304.481 640	1445.150 664	.000 692	.003 284	4.746 265	.210 692
31	368.422 784	1749.632 304	.000 572	.002 714	4.748 980	.210 572
32	445.791 568	2118.055 088	.000 472	.002 243	4.751 223	.210 472
33	539.407 798	2563.846 656	.000 390	.001 854	4.753 077	.210 390
34	652.683 435	3103.254 454	.000 322	.001 532	4.754 609	.210 322
35	789.746 957	3755.937 890	.000 266	.001 266	4.755 875	.210 266
36	955.593 818	4545.684 846	.000 220	.001 046	4.756 922	.210 220
37	1156.268 519	5501.278 664	.000 182	.000 865	4.757 786	.210 182
38	1399.084 909	6657.547 183	.000 150	.000 715	4.758 501	.210 150
39	1692.892 739	8056.632 092	.000 124	.000 591	4.759 092	.210 124
40	2048.400 215	9749.524 831	.000 103	.000 488	4.759 580	.210 103
41	2478.564 260	11797.925 046	.000 085	.000 403	4.759 984	.210 085
42	2999.062 754	14276.489 306	.000 070	.000 333	4.760 317	.210 070
43	3628.865 933	17275.552 060	.000 058	.000 276	4.760 593	.210 058
44	4390.927 778	20904.417 992	.000 048	.000 228	4.760 820	.210 048
45	5313.022 612	25295.345 771	.000 040	.000 188	4.761 008	.210 040
46	6428.757 360	30608.368 383	.000 033	.000 156	4.761 164	.210 033
47	7778.796 406	37037.125 743	.000 027	.000 129	4.761 293	.210 027
48	9412.343 651	44815.922 149	.000 022	.000 106	4.761 399	.210 022
49	11388.935 818	54228.265 800	.000 018	.000 088	4.761 487	.210 018
50	13780.612 340	65617.201 618	.000 015	.000 073	4.761 559	.210 015

$$S^n = (1+i)^n \qquad S_{\overline{n}|} = \frac{S^n-1}{i} \qquad \frac{1}{S_{\overline{n}|}} = \frac{i}{S^n-1} \qquad V^n = \frac{1}{S^n} \qquad A_{\overline{n}|} = \frac{1-1/S^n}{i} \qquad \frac{1}{A_{\overline{n}|}} = \frac{i}{1-1/S^n}$$

369

	1	2	3	4	5	6
Years	Amount of 1	Amount of 1 per Period	Sinking-Fund Factor	Present Worth of 1	Present Worth of 1 per Period	Partial Payment
1	1.220 000	1.000 000	1.000 000	.819 672	.819 672	1.220 000
2	1.488 400	2.220 000	.450 450	.671 862	1.491 535	.670 450
3	1.815 848	3.708 400	.269 658	.550 707	2.042 241	.489 658
4	2.215 335	5.524 248	.181 020	.451 399	2.493 641	.401 020
5	2.702 708	7.739 583	.129 206	.369 999	2.863 640	.349 206
6	3.297 304	10.442 291	.095 764	.303 278	3.166 918	.315 764
7	4.022 711	13.739 595	.072 782	.248 589	3.415 506	.292 782
8	4.907 707	17.762 306	.056 299	.203 761	3.619 268	.276 299
9	5.987 403	22.670 013	.044 111	.167 017	3.786 285	.264 111
10	7.304 631	28.657 416	.034 895	.136 899	3.923 184	.254 895
11	8.911 650	35.962 047	.027 807	.112 213	4.035 397	.247 807
12	10.872 213	44.873 697	.022 285	.091 978	4.127 375	.242 285
13	13.264 100	55.745 911	.017 939	.075 391	4.202 766	.237 939
14	16.182 202	69.010 011	.014 491	.061 796	4.264 562	.234 491
15	19.742 287	85.192 213	.011 738	.050 653	4.315 215	.231 738
16	24.085 590	104.934 500	.009 530	.041 519	4.356 734	.229 530
17	29.384 420	129.020 090	.007 751	.034 032	4.390 765	.227 751
18	35.848 992	158.404 510	.006 313	.027 895	4.418 660	.226 313
19	43.735 771	194.253 503	.005 148	.022 865	4.441 525	.225 148
20	53.357 640	237.989 273	.004 202	.018 741	4.460 266	.224 202
21	65.096 321	291.346 913	.003 432	.015 362	4.475 628	.223 432
22	79.417 512	356.443 234	.002 805	.012 592	4.488 220	.222 805
23	96.889 364	435.860 746	.002 294	.010 321	4.498 541	.222 294
24	118.205 024	532.750 110	.001 877	.008 460	4.507 001	.221 877
25	144.210 130	650.955 134	.001 536	.006 934	4.513 935	.221 536
26	175.936 358	795.165 264	.001 258	.005 684	4.519 619	.221 258
27	214.642 357	971.101 622	.001 030	.004 659	4.524 278	.221 030
28	261.863 675	1185.743 978	.000 843	.003 819	4.528 096	.220 843
29	319.473 684	1447.607 654	.000 691	.003 130	4.531 227	.220 691
30	389.757 894	1767.081 337	.000 566	.002 566	4.533 792	.220 566
31	475.504 631	2156.839 232	.000 464	.002 103	4.535 895	.220 464
32	580.115 650	2632.343 863	.000 380	.001 724	4.537 619	.220 380
33	707.741 093	3212.459 512	.000 311	.001 413	4.539 032	.220 311
34	863.444 133	3920.200 605	.000 255	.001 158	4.540 190	.220 255
35	1053.401 842	4783.644 738	.000 209	.000 949	4.541 140	.220 209
36	1285.150 248	5837.046 581	.000 171	.000 778	4.541 918	.220 171
37	1567.883 302	7122.196 829	.000 140	.000 638	4.542 555	.220 140
38	1912.817 629	8690.080 131	.000 115	.000 523	4.543 078	.220 115
39	2333.637 507	10602.897 760	.000 094	.000 429	4.543 507	.220 094
40	2847.037 759	12936.535 267	.000 077	.000 351	4.543 858	.220 077
41	3473.386 066	15783.573 025	.000 063	.000 288	4.544 146	.220 063
42	4237.531 000	19256.959 091	.000 052	.000 236	4.544 382	.220 052
43	5169.787 820	23494.490 091	.000 043	.000 193	4.544 575	.220 043
44	6307.141 140	28664.277 911	.000 035	.000 159	4.544 734	.220 035
45	7694.712 191	34971.419 051	.000 029	.000 130	4.544 864	.220 029
46	9387.548 873	42666.131 243	.000 023	.000 107	4.544 970	.220 023
47	11452.809 626	52053.680 116	.000 019	.000 087	4.545 058	.220 019
48	13972.427 743	63506.489 742	.000 016	.000 072	4.545 129	.220 016
49	17046.361 847	77478.917 485	.000 013	.000 059	4.545 188	.220 013
50	20796.561 453	94525.279 331	.000 011	.000 048	4.545 236	.220 011

$$S^n=(1+i)^n \quad\Big|\quad S_{\overline{n}|}=\frac{S^n-1}{i} \quad\Big|\quad \frac{1}{S_{\overline{n}|}}=\frac{i}{S^n-1} \quad\Big|\quad V^n=\frac{1}{S^n} \quad\Big|\quad A_{\overline{n}|}=\frac{1-1/S^n}{i} \quad\Big|\quad \frac{1}{A_{\overline{n}|}}=\frac{i}{1-1/S^n}$$

23%
Annual
Table

Years	1 Amount of 1	2 Amount of 1 per Period	3 Sinking- Fund Factor	4 Present Worth of 1	5 Present Worth of 1 per Period	6 Partial Payment
1	1.230 000	1.000 000	1.000 000	.813 008	.813 008	1.230 000
2	1.512 900	2.230 000	.448 430	.660 982	1.473 990	.678 430
3	1.860 867	3.742 900	.267 173	.537 384	2.011 374	.497 173
4	2.288 866	5.603 767	.178 451	.436 897	2.448 272	.408 451
5	2.815 306	7.892 633	.126 700	.355 201	2.803 473	.356 700
6	3.462 826	10.707 939	.093 389	.288 781	3.092 254	.323 389
7	4.259 276	14.170 765	.070 568	.234 782	3.327 036	.300 568
8	5.238 909	18.430 041	.054 259	.190 879	3.517 916	.284 259
9	6.443 859	23.668 950	.042 249	.155 187	3.673 102	.272 249
10	7.925 946	30.112 809	.033 208	.126 168	3.799 270	.263 208
11	9.748 914	38.038 755	.026 289	.102 576	3.901 846	.256 289
12	11.991 164	47.787 669	.020 926	.083 395	3.985 240	.250 926
13	14.749 132	59.778 833	.016 728	.067 801	4.053 041	.246 728
14	18.141 432	74.527 964	.013 418	.055 122	4.108 163	.243 418
15	22.313 961	92.669 396	.010 791	.044 815	4.152 978	.240 791
16	27.446 172	114.983 357	.008 697	.036 435	4.189 413	.238 697
17	33.758 792	142.429 529	.007 021	.029 622	4.219 035	.237 021
18	41.523 314	176.188 321	.005 676	.024 083	4.243 118	.235 676
19	51.073 676	217.711 635	.004 593	.019 580	4.262 698	.234 593
20	62.820 622	268.785 311	.003 720	.015 918	4.278 616	.233 720
21	77.269 364	331.605 932	.003 016	.012 942	4.291 558	.233 016
22	95.041 318	408.875 297	.002 446	.010 522	4.302 079	.232 446
23	116.900 822	503.916 615	.001 984	.008 554	4.310 634	.231 984
24	143.788 010	620.817 437	.001 611	.006 955	4.317 588	.231 611
25	176.859 253	764.605 447	.001 308	.005 654	4.323 243	.231 308
26	217.536 881	941.464 700	.001 062	.004 597	4.327 839	.231 062
27	267.570 364	1159.001 581	.000 863	.003 737	4.331 577	.230 863
28	329.111 547	1426.571 945	.000 701	.003 038	4.334 615	.230 701
29	404.807 203	1755.683 492	.000 570	.002 470	4.337 086	.230 570
30	497.912 860	2160.490 695	.000 463	.002 008	4.339 094	.230 463
31	612.432 818	2658.403 555	.000 376	.001 633	4.340 727	.230 376
32	753.292 366	3270.836 373	.000 306	.001 328	4.342 054	.230 306
33	926.549 610	4024.128 738	.000 249	.001 079	4.343 134	.230 249
34	1139.656 020	4950.678 348	.000 202	.000 877	4.344 011	.230 202
35	1401.776 905	6090.334 368	.000 164	.000 713	4.344 724	.230 164
36	1724.185 593	7492.111 273	.000 133	.000 580	4.345 304	.230 133
37	2120.748 279	9216.296 866	.000 109	.000 472	4.345 776	.230 109
38	2608.520 383	11337.045 145	.000 088	.000 383	4.346 159	.230 088
39	3208.480 071	13945.565 528	.000 072	.000 312	4.346 471	.230 072
40	3946.430 488	17154.045 599	.000 058	.000 253	4.346 724	.230 058
41	4854.109 500	21100.476 087	.000 047	.000 206	4.346 930	.230 047
42	5970.554 685	25954.585 587	.000 039	.000 167	4.347 098	.230 039
43	7343.782 263	31925.140 272	.000 031	.000 136	4.347 234	.230 031
44	9032.852 183	39268.922 535	.000 025	.000 111	4.347 345	.230 025
45	11110.408 185	48301.774 718	.000 021	.000 090	4.347 435	.230 021

$$S^n = (1+i)^n \quad\bigg|\quad S_{\overline{n}|} = \frac{S^n - 1}{i} \quad\bigg|\quad \frac{1}{S_{\overline{n}|}} = \frac{i}{S^n - 1} \quad\bigg|\quad V^n = \frac{1}{S^n} \quad\bigg|\quad A_{\overline{n}|} = \frac{1 - 1/S^n}{i} \quad\bigg|\quad \frac{1}{A_{\overline{n}|}} = \frac{i}{1 - 1/S^n}$$

24% Annual Table

Years	1 Amount of 1	2 Amount of 1 per Period	3 Sinking- Fund Factor	4 Present Worth of 1	5 Present Worth of 1 per Period	6 Partial Payment
1	1.240 000	1.000 000	1.000 000	.806 452	.806 452	1.240 000
2	1.537 600	2.240 000	.446 429	.650 364	1.456 816	.686 429
3	1.906 624	3.777 600	.264 718	.524 487	1.981 303	.504 718
4	2.364 214	5.684 224	.175 926	.422 974	2.404 277	.415 926
5	2.931 625	8.048 438	.124 248	.341 108	2.745 384	.364 248
6	3.635 215	10.980 063	.091 074	.275 087	3.020 471	.331 074
7	4.507 667	14.615 278	.068 422	.221 844	3.242 316	.308 422
8	5.589 507	19.122 945	.052 293	.178 907	3.421 222	.292 293
9	6.930 988	24.712 451	.040 465	.144 280	3.565 502	.280 465
10	8.594 426	31.643 440	.031 602	.116 354	3.681 856	.271 602
11	10.657 088	40.237 865	.024 852	.093 834	3.775 691	.264 852
12	13.214 789	50.894 953	.019 648	.075 673	3.851 363	.259 648
13	16.386 338	64.109 741	.015 598	.061 026	3.912 390	.255 598
14	20.319 059	80.496 079	.012 423	.049 215	3.961 605	.252 423
15	25.195 633	100.815 138	.009 919	.039 689	4.001 294	.249 919
16	31.242 585	126.010 772	.007 936	.032 008	4.033 302	.247 936
17	38.740 806	157.253 357	.006 359	.025 813	4.059 114	.246 359
18	48.038 599	195.994 162	.005 102	.020 817	4.079 931	.245 102
19	59.567 863	244.032 761	.004 098	.016 788	4.096 718	.244 098
20	73.864 150	303.600 624	.003 294	.013 538	4.110 257	.243 294
21	91.591 546	377.464 774	.002 649	.010 918	4.121 175	.242 649
22	113.573 517	469.056 320	.002 132	.008 805	4.129 980	.242 132
23	140.831 161	582.629 836	.001 716	.007 101	4.137 080	.241 716
24	174.630 639	723.460 997	.001 382	.005 726	4.142 807	.241 382
25	216.541 993	898.091 636	.001 113	.004 618	4.147 425	.241 113
26	268.512 071	1114.633 629	.000 897	.003 724	4.151 149	.240 897
27	332.954 968	1383.145 700	.000 723	.003 003	4.154 152	.240 723
28	412.864 160	1716.100 668	.000 583	.002 422	4.156 575	.240 583
29	511.951 559	2128.964 828	.000 470	.001 953	4.158 528	.240 470
30	634.819 933	2640.916 387	.000 379	.001 575	4.160 103	.240 379
31	787.176 717	3275.736 320	.000 305	.001 270	4.161 373	.240 305
32	976.099 129	4062.913 037	.000 246	.001 024	4.162 398	.240 246
33	1210.362 920	5039.012 166	.000 198	.000 826	4.163 224	.240 198
34	1500.850 021	6249.375 086	.000 160	.000 666	4.163 890	.240 160
35	1861.054 026	7750.225 106	.000 129	.000 537	4.164 428	.240 129
36	2307.706 992	9611.279 132	.000 104	.000 433	4.164 861	.240 104
37	2861.556 670	11918.986 124	.000 084	.000 349	4.165 211	.240 084
38	3548.330 270	14780.542 793	.000 068	.000 282	4.165 492	.240 068
39	4399.929 535	18328.873 064	.000 055	.000 227	4.165 720	.240 055
40	5455.912 624	22728.802 599	.000 044	.000 183	4.165 903	.240 044
41	6765.331 653	28184.715 222	.000 035	.000 148	4.166 051	.240 035
42	8389.011 250	34950.046 876	.000 029	.000 119	4.166 170	.240 029
43	10402.373 950	43339.058 126	.000 023	.000 096	4.166 266	.240 023
44	12898.943 698	53741.432 076	.000 019	.000 078	4.166 344	.240 019
45	15994.690 186	66640.375 775	.000 015	.000 063	4.166 406	.240 015

$$S^n = (1+i)^n \quad\Bigg| \quad S_{\overline{n}|} = \frac{S^n - 1}{i} \quad\Bigg| \quad \frac{1}{S_{\overline{n}|}} = \frac{i}{S^n - 1} \quad\Bigg| \quad V^n = \frac{1}{S^n} \quad\Bigg| \quad A_{\overline{n}|} = \frac{1 - 1/S^n}{i} \quad\Bigg| \quad \frac{1}{A_{\overline{n}|}} = \frac{i}{1 - 1/S^n}$$

25% Annual Table

	1	2	3	4	5	6
Years	Amount of 1	Amount of 1 per Period	Sinking-Fund Factor	Present Worth of 1	Present Worth of 1 per Period	Partial Payment
1	1.250 000	1.000 000	1.000 000	.800 000	.800 000	1.250 000
2	1.562 500	2.250 000	.444 444	.640 000	1.440 000	.694 444
3	1.953 125	3.812 500	.262 295	.512 000	1.952 000	.512 295
4	2.441 406	5.765 625	.173 442	.409 600	2.361 600	.423 442
5	3.051 758	8.207 031	.121 847	.327 680	2.689 280	.371 847
6	3.814 697	11.258 789	.088 819	.262 144	2.951 424	.338 819
7	4.768 372	15.073 486	.066 342	.209 715	3.161 139	.316 342
8	5.960 464	19.841 858	.050 399	.167 772	3.328 911	.300 399
9	7.450 581	25.802 322	.038 756	.134 218	3.463 129	.288 756
10	9.313 226	33.252 903	.030 073	.107 374	3.570 503	.280 073
11	11.641 532	42.566 129	.023 493	.085 899	3.656 403	.273 493
12	14.551 915	54.207 661	.018 448	.068 719	3.725 122	.268 448
13	18.189 894	68.759 576	.014 543	.054 976	3.780 098	.264 543
14	22.737 368	86.949 470	.011 501	.043 980	3.824 078	.261 501
15	28.421 709	109.686 838	.009 117	.035 184	3.859 263	.259 117
16	35.527 137	138.108 547	.007 241	.028 147	3.887 410	.257 241
17	44.408 921	173.635 684	.005 759	.022 518	3.909 928	.255 759
18	55.511 151	218.044 605	.044 586	.018 014	3.927 942	.254 586
19	69.388 939	273.555 756	.003 656	.014 412	3.942 354	.253 656
20	86.736 174	342.944 695	.002 916	.011 529	3.953 883	.252 916
21	108.420 217	429.680 869	.002 327	.009 223	3.963 107	.252 327
22	135.525 272	538.101 086	.001 858	.007 379	3.970 485	.251 858
23	169.406 589	673.626 358	.001 485	.005 903	3.976 388	.251 485
24	211.758 237	843.032 947	.001 186	.004 722	3.981 111	.251 186
25	264.697 796	1054.791 184	.000 948	.003 778	3.984 888	.250 948
26	330.872 245	1319.488 980	.000 758	.003 022	3.987 911	.250 758
27	413.590 306	1650.361 225	.000 606	.002 418	3.990 329	.250 606
28	516.987 883	2063.951 531	.000 485	.001 934	3.992 263	.250 485
29	646.234 854	2580.939 414	.000 387	.001 547	3.993 810	.250 387
30	807.793 567	3227.174 268	.000 310	.001 238	3.995 048	.250 310
31	1009.741 959	4034.967 835	.000 248	.000 990	3.996 039	.250 248
32	1262.177 448	5044.709 793	.000 198	.000 792	3.996 831	.250 198
33	1577.721 810	6306.887 242	.000 159	.000 634	3.997 465	.250 159
34	1972.152 263	7884.609 052	.000 127	.000 507	3.997 972	.250 127
35	2465.190 329	9856.761 315	.000 101	.000 406	3.998 377	.250 101
36	3081.487 911	12321.951 644	.000 081	.000 325	3.998 702	.250 081
37	3851.859 889	15403.439 555	.000 065	.000 260	3.998 962	.250 065
38	4814.824 861	19255.299 444	.000 052	.000 208	3.999 169	.250 052
39	6018.531 076	24070.124 305	.000 042	.000 166	3.999 335	.250 042
40	7523.163 845	30088.655 381	.000 033	.000 133	3.999 468	.250 033
41	9403.954 807	37611.819 226	.000 027	.000 106	3.999 575	.250 027
42	11754.943 508	47015.774 033	.000 021	.000 085	3.999 660	.250 021
43	14693.679 385	58770.717 541	.000 017	.000 068	3.999 728	.250 017
44	18367.099 232	37464.396 926	.000 014	.000 054	3.999 782	.250 014
45	22958.874 039	91831.496 158	.000 011	.000 044	3.999 826	.250 011

$$S^n = (1+i)^n \quad\bigg|\quad S_{\overline{n}|} = \frac{S^n - 1}{i} \quad\bigg|\quad \frac{1}{S_{\overline{n}|}} = \frac{i}{S^n - 1} \quad\bigg|\quad V^n = \frac{1}{S^n} \quad\bigg|\quad A_{\overline{n}|} = \frac{1 - 1/S^n}{i} \quad\bigg|\quad \frac{1}{A_{\overline{n}|}} = \frac{i}{1 - 1/S^n}$$

26%
Annual
Table

Years	1 Amount of 1	2 Amount of 1 per Period	3 Sinking- Fund Factor	4 Present Worth of 1	5 Present Worth of 1 per Period	6 Partial Payment
1	1.260 000	1.000 000	1.000 000	.793 651	.793 651	1.260 000
2	1.587 600	2.260 000	.442 478	.629 882	1.423 532	.702 478
3	2.000 376	3.847 600	.259 902	.499 906	1.923 438	.519 902
4	2.520 474	5.847 976	.170 999	.396 751	2.320 189	.430 999
5	3.175 797	8.368 450	.119 496	.314 882	2.635 071	.379 496
6	4.001 504	11.544 247	.086 623	.249 906	2.884 977	.346 623
7	5.041 895	15.545 751	.064 326	.198 338	3.083 315	.324 326
8	6.352 788	20.587 646	.048 573	.157 411	3.240 726	.308 573
9	8.004 513	26.940 434	.037 119	.124 930	3.365 656	.297 119
10	10.085 686	34.944 947	.028 616	.099 150	3.464 806	.288 616
11	12.707 965	45.030 633	.022 207	.078 691	3.543 497	.282 207
12	16.012 035	57.738 598	.017 319	.062 453	3.605 950	.277 319
13	20.175 165	73.750 633	.013 559	.049 566	3.655 516	.273 559
14	25.420 707	93.925 798	.010 647	.039 338	3.694 854	.270 647
15	32.030 091	119.346 505	.008 379	.031 221	3.726 074	.268 379
16	40.357 915	151.376 596	.006 606	.024 778	3.750 853	.266 606
17	50.850 973	191.734 511	.005 216	.019 665	3.770 518	.265 216
18	64.072 226	242.585 484	.004 122	.015 607	3.786 125	.264 122
19	80.731 005	306.657 710	.003 261	.012 387	3.798 512	.263 261
20	101.721 066	387.388 715	.002 581	.009 831	3.808 343	.262 581
21	128.168 543	489.109 781	.002 045	.007 802	3.816 145	.262 045
22	161.492 364	617.278 324	.001 620	.006 192	3.822 338	.261 620
23	203.480 379	778.770 688	.001 284	.004 914	3.827 252	.261 284
24	256.385 277	982.251 067	.001 018	.003 900	3.831 152	.261 018
25	323.045 450	1238.636 345	.000 807	.003 096	3.834 248	.260 807
26	407.037 266	1561.681 794	.000 640	.002 457	3.836 705	.260 640
27	512.866 956	1968.719 061	.000 508	.001 950	3.838 655	.260 508
28	646.212 364	2481.586 016	.000 403	.001 547	3.840 202	.260 403
29	814.227 579	3127.798 380	.000 320	.001 228	3.841 430	.260 320
30	1025.926 749	3942.025 959	.000 254	.000 975	3.842 405	.260 254
31	1292.667 704	4967.952 709	.000 201	.000 774	3.843 178	.260 201
32	1628.761 307	6260.620 413	.000 160	.000 614	3.843 792	.260 160
33	2052.239 247	7889.381 721	.000 127	.000 487	3.844 280	.260 127
34	2585.821 452	9941.620 968	.000 101	.000 387	3.844 666	.260 101
35	3258.135 029	12527.442 420	.000 080	.000 307	3.844 973	.260 080
36	4105.250 137	15785.577 449	.000 063	.000 244	3.845 217	.260 063
37	5172.615 172	19890.827 586	.000 050	.000 193	3.845 410	.260 050
38	6517.495 117	25063.442 758	.000 040	.000 153	3.845 564	.260 040
39	8212.043 848	31580.937 875	.000 032	.000 122	3.845 685	.260 032
40	10347.175 248	39792.981 723	.000 025	.000 097	3.845 782	.260 025

$$S^n = (1+i)^n \qquad S_{\overline{n}|} = \frac{S^n-1}{i} \qquad \frac{1}{S_{\overline{n}|}} = \frac{i}{S^n-1} \qquad V^n = \frac{1}{S^n} \qquad A_{\overline{n}|} = \frac{1-1/S^n}{i} \qquad \frac{1}{A_{\overline{n}|}} = \frac{i}{1-1/S^n}$$

27% Annual Table

Years	1 Amount of 1	2 Amount of 1 per Period	3 Sinking-Fund Factor	4 Present Worth of 1	5 Present Worth of 1 per Period	6 Partial Payment
1	1.270 000	1.000 000	1.000 000	.787 402	.787 402	1.270 000
2	1.612 900	2.270 000	.440 529	.620 001	1.407 403	.710 529
3	2.048 383	3.882 900	.257 539	.488 190	1.895 593	.527 539
4	2.601 446	5.931 283	.168 598	.384 402	2.279 994	.438 598
5	3.303 837	8.532 729	.117 196	.302 678	2.582 673	.387 196
6	4.195 873	11.836 566	.084 484	.238 329	2.821 002	.354 484
7	5.328 759	16.032 439	.062 374	.187 661	3.008 663	.332 374
8	6.767 523	21.361 198	.046 814	.147 765	3.156 428	.316 814
9	8.594 755	28.128 721	.035 551	.116 350	3.272 778	.305 551
10	10.915 339	36.723 476	.027 231	.091 614	3.364 392	.297 231
11	13.862 480	47.638 815	.020 991	.072 137	3.436 529	.290 991
12	17.605 350	61.501 295	.016 260	.056 801	3.493 330	.286 260
13	22.358 794	79.106 644	.012 641	.044 725	3.538 055	.282 641
14	28.395 668	101.465 438	.009 856	.035 217	3.573 272	.279 856
15	36.062 499	129.861 106	.007 701	.027 730	3.601 001	.277 701
16	45.799 373	165.923 605	.006 027	.021 834	3.622 836	.276 027
17	58.165 204	211.722 978	.004 723	.017 192	3.640 028	.274 723
18	73.869 809	269.888 182	.003 705	.013 537	3.653 565	.273 705
19	93.814 658	343.757 991	.002 909	.010 659	3.664 225	.272 909
20	119.144 615	437.572 649	.002 285	.008 393	3.672 618	.272 285
21	151.313 661	556.717 264	.001 796	.006 609	3.679 227	.271 796
22	192.168 350	708.030 926	.001 412	.005 204	3.684 430	.271 412
23	244.053 804	900.199 276	.001 111	.004 097	3.688 528	.271 111
24	309.948 332	1144.253 080	.000 874	.003 226	3.691 754	.270 874
25	393.634 381	1454.201 412	.000 688	.002 540	3.694 295	.270 688
26	499.915 664	1847.835 793	.000 541	.002 000	3.696 295	.270 541
27	634.892 893	2347.751 457	.000 426	.001 575	3.697 870	.270 426
28	806.313 974	2982.644 350	.000 335	.001 240	3.699 110	.270 335
29	1024.018 748	3788.958 324	.000 264	.000 977	3.700 087	.270 264
30	1300.503 809	4812.977 072	.000 208	.000 769	3.700 856	.270 208
31	1651.639 838	6113.480 882	.000 164	.000 605	3.701 461	.270 164
32	2097.582 594	7765.120 720	.000 129	.000 477	3.701 938	.270 129
33	2663.929 895	9862.703 314	.000 101	.000 375	3.702 313	.270 101
34	3383.190 966	12526.633 209	.000 080	.000 296	3.702 609	.270 080
35	4296.652 527	15909.824 175	.000 063	.000 233	3.702 842	.270 063
36	5456.748 710	20206.476 702	.000 049	.000 183	3.703 025	.270 049
37	6930.070 861	25663.225 412	.000 039	.000 144	3.703 169	.270 039
38	8801.189 994	32593.296 273	.000 031	.000 114	3.703 283	.270 031
39	11177.511 292	41394.486 267	.000 024	.000 089	3.703 372	.270 024
40	14195.439 341	52571.997 559	.000 019	.000 070	3.703 443	.270 019

$$S^n = (1+i)^n \qquad S_{\overline{n|}} = \frac{S^n - 1}{i} \qquad \frac{1}{S_{\overline{n|}}} = \frac{i}{S^n - 1} \qquad V^n = \frac{1}{S^n} \qquad A_{\overline{n|}} = \frac{1 - 1/S^n}{i} \qquad \frac{1}{A_{\overline{n|}}} = \frac{i}{1 - 1/S^n}$$

28% Annual Table

Years	1 Amount of 1	2 Amount of 1 per Period	3 Sinking- Fund Factor	4 Present Worth of 1	5 Present Worth of 1 per Period	6 Partial Payment
1	1.280 000	1.000 000	1.000 000	.781 250	.781 250	1.280 000
2	1.638 400	2.280 000	.438 596	.610 352	1.391 602	.718 596
3	2.097 152	3.918 400	.255 206	.476 837	1.868 439	.535 206
4	2.684 355	6.015 552	.166 236	.372 529	2.240 968	.446 236
5	3.435 974	8.699 907	.114 944	.291 038	2.532 006	.394 944
6	4.398 047	12.135 880	.082 400	.227 374	2.759 380	.362 400
7	5.629 500	16.533 927	.066 482	.177 636	2.937 015	.340 482
8	7.205 759	22.163 426	.045 119	.138 778	3.075 793	.325 119
9	9.223 372	29.369 186	.034 049	.108 420	3.184 214	.314 049
10	11.805 916	38.592 558	.025 912	.084 703	3.268 917	.305 912
11	15.111 573	50.398 474	.019 842	.066 174	3.335 091	.299 842
12	19.342 813	65.510 047	.015 265	.051 699	3.386 790	.295 265
13	24.758 801	84.852 860	.011 785	.040 390	3.427 180	.291 785
14	31.691 265	109.611 661	.009 123	.031 554	3.458 734	.289 123
15	40.564 819	141.302 926	.007 077	.024 652	3.483 386	.287 077
16	51.922 969	181.867 745	.005 499	.019 259	3.502 645	.285 499
17	66.461 400	233.790 714	.004 277	.015 046	3.517 692	.284 277
18	85.070 592	300.252 113	.003 331	.011 755	3.529 447	.283 331
19	108.890 357	385.322 705	.002 595	.009 184	3.538 630	.282 595
20	139.379 657	494.213 062	.002 023	.007 175	3.545 805	.282 023
21	178.405 962	633.592 720	.001 578	.005 605	3.551 410	.281 578
22	228.359 631	811.998 682	.001 232	.004 379	3.555 789	.281 232
23	292.300 327	1040.358 312	.000 961	.003 421	3.559 210	.280 961
24	374.144 419	1332.658 640	.000 750	.002 673	3.561 883	.280 750
25	478.904 857	1706.803 059	.000 586	.002 088	3.563 971	.280 586
26	612.998 216	2185.707 916	.000 458	.001 631	3.565 602	.280 458
27	784.637 717	2798.706 132	.000 357	.001 274	3.566 877	.280 357
28	1004.336 278	3583.343 849	.000 279	.000 996	3.567 873	.280 279
29	1285.550 435	4587.680 126	.000 218	.000 778	3.568 650	.280 218
30	1645.504 557	5873.230 562	.000 170	.000 608	3.569 258	.280 170
31	2106.245 833	7518.735 119	.000 133	.000 475	3.569 733	.280 133
32	2695.994 667	9624.980 953	.000 104	.000 371	3.570 104	.280 104
33	3450.873 173	12320.975 619	.000 081	.000 290	3.570 394	.280 081
34	4417.117 662	15771.848 793	.000 063	.000 226	3.570 620	.280 063
35	5653.910 607	20188.966 455	.000 050	.000 177	3.570 797	.280 050
36	7237.005 577	25842.877 062	.000 039	.000 138	3.570 935	.280 039
37	9263.367 139	33079.882 639	.000 030	.000 108	3.571 043	.280 030
38	11857.109 938	42343.249 778	.000 024	.000 084	3.571 127	.280 024
39	15177.100 721	54200.359 716	.000 018	.000 066	3.571 193	.280 018
40	19426.688 922	69377.460 437	.000 014	.000 051	3.571 245	.280 014

$$S^n = (1+i)^n \quad S_{\overline{n}|} = \frac{S^n - 1}{i} \quad \frac{1}{S_{\overline{n}|}} = \frac{i}{S^n - 1} \quad V^n = \frac{1}{S^n} \quad A_{\overline{n}|} = \frac{1-1/S^n}{i} \quad \frac{1}{A_{\overline{n}|}} = \frac{i}{1-1/S^n}$$

29% Annual Table

Years	1 Amount of 1	2 Amount of 1 per Period	3 Sinking-Fund Factor	4 Present Worth of 1	5 Present Worth of 1 per period	6 Partial Payment
1	1.290 000	1.000 000	1.000 000	.775 194	.775 194	1.290 000
2	1.664 100	2.290 000	.436 681	.600 925	1.376 119	.726 681
3	2.146 689	3.954 100	.252 902	.465 834	1.841 953	.542 902
4	2.769 229	6.100 789	.163 913	.361 111	2.203 064	.453 913
5	3.572 305	8.870 018	.112 739	.279 931	2.482 996	.402 739
6	4.608 274	12.442 323	.080 371	.217 001	2.699 997	.370 371
7	5.944 673	17.050 597	.058 649	.168 218	2.868 214	.348 649
8	7.668 628	22.995 270	.043 487	.130 401	2.998 616	.333 487
9	9.892 530	30.663 898	.032 612	.101 086	3.099 702	.322 612
10	12.761 364	40.556 428	.024 657	.078 362	3.178 064	.314 657
11	16.462 160	53.317 792	.018 755	.060 745	3.238 809	.308 755
12	21.236 186	69.779 952	.014 331	.047 089	3.285 899	.304 331
13	27.394 680	91.016 138	.010 987	.036 503	3.322 402	.300 987
14	35.339 137	118.410 819	.008 445	.028 297	3.350 699	.298 445
15	45.587 487	153.749 956	.006 504	.021 936	3.372 635	.296 504
16	58.807 859	199.337 443	.005 017	.017 005	3.389 640	.295 017
17	75.862 137	258.145 302	.003 874	.013 182	3.402 821	.293 874
18	97.862 157	334.007 439	.002 994	.010 218	3.413 040	.292 994
19	126.242 183	431.869 596	.002 316	.007 921	3.420 961	.292 316
20	162.852 416	558.111 779	.001 792	.006 141	3.427 102	.291 792
21	210.079 617	720.964 195	.001 387	.004 760	3.431 862	.291 387
22	271.002 705	931.043 812	.001 074	.003 690	3.435 552	.291 074
23	349.593 490	1202.046 518	.000 832	.002 860	3.438 412	.290 832
24	450.975 602	1551.640 008	.000 644	.002 217	3.440 630	.290 644
25	581.758 527	2002.615 610	.000 499	.001 719	3.442 349	.290 499
26	750.468 500	2584.374 137	.000 387	.001 333	3.443 681	.290 387
27	968.104 365	3334.842 636	.000 300	.001 033	3.444 714	.290 300
28	1248.854 630	4302.947 001	.000 232	.000 801	3.445 515	.290 232
29	1611.022 473	5551.801 631	.000 180	.000 621	3.446 135	.290 180
30	2078.218 990	7162.824 104	.000 140	.000 481	3.446 617	.290 140
31	2680.902 497	9241.043 095	.000 108	.000 373	3.446 990	.290 108
32	3458.364 222	11921.945 592	.000 084	.000 289	3.447 279	.290 084
33	4461.289 846	15380.309 814	.000 065	.000 224	3.447 503	.290 065
34	5755.063 901	19841.599 660	.000 050	.000 174	3.447 677	.290 050
35	7424.032 433	25596.663 561	.000 039	.000 135	3.447 811	.290 039
36	9577.001 838	33020.695 993	.000 030	.000 104	3.447 916	.290 030
37	12354.332 371	42597.697 831	.000 023	.000 081	3.447 997	.290 023
38	15937.088 759	54952.030 203	.000 018	.000 063	3.448 059	.290 018
39	20558.844 499	70889.118 961	.000 014	.000 049	3.448 108	.290 014
40	26520.909 403	91447.963 460	.000 011	.000 038	3.448 146	.290 011

$S^n=(1+i)^n$	$S_{\overline{n}|}=\dfrac{S^n-1}{i}$	$\dfrac{1}{S_{\overline{n}|}}=\dfrac{i}{S^n-1}$	$V^n=\dfrac{1}{S^n}$	$A_{\overline{n}|}=\dfrac{1-1/S^n}{i}$	$\dfrac{1}{A_{\overline{n}|}}=\dfrac{i}{1-1/S^n}$

377

30% Annual Table

Years	1 Amount of 1	2 Amount of 1 per Period	3 Sinking- Fund Factor	4 Present Worth of 1	5 Present Worth of 1 Per Period	6 Partial Payment
1	1.300 000	1.000 000	1.000 000	.769 231	.769 231	1.300 000
2	1.690 000	2.300 000	.434 783	.591 716	1.360 947	.734 783
3	2.197 000	3.990 000	.250 627	.455 166	1.816 113	.550 627
4	2.856 100	6.187 000	.161 629	.350 128	2.166 241	461 629
5	3.712 930	9.043 100	.110 582	.269 329	2.435 570	.410 582
6	4.826 809	12.756 030	.078 394	.207 176	2.642 746	.378 394
7	6.274 852	17.582 839	.056 874	.159 366	2.802 112	.356 874
8	8.157 307	23.857 691	.041 915	.122 589	2.924 702	.341 915
9	10.604 499	32.014 998	.031 235	.094 300	3.019 001	.331 235
10	13.785 849	42.619 497	.023 463	.072 538	3.091 539	.323 463
11	17.921 604	56.405 346	.017 729	.055 799	3.147 338	.317 729
12	23.298 085	74.326 950	.013 454	.042 922	3.190 260	.313 454
13	30.287 511	97.625 036	.010 243	.033 017	3.223 277	.310 243
14	39.373 764	127.912 546	.007 818	.025 398	3.248 675	.307 818
15	51.185 893	167.286 310	.005 978	.019 537	3.268 211	.305 978
16	66.541 661	218.472 203	.004 577	.015 028	3.283 239	.304 577
17	86.504 159	285.013 864	.003 509	.011 560	3.294 800	.303 509
18	112.455 407	371.518 023	.002 692	.008 892	3.303 692	.302 692
19	146.192 029	483.973 430	.002 066	.006 840	3.310 532	.302 066
20	190.049 638	630.165 459	.001 587	.005 262	3.315 794	.301 587
21	247.064 529	820.215 097	.001 219	.004 048	3.319 842	.301 219
22	321.183 888	1067.279 626	.000 937	.003 113	3.322 955	.300 937
23	417.539 054	1388.463 514	.000 720	.002 395	3.325 350	.300 720
24	542.800 770	1806.002 568	.000 554	.001 842	3.327 192	.300 554
25	705.641 001	2348.803 338	.000 426	.001 417	3.328 609	.300 426
26	917.333 302	3054.444 340	.000 327	.001 090	3.329 700	.300 327
27	1192.533 293	3971.777 642	.000 252	.000 839	3.330 538	.300 252
28	1550.293 280	5164.310 934	.000 194	.000 645	3.331 183	.300 194
29	2015.381 264	6714.604 214	.000 149	.000 496	3.331 679	.300 149
30	2619.995 644	8729.985 479	.000 115	.000 382	3.332 061	.300 115
31	3405.994 337	11349.981 122	.000 088	.000 294	3.332 355	.300 088
32	4427.792 638	14755.975 459	.000 068	.000 226	3.332 581	.300 068
33	5756.130 429	19183.768 097	.000 052	.000 174	3.332 754	.300 052
34	7482.969 558	24939.898 526	.000 040	.000 134	3.332 888	.300 040
35	9727.860 425	32422.868 084	.000 031	.000 103	3.332 991	.300 031
36	12646.218 553	42150.728 509	.000 024	.000 079	3.333 070	.300 024
37	16440.084 119	54796.947 062	.000 018	.000 061	3.333 131	.300 018
38	21372.109 354	71237.031 180	.000 014	.000 047	3.333 177	.300 014
39	27783.742 160	92609.140 534	.000 011	.000 036	3.333 213	.300 011
40	36118.864 808	120392.882 695	.000 008	.000 028	3.333 241	.300 008

$$S^n = (1+i)^n \qquad S_{\overline{n}} = \frac{S^n - 1}{i} \qquad \frac{1}{S_{\overline{n}}} = \frac{i}{S^n - 1} \qquad V^n = \frac{1}{S^n} \qquad A_{\overline{n}} = \frac{1 - 1/S^n}{i} \qquad \frac{1}{A_{\overline{n}}} = \frac{i}{1 - 1/S^n}$$

Index

in mass appraisal
analysis of differences among comparables in, 300–306
differences among comparables in, and assimilation function, 299–300
improvement of, through mathematical techniques, 305–6
use of computer in, 303
methods used in, 41, 92–95, 114–29
and principle of substitution, 105
sources of data for, 110–11
for special-purpose properties, when applicable, 123
when applicable, 41, 108
Comparative sales data
in comparative sales data method of estimating depreciation, 162
See also Comparative sales approach to value; Comparative sales data method of estimating depreciation; Data; Sales data
Comparative sales data method of estimating depreciation, 160, 161–63
Competing commercial neighborhoods, as factor affecting value of commercial property, 58
Competition, principle of, 27, 213
and principle of balance, 27
Compound interest, 258, 259, 260, 268
Compound interest tables, explanation of, 313–17
Computer, applications of, in mass appraisal, 307–10
Computer graphics, 81–82
Conformity, principle of, 28
and principles of progression and regression, 30
Conformity of houses, 51
Consistent use, principle of, 28
Construction
new
analysis of, in abstraction (allocation) method of land valuation, 95
as economic factor affecting value, 52
quality of
in estimate of economic life, 178
and selection of benchmarks, 129
type of, in estimate of economic life, 178
Construction cost
estimating, 133–54
in preparing cost manual, 150–54
unit basis for, 140
Construction type. *See* Classification of buildings
Contract for deed method of real estate financing, 191
Contract for sale method of real estate financing, 191
Contribution, principle of, 28–29, 114–15, 119

and principle of balance, 26
and principle of increasing and decreasing returns, 30
and principle of surplus productivity, 31
Contributory value of improvements, 121, 122, 123, 161
Coordinate method. See *X, Y* coordinate method
Coordinate parcel identification system. *See* Parcel identification system
Coordination (management), as agent of production, 26
Co-owners, rights of, as limitation on property rights, 14
Correlation of value indications, 41, 42–43
Correlation (statistical), 300–304. *See also* Coefficient of correlation
Cost
definition of, 17
and price, 17–18
replacement; *see* Replacement cost
reproduction; *see* Reproduction cost
and value, 28, 136
Cost and depreciation schedules, and mass appraisal, 131
Cost approach to value, 39–40, 96, 106, 131
accrued depreciation in; *see* Depreciation, accrued
cost estimation in, 133–54
gross rent multiplier as check on, 125
improvements rated in, 132–33
income approach to value as check on, 204
in mass appraisal, 131, 297–98
primary use of, 131
and principle of substitution, 131
steps in, 131–32
value estimate in, how obtained, 39
Cost data, 37, 108, 150
analysis of, 151
in preparation of cost manual, 150–51
Cost estimation. *See* Cost approach to value
Cost factors, 135, 147, 149
Cost index, use of, in updating cost manual, 298–99
Costing table, 298–99
Cost manuals, 108, 143, 145, 150–54, 298–99
Cost-of-living index, 46
Costs
changes in, and cost factor tables, 147
direct, 134
indirect, 134, 140
in land residual capitalization method, 100
recapture of, by builder, 133–34
summary of (example), in observed condition (breakdown) method of estimating depreciation, 174–75
unit-in-place, 151
See also Building costs; Construction cost; Development costs